Sloth, like ruft, confumes fafter than labor wears ; while the uſed key is always bright.

God helps them that help themſelves . Loſt time is never found again.

Doſt thou love life ; then do not ... that is the ſtuff life is made of.

The ſleeping fox catches no poultry . There will be ſleeping enough in the grave.

He that hath a trade hath an eſtate. At the working man's houſe hunger looks in, but dare not enter.

Induſtry pays debts , while deſpair encreaſeth them .

How deep, while ſluggards ſleep ; and you ſhall have corn to ſell and to keep.

Work to day, for you know not how much you may be hindered to morrow.

Fly Pleaſure and it will follow you. The diligent ſpinner has a large ſhift.

Now I have a ſheep and a cow every body bids me good morrow.

I never ſaw an oft removed tree, nor yet an oft removed family that did ſo well as thoſe that ſettled be.

Three removes are as bad as a fire; and a rolling ſtone gathers no moſs.

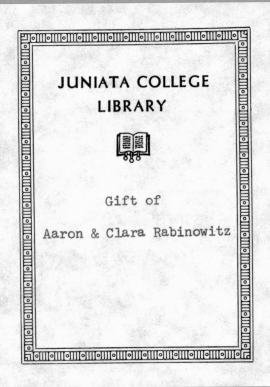

Benjamin Franklin
and the Zealous Presbyterians

Benjamin Franklin

and the Zealous Presbyterians

Melvin H. Buxbaum

The Pennsylvania State University Press
University Park and London

Endpapers from Bowles's Moral Pictures; or Poor Richard Illustrated. Being
Lessons For the Young and the Old, on Industry, Temperance, Frugality, &c. by
the late Dr. Benj. Franklin. Courtesy of the Yale University Library.

Library of Congress Cataloging in Publication Data

Buxbaum, Melvin H
   Benjamin Franklin and the zealous Presbyterians.

   Includes bibliographical references.
   1. Franklin, Benjamin, 1706-1790. 2. Presbyterians
in the United States. I. Title.
E302.6.F8B94   973.3′2′0924 [B]   74-14932
ISBN 0-271-01176-9

Designed by Glenn Ruby

Printed in the United States of America

For My Parents, Herbert and Evelyn Buxbaum

Contents

Preface

This book attempts to accomplish two distinct but closely related goals. The first chapter is basically literary. It seeks to analyze Franklin's *Autobiography* as a personal and national propaganda piece, responding to assaults on him and on America by presenting very positive images of both. The reader is asked to consider the unique promotional value of the *Autobiography* in light of Franklin's actual relationship with Presbyterian groups in America from about 1720 to 1770, a relationship in which he was more polemicist than promoter. The second through sixth chapters, though occasionally concerned with such literary matters as persona and rhetoric, are primarily historical and trace Franklin's involvement with Presbyterians from his youth in Boston to the decade of the Revolution. Although the initial chapter is an integral part of the book, some readers might prefer to move through it quickly and pick up the narrative which begins with the second chapter.

In the course of writing this book, I have incurred a heavy debt of gratitude, which it is my pleasure to acknowledge. The National Endowment for the Humanities made it possible for me to do much of the research free from teaching responsibilities. I was therefore able to spend many months researching the splendid manuscript collections at the Historical Society of Pennsylvania, the American Philosophical Society, the Presbyterian Historical Society, and the Friends Historical Society Library at Swarthmore College. I was privileged also to work at the Massachusetts Historical Society, the Houghton Library of Harvard University, and the Harvard Archives, as well as at the libraries at Princeton and Yale universities. At each of these institutions the members of the staff were very helpful, and I wish to express my appreciation to them. A good deal of the early research and most of the writing were done at the Newberry Library in Chicago, and I am happy for the opportunity to extend a special thanks to Dr. Lawrence W. Towner and his wonderfully cooperative staff for their help and patience. It would be difficult to find anywhere a better place to work than "the Newberry." More recently I have benefited from the fine American literature and history collections and helpful staff of the Freeport Memorial Library in Freeport, New York.

The nucleus of the present study profited from the criticism and encouragement of Professors Robert E. Streeter, Martin E. Marty, and Gwin J. Kolb of The University of Chicago. Professor Streeter guided the initial research, making me the recipient of his vast knowledge and unfailing good sense. He and Professors Harrison T. Meserole and John B. Frantz of The Pennsylvania State University read the final manuscript, which has been improved by their valuable suggestions. John M. Pickering, Editorial Director of The Pennsylvania State University Press, and his able staff have labored to save me from a variety of errors. It is only I, however, who am responsible for any faults.

It would have been impossible to have completed this book without the cooperation of my family. Julie and Laurel never, or almost never, touched my papers. And my wife, Maxine, who for years read, proofread, typed, and tried hard to drive me to clarity, lends a special meaning to all undertakings and events.

Prologue

Writing to his sister, Jane Mecom, Benjamin Franklin once complained of Congregationalists and Presbyterians, whom he lumped together as "zealous Presbyterians," for their bigotry and utter lack of charity toward any who disagreed with them. He had been born and raised in the faith and, though he became a deist while still a youth, thought he knew the denomination and its adherents well. What he knew of its doctrine he could reject easily enough, but he could not dismiss the social and political influence of the most powerful religious group in America. Nor could he learn to live comfortably with it, and when Presbyterianism threatened to intrude itself into the secular life of his province—whether his native Massachusetts or his adopted Pennsylvania—Franklin often battled against it. Though his last years, 1770 to 1790, were marked by an acceptance of zeal, both republican and Calvinist, the sage's capitulation came only after five decades of resistance.

This book attempts to explore that struggle and in so doing to present a way of seeing Franklin, half a century of his career, and a number of his works, particularly the *Autobiography,* or memoirs, in a substantially new way. It seeks also to separate the historical man from the carefully wrought image of himself he left behind him. What we find in the memoirs and other late pieces is less the actual Benjamin Franklin than the good man of moderate abilities who, because of his diligence, frugality, tolerance, and practical virtue, gains success and reputation in a young country that is filled with opportunity for such people. Such personal and national images have become central to the American dream. Both images, however, are here tested against one of the major concerns of Franklin's life before 1770: the growing authority of Presbyterianism. It is ironic that in dealing with it Franklin was as guilty of censoriousness and bigotry as he accused Presbyterians of being.

We have been slow to recognize this truth about Franklin and his relationship with Calvinist Establishments because we have generally accepted the image that he fashioned of himself as being the actual man. To be sure, we have long known him to be an adroit and persistent controversialist on political topics. But just as important to understanding him, his intentions, and his literary achievements is realizing that he was, despite his frequent claims to the contrary, an equally astute and dedicated polemicist on religious matters. He was, in fact, a rhetorician: always sensitive to the nuances in a highly charged situation and alert to protect himself from the thrusts and mockery of his enemies so that he could accomplish his aims, yet careful to leave behind him a reputation that would serve as an inspiration to his countrymen and to potential settlers as well as a credit to his long career.

Playing this dual role was no easy task. Although Franklin's activities are by no means as checkered as those of some later American politicians, he nevertheless engaged in schemes that suggest a person considerably different from the protagonist of the *Autobiography*. In his dealings with Presbyterian groups, he was customarily antagonistic and often vicious. These are not matters which he reveals about himself or about his fellow Americans in the memoirs and other works designed to present a positive view of both. He and his country had enough foes eager to do them harm. Franklin had made enemies long before 1771, the year he began to write his memoirs, and when it became clear that America and England were heading for final separation, the young country was assaulted steadily in the British press and made to seem a hostile place for potential emigrants. Franklin knew well that his country needed to attract useful people from Europe and that anti-American propaganda might keep them away. He therefore conceived of his *Autobiography* as a public relations piece not only for himself but for America, and in developing the hero of his memoirs he created a typical American of the kind he wanted to see settle in his country. This man prospered in a friendly, growing land of boundless opportunity. Unpleasant truths about Franklin himself or America were ignored, slighted, or altered for the sake of his image.

Nowhere is this propagandistic intention more evident than in Franklin's portrayal of himself as a benevolent live-and-let-live deist who does well by working hard and doing good for his fellow men regardless of such matters as their station in life, politics, or religion. Though charming, the picture is not a very accurate one of Franklin's career or of life in America.

Denominational rivalry was intense in most of the colonies, and Presbyterianism in particular was often too much of a threat for Franklin to rest easy. Its increasing strength and influence were a source of fear and dismay to him. New England had always been controlled by Presbyterians, who were now moving to seize a major share of the political and social power in Pennsylvania and New Jersey from Franklin's political allies. Presbyterian churches were multiplying everywhere, and Presbyterians were either in charge of or prominent in most northern colonial colleges. Harvard, Yale, and the College of New Jersey (Princeton) were theirs. Queen's College (Rutgers), though not Presbyterian, was Dutch Calvinist, and King's College (Columbia) was embroiled in a bitter contest between Anglican and Presbyterian forces for control. A similar struggle in his own College of Philadelphia (later the University of Pennsylvania) was especially grievous, and to make matters worse he feared Presbyterians might take over the institution. The number of ministers they would be able to graduate one day might well be the significant factor in determining the character of life in the Middle Colonies as it had in New England. They were already winning against Anglicans, their nearest rivals, in local competition to see who would capture most of the unchurched in areas without regular ministers. Moreover, after the dramatic revivals known as the Great Awakening, the reorganized Presbyterian Church, while rejecting the excesses of the Awakening, committed itself to evangelism. Franklin had seen first-hand the vulgarity of sanctimonious, self-styled saints and the irrationality and indecency of the instantly converted, who all too frequently rushed to condemn as unregenerate those who disagreed with them.

Presbyterians were most effective in the North and traditionally had their home base in Philadelphia, but they were gaining in numbers and importance all over the country. The Presbyterian minister and scholar John Ewing, who eventually became Provost of the College of Philadelphia, envisioned a time when his steadily increasing denomination, served by a plentiful supply of clergymen, would become the dominant force in American religious, political, and social life. Wary Anglicans had, with reason, often charged that Presbyterians looked upon theirs as the national church of America. The prospect of Presbyterian control was frightening to Franklin, and he flatly declared that if the denomination seized power in Pennsylvania, he would settle in London.

He had tried to prevent such a circumstance in ways that would startle the benevolent persona of the memoirs. Beginning in the Boston of his youth, he and his brother and their allies tried to curb the power and influence of the clergy and their friends in government. Launching all-out attacks on them in James Franklin's *New England Courant,* the small group of dissidents gained much notoriety and some success. Of all the *Courant* pieces which assaulted the ministers and politicians, however, the most effective were those written secretly by the young Benjamin, the Dogood letters. These pieces show that while still in his teens, he had determined that the local Calvinist Establishment must be made to appear authoritarian, irrelevant, and dangerous and therefore had to be held in check. Those in government who supported the clergy, then, were also a threat to the well being of the common people and had likewise to be opposed.

Once permanently established in Pennsylvania in 1726, the mature Franklin grew even more hostile to what he called Presbyterianism. The ruling Quakers had long feared and disliked Presbyterians, and so the environment in the province did little to militate against anti-Presbyterianism. Franklin responded to this situation by using his newspaper, the *Pennsylvania Gazette,* to attack the faith and to promote deism. Further, in the mid-1730's he lashed out viciously for months at the Church for silencing a heterodox minister, Samuel Hemphill. Even after others who, like Franklin, had been refreshed by the preacher's rationalistic sermons deserted him when he proved to be dishonest, Franklin himself continued to defend him anonymously and in so doing scored the Church and its beliefs. The Hemphill affair produced some of Franklin's most violently anti-Presbyterian writing and is discussed in light of the critical struggle for power within the young Church.

Considering Franklin's increasing antipathy toward the denomination, it is surprising that just a few years later we find him leading all other secular printers in ardent support of George Whitefield and the Great Awakening. Whitefield, though an Anglican minister, had come under the influence of hellfire evangelical Presbyterian ministers in Pennsylvania and New Jersey. These were men whose frightening and disruptive tactics were rejected by traditionalists and others in the Church, but Whitefield thought them the best servants of God in America and soon became a thorough Calvinist himself. That Franklin could have promoted one who condemned deists as well as other opponents, and who created chaos among thousands, is at the outset a tribute to Whitefield's great oratorical powers and to the widespread excitement caused by the spreading revivalism. Franklin was, for a time, a good deal more moved by the minister than he was later willing to admit in the *Autobiography* and other pieces. More significantly, though, he changed his mind about Whitefield and the Awakening and, switching his support to their opponents, added to the confusion in the sorely divided Presbyterian Church. This he did in ways that have not been previously recognized; however, his efforts testify to his continuing hostility toward Presbyterianism.

Since an important key to supremacy in American religious and political life was the ability to graduate clergy and thus establish new churches, it is understandable that Franklin's anti-Presbyterianism should have surfaced in the arena of higher education. Although he was the founder and, for a time, the guiding force behind the Academy and College of Philadelphia, religious and political infighting drove him from any position of authority in the school. Complicating matters was the rivalry between conservative Presbyterians at the College of Philadelphia and the more evangelical Presbyterians who controlled the College of New Jersey. Both of these groups, while working against each other, battled Anglicans in the Philadelphia institution. Franklin keenly resented being forced from power in the school. Moreover, he was disgusted that it had become, as he believed, a mere prize sought by warring factions. He had reason to be distressed, yet his reaction to the situation was unfortunate. He had no desire to see the College of Philadelphia become an Anglican seminary, but he looked with alarm on the possibility of its falling into the hands of local Presbyterians. He therefore used the serious financial troubles in the school to injure it. Further, his son, William, Royal Governor of New Jersey, proved to be his father's surrogate. Having learned his anti-Presbyterianism from the elder Franklin, William tried to seize control of the College of New Jersey, and when this move failed, he found other ways to check its growth. These events, occurring in the 1750's and 1760's, show that middle age did nothing to lessen Franklin's animosity. He had yet to achieve the disinterested benevolence he would claim for himself in the memoirs.

The same can be said for his using the strife which existed between settlers and Indians on the frontier to effect royal government for Pennsylvania. The effort to bring the province under the Crown lasted almost until 1770. Franklin came to believe that the Presbyterians in the Philadelphia area and in the West stood a good chance of winning control of the province in the near future. He therefore determined that the most effective way of stopping them and of punishing his old political enemy, Thomas Penn, the proprietor, was to make Pennsylvania a Crown colony. In addition to ridding the colony of proprietary government, the change would soon bring to the province the Church of England and perhaps an American bishop. Presbyterians had every reason to fear and work against such a plan, and many of the Quakers, who considered Presbyterians their chief enemies, were no happier with Franklin's scheme. They and others who opposed it helped to defeat him in the election of 1764, hoping thereby to end his attempts to change the government. Franklin, however, worried as never before about Presbyterian power and had himself appointed agent to England, ostensibly to work against the Stamp Act, but chiefly to promote royal government.

These are not matters that Franklin deals with or intended to treat accurately in his memoirs and other later writings. By 1770 the politics of the Empire had changed his thinking about England and his old enemies: Presbyterians and Congregationalists were now in the forefront of the patriotic movement, and Franklin was defending them and himself from brutal attacks in the British press while trying to promote the American cause. When in 1771 he began to write his *Autobiography*, he therefore created a Benjamin Franklin and an America that were less realistic portrayals than propagandistic ones. Franklin became the typical American who gained success by hard work and general benevolence, and his country was depicted as a haven for just such people, young Americans and Europeans alike, who would be made to understand that America offered them the chance to achieve security, prosperity, and happiness for themselves and their children.

I

Franklin's *Autobiography:*
A Persona for the Abused

Much of what is popularly known about Benjamin Franklin we have learned from his *Autobiography*. So great is the force of these memoirs that their protagonist has become firmly entrenched in the public mind as the real and complete man. Consequently, we know Franklin as the industrious, frugal, wise man whose good and useful works, moralisms, scientific achievements, patriotism, and disinterested benevolence to men, regardless of such extraneous matters as their nationality and religion, prove that a professional do-gooder can do very well for himself in America. This is the Franklin that has become a central part of the national folklore. His life seems to point the way to pragmatic virtue and a neat little bundle in the bank at the same time: "Nothing so likely to make a man's fortune as virtue," was the theme of a work he had long hoped to write, "The Art of Virtue," a summary of his thinking on how to live successfully. Small wonder that he makes many of his middle-class descendants uncomfortable. He seems to stand for much that is unlovely in American life of the past and the present. Often enough our goals have seemed to be predicated upon Poor Richard's aphorism: "'Tis hard for an empty Bag to stand upright." Yet many of us pride ourselves on the fact that we set our sights on higher things, which Franklin was either unconcerned with or involved with in only a grubby, utilitarian way. Thus it is that many of us laugh at him, scorn him, or relegate him to the irrelevant, convincing ourselves that we are his moral and cultural superiors. The picture of the Franklin most of us know seems appropriately placed on thrift stores and savings banks.

We do not feel this way about Washington, who hangs forever dignified, austere, and aloof, if undusted, in classrooms throughout America. Nor have we so condemned Jefferson, who is almost entirely identified with the lofty idealism and moving rhetoric of the Declaration of Independence and with the obsolete dream of self-sufficiency on the land. Still, there is a folksy quality in Franklin, so atypical of national heroes, and we admire him for it. There is ultimately a common-as-shoes, human quality in him that prevents us from shoving him aside altogether. His commonness, his humor, and his rise from poor beginnings to great success remind us of Lincoln, which is a compliment to both men.

As one scholar noted, however, Lincoln has fared much better than the often maligned Franklin.[1] Historians have, of course, attacked Lincoln's policies and his motivations, but the *man* has hardly been vilified as Franklin has. We are safe in concluding, as Carl Van Doren does, that some of the hostility toward Franklin on the part of a contemporary like John Adams is the jealousy of a less gifted and less popular man toward a greater one.[2] But why the vituperation of twentieth-century detractors who insist that Franklin is a money-hungry, vulgar, "two-penny" philosopher, the very wellspring of polluted American values?[3] Why the more subtle but nevertheless damaging view of Franklin as a very talented but completely unspiritual man to whom utilitarianism was a substitute for principle?[4]

Of the many diatribes against Franklin, probably the most famous is the amusing, wrong-headed, but perceptive one made by D.H. Lawrence. He admits that there are some things to admire in the philosopher, "his sturdy courage, first of all, then his sagacity, then his glimpsing into the thunders of electricity, then his common-sense humor." But this is a list used merely as a rhetorical device to set up Franklin for the onslaught that follows: "All the qualities of a great man, and never more than a great citizen. Middle-sized, sturdy, snuff-coloured Doctor Franklin, one of the soundest citizens that ever trod or 'used venery.' I do not like him." Lawrence, to be sure, is having a good old time indulging himself at his antagonist's expense, but he is also quite serious. Franklin had committed the unpardonable sin of defining and seeking perfection. Worse yet, he had suggested in his memoirs that other people do the same, and he tried to show them what virtues had to be attained and how one could make them a part of himself, or at least make others think they were part of his fiber! Lawrence had often enough been driven to rage by lesser offenses. "The Perfectibility of Man! Ah heaven, what a dreary theme! The perfectibility of the Ford car! I am many men. Which one of them are you going to perfect? I am not a mechanical contrivance." Franklin's chart of virtues leading to perfection does seem terribly mechanical to anyone choosing to ignore the obvious humor with which the scheme, though not the intention, is treated. Throughout the *Autobiography* the protagonist that moves blandly from one success to another appears to many modern readers the very Anti-Christ of spirit and imagination. And Lawrence, an artist with an active imagination and very delicate sensibilities, which he cultivated with loving care and self-conscious passion, feared for his wolf:

> The ideal self! Oh, but I have a strange and fugitive self shut out and howling like a wolf or a coyote under the ideal windows. See his red eyes in the dark? This is the self who is coming into his own.
>
> The perfectibility of man, dear God! When every man as long as he remains alive is in himself a multitude of men. Which of these do you choose to perfect, at the expense of every other?
>
> Old Daddy Franklin will tell you. He'll rig him up for you, the pattern American. Oh, Franklin was the first downright American. He knew what he was about, the sharp little man. He set up the first dummy American.[5]

Franklin had made a virtue of work, Lawrence charges: " 'Work, you free jewel work!' shouts the liberator cracking his whip. Benjamin I will not work. I do not choose to be a free democrat. I am absolutely the servant of my own Holy Ghost." It is with good reason that the Puritan authorities banished Mistress Hutchinson and other Antinomians who followed the uncertain promptings of their piece of the Holy Ghost instead of working on more practical if mundane levels for the good of Massachusetts. But the charges are true: if Franklin could have spotted Lawrence's wolf, he would have organized a posse to shoot it in the interest of the community. We are dealing here with two very different men and two very different times.

Though this psychological and generational gap is not a fact Lawrence seems to appreciate, his criticism is nevertheless important. In fact, it would be difficult to find a criticism of Franklin that is at once so right and yet so wrong. The hero of the *Autobiography* does indeed make a virtue of work, exalts what appear to be the more superficial aspects of man, exorcises from him his lurking wolf, the mystery of his soul, and in doing these things creates as the center of his memoirs an efficient machine of sorts. Lawrence, aware that the protagonist is a persona, wonders "why Benjamin set up this dummy of a perfect citizen as a pattern to America." The question is very important, but Lawrence's answer is disappointingly superficial: "He thought it simply was the true ideal."[6] The persona was, to be sure, the ideal American as far as Franklin was concerned, the kind of person he thought would be successful in the young country and the kind America needed. But the persona is not the whole Franklin. We will, I believe, understand him and his *Autobiography* better if we look upon the persona as the result of necessity more than as the man himself or as his personal ideal left to his son and descendants.

It would seem, in fact, that the salutation of the memoirs is purely a literary device. Franklin begins in a charmingly personal way as if he were writing a letter to his "Dear Son," William. He justifies the form of this part of his story on the grounds that there were "Circumstances of *my* Life, many of which you are as yet unacquainted with." Yet at the time Franklin wrote the first part of his life, William was forty years old and certainly knew much of his eminent father's past.[7] Franklin then proceeds to tell William facts of family history, many of which the two men had discovered while visiting Ecton in Northamptonshire, where the rector and his wife showed both Franklins the church registers and the Franklin family gravestones. Indeed, the father expresses his confidence that William remembers the trip. The two also had been together at Birmingham when they looked up a number of Deborah Franklin's relatives, and again at Banbury when they visited another ancestral home. William, then, surely would recall the essential facts his father relates, especially since only thirteen years had elapsed from the time of the 1758 trip. Moreover, in 1758 William had been a twenty-seven-year-old man and capable of sharing his father's interest. The address, then, is actually a plausible means for the author to introduce his persona.

The *Autobiography* constitutes Franklin's most significant attempt to create the personal image of himself that he wanted to leave behind. This is especially true of the first part of the work, which was written in 1771. Although Franklin was not as great or as widely admired as he later became, he was nevertheless at this time very important and well known in Europe as well as in America. The remaining parts of the memoirs were written in 1784, 1788, and 1789-90, and deal largely with public matters, though they also contribute to his personal image.[8]

Franklin had achieved philosophical eminence before 1771 and was widely respected, but he also had a good many political, social, and religious enemies. He began acquiring them early in life when his activities and harangues in favor of deism made him something of a horror to the pious citizens of Boston. They, along with his political foes in government, had their revenge on the young apprentice as well as his older brother James, whose newspaper, the *New England Courant,* satirized the political and religious Establishments by harassing them as no other paper had ever dared to do. James, one of the more obnoxious writers for the *Courant,* was imprisoned and young Benjamin was called before the General Court and made to feel that the Boston of 1723 was no place for a satirical, outspoken deist and democrat who also wanted to get ahead.[9]

But as the sixty-five-year-old Franklin sat down in the garden study in the pleasant Twyford house of his good friend and champion of the American cause, Jonathan Shipley, Bishop of St. Asaph, and began to re-create seemingly more pleasant and innocent times, he did not have to turn his thoughts back to his boyhood and recall ancient foes. He had made enemies of more recent vintage. He could not have forgotten, for example, that before he had left for England on his first public mission abroad in 1757 as agent for the Pennsylvania Assembly in their dispute with the proprietor, he had been ousted by enemies from any active role in the Academy and College of Philadelphia, which had been his particularly beloved brainchild.

Or certainly he could have recalled that as recently as 1764 he had been reviled in an especially vicious election campaign and had lost his seat in the Assembly to his political and religious opponents. Though he was defended, they played havoc with his character and reputation. Selections from one anti-Franklin piece, *What is Sauce for a Goose is also Sauce for a Gander.* BEING A *small Touch in the* LAPIDARY *Way.* OR TIT *for* TAT, *in your own Way.* AN EPITAPH *On a certain great Man . . . ,* indicate the tone of the election campaign in general. It is dedicated "TO the much esteem'd Memory of/B_____ F_____ Esq; L.L.D;/The only man of his day/In Pennsylvania,/Or perhaps of any age or in any country,/Whose *ingrate Disposition* and *Badness of Heart* . . ./Ever introduced to/POPULARITY./" Among Franklin's "enormous Vices" are his mistreatment of his "PATRONS," the Quakers. Furthermore, his fame in science was gained by disgusting means, we are told, since he assumed "the merit/Of other mens *discoveries.*" As for his honorary degrees, he stooped not only to "meanly *begging*" them, but to "*buying*" them as well. His political success in good measure can be traced to his knowledge of "every Zig Zag Machination,/And triming Contrivance."[10] His chief goal is to destroy the government of Pennsylvania and "dispossess the People of/Their CHARTER RIGHTS,/And inestimable Privileges." He had lived in the grand style in England at the public expense after being appointed agent for the province in 1757. Yet he is so low that now he seeks to destroy those very men who brought him into power. Finally, Franklin never even performed those tasks he was assigned, presumably because he was too busy.

The attacks on his political activities could be dismissed easily enough, for such abuse was part of the life of a public man; however, the personal smears, the malicious charges against him as a man, were harder to live with. Probably his greatest personal hurt was the writer's assault on a part of Franklin's earlier life that involved his son, William, the governor of New Jersey. Since the author considers this his best thrust and a credible summary of Franklin's true character, it is worth presenting in its entirety:

> His principal Estate, *seeming* to consist,/Till very lately,/In his Hand Maid BARBARA/A most valuable *Slave,*/The *Foster-Mother*/Of his last Offspring,/Who did his dirty Work,—/And in two *Angelic* Females,/Whom Barbara also served,/As Kitchen Wench and Gold Finder./But alas the Loss!/Providence for wise, tho' secret Ends,/ Lately depriv'd him of the Mother/Of EXCELLENCY./His Fortune was not however impair'd,/For he piously witheld from her/MANES,/The *pitiful* Stipend of *Ten Pounds per Annum,*/On which he had cruelly suffered her/To STARVE;/Then stole her to the *fably mean;*/Whose Ambition is/POWER;/And whose Intention is/TYRANNY/Remember then O Friends and Freeman,/And be in-*Monumental Inscription.*/Reader behold this striking Instance of/Human Depravity and Ingratitude;/An irrefragable Proof,/That nei-ther the Capital Services/Of *Friends,*/Nor the attracting Favours of the Fair,/Can fix the Sincerity of a Man,/*Devoid of Principles* and/*Inef-fably mean;*/Whose Ambition is/POWER;/And whose Intention is/TYRANNY/Remember then O Friends and Freeman,/And be in-treated to consider,/That in the howling Wilderness/When we would guard ourselves against/The covered Wolves of the Forest, or/The stinging Snakes of the Mountains,/Our Maxim should be/*Beware of taking them to our*/BOSOMS./FINIS.[11]

Much more restrained, though nevertheless damaging to Franklin's repu-tation, was the protest against his being sent to England for the province after he lost the 1764 election. The protestors, who included such eminent Pennsyl-vanians as John Dickinson and the Chief Justice of Pennsylvania, William Allen, one of the colony's most influential Presbyterian leaders, made clear their objections to Franklin. First, he was the cause of recent "Distraction" in the province with his efforts to make Pennsylvania a Crown colony. Sec-ond, his "fixed enmity" to the proprietary family prevented him from acting rationally with them and made accommodation impossible.

Representing the colony, Franklin would force the continuation, therefore, of the "fatal Dissensions" that he had caused in the first place. Third, Franklin, the protestors asserted, was "very unfavorably thought of by several of his Majesty's Ministers" and even by the King himself. Fourth, his appointment would be "extremely disagreeable to a very great Number of the most serious and reputable Inhabitants of this Province of all Denominations and Societies," who recognize that he would use his position once more to cause further "Convulsions" in the colony. Fifth, his appointment was rammed through the Assembly unfairly by his supporters. Sixth, his very honesty is, the protestors charged, open to grave suspicion, for on an earlier trip abroad he had used public funds irresponsibly and for his own advantage. For these reasons the protestors predicted that a host of "Mischiefs" would result from his appointment.[12]

Once he was in England, officially to oppose the Stamp Act but also to end proprietary government in Pennsylvania, Franklin continued to bear the burden of savage attacks on his character. His very patriotism was challenged, as he was accused of being a traitor to his country and of privately supporting the obnoxious tax. So successful were his enemies in working up sentiment against him that a mob swore it would level his house, and his family had to be protected by friends.[13] This is a fact, of course, which demonstrates the effectiveness of the Proprietary Party in the colony as well as the political emotionalism of the time, but it also indicates that Franklin stood at a very low level in the opinion of many of his neighbors. Eventually it became clear to objective people that in spite of some lapses of political wisdom and common sense which led him to have his friends appointed distributors of the stamps, Franklin opposed the act. His opponents, however, continued to accuse him of treachery. His brilliant performance during his examination before the House of Commons, which proved his opposition to the tax and his loyalty, was called a fraud, and the calumnies continued in all their damaging malevolence.[14]

Such criticism and disparagement of one's character, particularly endured by one who traded on his reputation for disinterested virtue, are not easy to forget or to ignore. Had he been attacked by nobodies, Franklin could have remained aloof. His detractors, however, included not only Dickinson and Allen, but such very prominent men as Hugh Williamson, professor of mathematics at the College of Philadelphia and one of the foremost Presbyterian leaders in the colony; the Reverend Francis Alison, eminent Presbyterian minister and Vice Provost of the College; Samuel Purviance, Jr., influential Presbyterian politician and ardent opponent of Franklin; the wealthy Edward

Shippen, Sr., and other members of that leading Presbyterian family; Governor Robert H. Morris; the Reverend William Smith, Provost of the Academy and College of Philadelphia and Franklin's archenemy; and Richard Peters, President of the Trustees of the College, Thomas Penn's provincial secretary, and long a foe to Franklin's political policies. There were also such opponents in America and in England as Andrew Bradford, his fellow printer, and later, when their partnership ended and he was able to move freely, David Hall. Though he retained much of his personal regard for Franklin, Hall believed the colony was better off as it was than in the hands of the King. He thus refused to promote royal government in his *Pennsylvania Gazette* and believed that Franklin's allies, who also desired the change, tried to ruin him by promoting competition from another newspaper. Even some of Franklin's presumed friends rejected his policy of taking the government away from the proprietor. These were men who had no more use for Thomas Penn and his supporters than Franklin himself had, but they either publicly or privately worked against Franklin in his attempt to bring Pennsylvania under the Crown. Moreover, many of them expressed serious reservations about Franklin's motives and character.

Among these men were two of the foremost Quaker pacifists in the country, the wealthy and widely known merchants Israel and James Pemberton. There was also the nonpacifist Friend Isaac Norris, the universally respected Speaker of the Assembly and Franklin's usual ally; the English Quaker merchant David Barclay, Sr.; and the great London Quaker and physician John Fothergill, F.R.S., who worked with Franklin in England and against him at the same time, a man whom Franklin called "among the best Men I have known, and a great Promoter of useful Projects." Some of these people were content to confine their objections to Franklin to private letters, but others made known in print their antipathy toward him and his plans. The newspapers of the time were often enough vehicles for character assassination and Franklin, despite disclaimers to the contrary, was sensitive to attack. As he grew older and increasingly involved in the strained events leading up to the Revolution, he became more obviously defensive when he felt his reputation had been damaged. Ironically, though, his severest detractors, even for a time after 1771, were his American enemies, men who in general knew him well. It was such enemies who spread the report of his allegedly treacherous conduct in the Stamp Act proceedings.[15] Deeply hurt and resentful, Franklin denied the charge,[16] but there was little that he could do to preserve his character except assert his patriotism, continue to work for repeal, and hope that his friends could defend him adequately.

Franklin found it easier to respond to abuse from writers for the Ministry. He turned their hostility to his advantage in revealingly defensive terms: he was, he said, "too much of an American" not to incur the wrath of his country's adversaries. Thus his reputation among many in England suffered because of his patriotism. Such a statement, made in this case to his son, was certain to be spread around and increased Franklin's reputation among most of his countrymen. He rightfully but nonetheless consciously identified himself with the American cause and therefore shared in its nobility.[17] Franklin had British friends who defended him, if not always his country, but he was still concerned enough over the effect of many personal attacks on his reputation in England to write an apologia.

There were those who argued that since he and his son held Crown offices, he had to defend the government's position regardless of what his fellow Americans thought. His failure to act an appropriate part proved him guilty of the basest ingratitude.[18] Other Ministry writers learned from Americans and sought to get Franklin off the political stage by accusing him of disloyalty to America,[19] knowing well that there were people on both sides of the Atlantic who believed that his loyalties were determined essentially by the favorability of the political winds, that he always sought his own interest above all else, and that in stormy weather he could be counted on to steer his own ship to the safest and most prosperous harbor.[20] One of the reasons for Franklin's rise in life was his well-publicized moral character. Small wonder, then, that a concerned Franklin sought diligently to preserve his image. In private and public letters written in the colonies and in England he tried hard to defend himself. He insists repeatedly on his loyalty to and love for his country and, in fact, on his benevolent good will to all men, on the unswerving integrity with which he has served, and on the fact that his great desire to do good to both England and America and thus prevent the fatal division of the Empire made him enemies in each country, just as his defense of the liberties of his fellow Pennsylvanians made for him political foes among the proprietor's friends. The kind of protective image Franklin was seeking to create for himself he summarizes in a letter to John Jay in 1784, about the time that he resumed his *Autobiography*. Franklin knew, of course, that the career of the young and promising statesman was on the rise and that Jay was almost certain to outlive him by decades. Franklin was therefore careful to present the best possible picture of himself, realizing that long after his death he would be discussed and written about by just such influential people as Jay. He therefore addresses himself to what he believed essential to his reputation. He admits to having "some Enemies in England," but he insists that they are "my enemies as an American." He continues:

> I have also two or three in America, who are my Enemies as a *Minister,* but I thank God there are not in the whole world any who are my Enemies as a *Man;* for by his grace, thro' a long life, I have been enabled so to conduct myself, that there does not exist a human Being who can justly say, "Ben Franklin has wrong'd me." This, my friend, is in old age a comfortable Reflection.[21]

Putting aside the dubious logic with which he separates the man from his roles and activities, Franklin's claim is, to say the least, extravagant. As a son, brother, husband, businessman, politician, and writer, he often hurt others. Yet so worried was he about his reputation that he consciously, even self-consciously, spread what he called his "good Fame."[22]

The attacks on his character, however, were not without benefit to Franklin. During his earlier life, and especially after his first political mission to England, he had come to be a thorough Anglophile. His detractors and the worsening political situation forced him to reevaluate his feelings with the result that he became very critical of England and much more the defender of his own country. This matter will be explored more fully below, but for the present it is worth noting that this change enabled Franklin to identify closely with the cause of his countrymen, and in defending them he also defended himself and worked at creating a positive image of himself as a man and as a public figure.

Charged frequently by opponents with disgraceful ingratitude to a government that had given him a profitable office, he replied sharply that the Ministry had offered him even a better place recently. His for the asking could be a place in the Salt Office, one that paid the handsome sum of "five hundred a Year," if only he would betray the American cause. Asserting his patriotism and personal honor, Franklin treats the offer with contempt. Though the Ministry may have been shocked at his refusal, he was not surprised by the offer for, he said, it was "a settled Point in Government here, that every man has his Price."[23] This was directed as much at his American audience as at British readers. He would prove himself the patriot and insure his reputation on that score during and, insofar as he could, after his lifetime.

In this he had the help not only of William and other political allies but of his sister Jane Mecom who, as Franklin knew, read his letters aloud and showed them to family and friends eager to hear of the great man's doings. Franklin made certain they would know of his selfless patriotism and integrity. He wrote to his sister that his love for his country and his honor led him to reject lucrative offices and might also cost him his position in the post office. This would, he said, surely cause him inconvenience, for he was old now and had spent much of his own money living abroad in the service of his country. Nevertheless, his letters urging nonimportation, the chief cause of the financial danger to him, were "written in compliance with another Duty, that to my Country; a Duty quite distinct from that of a Post Master."[24] And less than half a year before composing the first part of his memoirs, he wrote to a friend in Boston that his loyalty to America was making his labors in England very difficult to bear. Yet though he had gone through much, he gladly suffered all in the hope that he might be of some use to his country.[25] Even before he began his *Autobiography,* then, Franklin was very much concerned with overcoming the effects on his reputation of the many attacks he had borne through the years, for they were certain to be inimical to the "good Fame" that he had so much in mind and worked hard to preserve and even improve.

When his respite at Twyford ended in mid-August of 1771 and he returned to London and politics, having finished the first part of his life, he once again continued to create defensive and positive images of himself. Naturally, he concentrated on his loyalty, but he also emphasized his other virtues: his philosophical temper, which made him a disinterested well-wisher to England, though an implacable foe of Tories, and his personal sacrifice which kept him from the family and friends he loved and longed for desperately. He refers to himself as being in "Exile" from his "dear Country" for which he harbored an "indelible Affection," and stresses again his loneliness. Doubtless he missed his family and friends in America, but he had left them before without undue hardship. His good friends throughout Great Britain and his enormous prestige in learned circles surely helped offset his sense of loss and isolation. His use of the word "Exile" therefore seems, like the tone of his comment in general, self-conscious and sentimental. Moreover, even allowing for the patriotic feeling of the time, his claim to an "indelible Affection" for a country that he had always before considered indisputably inferior to England in nearly every way seems somewhat contrived and designed to enhance his image among his countrymen rather than to be an accurate rendering of his usual feelings.

It was also good public relations for him, as the two countries moved closer to war, to make certain that his fellow Americans would know how valuable a sacrifice he was making for them, and how important his services were. For example, although his justly famous satires, "The Sale of the Hessians" and "Rules by Which a Great Empire May be Reduced to a Small One," were not written under his name, once they proved successful he lost no time in telling such key people as his son and Thomas Cushing, the Boston patriot and political leader, that he was their author.[26] After he was viciously attacked by Solicitor General Wedderburn and disgraced in 1774 for sending to Boston the Hutchinson-Oliver letters, he wrote a strong defense of his character. So angry was he that his apologia is practically a personal declaration of war against England.[27] And when he lost his place in the post office, he declared that the Ministry wanted only slavish types who would follow orders regardless of the consequences to their country,[28] and not men of patriotism, integrity, and courage like himself. As Verner Crane points out in commenting on Franklin's responses to criticism, the experience at the hands of Wedderburn had made him unusually sensitive to what others said about him.[29] This is true, but the trial in the cockpit was not the beginning of his acute sensitivity to his reputation; it was rather a culmination of a growing concern.

It was even important to him that he impress upon the public an image of himself as an old man who had long served others and was therefore entitled to respect instead of abuse. In defending his role in the Hutchinson-Oliver affair, Franklin wraps around himself the kindly protective mantle of age. Stressing the point that for decades he has worked for the public good in many ways and always with honor, he implies that he was not about to begin acting dishonorably at so advanced a stage in his life. People might disagree with his politics, but not with his motives or integrity. The proof he offers to support this contention is that "I have had the Felicity of bringing down to a good old Age as fair a Reputation (may I be permitted to say it?) as most publick Men. . . ." He continues, calling attention again to his years, when he justifies striking back at his detractors: "I should therefore (persisting as old Men are apt to do, in old Habits) have taken no Notice of the late Invective of the Solicitor-General, nor of the abundant Abuse in the Papers, were I not urg'd to it by my Friends. . . ." The "Friends" are a handy device who enable Franklin to defend himself and to plant sympathetic and positive images of himself in the minds of his readers. It is a literary vehicle he would use again in the *Autobiography*. He decided not to publish this work intended for the newspapers, likely concluding that given the furor over the affair, he had best remain silent about his role and intentions. Yet the piece indicates clearly his concern about his reputation and shows that he was beginning to portray himself as the moral, disinterested and benevolent lover of mankind, who, above petty and vicious conduct, had always been faithful to the people he served and to his sense of honor.[30] It was good judgment on his part not to have published his defense, for it fails. Franklin makes himself too theatrical and idealized a figure and therefore is unpersuasive and even irritating. He was much more effective as the down-to-earth and winning American of his memoirs.

Even in France, where Franklin was widely admired and loved, he still remained self-consciously aware of his image. With an instinct for public relations he announced to his friends just how immediately recognizable he was in Paris because of his unique appearance. He pictured himself as the plain, average American, unwigged and in a fur cap "which comes down my Forehead almost to my Spectacles. Think," he wrote, "how this must appear among the Powder'd Heads of Paris!"[31] The costume was very successful, indeed, and Franklin, who had already achieved fame for his scientific work and for Poor Richard's sayings, was revered in a France that knew him instantly and identified him as the representative New Man whose life and nation offered hope for all the common people of the world. He delighted in his French image, which was spread by the countless medallions with his likeness on them, "some," as he happily reported to his daughter, "to be set in the lids of snuff-boxes, and some so small as to be worn in rings; and the numbers sold are incredible. These, with the pictures, busts, and prints, (of which copies upon copies are spread everywhere,) have made your father's face as well known as that of the moon. . . ." Then, unable to contain his pride— to which he was entitled after so much abuse—he went on: "It is said by the learned entymologists, [sic] that the name *doll*, for the images children play with, is derived from the word Idol. From the number of *dolls* now made of him, he may be truly said, *in that sense*, to be i-doll-ized in this country."[32] The pun notwithstanding, his genuine happiness was apparent.

He would never attain so completely positive an image in his own country, where there were yet many alive who had once been his enemies; but he worked at making his American image as positive as he reasonably could. He represented himself again as the benevolent patriot and statesman who had "long laboured in England, with a great deal of sincerity" to prevent war, suffering many attacks for his pains. As he said, though, with no great accuracy, "I keep a separate account of private injuries, which I may forgive; and I do not think right to mix them with public affairs."[33] His relationships with such men as William Allen, William Smith, Thomas Penn, and others show, however, that he often let personal bitterness interfere with public matters.[34] It is not surprising therefore that soon after his experience with Wedderburn, he became convinced of the futility of trying to reunite America and England. Moreover, he did not hesitate to convey his sense of hopelessness to influential Americans. He told his son that it was now useless for him to think of ever being promoted to a higher office and, suggesting strongly that service in the King's government was disgraceful, urged William to resign his governorship and take up farming, which was more honorable.[35] To Cushing he wrote two letters in less than two weeks, expressing the impossibility of ever getting a fair hearing in England for the American cause, since the whole of England now seemed to Franklin hostile to the colonies. Anticipating that the Massachusetts House might believe him to be painting an unduly bleak picture because of his personal situation, he stressed his disinterested patriotism again:

> But, indeed, what I feel on my own account is half lost in what I feel for the public. When I see, that all petitions and complaints of grievances are so odious to government, that even the mere pipe which conveys them becomes obnoxious, I am at a loss to know how peace and union are to be maintained or restored between the different parts of the empire.

He knew that the Ministry had vilified him not only because he was conveying unpopular petitions and defending unpopular positions, but because his treatment of the Hutchinson-Oliver letters was embarrassing. Yet he concluded his letter to Cushing on a note designed to show the utter senselessness of continuing a part of the Empire: "But where complaining is a crime, hope becomes despair."[36] This was now the usually optimistic Franklin's attitude and his approach to his task in England, as many other letters show, including some that were printed in America.[37] His loyalty to his own country and his disillusionment with England had been established before the smear by Wedderburn, but it is nonetheless true that this affair, which injured Franklin's reputation and image, helped to make him a revolutionary.

He continued to work at enhancing his image even after he returned to America. For many years, he said, his only personal ambition had been to leave behind him the "fair Character" he had "so long endeavoured to deserve." This was of crucial importance to him, he had earlier told a correspondent whom he encouraged to counter Arthur Lee's attacks on him, for he had "lived beyond all other Ambitions."[38] Still, there were always detractors like Lee about whom Franklin worried. He therefore sacrificed accuracy of description to image-building when discussing himself. To his much younger friend and admirer, the lovely Madame Brillon . . . he took care to make himself appear as adored in his own country as he was in France. Ignoring the abuse still being hurled at him by his enemies, he reported to her that "I am in a country where I have the happiness of being universally respected and beloved. . . ."[39] This he said in the spring of 1788. Two years later, just before his death, which he knew was imminent, he wrote his fellow scientist and friend, Ezra Stiles, Congregationalist minister and President of Yale College, a delightfully urbane and charming, but almost incredible, letter. Stiles had questioned Franklin about his religion, for the minister was bothered that a man so close to the end should remain a deist. Enjoying a brief respite from terrible pain and from the opium he took to relieve it, Franklin used the opportunity of a reply to once more improve his reputation. Addressing himself specifically to Stiles' important concerns, he images himself significantly as the benevolent, generous, live-and-let-live deist who supported "all sound Religion." He would not, however, become dogmatic on the subject, for he has never done so, he writes, and it is now much too late in the day for him to begin. He will soon enough know the truth.[40]

In general, then, many of Franklin's letters express a deep concern for his public and personal images. As the public man he is the disinterested, loyal, and sacrificing patriot who, prompted by his love for his fellows, had always served them with honor and with disregard for his own desires or well being. The man himself is the good person of decent ability whose benevolence, honesty, and common-sense wisdom make him beloved. His rewards for a lifetime of service are appropriately not the material kind, but a sense of satisfaction at having done good and remained good. This is a pleasing picture of a national and even international hero, but it is one created in letters which, written amid great tension and a multitude of duties to so many different people, might cause the overall image of him to lack coherence and fail to achieve the effect he desired. Furthermore, there was no guarantee that most of his letters would survive. Franklin therefore created the image of himself he wanted left behind in a permanent, carefully wrought form that would survive to his benefit.

In the course of building a positive image of himself in the *Autobiography,* Franklin, in effect, answers his critics. Charged often with being a grubby politician who is interested chiefly in his own advancement, Franklin reminds his readers of his life-long devotion to useful projects that benefited the public. Indeed, the compactness of the memoirs makes it seem that its hero is a professional do-gooder. As a boy, to be sure, he admits to allowing his "early projecting public Spirit" to overcome his sense of scrupulous honesty: he led his comrades in pilfering some stones intended for use in a new house and they built a wharf with them so that the whole community could fish for minnows more conveniently—especially the boys of Philadelphia! As he grew older, however, his zeal for good works became less clouded by personal desire, and it is not far along in the *Autobiography* that we come across Franklin's "first Project of a public Nature," the founding of the Library Company of Philadelphia in 1731, when he was just twenty-five years old. Laboring to make his newspaper and shop prosper, he did not undertake another significant project for the public good until 1736, when he formed the very useful Union Fire Company. Thereafter, events move more quickly: we learn about the improved fireplace he invented, the famous "Franklin stove"; of his far-reaching *Proposal for Promoting Useful Knowledge,* a piece that led to the founding of the American Philosophical Society; about his achievements in electricity, which were most pleasing to him because they had humane and practical value in saving lives and property; and about another useful project which he began, the Association for the defense of Pennsylvania.

Upon his retirement from business in 1748, he ardently wished to spend his life studying the wonders of electricity and visiting his family and friends. Instead, however, he tells us, he could not refuse the call to community service, so that in leaving his business with his partner, he did not gain the leisure he wanted. Now he was busy with public matters. Though he was at times upset over petty disputes, he writes that he was happy in having the opportunity and influence to promote useful measures for his fellows. Ten months after his retirement he was elected to the Philadelphia Common Council, and soon afterward, he published his *Proposals Relating to the Education of Youth in Pennsylvania,* which expressed his great desire to found a school in Philadelphia. His indefatigable zeal and the effectiveness of the *Proposals* made him the chief instrument in the birth of the Academy of Philadelphia. In recognition of his efforts he was elected a trustee of the institution, later the Academy and College of Philadelphia, and after 1791 the University of Pennsylvania. This is an office, he says in the 1788 section of his memoirs, that he had always held and presumably discharged faithfully, insofar as his other responsibilities

permitted. The impression we are left with is that Franklin's role in the
school and his relationship with the other trustees and with the faculty had
always been a happy and productive one, but here, as in many instances in the
memoirs, the image of the respected, useful, and benevolent founder-trustee,
as we shall see below, does not correspond to the facts.

Reading on, we discover that in 1751 Franklin used his political influence
and his growing fame as a promoter of good works to help found the Pennsylvania Hospital. In the same year, still unable to capture the leisure that by this
time must have seemed very elusive to him, he undertook more responsibility
and became a member of the Pennsylvania Assembly and also was elected al-
derman of Philadelphia. In the last five years covered in the *Autobiography,*
we discover that Franklin developed the essence of his farsighted Albany Plan
of Union for the mutual defense of the colonies; that he was very active in
supplying horses, wagons, and provisions for General Braddock's intended
campaign against the Indians; that he was one of the commissioners who en-
deavored to organize the defense of Northampton County; that as commander
of that County he supervised the building of three forts there in the dead of
winter; that he was commissioned colonel of the Philadelphia militia which he
organized; and that he left his family and friends and went to England as the
Assembly's agent, hoping to protect the rights of the people of Pennsylvania
against the avarice of the proprietor. It seems understandable, as Franklin
points out, that the people love him.

These are some of his most notable achievements, but by no means all of
them, for he delighted in useful works of lesser note as well. He was interested
in anything that would benefit his fellow men. We are told of his efforts to
increase the amount of colonial currency, and to improve the city watch, light
and clean the streets. It is impossible not to be impressed at the range
of his concern as well as with his accomplishments for the public welfare.
They were important to him, and he obviously felt that posterity would have
the same regard for them and for the man who engaged in so many projects as
he himself had. Franklin, then, uses his memoirs to do for his early and
middle years, at least, what his letters do for his later ones. He could not
know, of course, that future generations would be more selective than his own
time in appreciating useful projects or that many people would find it easy to
ridicule do-gooders, no matter how benevolent they were. And Franklin
makes certain that his readers will know that in all his work for the public it
had been a standing principle of his *"That as we enjoy great Advantages from
the Inventions of others, we should be glad of an Opportunity to serve others*

by any Invention of ours, and this we should do freely and generously."[41] Franklin, of course, did actually perform these and other good works. His facts as such are nearly always correct; however, as will be made clear, in some important areas they would not stand up very well in courts that require not only the truth, but the whole truth.

His enumeration of his deeds protects him not only from the charge of being self-seeking but also from that of disloyalty, for much of what he did proved his patriotism to America as well as his good will to England. During the years he was working at his memoirs, the matter of patriotism was necessarily a more important point than the fact that he had been a loyal subject and well-wisher to the Crown also. He is therefore careful to point out that he rejected with utter contempt the offer of a favor Thomas Penn had made through Governor Denny. Penn wanted Franklin at least to relinquish his role as the champion of the popular party against the proprietor in their ancient tax disputes. Franklin, then, scorned the advantages he could have gained from the wealthy and powerful proprietor, who had positions and land to give to those who served him well. All Franklin could get, we are left to believe, was the love of a people who knew he was working for them and also the sense that he had conducted himself honorably. But the author of the *Autobiography* further realized that his readers would likely see this early event as a forerunner of later bribe attempts made by the Crown, in which he would once again prove and report himself to be the patriot of the people rather than the lackey of the rich.[42] It was therefore for good reasons that the people honored him at times more highly than they had even Penn when he was in the province.[43] Further, the incident with Denny would seem a prefiguration of his later loyalty and integrity in England. The hero of the memoirs would no more betray the cause of his country than that of his province.

In the *Autobiography* Franklin hardly misses addressing himself to any charge that had been made against him. In letters and documents, as in the memoirs, for example, he vehemently denied the accusations made by eminent men, including the proprietor, that he had lived luxuriously abroad at the public expense and even embezzled public funds for private use.[44] In writing his life he offsets these claims by presenting examples of his well-publicized frugality and the benefits he derived from it. It was, of course, impossible for him to know how later generations would take to this virtue, that what the eighteenth century thought so well of would be scorned by many in the twentieth. He therefore points out that frugality had been impressed upon him when he was a boy, and that he had learned his lesson so well as to have lived modestly all the years covered in the memoirs and, by extension, afterward. Frugality is the fifth of his famous thirteen virtues and one, we are told, that contributed mightily to "the constant Felicity of his life down to his 79th Year." This was a major lesson taught by Poor Richard and one of the cardinal principles of his creator's *"great and extensive Project,"* his worldwide "united Party for Virtue," otherwise known as the "Society of the *Free and Easy;* Free as being by the general Practice of the Virtues free from the Dominion of Vice, and particularly by the Practice of Industry and Frugality, free from Debt, which exposed a Man to Confinement and a Species of Slavery to his Creditors."[45] Frugality is actually made, for most men, a precondition of morality. The world would certainly know that Benjamin Franklin did not live high off the hog either at his own expense or that of anyone else.

At least until he went abroad, Franklin was indeed frugal, and even in Europe he normally lived moderately if quite comfortably. It was no great problem, then, for him to defend himself on this ground, especially since he readily admits to some forgivable luxury in his household once he was established in his trade.[46] Other charges, though, took real skill in combating, and Franklin's responses to them at times account for a number of the most enjoyable parts of his memoirs. Rebuked severely for William's illegitimacy by enemies who sought to ruin Franklin politically, he is forced to admit to "some foolish Intrigues with low Women."[47] Presumably, one of these intrigues was with William's mother-to-be, though Franklin never mentions her specifically. Promiscuity was a touchy matter and his admission was not without danger to the success of his memoirs. Americans took a self-righteous pleasure in their morality and proclaimed it everywhere. Yet Franklin also knew them to be quite human and reasonably assumed that future readers would commit follies of their own which they also would keep from the world or mention only in general terms. His ready admission of his indiscretions therefore gains him sympathy. Moreover, he eases our consciences by handling his "errata" with a lightheartedness that makes his defensiveness and even his moralism appealing and charming. And everything comes out all right in the end![48] He says of his affairs, for example, that the women merely "fell in my Way"; he did not go hunting for them. Further, he had suffered properly for his escapades because of the "Expence and great Inconvenience" involved, and because of the "continual Risque to my Health by a Distemper which of all Things I dreaded, tho' by great good Luck I escaped it." He hardly seems to have enjoyed himself at all, and so parents could let their boys read about his life knowing that Franklin had provided another object lesson. Yet for the adults, it was good to know that for all his fame and moralism, the great man was altogether human and subject to human frailties. His readers are made to accept his defense because of his candor and humor. It is, after all, fun to think of him giving in to "that hard-to-be-govern'd Passion of Youth." The audience is relieved for itself as well as for the author to discover that he was not always the moralistic Father Abraham and is thus entirely disposed to forgive him his early adventures, as it does its own.

For those who uncharitably insist on more suffering, Franklin notes that his attempted advances to the mistress of his friend James Ralph were thoroughly resented by the woman and by Ralph. The lady repulsed his attempts, and his friend, who had been sponging off Franklin, let him know his conduct "cancel'd all the Obligations" Ralph had been under to him. "So I found I was never to expect his Repaying me what I lent to him or advanc'd for him."[49] In one way or another Franklin shows that he makes or is compelled to make amends for his errors. Usually he pays their price in so humorous and typically human a way that he succeeds in portraying himself as engaging and sympathetic in part because of his faults. What is more, he learns from his mistakes. He had been squandering money with Ralph but now turned his thoughts to frugality and decency. Upon resolving to reform, he finds a better paying job, decreases his lodging expenses and other appetites, and even has some success in reforming the habits of his fellow workers.[50] We are made to feel that with perhaps rare slips his conversion was genuine and that, accordingly, he persevered. His well-known success, humanitarianism, and moral character—all of these attest to his reformation. Thus he is able to defend himself against accusations of immorality as he does against charges of luxurious living at the public expense. Indulgence of any kind, he discovers, is not only unwise, bad, and unhealthful—it is expensive!

Another way in which the *Autobiography* serves to defend him against charges made about matters that occurred after 1757, the year the narrative ends, concerns his alleged base ingratitude to England. Although that nation, he says, had given him love, honors, and profitable positions, he owes it nothing. Not only did he perform his duties well, but he demonstrated his affection for England in a host of ways from trying to prevent war to suggesting in detail ways of improving the street lighting in London and "of keeping clean the Streets of London and Westminster." He repeats his proposals in the memoirs, hoping "they may afford Hints which some time or other may be useful to a City I love, having lived many Years in it very happily."[51] This was written in 1788, after the long and bitter war, and after Franklin had suffered great personal abuse from British writers and Wedderburn. No reader could fail to be impressed by the generosity of Franklin's sentiments or was likely to believe its benevolent author guilty of ingratitude or baseness.

Continuing his apologia, Franklin becomes more than irritated with detractors who argued that he owed his allegiance to the Crown because of his place in the post office. His tone is sharp as he says that he had been appointed postmaster of Philadelphia because his predecessor was negligent and incompetent, and that he had been promoted to deputy postmaster of America because of his success in the lower station. When he assumed charge of the American post office it had been a sorry, hodgepodge affair that was losing money. It was he who had made it not only profitable, but more profitable even than the post office of Ireland. And he therefore felt unindebted to England. Further, he is careful to point out, since he had been replaced for political reasons, the Crown had received "Not one Farthing" from the American post office. Franklin leaves the reader with the impression that his appointment as deputy postmaster general had been made solely in recognition of his achievements in the Philadelphia office. In the memoirs, hard work and competence are rewarded. While Franklin's diligence and success are not arguable, it is also true that he was promoted because he had solicited the higher position more than two years before he finally received his commission.[52] Here, as elsewhere, Franklin is perpetuating myths: a national one concerning opportunity and advancement in America, which will be discussed below, and the myth that he had always been above seeking political favors. The latter, designed to enhance his image, is simply false. Although his readers are led to believe differently, he had earlier in his career also asked for the clerkship of the Pennsylvania Assembly.[53]

When the facts do not jibe with the defensive myth of Franklin as the good man of tolerable abilities, who necessarily succeeds in the Land of Opportunity, they are altered, ignored, or subsumed. The Crown did not care about the advancement of Benjamin Franklin, but it did want to make money on the post office, and Franklin made it lucrative. The man, like the hero of the *Autobiography*, does not have to beg favors in a country where there are so many possibilities and so many things to be done. These are Franklin's facts and the interpretation one is forced to read into them. Further, he would have us conclude that the complete unprofitability of the post office after his dismissal results from the Crown's insistence on slavishly loyal rather than competent servants; therefore the Crown suffers justly, and Franklin's experience is made to seem a microcosm of the larger event of the war and independence. What he does, however, is to ignore the facts of history for the sake of his image. He had been dismissed from his post on January 30, 1774, and independence was declared officially only eighteen months later! Moreover, the colonies had been at war with England long before July 4, 1776. The post office could not likely have remained profitable regardless of who had been in charge. But again, Franklin is less interested in strict historical accuracy than in defending himself against damaging attacks on his character by inventing a plausible, delightful, and very useful but imaginative protagonist for his memoirs who, especially in the future, would stand for the actual man.

Given the fact that the persona was not only good and competent but also a lover of mankind, Franklin had to make certain that his memoirs addressed themselves to the serious charges of bigotry that had been hurled at him before and after he began writing about his life. Such an omission would have done irreparable damage to the image he wanted to create and leave behind. He had endured acute social and political embarrassment for unfortunate remarks he had made about various religious groups. Perhaps his most infamous public slip in this connection was his reference to the Germans as "Palatine Boors" who should not "be suffered to swarm into our Settlements, and by herding together establish their Language and Manners to the Exclusion of ours."[54] Franklin had cause to regret this comment, with its picturesque imagery, when thirteen years later the Germans, reminded of it, turned out in mass to help defeat him in the election of 1764.

This is his best known expression of bigotry, but he was guilty of others as well. The Friends, for example, he had once said, were the chief mischief-makers in the province, and in this respect were worse even than Jesuits.[55] As for Roman Catholics, Franklin often used Protestant hatred and distrust of them in comparing an opponent with Jesuits or "Popish" priests to make him obnoxious; and he made a bugbear of Catholics in his *Gazette*. In fact, a rhetorical technique that he seemed to enjoy using to discredit a non-Catholic institution or person was to compare either to Catholic counterparts.[56] Although he capitalized on a fear of Catholics to work up enthusiasm for defense against the Catholic French and their Indian allies during the wars against them, it is nevertheless true that Franklin did not overcome his Protestant antipathy for Catholics generally until he went to France in 1776 as the American commissioner.[57]

It was the dominant religious group in America, however, the Calvinists, whom Franklin lumped together as Presbyterians, that he most feared and disliked. Since the exploration of this situation is the province of the major part of this study, it is enough now to point out that he used his influence to work against organized Calvinism whenever it threatened to move out of the churches and become a viable part of the political and social life of the colonies. He had begun his career of anti-Calvinism as a youth in Boston and did not really accept Congregationalists or Presbyterians as groups until at least the late 1760's, nearly half a century later. He had frequently been accused of hating Calvinists by men who knew him and were active in church-related affairs. It is also true that Calvinists were among his chief opponents and although some of them hated Franklin for political reasons essentially, others recognized him as an enemy on religious grounds.

Religious bigotry, though, was thoroughly at odds with the image of himself Franklin wanted to leave behind. He therefore used his memoirs as he had his letters, like the one in 1790 to Stiles, to create a contrary picture of himself as the genial deist who, in his benevolence, is a friend to all religions and sects, though a member of none himself. He formulated his own well-known religious creed, he says, from "the Essentials of every Religion," especially those found in America, and he claims to have "respected" all of them, "tho' with different degrees of Respect as I found them more or less mix'd with other Articles which without any Tendency to inspire, promote or confirm Morality, serv'd principally to divide us and make us unfriendly to one another."[58] The statement, though carefully guarded, actually betrays some of Franklin's hostility toward religions that stressed theology, the "other Articles" he mentions, rather than general morality. What Franklin is saying here is that religion is acceptable if it conforms basically to his deistic principles. Yet he makes a point of noting, correctly, that he always gave his "Mite" for the erection of new houses of worship. It was good public relations to do so and sound image-building to note the fact; however, it was by no means an uncommon practice to make such donations and the act proves nothing about his relationships with different religious groups in America. Unfortunately, the Congregationalism Franklin knew in Boston and the Presbyterianism he lived with uncomfortably in Pennsylvania did not coincide with his notions of what religion should be and do. His troubles with these groups are matters that remain hidden from most people, for of necessity he either ignores them or plays them down skillfully in the *Autobiography.*

He does, to be sure, take upon himself some of the wrong for his early difficulties in Boston with the Congregationalist ministers and the Governor's party, but these he describes in only the vaguest and most fragmentary terms.

He is careful to mention that he did defend a Presbyterian preacher in Philadelphia; become a friend to the great evangelist George Whitefield; admire the open-mindedness of the Pennsylvania Dunkers; say kind things about Moravians and about a pious Catholic lady in London; and hold in high regard Quaker moral principles. To one degree or another all these things are true and there is indeed other evidence which supports Franklin's claim to religious tolerance. As this study will make clear, however, the general tolerance Franklin extended to religious groups leaves ample room for at least one crucial exception—his anti-Calvinism. In discussing this relationship one must come to grips with the brilliantly wrought picture of himself he has left us, a picture so plausible and so accurate in parts that the whole image has been accepted, as Franklin intended it to be.

None of this is to say that in defending himself against charges of bigotry, disloyalty, and other failings Franklin makes himself perfect. To have done so, of course, would have been disastrous. He owns up to his follies with humor and evident candor. Furthermore, his subsequent embarrassment or suffering and reformation (he nearly always reforms his ways) are treated with grace and charm. All of this is positively disarming, and though we may reject, or like to think we reject, his utilitarianism, we are forced to identify with him and even to like him. Our awareness that the writer is a great man and patriot contributes to our delight in discovering that he is also quite human. Franklin's treatment of himself makes us feel better about him, ourselves, and men generally.

A good example is the clever manner in which he deals with his pride. In making his confession of this, the oldest and most troublesome of human failings, he uses the ironic device of turning the tables on tradition and argues that vanity is often productive of good because it encourages people to live up to their inflated images of themselves; we should therefore give thanks to God for our vanity as for the other "Comforts" of life. In this way Franklin creates a charming defense not only for himself but for his fellow men. Surely, then, we must be ready to forgive him such minor sins if we are to forgive our own and want others to overlook them. Moreover, the man who is so perceptive, candid, and altogether human, we feel, is one in whom we can have confidence and, given the slightest bit of fudging here and there, is one in whom we can believe.

Further, the historical evidence is overwhelming: Franklin is certainly a great and good man, and unlike other such men he does not bludgeon us with his importance, abilities, or virtues. Although he is serious about morality, he treats his own well-known virtue lightly in the memoirs. This is true even for the latter parts, written during the period he was becoming an increasingly significant figure in politics and when he was already one of the greatest scientists and moral philosophers of his era. In light of his achievements, it is fair to say that the *Autobiography* is truly a very modest document, and this modesty contributes to his image as one of our most down-to-earth national heroes. Yet there is ample evidence in the *Autobiography* that he achieved a great deal, and we are left with the unmistakable impression that the author of so many deeds which benefited others is a man not only of ability but of genuine good will.

Such a man could hardly have been guilty, it seems, of such really serious faults as disloyalty, dishonesty, or bigotry. Accusations to the contrary seem too inconsistent with the image created in the memoirs to be true. This is perhaps especially true of the charge of bigotry, for it contradicts directly the image of the good man at the center of his life. Further, given the pervasive Calvinist origins of most Americans and yet the denominational and sectarian heterogeneity in the Middle Colonies, it would seem difficult for one to have been an active bigot and still have retained anything of a character, much less for one to be effectively hostile to Calvinist groups. Then, too, as Franklin is careful to point out, his views on religion were liberal and he had long been respected and loved by people whose religious beliefs were quite different from his own. He was, he reminds us, elected a trustee of the "New Building" that had been built for Whitefield during the Great Awakening and which was soon to house the students of the Academy of Philadelphia. Franklin was the only trustee who belonged to no sect or denomination; his colleagues chose him because "I was merely an honest Man. . . ."[59] The overall image of Franklin—the persona he creates for his life—is the good man of tolerable abilities who does many things and goes far in America; and the essence of that goodness, we are made to believe, is his altruism.

But this treats Franklin's self-created image and his achievement on a personal level, whereas the greatness of the *Autobiography,* and to a degree of the man, rests on our understanding of the memoirs as a national document, albeit a propagandistic one. What Franklin did for his own reputation he did for that of his country as well. If he is the man of "tolerable abilities," not unusual brilliance, who goes far personally and as a public figure, it is also true that he makes this rise seem almost inevitable, for America is the Land of Opportunity. The kind of man who fits into this country, exemplified chiefly by the protagonist of the memoirs, can hardly fail to succeed. It is this representative persona that Lawrence calls "the first dummy American," but to Franklin he was a necessary device for his country.[60]

In England almost continuously from the end of 1756 to the eve of the Revolution (he was in America from November 1762 to November 1764), Franklin saw emerge in the British press a horrifying image of America. Until the middle of the eighteenth century the colonies were considered by the journalists primarily as a source of wealth and power to the Empire. This situation changed dramatically, however, when Americans resisted the Stamp Act. Many in England came to see the refusal to pay the tax as the most unprincipled niggardliness. By the time Franklin began writing his memoirs his countrymen had long been represented in much of the British press as a rapacious, ungrateful pack of religious bigots, cowards, and intellectual inferiors, who might have to be taught a sharp lesson by their too lenient Mother country. Moreover, the writers for the King and the Ministry continued, the quality of life in America was vastly inferior to that enjoyed by Englishmen, and persons who went to America were traitors (after the outbreak of hostilities) or at best fools, since there were so few possibilities for success or happiness there.

This emerging image caused Franklin great personal distress, for his first mission in England (1757-1762) and the honors and friendships it brought him had made him a thorough Anglophile. Understandably his love for England diminished slowly. Until about the middle of 1765, he responded to the attacks with pointed but gentle humor;[61] however, as the vituperation increased and became more vicious, his defenses became sharper in tone.

It would not be surprising if he at times felt overwhelmed by his task, for the abuse flooded the press. The colonists were "wild" men,[62] a mere "mob"[63] led by a band of smugglers and traitors.[64] By 1766 the image of America had become so bad that Anti-Sejanus found himself the spokesman for many Englishmen when he called the colonists "scum and refuse" that, like an insensible and recalcitrant beast, had to be beaten severely.[65] Vindex Patriae revealed a root cause of the brutal attacks on the Americans: they were, he wrote, as if to explain all, in their religion, customs, indeed in their very morals, like the despised Scots! Small wonder, then, that the worst that could be said of them was true. They were necessarily intolerable boors who, as a matter of tradition, "persecute old women for witches."[66]

For others the Puritan background of so many Americans made them naturally immoral and riotous.[67] One journalist, playing on old English prejudices, asked: "Do we not know that Glasgow may be considered the capitol of Virginia," and that "New England is indebted to the Scotch kirk for her confession?" This meant to him that the Americans had to be taught a lesson and restored "to their inferior rank which they are only entitled to."[68] Astea charged that the rude life in America had made its white inhabitants "half Indians" who had to be treated as savages.[69] After all, one could not expect civilized behavior from people of such "pernicious doctrine."[70] It is clear that many Englishmen never forgave the majority of colonists for not having the good taste to be Anglicans. Moreover, among the bigots were members of the clergy. John Ewer, Lord Bishop of Landaff, tried to exploit the political hostilities to belittle Calvinism and further Anglican claims for the necessity of an American bishopric, a cause which was being hotly contended in America. The Dissenters, he said, had "abandoned their native manners and religion" when they left England, and now they had become as brutal and profligate as their Indian neighbors. They could be saved only by a bishopric and the establishment of Anglican seminaries throughout America.[71] The Bishop of Bristol agreed that the Church of England had to undertake civilizing the colonists,[72] and another penman for the Ministry condemned all Americans as "deformed Pharisees."[73] But it was the Boston "Puritans" who came in for the worst treatment. Not only were they "Philistines" and "sanctified hypocrites,"[74] but they were unparalleled examples of human "depravity."[75] Veritas declared flatly that all Americans were so degenerate and inferior by nature as to be "contemptible" even to their own slaves.[76]

Throughout his second mission in England (1764-1775) Franklin responded to these hostile attacks on his countrymen and on the quality of life in America. During this period he published at least 125 letters in the British press in addition to dispatching a great many more private letters to influential people in which he countered the charges.[77] The task of replying required a man of Franklin's abilities, knowledge, and energy, for he found himself defending his country on such grounds as its spiritual state, morality, the intelligence of its citizens, its culture, liberality, rationality, and climate. He even defended Americans on such matters as their breakfasts and their virility!

Yet people still left Great Britain to escape poverty. Moreover, the Ministry did not really believe its own propaganda would succeed, and throughout the Empire instituted policies unfavorable to emigration. The much despised Scots, too, were told to stay where they were and give up all thoughts of removing to America. Eventually the Crown declared it unlawful to emigrate and threatened severe punishment for those who tried to leave for the colonies. Even before war was actually declared, English policy made emigration synonymous with treason.[78]

To some degree the propaganda by itself was effective, for during his second mission Franklin had received many letters from people who wanted to go to America but who were afraid of what they would find when they arrived. Franklin responded to such letters patiently, but he was disgusted by English policy. He had long promoted emigration and knew better than most men that the country had a real need for decent, industrious settlers who, eager to practice their skills to advantage, would benefit the country in which they prospered.[79] He therefore sought in the latter parts of his memoirs to prove that such persons not only could but almost had to succeed in the new nation. In all parts of the *Autobiography* we find not only a reconstructed Franklin but also an America that is made to seem something like a utopia for common folk. Toward the end of his life he used his great prestige in pleading with Americans to desist from printing the libelous and scandalous pieces that had become so common a product of the native press, and thereby protect the image of their country and countrymen from enemies who were only too glad to read negative things about America.[80]

This promotional principle guided him in his representation of America in the memoirs. He could address himself to the claims of British military superiority and colonial incompetence by reminding everyone of the arrogant Braddock's disastrous campaign against a few French and Indians and of the colonists' skill and courage in battle. Such unsavory matters as political infighting, religious and social animosities, frontier versus city tensions, lawlessness, the ugly effects of provinciality, dishonesty in high places—all were treated humorously, glossed over, or ignored. Instead we find a country that produces a great number of successful, solid people, less famous than the protagonist of the memoirs, but nevertheless valued and comfortable citizens. We find a people who are concerned about the well being of their fellows and who promote useful projects to benefit the whole community, especially the less fortunate. For example, there is the old woman at Burlington, New Jersey, who kindly takes in the youthful Franklin for a time and tries to help him make his fortune as a printer by encouraging him to settle there and open up shop. Or there is Vernon, who conveniently leaves money with the young apprentice and neglects asking for it for years. Even Bradford and Keimer aided him before he proved to be a threat to them. Others, like the "grave, sensible, matron-like Quaker Woman" who saved the teen-aged Franklin from a couple of theiving "strumpets" helped in less monetary ways; but they nevertheless share in the honest concern among most of the Americans in the *Autobiography* to promote the interests of their country by giving aid to decent and industrious people of competence. The typical American, then, is very unlike the English Governor Keith who, with empty promises of patronage—promises he knew to be worthless—duped the young Franklin into going to England to buy type and set up shop in Philadelphia. Perhaps the single most significant contrast to Keith is furnished by the story of the good Quaker merchant, Mr. Denham of Philadelphia. This man speaks not only for the benevolent interest of Americans but also for their general integrity as well as for the opportunity that abounds in the new country. Having gone bankrupt in England, he moved to Philadelphia where, through diligence in his calling, he prospered. He returned to England to pay off his debtors—all that he owed them, plus interest. It is Mr. Denham who, in his kindness, saves Franklin from a career as a vagabond swimming instructor in Europe by the offer of a position in Denham's establishment.

The America of the memoirs is one in which poor apprentices, if they work hard and live decently, succeed. This is the story of most of the members of the Junto. We are told about Nicholas Scull, who rises from being a surveyor to surveyor-general, and also of William Coleman, who, beginning as a "merchant's clerk," eventually becomes "a merchant of great note, and one of our provincial judges." Those who, like Hugh Meredith, are unfit for trade can begin again in agriculture or some other field to which they are suited. Good, able men are needed in America and were, in the memoirs, sure to find help from a Mr. Denham, or even from so eminent a figure as the attorney Andrew Hamilton, another one of Franklin's patrons. Like David Hall they might one day become their master's partner in a business which would eventually become theirs to enjoy and profit from. Competent women, like the widow of Franklin's partner, Peter Timothy, if they possess the same qualities, can carry on businesses successfully. Opportunity necessarily abounds in an America which, in the *Autobiography*, is presented as a land of peace and plenty, comradeship and good will. So insistent was Franklin on this point that after the Revolutionary War he pleaded with President John Witherspoon of the College of New Jersey (Princeton) not to solicit funds in Europe for the school, for such solicitation would make America seem a beggar to Europeans and lower the new nation in the eyes of foreigners, whose good opinion it had to gain and keep.[81] In short, the America of the memoirs is consciously made both the

Land of Opportunity and, for the poor of the British Empire and Europe, the Land of the Second Chance. Good things happen in such a country materially and, as Franklin shows by using himself as an example, morally.

Indeed, his first serious moral failings occur while he is living in England. There the nineteen-year-old squanders his own money and uses what had been entrusted to him by Vernon; he attempts to seduce his friend's mistress; he ignores his obligations to Deborah Read; and it is in England that he falls into danger of becoming an itinerant swimming instructor. He is saved by Mr. Denham and brought back to America. The very thought of returning prompts the young man to reform his life, and while still on the ship bound for Philadelphia he develops plans for regulating his future conduct. America and immorality are nearly made incompatible. This is only appropriate, for just as Franklin created a favorable image of himself to offset the effects of frequent personal attacks, he tried to promote much needed emigration by making America seem as desirable a place as one could find for poor but good, industrious, and competent Europeans.

His treatment of his country, however, had not always been so sanguine and generous. In fact, it is fair to say that the overriding image of America Franklin created in his writings before his second mission to England was negative. Even when one considers that much of what he wrote is humorous and satiric, it is nevertheless true that he must have considered his humor and satire to have factual bases which would make them effective. When as Silence Dogood the young Franklin scores different groups of his countrymen as bigots, hypocrites, ignorant, stupid, and immoral dunces and drunken idlers, who are nonetheless proud, vain, and dull,[82] he is anticipating the accusations made by the hacks for the Ministry half a century later. Franklin, indeed, goes further than many journalists, for in the guise of the Widow Dogood and such other women reformers as Martha Careful and Caelia Shortface, he criticized American women for their alleged scandalous gossiping, vanity, immodesty, immorality, and prostitution.[83] As the male Busy-Body he expresses his great concern about "the growing Vices and Follies of my Countryfolk," and in pointing out what is still good in their character condescends to them just as English friends of America frequently condescended before the Revolution. About the best the Busy-Body can find to say about his countrymen is that while they are good people, they are never able to realize the potential they were born with, living as they do in an underdeveloped place short on opportunity.[84] Readers of Franklin's Casuist letters, his defenses of the Reverend Samuel Hemphill,[85] as well as many of his political pieces, feel that the Busy-

Body is being charitable, since these works picture Americans as a very sorry lot with whom no reasonable and moral person could live comfortably. And writing to his sister Franklin condemned the arbitrariness and arrogance of the majority of Americans—Calvinists—on religious matters.[86] His own condescending attitude toward his country he expressed in a letter to his friend, the prominent English printer William Strahan: "We have seldom any Newes on our Side of the Globe that can be entertaining to you or yours. All our Affairs are *petit* . . . [and] can seem but Trifles to you."[87] Franklin was not beyond treating his country in Lilliputian fashion to ingratiate himself to an Englishman of note. He was not a youngster lacking discretion when he wrote this letter, but a firmly established and very successful tradesman and citizen of Philadelphia. Even in his middle age he wrote to a friend in England that America was militarily incompetent,[88] a position quite different from the one he was later to uphold; and during his first mission in England, and even during part of his second crucial period there, he imaged America from time to time in negative terms.[89] He stopped downgrading his country only toward the latter part of 1766 when, responding to political changes and the attacks of pro-Ministry writers, he consistently defended America and reconstructed its image.

This change is mirrored in Franklin's treatment of England. One finds occasional unpleasant images of England created by him during his first mission, usually when he was upset by bureaucratic haggling or stupidity which delayed the resolution of matters important to him;[90] however, his basic Anglophilia remained undisturbed until about 1769. Only when he lost confidence in the justice of England, became increasingly intolerant of slanders in the British press, and began to see his countrymen in a more favorable light as an ardent patriot, did he depict England in essentially unfavorable terms. As his regard for his own country grew, his respect for the Empire waned; and these changes are reflected in Franklin's treatment of both countries. It should also be noted that even when England stood higher than America in Franklin's esteem, he tolerated no attacks on the colonies from English opponents. When during his first mission in England an Anglican attacked American Dissenters on the grounds that they universally hated the Church of England, Franklin defended them well, if not accurately. He replied that America was a country not only of tolerance but of complete religious harmony in which Anglicans and Dissenters lived in a state of peace and "good will" that was "both mutual and equal."[91] It is accurate to say that the America of the *Autobiography* was created as much in response to hostile English attitudes as it was to the need for settlers; and since the numerous Calvinists of America were often the most severely maligned, Franklin felt compelled to defend them.

Although he conceived of the propagandistic value and scheme of the memoirs himself, it is nevertheless true that others also recognized that the record of his life could inspire young people to accomplishment. Abel James, Quaker merchant and long-time ally of Franklin, knew "of no Character nor many of them put together, who has so much in his Power as Thyself to promote a greater Spirit of Industry and early Attention to Business, Frugality and Temperance with the American Youth." Benjamin Vaughan, Franklin's English editor, was perhaps even more influential. Writing in 1783, he told Franklin that if he did not write his life someone else surely would, and likely "do as much harm, as your management of the thing might do good." Considering what he elected to gloss over or quietly ignore in the *Autobiography,* these words may have served as a particular encouragement to Franklin. Vaughan also saw, as did Franklin, that the memoirs would "present a table of the internal circumstances of your country, which will very much tend to invite to it settlers of virtuous and manly minds."[92] Both correspondents, then, see Franklin's life not only as a personal document, but as a guidebook for living well and successfully. Franklin himself conceived of the work as a model to be used by "my Posterity," as he says in Part One and Part Two of the *Autobiography.*[93] Though he may have been referring specifically to his family descendants as well as to a general posterity in 1771, it seems more than likely that his reputation after the war and the condition of the struggling nation made him think of his posterity in the broadest possible terms. This had to include Europeans who, he knew, saw the American experiment as the hope for mankind and Franklin himself as the living embodiment of hope for the future of the average man.

Franklin was pleased by James' and Vaughan's letters, but he was also responsive to warnings such as the one sent by his French friend Louis Le Veillard, who said that printed accounts of Franklin's life contained serious errors. He called upon his American friend to set the record straight by finishing his memoirs. Though his personal reputation was important to him, Franklin was at least as concerned about defending his country, which, after 1765, had been steadily attacked.[94] These concerns dictate in great measure the form and persona of his memoirs, and influence much of his political writing, even to the extent that he defended the frequently maligned Calvinists.[95]

This suggests quite a different state of mind on the part of one who formerly believed that England represented the crowning achievement of liberty and progress.[96] He wrote to his young friend Mary Stevenson in 1763 that of all the splendid things England could boast of, he envied it most "its People," of whom there were so many more superior ones than in his own much larger country.[97] To Strahan Franklin wrote that he hoped to finish his affairs in America very soon and spend his remaining years in England.[98] Even during his second mission in England, while working against the Stamp Act and defending his country, he found it difficult to alter his views of the Mother country. He made it clear to Peter Collinson that America could not hope to withstand the thrust of English policy and had to have faith in the justice of Parliament.[99] Once the Stamp Act was passed, an impressed if dismayed Franklin described the power of England over America in cosmological terms. He told his friend Charles Thomson, in the summer of 1765, "We might as well have hinder'd the Suns setting," and he advised acquiescence to the decision.[100] If Franklin's confidence in England was in the least shaken, repeal of the tax made all well again and he wrote five letters in a week congratulating friends on the news and pleading with the colonies to remember their subordinate position and be dutiful children to their Mother.[101]

When it became clear to many Americans that the Declaratory Act, which accompanied the repeal and gave Parliament the power to make binding laws for America "in all Cases whatsoever," was a real threat, Franklin still remained naïvely sanguine. The Act, he said, was merely a face-saving gesture, and his countrymen could be certain that a wise Parliament did not mean to use such power as long as the colonists were generous and compliant subjects.[102] Though before long he would become less optimistic about Parliament, he continued to have faith in the benevolence of the King until after he had completed the first part of his memoirs in the summer of 1771. In fact, his most important personal reason for returning to England as agent in 1764 was to improve life in Pennsylvania by working to take it out of the hands of the proprietor and turn it over to the Crown. Even when the political situation grew very tense, Franklin persisted in working actively for the change of government until 1769, and he still desired it afterward for a time.[103]

It is interesting to follow the gradual change in his feelings. In the early spring of 1765 he was able to write a pleasant but effective satire on the unreliability of English news writers in the hope of discrediting the anti-American campaign in the press.[104] By the next year, though, his satires had become Swiftian. In "Pax Quaeritur Bellow" he is one Pacificus who ironically calls for a body of Scottish highlanders, Canadians, and Indians to massacre the bothersome colonials and replace them with felons transported from England in the interest of securing a lasting peace.[105] In general, Franklin's best satires were the result of his efforts to head off the war, and we find in 1773, for example, his "Rules by Which a Great Empire May be Reduced to a Small One." This, like other pieces, depicts England as a nation duped by vicious and self-seeking ministers and their allies who are stupidly and arrogantly leading the country into a disastrous war. The intensity of his criticism grew in nonsatirical pieces, too, as he attacked English vices and follies while defending his own country. England was denounced for its own riots and lawlessness, its traditional religious bigotry, insolence, general illiberality, narrow-minded nationalism, barbarism, selfishness, vanity, ignorance of America, unreasonableness, injustice, and virtually total political corruption.[106] From top to bottom English society was vile, and Franklin warned his fellow colonists that their enemies would demolish the posts in the Indian country so that the settlers would be subject to attack and have to become dependent on England for protection, a policy that would leave them, it was thought, at the mercy of Tory politicians.[107] The baseness at the highest level of society filtered down, and Franklin depicted the laboring but poor English workingman as a lazy good-for-nothing who squandered his time and money in alehouses and was therefore responsible for his own destitute condition.[108] Even the Anglican clergy were rebuked. Franklin charged that the missionaries of the Venerable Society for the Propagation of the Gospel in Foreign Parts were a source of bitterness against America. These men and their superiors would control religion in the colonies, whose population was comprised overwhelmingly of Dissenters; thus they poisoned the minds of Englishmen against Americans, representing them as destitute of religion and morals, enemies to the Anglican Establishment, and a threat to England, in the hope of forcing the government to establish the Church of England in America.[109] By 1770, the year before he began the memoirs, Franklin, still working for peace and trying to be a friend to both countries, was thoroughly fed up with the English ministers, whom he called a group of debased fools bent on risking war so that they could tax the colonies at will and thereby gratify a useless group of jobless "Court Harpies." He suggested that the Ministry could raise all the revenue it needed by taxing instead the "Luxury and Vice" that was universal in England.[110] As for average Englishmen, of whom Franklin once thought well, he attacked them for their arrogant and contemptuous attitude toward America.[111] By the autumn of 1770, there was no group in England that was sacrosanct.

Franklin's efforts at image-building continued into the crucial years after 1771. Early in 1772 he looked upon New England in a way that would have surprised the young apprentice of half a century earlier. He contrasted vividly "the Happiness of New England, where every Man is a Freeholder, has a Vote in public Affairs, lives in a tidy, warm House, has plenty of good Food and Fewel, with whole cloaths from Head to Foot, the Manufacture perhaps of his own Family," with the condition of the common people of Scotland and Ireland. These unfortunates had to do without the necessities of life so that the manufacturers and merchants could carry on an extensive and very profitable trade. Moreover, America was blessed in not having the "enormously wealthy" gentry who kept British farmers mere tenants, "poor, tattered, dirty, and abject in Spirit." In comparison to the depressing existence of these wretches, savages enjoyed real comfort and "every Indian is a Gentleman. . . ."[112] His words were double-edged: they were not only a criticism of social conditions within the Empire, but a promise of a better life to potential emigrants.

Later that year Franklin further indicated that his alienation from England included its basic institutions, as once more he attacked the Church of England in defending the liberality and good will of American Calvinists.[113] Though he could hardly be called an Anglican, Franklin had long held a pew in Christ Church of Philadelphia and formerly thought well of the Church of England. His open criticism of the Church expresses the fact that he was preparing himself and many of his countrymen psychologically for the final break with England. To Cushing he wrote, "our great Security lies" not in a benevolent or even wise and fair Parliament and King, but "in our growing Strength, both in Numbers and Wealth; that creates an increasing Ability of assisting this Nation in its Wars, which will make us more respectable." More important, though, was the fact that the growing strength of America would make "our Friendship more valued, and our Enmity feared."[114] This is not the language of the peacemaker and diplomat, but of an angry, disgusted, and abused man who is forgetting to keep separate accounts of private and national injuries. English hostility and intransigence only confirmed his deepening conviction that separation was inevitable. Franklin came to believe that liberty was vanishing in England and that all who truly valued this blessing would seek a haven in America.[115]

In the winter of 1775 he warned his countrymen that all Europe saw America as a refuge, and that as Americans they had to guard their reputations. In fact, he announced, the "eyes of all Christendom are now upon us, and our honor as a people is become a matter of the utmost consequence to be taken care of."[116] A good image among foreigners would make friends for the colonies and encourage emigration among useful people who would increase America's growth, power, and wealth. He determined, then, to do what he could to make its reputation as positive as possible. He tried to inculcate patriotism in his son and in another Tory, his former political ally Joseph Galloway. Inspired by his own enthusiasm for the American cause, Franklin seems to have ignored the fact that Galloway was also experienced in colonial politics and knew how vicious it could be. There seems no better explanation to account for Franklin's idealized picture of American public affairs which he praises as "the glorious public Virtue so predominant in our rising Country." Indeed, he seems ready for a declaration of independence and full scale war when he declares, "I cannot but apprehend more Mischief than Benefit from a closer Union"[117] with Great Britain. In the *Public Advertiser* for February 7, 1775, he again defended American religion, courage, and gallantry and reminded his British opponent that the population of America was increasing rapidly while that of England and Scotland was declining.[118] For years, beginning with his frequent claims that England was dependent on America, Franklin's public pronouncements created the impression that while England's star was clearly descending, that of America was steadily and certainly rising on the horizon.

What had been developing in the course of his years of defending his country and having second thoughts about England was a love affair between him and America, stronger by far than the one he had once had with the Mother country. He lauded the bravery and nobility of his suffering countrymen and their pervasive idealism. These were not things, he wrote to Joseph Priestley, that would be believed in England. It would seem incredible there that "men can be as diligent with us from zeal for the public good, as with you for thousands per annum. Such is the difference between uncorrupted new states, and corrupt old ones."[119] Some of Franklin's idealism doubtless can be attributed to the political situation and also to the fact that he had been away from home for so long; yet he knew America well, especially the bare knuckles world of colonial politics. The utopian picture he paints, then, is in large measure prompted by his ardent desire to enhance the image of his country.

In his lyrical idealization of Americans and of the nation that was developing, he reverted to Calvinist modes of thought which he had rejected half a century earlier. America was God's country, a kind of secularized or nondenominational City on a Hill, the center of God's consciousness and predestined to victory and true greatness as it became a vital symbol of promise and fulfillment. It was useless to contend, he told an English correspondent. With the exception of a few Tories and placeholders, all the country was united against England. While the British regulars, at an expense of £3,000,000, had managed to kill 150 Americans, "sixty-thousand children have been born in America."[120] "God," he wrote to another Englishman, "will protect and prosper America."[121] Addressing himself to foreign readers, he imaged the America of the future as a powerful and virtuous nation comprised of hard-working, frugal, honest, and reliable people who, as a natural result of their fine character and great opportunities, would surely thrive.[122]

Writing from France in 1777 he saw his country again as the refuge for good and industrious but sometimes oppressed Europeans, men who longed for liberty and a chance to improve their lives. There were, he said, men everywhere "who talk of removing to America with their families and Fortunes, as soon as Peace and Independence shall be established." Thus, he enthusiastically reported, all Europe felt "that our Cause is *the Cause* of all Mankind, and that we are fighting for their Liberty in defending our own. 'Tis a glorious task assign'd to us by Providence" and was certain of "Success."[123] The new nation's messianic role in history was, as Franklin envisioned it, to offer not magnificence or opulence that thrives on poverty and great inequality, but instead a decent life with all the necessities for a "virtuous and laborious people." Given the prospects of the country, its excellent and cheap farm land, the growing need for tradesmen and businessmen in a dramatically increasing population, the mildness of the laws, and inexpensiveness of small and honest government, the proper people could hardly fail to succeed.[124] A mission so humane was bound to meet with the approval and favor of a benevolent and just God. "It is with great Sincerity," he exclaimed to Josiah Quincy in 1779, "that I join you in acknowledging and admiring the Dispensations of Providence in our Favour. America has only to be thankful, and to persevere. God will finish his Work, and establish their Freedom; and the Lovers of Liberty will flock from all Parts of Europe with their Fortunes to participate with us of that Freedom, as soon as Peace is restored."[125]

Privately Franklin worried a good deal about unpleasant realities that did not seem appropriate to the nation he was describing. He was very concerned about such developments as the "Corruption of Manners" that arose from a depreciating currency,[126] and he protested the widespread practice in America of newspaper libeling. He appealed to his countrymen to end the practice and he pleaded with printers to realize that they were the guardians of their country's reputation and thus to refrain from printing libels. These pieces, he warned, would provide British newspaper writers additional grounds for attack and make our friends uncertain about Americans. Ultimately, the practice would keep potential emigrants in Europe out of fear.[127] Until he returned home and wrote a piece on the subject for a newspaper, such complaints were confined to personal letters to printers, and he continued ignoring this and other unpleasantness about America while promoting it as the new promise of God to the common man of virtue, diligence, and competence. Although he had on occasion promoted emigration before 1771,[128] his greatest efforts in this direction began in 1773. He enlisted the support of Galloway in electing Samuel Dunn, "a very ingenious Mathematician and universal Mechanic, very fond of America," to the American Philosophical Society. Franklin thought that since Dunn was "very desirous of the honour," he might be moved to settle in America once he had been elected.[129] When he discovered one Robert Hare, who was thinking of moving to Philadelphia to start a brewery, Franklin again called on Galloway, and also on the Reverend Thomas Coombe of Philadelphia's Christ Church, asking them to make Hare, who was known to be a good and able man, welcome in the city.[130]

Franklin was intensely bitter over plans to halt emigration to America. In a piece that he probably left unpublished, he responded to a Scottish writer who charged that emigrants to America "must suffer" great "misery." Franklin promised them instead the same "felicity" earlier settlers had always enjoyed, ample opportunity to succeed, the good will of the people and an end to privation.[131] The prospects in America were far better than those in the compliant British colony of West Indies where, as the memoirs show, people who left Philadelphia to settle often perished miserably or died young.[132] To Charles W.F. Dumas he wrote that while America was no place yet for "gentlemen of mere science in *les belles lettres*," it was certainly "a good country for artificers or farmers."[133] After independence had been declared, Franklin called on all "Friends of Liberty and of Man"[134] to leave England and come to America. He told David Hartley that all English Whigs, provided they did not support the Tories, would one day be able to emigrate and thus enjoy liberty once again.[135] To the wealthy Charles Epp, he praised not only the people, government, and laws in America, but its very air in urging Epp to settle in the country after the war.

Most of the people who inquired about emigrating, however, and the ones to whom Franklin addressed himself generally, were the middling sorts. When three English manufacturers expressed their desire to settle in Pennsylvania, Franklin encouraged them in every way he could. But these men, like others, thought they were doing the struggling nation a favor and demanded special consideration. This attitude always irritated Franklin. The men would not, as they had wanted, have their transportation paid by the government. Franklin would not allow his country to seem a beggar after talent or mere bodies. The government, he therefore wrote, could not possibly pay their way, for so great a number of worthy Europeans were moving to America that the transportation costs would be astronomical. All who came here would have to be content with excellent prospects, a fine climate, and mild government and laws.[136]

So considerable was the desire to emigrate and so assiduously did Franklin encourage it, that he found himself pestered continually, often by the wrong kind of people. He therefore wrote his comprehensive "Information to Those Who Would Remove to America," in which he clearly identified the kind of people he wanted to see settle in his country. They were, on the whole, the kind of people represented by the persona of the *Autobiography*. These people would find that they could buy large estates for very little money, and that the land was continually increasing in value. As they prospered they could add to their land and would be able to start their children out in life with good farms of their own. And, as Franklin points out, there is no better place for children, since America is made up of moral, hard-working, and thrifty people who praise God for His goodness to them. They are a happy people, and newcomers will encounter none of the religious hostility so typically and destructively prevalent in Europe. Rather, as Franklin continues his myth-making, they will discover that "the Divine Being seems to have manifested his Approbation of the mutual Forebearance with which the different Sects treat each other, by the remarkable Prosperity with which He has been pleased to favour the whole Country."[137]

Franklin knew better than this. There was widespread religious rivalry and bigotry in America. He had had long experience with the bitter religious struggles between Dissenters and the Church of England and among Dissenters themselves. What is more, he knew that he had himself been involved deeply, and often shamefully, in hotly contested battles in which religion, especially denominational power, was the major source of contention. These facts corroborated charges of religious bigotry made against him and his countrymen. He would therefore betray neither this nor other unhappy facts about America and himself, for both needed good publicity. Franklin wanted to leave behind a positive picture of himself, and America had to be depicted as a place receptive to good, industrious people regardless of their religious persuasion. Facts that seriously marred his own reputation or that of the nation obviously did not fit into his image-making and were generally changed, subsumed, or ignored—and this is what Franklin perpetuated in personal letters and in publications for the press. He continued to promote America and himself, as only he could, even in the face of great official opposition from England.[138] Essentially the same plan holds true for the *Autobiography* as well, and it is small wonder that toward the end of his life Franklin was disturbed by biographies of him that appeared filled with errors. He tried to dissuade publishers from printing any accounts of his life,[139] hoping that he would have time to write his own version. In doing so he created for the world not only a picture of Benjamin Franklin, but even more of a typical American who acts out the success story that is America. This character is Lawrence's "dummy," who automatically prospers in a land of unbounded promise. If, indeed, the persona of the memoirs is a dummy, his creator is manipulating the strings to make him play a carefully conceived and vital role in the national drama. And nowhere is the disparity between the Franklin and the America of the memoirs and writings—and those that actually existed—more dramatically seen than in his relationship with the Congregationalist and Presbyterian Establishments before the Revolutionary period. This relationship, though characterized by sentiments utterly antithetical to those he created for himself and his country, is fascinating and revealing, and it takes shape first in the Boston of his youth.

II

Doing Good in Boston

Franklin was born in Boston in 1706 and grew up at a time when the piety that had been a hallmark of Puritanism had waned. Secularization, political unrest, and economic dissatisfaction were coming to the surface in a number of anti-Establishmentarian ways. Political conservatives like the Dudleys and the clerical power structure in the Boston area tried to make the people more amenable to law and authority. Against these forces was the anti-Court party led by the two Elisha Cookes and their followers, who wanted to liberalize the colony and assume a greater share of power. For the ministers, especially, the times seemed very bad—a sad contrast to a time in the recent past when a core of godly citizens and a good government controlled the insubordinate. By 1721, however, the clergy felt they had been shoved aside in many areas which they considered part of their legitimate province. The fragmentation of authority was part of the secularizing thrust. Judge Samuel Sewall complained, "we live in Such An Age that Its too Often a flouting expression to be called a Ministerial man," and he warned "that ye present Contempt of Our Ministry carries with it a Very Ill Omen." Yet even the orthodox Sewall feared being too thoroughly identified with the clergy and refused to allow his name to be used by the ministers when they solicited contributions.[1] Clearly, unless New England was going to continue to deteriorate—and Cotton Mather had pronounced Boston "an Hell upon Earth" already in the possession of Satan[2]—the clergy would have to reassert themselves as a central force in everyday affairs as well as in theology and morals. Led by Mather, they largely overcame divisions within their own ranks for a time and did try to reaffirm the universality of their proper concerns by assuming authority in medicine and public health.

The smallpox epidemic which wracked the Boston area in 1721 proved to be socially explosive as well as deadly.[3] Coming as it did when Bostonians were growing very hostile to English economic and cultural domination and increasingly negative to the way their own secular and religious Establishments treated them,[4] the plague and the confusion and animosity attending it posed grave dangers. Zabdiel Boylston, though he had no medical degree, was trained as a physician and inoculated ten persons in July 1721. The method of inoculation he used was correct in its time and has become the basis for modern practice. It was new, however, and the majority of people were in no mood to experiment and perhaps spread the disease, which was already becoming an epidemic. They were therefore furious at Boylston and his chief supporter, Cotton Mather; and the House of Representatives, expressing widespread fear, forbade inoculation. But the Governor's Council turned down the House bill and Boylston continued his inoculations. Dr. William Douglass, a European-trained physician with a medical degree, renewed the attack against the practice that had been carried on with Mather's support. Douglass ridiculed inoculation, Boylston, Mather, and all who agreed with them. Boston was essentially divided into two camps. Most of the clergy, though often at odds over religion and politics, united with Mather on this issue. From the lower end of the social scale, however, came the vehement opposition of a group of freethinkers and liberal Anglicans who gathered around James Franklin's *New England Courant*.

This newspaper, published without government sanction, was born to do battle with the religious and civil Establishments. It had attacked the government on matters of its competence and policy and had been chiding the magistrates and particularly the clergy for failing miserably to keep New England moral. Had the ministers, the Couranteers argued, been doing their job of watching over the conduct of the people instead of interfering in politics and economics, areas in which they were completely ignorant, everyone might be better off. Inoculation was yet another instance of the clergy putting their two cents into affairs that were in no way connected with their proper concerns. Although Douglass may have had professional reasons for opposing inoculation, the viciousness of his attacks on Mather and his allies indicates that he, like the other Couranteers, was using the smallpox scare to blister the ministers and their political supporters. As *Courant* readers were to discover, even New England's traditional religious beliefs were fair game.

The first issue of the *Courant* appeared when the disease had already caused hysteria in Boston, and when the battle over inoculation was red hot. In this issue John Checkley, a bookselling apothecary who was later to become an Anglican minister, took on the clergy. Checkley, who was one of

James Franklin's friends, had earlier driven the Mathers and their friends to rage with his defenses of the Apostolic origins of the Church of England and his diatribes against Calvinism. Now as an anti-inoculator he was again insulting the clergy. He attacked them and Boylston in a brief but effective satirical poem. They, he wrote, "like faithful Shepherds take care of their Flocks,/By teaching and practising what's Orthodox,/Pray hard against Sickness, yet preach up the POX!"[5] The implication is that the ministers are deficient not in good will or in works, but in intellect, at least when they roam outside the familiar realm of theology. Checkley's attack poses the very real problem of whether one should accept the word of a man simply because he wears the cloth. Many good people in Boston were saying no and insisting that in secular matters practical knowledge and experience meant more than an old name, a good character, piety, or expertise in theology.[6]

The Reverend Thomas Walter of Roxbury retaliated anonymously in *The Little Compton Scourge: Or, the Anti-Courant,* which James Franklin, with a sense of the ridiculous and an eye on business, printed. In what is intended to be a satire, Walter chides "the miserable and dull *Couranto,*" who writes with nerve rather than mind. The minister condemns his opponents for taking up a pen without first having acquired a degree from Harvard or without even any "Pedigree."[7] Walter's performance betrays not only the sensitivity of the Boston area clergy, who were desperately trying to regain something of their former status and influence, but also their bankrupt power for he had to fall back on worse than irrelevant arguments to defend his colleagues and profession against a physician and a group of tradesmen.

Checkley was not disheartened or chastened and again insisted that the ministers confine their endeavors to the realm of the spirit.[8] In this demand he was supported by Douglass, who once more tried to force the clergy back into their churches and thereby limit the scope of their activity and power. No longer, he declared, could the people allow their ministers to use "a Cloak of Piety and Devotion" to cover up half truths and "Quack Recommendations."[9] Mather was hurt but undefeated. His concern for Boston, his conviction that he was correct, his great desire to reaffirm the right of the clergy to intervene in practical affairs—a matter central to his perception of the universe—and the encouragement of agent Jeremiah Dummer, who wrote that inoculation was a great success in England—all these drove Mather to insist on the benefits to be gained from the practice.[10] Thus the verbal struggle continued on both sides, adding to the confusion and excitement of the people, the amusement of the Couranteers, and to the frustration of the clergy. Surely one of the most dangerous and demoralizing attacks, from the point of view of the ministers, was the attempt to make their positions untenable by calling into question their morality. Douglass, for example, had charged that Mather, in his colossal vanity and conceit over his exaggerated intellect, was defending inoculation only because he desired the reputation of a scientist. He was willing, in other words, to criminally sacrifice the very lives of his fellows at the altar of personal aggrandizement.[11] Not content with their proper functions, Mather and his ministerial supporters would lord it over the community regardless of the disastrous consequences of their actions. The whole situation reminded Douglass of another ministerial "Infatuation . . . of about Thirty Years" earlier: many innocent persons had suffered at Salem, too, as Mather and others should well remember.[12]

William Cooper, who shared the duties at Brattle Street Church with Benjamin Colman, tried to turn back history by establishing theology as the basis for the argument. Inoculation, he said, is approved by God because the first law of nature "is GOD'S Law." It is one of God's means which He provides degenerate man to escape from just punishment, and therefore inoculation is a holy instrument in the divine plan.[13] Later, Mather went beyond science, suggesting that after all bodily sickness was but a metaphor for the condition of Boston's collective soul, and for such a malady the only certain cure was a speedy return to the old piety.[14]

The Couranteers and their allies failed to be convinced by such poetic reasoning and continued their onslaught. Thomas Robie, a Harvard tutor in science who had also been inoculating, complained of the furious "Boston-Mobb" that had harassed him and his patients.[15] An old, tired, but still useful Increase Mather bemoaned, Jeremiah fashion, the sinful times and, perhaps thinking of particular persons, complained that *"the Sons of Good Men"* sometimes turn out badly.[16] The Reverend John Webb, who apparently saw no victory for his side in the pamphlet war with the *Courant* group, significantly reminded the civil officials of their duty to work for the Reformation by "a diligent search into the several steps and grounds of a People's Degeneracy."[17] Soon the politicians, some of whom supported inoculation and many of whom resented the attacks on the clergy and government made by James Franklin and his friends, would join the contest on the side of the ministers, the side of God and, as they saw events, the side of law, order, and traditionally established authority. They would, a good number of them, especially dislike James Franklin because as printer of the *Courant* he was responsible for the abuse heaped on the men of God and for attacks on government policy and competence. Not only had James accused the public officials of laxity in protecting the colony,[18] he boldly criticized them for supporting the lies hurled by the clergy at him and his friends.[19] Such attacks on the politicians were poor judgment. Liberal and conservative factions alike had to make a show of defending the dignity of government; they therefore imprisoned James and called his apprentice, Benjamin, before the General Court to give an account of himself.

By the time the younger Franklin entered the lists as Silence Dogood, the Boston area press had become a battleground for a war between those who favored inoculation, piety, and sanctification and those who were against the practice, covertly or openly impious, and happily unsanctified, at least by the New England standards of April 2, 1722. Franklin was only sixteen at the time, but was already "a thorough Deist,"[20] to the concern of his piously dissenting parents.

They would have to grow accustomed, however, to sons who dissented in their own way. Writing in the guise of Mrs. Dogood, Franklin picked up the anti-ministerial and anti-government themes that had already appeared in the *Courant,* and with his charming and felicitous prose and first humorous persona, joined his brother and James' friends in attacking both Establishments in an effort to undermine their positions. For Benjamin—who had been destined for the clergy by his father, but who, after family plans changed, rejected Congregationalism[21] as incredible—the chance to attack the clergy seems also to have served the purpose of justifying his adoption of deism. Benjamin not only delights in ridiculing the ministers and their faith, but in the *Dogood Papers* he actually launches what became a career of hostility toward major Calvinist groups, at least when they threatened to become an important force in secular life.

Considering his purposes, his choice of a persona is excellent. Mrs. Dogood, the moralistic widow of a good country parson, is an example of a mask that meets the rhetorical requirements of satire.[22] The classical rhetoricians pointed out that the essential elements of communication involve the ethos of the speaker since the audience evaluates him, the power of the speaker's arguments because he had to persuade his audience, and the effectiveness of the speaker's appeal to the emotions and interests of his audience. In satirizing his opponents Franklin's chief obligation is to establish the Widow's ethos in such a way as to make her character not only acceptable but engaging, and therefore to create in the audience a disposition to accept her arguments. It should be remembered, moreover, that though they are couched in humor, these arguments are generally quite serious. Basically, then, the character Franklin chooses for his persona is the best possible, the good common person—the mask we encounter in the *Autobiography*. That Silence is female adds to the satirical effect of her pieces, for she is commenting on problems that were normally considered the concern only of men. The Widow, of course, is helped a good deal by the fact that her views were shared by many other average decent people who, for one reason or another, were dissatisfied with the ministry or the government or both. In identifying Mrs. Dogood with the middling sort of town person,[23] then, Franklin is trying to make sure that her arguments will enjoy the authority that comes conveniently from articulating views that, at least in some quarters, are current. Further, the Widow not only appeals to the emotions and interests of her audience, but as her attacks express the views of others as well as those of her creator, they are made to appear synonymous with the welfare of the good people. It is their true interest she is determined to protect against all foes, regardless of their status and power. Her enemies are therefore the enemies of the people, even if they are found particularly among the Governor's party and in pulpits.

The second sentence from her pen is, in fact, a gibe at the snobbery of the clergy, a sore point with many New Englanders. Silence feels called upon to defend her right to make use of the press because "the Generality of People, now a days, are unwilling to either commend or dispraise what they read, until they are . . . informed" whether the writer is "*poor* or *rich*, . . . a Schollar or a Leather Apron Man."[24] One of the chief claims to importance left to the ministers was the tradition of an educated clergy. In times of declining piety their education became increasingly significant to them because it placed them above the majority of people, even the wealthy merchants. Perry Miller has pointed out the weight the ministers placed on their college training and degrees,[25] since it gave them, in their minds, the right to decide or at least have an important say in critical secular matters regardless of the objections that might be raised by a population that was becoming less godly and respectful. Like Checkley and Douglass, then, Silence is challenging the supremacy of the ministers in intellectual matters by saying that the proof of one's ability is in what he says and how he says it, and not in the facts of his biography.

We learn that these pragmatic criteria of the workaday world apply to politicians as well as ministers. Effective performance of duty rather than family name, community status, or private wealth would determine one's skill in government. Though events later proved that most of the politicians resented being treated in such a manner, the insistence on tangible evidence of ability rather than position came at an especially difficult time for the clergy. They had become involved in the controversy over paper money as a solution to Boston's financial crisis, a fact which in itself was enough to anger a substantial number of people. When the ministers actually took one side or the other in the controversy, or advocated prayer and frugality as the means of resolving economic problems, they alienated a substantial part of the community. They were told openly to concentrate on theology and leave financial matters to those best able to handle them. Worse yet, there were those who had the nerve to accuse ministers who favored paper money with adopting this position solely out of greed.[26] Such attacks were very rare and hardly constituted a sustained assault. It remained for the Couranteers to launch a full scale war. Nevertheless, the first Dogood piece was itself a significant attempt to remove the clergy from what was becoming the essentially secular mainstream of Boston area life. Silence's first contribution also corroborates earlier *Courant* barbs on the scope of the clergy's role and on the limits of their authority and ability. Perhaps just as important, the letter establishes a precedent for further attacks on the ministers, attacks one feels she had been planning for some time.

In her second letter we discover that she is a lover of virtue and charity and "a great Forgiver of *private* Injuries." The italics tell an interesting story: they inform her readers that the groups and vices she attacks will be assailed not out of a personal desire for revenge or because of private antipathy, but because of her concern for the common good. Moreover, the injuries will be public and should therefore be remedied by average citizens like herself. Of course, the most public people of authority were the clergy and civil officials. The next part of the sentence, following the point about "*private* Injuries," calls the reader's attention to the ministers, for Silence goes on immediately to say that she is "A hearty Lover of the Clergy and all good Men."[27] This phrase anticipates a forthcoming charge against the Widow and also relates the ideas of public injury and the ministers. The "all good Men" is much too generalized to evoke any kind of picture or attach itself to any specific group, and so we are left with the notions of public harm and the clergy. Silence follows her reference to the ministers and good men generally with the warning that she is "a mortal Enemy to arbitrary Government and unlimited Power." Here she not only suggests that at least some in government are arbitrary and power-mad, but she makes us feel that she will rebuke only them, or others in positions of authority. Just as we were given the contrast between private injuries which Mrs. Dogood could easily forgive, and the presumed public injuries which she could not and should not forgive readily, we now have the contrast between good men and those who would do harm to the public, in this case those who would make government arbitrary and who seek tyrannical power. The whole sentence—"I am one of an extensive Charity, and a great Forgiver of *private* Injuries: A hearty Lover of the Clergy and all good Men, and a mortal Enemy to arbitrary Government and unlimited Power"—creates positive and negative categories, and in doing so exposes the objects of the satires: evil men who, for their own purposes, would bring the public to their knees. As defender of the good people, whose goodness she shares, the Widow presumably also represents them and speaks for them, giving voice and form to what they feel about the groups who are made to be their common enemies. These men, Silence warns her readers, are very dangerous for they are usually thought to be pillars of morality and Christianity and are held up as models by those in power, leaders who themselves are too often deceived by hypocrites.[28] Why so many in the Establishments should be easily deceived is a matter Silence is confident her readers will figure out for themselves. Yet in the remaining letters we learn again that there are clearly among the religious and political leaders those who would strip the good common people of their liberties so that they could have things their own way. This was a position that met with support among many self-reliant and alienated people; however, the clergy and the Governor's party especially, among the politicians, were less happy with the Widow's satires.

Undaunted by the opposition to herself and the other Couranteers, Silence continued her thrusts. In her fourth letter, for example, she once more attacks the clergy, this time through Harvard College, the breeding ground of most New England ministers and a substantial number of politicians. She discovers that most of those who attend the College are "little better than Dunces and Blockheads," their sole preparation for learning being their family's wealth. Poverty prevents far worthier boys from attending. What is worse, those who gain entrance, unmindful of their opportunity, ignore learning and keep company with idleness and ignorance.[29] Mrs. Dogood is little concerned about accuracy here, for the lengthy lists of promising but impoverished students who attended Harvard on scholarships or other aid were regularly made public.[30] In fact, for the period of 1712-1732, Harvard actually spent as large a percentage on financial aid for students as it did in 1964-1965; and in 1723, 11.6 percent of its budget was allocated for student aid, a figure that has not yet been equalled![31] Facts, like accuracy, however, were unimportant to

Silence, who was intent on increasing popular hostility toward the Establishments and their symbols. She could therefore belittle the frequent and well-grounded complaints of the clergy that they could not live decently on their salaries and, taking advantage of the financial crisis in New England, charge that the ministerial candidates at Harvard were foreshadowings of the settled clergy in that they all had been called to their profession not by God, but by "Pecunia," who alone is their sole motivation to continue their studies.[32] This must have seemed an incredible thing to say to the ministers and Harvard faculty who were in dire straits and needed salary supplements to get along.[33] Their fixed incomes were inadequate during times of inflation and depressed currency, and these were frequent problems in New England. Secular people also complained of the pinch, but the Widow singles out the ministers for attack, arguing that their complaints were another indication of their well-known greed. Though the facts were, in the case of finances, on the side of the clergy, Silence knew that many *Courant* readers would readily believe the worst about the ministers.

She does not stop here in her effort to discredit them and the College, for her next piece challenges their usefulness, orthodoxy, and morality. The clergy are nothing more than cheats, she charges, and are not even true to their own particular religious group, for they plagiarize from the Anglican Archbishop "Tillotson's *Works* . . . to embellish" their own.[34] The reference to Tillotson may be a slap at Harvard President John Leverett's well-known sympathy with Episcopalianism. His religious liberalism made for him influential enemies among strictly orthodox ministers in New England, and Silence may be fanning smoldering coals. In any case, such dishonesty, she says, is part of the game played by all concerned with the school, and Harvard is actually no better than "a Dancing School" whose graduates leave "as great Blockheads as ever, only more proud and self-conceited."[35] Obviously, then, there was little need to show respect or pay attention to the ministers. Samuel Mather's satire on a bit of inept metaphor used by Mrs. Dogood[36] seems hollow next to the letter that verbalized what many, who did not understand such literary things even as well as Silence, felt about the pretensions and quality of some clergy, but did not have the courage or ability to express. It is not surprising that Harvard conducted its profitable printing business with Samuel Gerrish and gave none of it to James Franklin.[37]

In her next piece, the Widow hit hard on delicate matters that had bothered the College. Though the Harvard Corporation knew it had given aid to many students, its members were also aware of the fact that there had been too many serious problems concerning the morality and evident sanctity of Harvard students who liked to live high and whose occasionally scandalous behavior was public knowledge.[38] President Leverett himself was not exempt from being questioned about his role in the moral and spiritual conduct of his charges. Arch-conservatives such as Sewall and Paul Dudley continued an old battle with the liberal Leverett by accusing him of having neglected chapel exhortations and thereby contributing to the obvious decay of the scholars and the College.[39] Attacked from within the ranks and without, Leverett must have wondered how much more he and the College would have to endure. Silence had even brought up the ancient and troublesome matter of disorders breaking out at Harvard parties. Leverett tried, but with no great success, to stop unseemly behavior by demanding on June 28, 1722, that the commencement parties be curbed and that "no preparacon nor pvision either of plumb-cake, or Rosted, boyled, or baked meats or pyes of any kind shalbe made by any Comencer, nor shal any Such have any distilled Liquors, or any composition made therewth. . . ." Violators, he warned, would have the food confiscated and be fined twenty shillings. The Corporation supported the measure unanimously on the same day it was made, which was just six weeks after the appearance of the fourth Dogood piece with Silence's estimation of Harvard.

In addressing the Corporation and insisting on an end to the wild parties, Leverett undoubtedly also had in mind the smallpox epidemic and other serious matters. He spoke of the plight of the "Countrey in Genl." It is likely, however, that he was thinking too of the Couranteers and Mrs. Dogood when he brought up the troubles of "ye College in pticular," for it had "bin under Such Circumstances, as call alloud for humiliacon, and all due Manifestations of it."[40] The very next day the vote of the Corporation was read to the students, fellows, and tutors, and they were all warned to watch their conduct[41] and avoid providing ammunition to the enemies of the College. Mrs. Dogood's thrusts constitute Franklin's first attack on a school, but as later events would prove, not his last. As a middle-aged, very prominent man he would operate covertly in his own person and also through his son to thwart other colleges. These intrigues, like the youthful assault on Harvard and the Dogood pieces generally, would find no place in the memoirs of one who portrayed himself as a live-and-let-live deist who respected and supported all religious groups because he believed them useful in promoting morality and happiness. Such intrigues would seem most out of place in the idealized America he created as the essential background for his successful life.

Having discredited the clergy and politicians, the Widow's next move in the difficult time of 1722, as the self-appointed spokesman of the "good" people, was to assume, in a secular and unofficial way, the prerogatives of both Establishments by showing that they had failed in their duties. This is an important matter to her, and so she devotes most of her fifth, sixth, twelfth, and thirteenth letters to usurping authority, showing that government and other social affairs are entirely secular concerns, and that common sense and practical virtue rather than piety or orthodoxy were what New England needed. These are crucial points in the letters. Satire, as one student of the subject has said, "asserts the validity and necessity of norms, systematic values, and meanings that *are* contained in recognizable ethical codes."[42] What Mrs. Dogood is saying in her satires is that the old orders regulating civil, religious, and moral life are no longer workable in the first quarter of the eighteenth century. Of course, then, as the representative of the "good" people, she feels compelled to strike out at what is detrimental to her community. She chastises the guardians of the old codes for not making them relevant to modern life—in other words, for not doing their job. Finally, as a decent person who sees the unhappy effects of outmoded values and institutions and bankrupt leadership, she calls for changes. Piety, the heart of Puritan experience, must now be supplanted by practical morality, and people like herself must assume the leadership in New England, taking over from a largely irrelevant, elitist corps of Harvard graduates. Silence thus encourages not only increased secularization, but actually the complete restructuring of society.

In her fifth letter she undertakes to do something about the "present reigning Vices in the Town,"[43] for the ministers and officials have failed to control them. In her next piece she therefore sets herself up as the judge of New England's moral condition, which she finds to be poor.[44] It was, to be sure, standard procedure for the clergy to rebuke the community for its vices and to predict the wrath of God. Magistrates, too, had a right to punish offenders. But for a mocking satirist of no particular education, status, or other authority to pretend to be a Yankee Spectator and assume such authority, indeed to make light of traditional authority, if not of the problems, was an insult to the Establishments.[45] Addison could influence and charm London with such efforts, but unlike New England, London was unencumbered by the image of itself as a covenanted community with a special mission.

Similar in tone and intention, letters twelve and thirteen attack pride, drunkenness, and prostitution, among other vices, that the ministers and officials had failed to control, much less eradicate.[46] To make matters worse for the clergy and civil authorities, they generally responded with deadly seriousness to these and other satires in the *Courant,* and thus played into the hands of their opponents. In writing satire, one may use either the rapier or the bludgeon, the indirect thrust or direct onslaught. Franklin chose the former, which is normally more effective, and has the additional advantage of creating a distance between the satirist and the object of the satire. This distance is increased by virtue of the persona, and so the result of such pieces as the *Dogood Papers* is that the object of attack, if he responds seriously, is left alone on center stage spitting at the wind; for the Widow has identified herself with the generalized and inclusive "good" people of New England, who by this time are made to be on the side of virtue, honesty, liberty, and common sense, and therefore oppose contrary qualities and those who promote them— the clergy and their political allies. Some of the ministers and politicians recognized what Silence was doing and took measures to curb her and the other Couranteers.

James Franklin and his friends persisted in their abuse, however, and the mysterious Mrs. Dogood added to their success with the best satires in the colonial American press. In fact, it is fair to say that although the Franklins got into trouble because of the *Courant*'s attacks in general, Mrs. Dogood's are by far the most effective. Her seventh letter, the famous "RECEIPT to make a New England Funeral ELEGY," is one of her best and a case in point. The religious, literary, historical, and social contexts of this satire could easily be the subject of a large study. Although this is not possible here, the piece nevertheless demands special attention.

Benjamin, an avid reader with a limited number of books at his disposal, read just about everything he could get his hands on, including a good deal of poetry. Until his father dissuaded him, in fact, he had given some thought to becoming a poet. Yet most of the native models he could get were indeed wretched. As the Widow notes, Americans used their poetic talents, such as they were, to compose funeral elegies, and the vast majority of them were written by New England ministers. The "RECEIPT" is, of course, a spoof on the poor quality of these stilted poems; but it is also an attack on the clergy and civil officials who, the piece suggests, permitted the decline in piety that is clearly betrayed by the content and style of the elegies. Before 1665 the earliest Puritan fathers in England and America had developed what they considered to be the proper matter and form of the pious Puritan funeral elegy. Briefly, the tribute had to provide an example of the life and rewards of a saint in such a manner as to define the characteristics of saintliness. The style of the poem had to be plain and somber (except for the part dealing with the

saint's translation, which was joyful) to express the humility of the subject
and the poet. Moreover, the pious elegy often included a jeremiad, forcing the
community to see that the death of a saint was a sign of God's displeasure
with the community.

Since the substance of these elegies was made appropriate to the particular
life of the deceased, the poems were usually free of apparent formulism.
Perhaps the most important point to be made about their style is that the
elegists, as much as possible, subsumed the normal literary concern for technique in order to concentrate on the content of the poem, a fact which undoubtedly helps explain why few of the poems have any literary merit.[47] The
earliest elegists, however, would not have been bothered in the least by such a
criticism as this, for they did not think of themselves as poets and believed
wholeheartedly in the dictum: "God's altar needs not our polishings."
What was important, after all, was to praise a saint and to show that his loss
was a chastisement from God for the backsliding of the community; in this
way, perhaps, the elegy could be used, like the sermon, to inculcate or
increase piety. Given the clear intention and model developed by the Puritian
forebearers, the elegy should at least have resisted literary fashion, if not
remained immune to it, as long as the people upheld the original pious ideals.

Typical of the early elegies is the following one by the first Peter Bulkeley
on Thomas Hooker,[48] who died in 1647. Bulkeley's elegy goes on for 100
lines and so will be excerpted here:

> Comes sighs, come sorrows, let's lament this rod,
> Which hath bereav'd us of this man of God:
> A man of God, who came from God to men,
> And now from them is gone to God again.

It is Hooker's piety, the heart of Puritanism, and consequently the essence of
the early elegies, that is expressed. The man of God is His instrument, sent for
a time to be a model of a Christian in the literal sense—a Christ in
miniature—and to open men's hearts and point the way to God. The first
two lines quoted, however, introduce another feature commonly found in the
elegies as well as in Puritan sermons. Hooker's death is "A fatal day, a day
of sad presage," and, as the elegist says further on, it is a chastisement
from God for New England's sinfulness. The people were not, in other
words, living up to the national covenant and were consequently being

punished by having a saintly minister and guide taken from them. The people therefore do not "lament" the departed Hooker, who is saved, but rather bemoan their loss and its significance in terms of their spiritual condition. This part of the elegy, carefully designed to inspire piety and reform, is the equivalent of the jeremiad in the sermons. To make certain that the survivors understand the importance of what has happened, Bulkeley continues his jeremiad:

> O happy days, when such lights shine on earth!
> O bitter days, when they are hid beneath!
> . . . .
> Let Hartford sigh, and say, *I've lost a treasure*;
> Let all New England mourn at God's displeasure,
> In taking from us one more gracious
> Than is the gold of Orphir precious.

Bulkeley, to be sure, is unsparing in his praise of Hooker; however, knowing what we do of the deceased minister and of his central place in New England Puritanism, the praise is by no means excessive. Hooker was widely thought to have "Each moral virtue, with rare piety, pure zeal, yet mixt with mildest clemency." In brief, he is portrayed as a Christian, again in the literal sense of the word. In the rest of the poem, though Bulkeley has brought up the saint's civil virtues and morality, the emphasis is on Hooker the pious and effective preacher, the physician of the soul who was able to speak as a dying man to dying men:

> To mind he gave light of intelligence,
> And search'd the corners of the conscience.
> To sinners stout, which no law could bring under,
> To them he was a son of dreadful thunder,
> When all strong oaks of Bashan us'd to quake,
> And fear did Lebanus his cedars shake;
> The stoutest hearts he filled full of fears,
> He clave the rocks, they melted into tears.
> Yet to sad souls, with sense of sin cast down,
> He was a son of consolation.
> Sweet peace he gave to such as were contrite;
> Their darkness sad he turn'd to joyous light.

Then, in what is one of the most moving compliments that can be paid a preacher of this kind, a compliment which also suggests the importance of soul-searching preaching and piety to the elegist and to his readers, Bulkeley says that Hooker "had learn'd the rightest art" of preaching so that "Each ear that heard him said, He spake to me. . . ." Of course Hooker's ministry was a manifestation of his own piety, and he is therefore now enjoying his reward:

> Yet thou, O blessed saint, art now at rest,
> I' the bosom of thy Christ, which is the best;
>
> . . . .
>
> To honour God . . . was thy whole intent.
> From God thou camest forth, who sent thee hither,
> And Now hath call'd thee back to live together.
> Him didst thou serve while life and breath did last,
> With him now blest, while life and breath is past.

The elegy is not good poetry, but Bulkeley, his subject, and his contemporaries were not interested much in poetry as an art form and even less in gaining reputations as poets. They therefore paid little attention to poetic devices or fashions. What chiefly concerned them was the expression of regard for the deceased and showing what the loss of a saint meant to them and should mean in a community that had set its sights on achieving godliness. To accomplish their ends the elegists wrote in the poetic equivalent of the plain style of the sermons; for like God's alter, God's saints needed no human polishings. Moreover, the earliest elegists were not forced to make their subjects more than they believed they were: Puritan saints. This confidence in the piety and sanctity of their subjects also made poetic embellishments unnecessary and inappropriate. Anyone who reads these elegies written by the first settlers, men like Bulkeley, the first John Cotton, and John Wilson, for example, must realize that they are very serious and often somber in tone. These men and their fellows did not look upon death as a subject for levity or as an excuse for writing poetry; an ostentatious display of wit, or relish in being literary, they regarded as unseemly and impious. Such feelings were central to their refusal to write broadside elegies until the Cavaliers had abandoned them and the form was no longer identified with joking or license. The task of the Puritan elegist was to deal with such crucial matters as the Christian life and death of a departed saint and the lessons the community had to learn from both. Their efforts were not intended to show off wit, or the poetic skill of the elegist, or to pander to literary fashion. It is not hard to discover, then, why most New England elegies are poor as poetry. They are really rhymed funeral sermons. As such they are hardly poetic, but they are occasionally graceful, sometimes moving, and always pious.

Over the years, however, it became increasingly evident that the elegies had changed in content and form, the major difference being that they became literary exercises designed to display the intellectual and literary wares of the poet. Death had become a rationale for artistic achievement, for making puns and jokes in the covenanted community; and even before 1680 the pious elegy had, in most cases, lost its piety. The ministerial elegists, who were guilty of impiety and conscious literariness in their own tributes, called for an end to such practice and a return to the original models when they commented on the elegies of others. Such Puritans as Joseph Capen, Thomas Tileston, Daniel Gookin II, Benjamin Tompson, John Norton II, Nicholas Noyes, Nehemiah Walter, Edward Taylor, and Cotton Mather are all guilty of expressing the decline of piety in New England in their elegies by their joking, punning, and conscious attempts to be literary, as well as by their omissions of the characteristics of saintliness, the jeremiad, the saint's rewards, and even, on many occasions, by their failure to mention God at all in their poems. This constitutes quite a falling away from the pious model created by Bulkeley, Cotton, Wilson and by such other early settlers as Percival Lowell, Thomas Dudley, John Norton I, and William Bradford. These men were not all ministers; in regard to piety, though, there was little to distinguish the laity from the clergy.

While there are numerous examples of impious elegies that in their clowning and conscious literariness reflect the often lamented decline in piety, a few will indicate what was happening. In 1681, about twenty years after the decline became apparent,[49] Joseph Capen wrote an elegiac tribute to John Foster, who served New England as a printer, almanac maker, astronomer, mathematician, and school teacher. Foster was not only versatile, but was a good man, and his death at the age of thirty-three was felt keenly. Capen, though, opens his elegy with two gruesome puns that immediately call attention away from Foster and to the poem itself and the poet:

> Here lye the relict Fragments which were took
> Out of Consumption's teeth by Death the Cook.
> Voracious Appetite dost thus devour
> Scarce ought hast left for worms t' live on an Hour

> But Skins & Bones, (no bones thou maks't of that,
> It is thy common trade t' eat all the fat.)[50]

Having achieved these successes, Capen rounds out his elegy with a series of jokes and puns that, along with the increasingly popular sentimentality in such tributes, appear just at the point which is supposed to express the poet's sincere conviction that the deceased, because of his piety, has gained salvation:

> Yea, though with dust thy body soiled be
> Yet at the Resurrection we shall see
> A fair Edition and of matchless worth,
> Free from Errata, new in Heaven set forth:
> 'Tis but a word from God the Great Creatour,
> It shall be done when He saith *Imprimatur.*

Thomas Tileston's tribute to Foster reflects even more clearly the extent to which many of the Puritans were losing the old piety. Foster was survived by his brothers and sisters: Elisha, James, Standfast, Comfort, Patience, Thankful, and Mary. The opportunities for comedy are too great for Tileston to resist, and so not all of the survivors escape being immortalized by Tileston's piety, as he writes:

> Let James and let Elisha too
> With Comfort, Standfast weeping go,
> Thankful, Patience, Mary likewise
> Like loveing Sisters solmenize
> With Sighs your greatest loss, but yet
> Your *Thankful, Hope* do not forget
> With Perseverance to fulfill.
> Know your Elijah's God lives still.
> *Standfast* therefore with *Patience,*
> *Comfort* shall be your recompence.[51]

The italics make certain that even unpoetic readers caught the full brunt of the poet's wit, for Tileston did not want them to forget who wrote this tribute. Moreover, he and the other later elegists had to assume that their efforts would be appreciated by their readers. All writers must assume a variety of things about their audiences and what they would find good. This was true for the earliest elegists, and it was equally true for those who came after them. The elegies therefore express not only the declining piety of the elegists but that of the community at large. In the case of Tileston, he is undisturbed by the fact that his clowning detracts from the sense of loss one is supposed to feel over Foster's death as well as from whatever expressions of piety are intended. In fact, though what he self-consciously calls his "homely Country verse" and "poor Rural Poetry" runs 104 lines, only the last 6 deal with salvation at all, and these few are pale and mechanical:

> Grieve not too much, for the time draws near
> You'll re-enjoy Relations dear,
> And all together will on high
> With everlasting Melody
> And perfect peace His praises sing,
> Who through all troubles did you bring.

Tileston, it seems, had to warm up to his subject and whereas the chance to display his wit excited him enough to write verse that is at least mildly interesting, the prospect of writing about salvation in a straightforward manner, without built-in verbal aids to humor, moved him to only the most perfunctory statement. But then by 1681, the year the elegy was written, there may have been some doubt concerning how eager Foster's brothers and sisters would have been at the prospect of "re-enjoy [ing] Relations dear."

Benjamin Tompson was obviously proud of his comparatively impressive abilities as a poet and wit, and he often used the occasion of someone's death to display his talents. He puns and jokes in his 1679 elegy on Governor John Endicott when, saying that Endicott's death caught by surprise even the best almanac prognosticators, he concludes that this fact "proves Star-prophets sometimes in the dark."[52] Tompson's most clowning elegy, though, is "The Grammarian's Funeral." This piece was originally written in 1667 in honor of the Boston schoolmaster Robert Woodmancy, but the poet used it again forty-one years later for Ezekiel Cheever, another of the town's teachers. There are a dozen or more puns and a great deal of conscious literariness in the poem as Tompson extracts every drop of comedy he can out of the deceased's profession. Because of the grammarian's death the different parts of speech "were in most lamentable Cases."[53] "The five *Declensions* did the work of burying their master decline. ..." Of the preparations for the funeral: "O *Verbs* the *Active* were, Or *Passive* sure,/*Sum* to be *Neuter* could not well endure." In general it was "A doleful Day for *Verbs, they* look so *moody."* "The Verbs irregular . . . / Would break no rule. . . ." And as one more example:

> *Volo* was Willing, *Nolo* some-what stout,
> But *Malo* rather chose, not to stand out.
> *Possum* and Volo wish'd all might afford
> Their help, but had not an *Imperative Word.*

All this punning detracts from the supposed seriousness of the situation and is hardly designed to inspire piety or encourage reform. Moreover, Tompson's poem is a further departure from the early elegies in that it is obviously not intended for the unschooled. This, however, makes little difference for there is no lesson to be learned from the death of either schoolmaster. What concerns Tompson is that his readers remember his wit and ability to sustain a joke in verse. Indeed, "The Grammarian's Funeral" reveals the decline in Puritan zeal because it never deals in the least with piety, salvation, or even with God!

Ministers, guilty themselves of impious elegies, would try to put a stop to the new elegies. But they had as little success in bringing back the older kind as they had in coping with the increasing secularization of life and the diminution of their once pervasive influence in the community. Daniel Gookin II could insist on genuine piety and an end to telltale flattery in the tributes, and Nicholas Noyes might warn that too many recent elegies "seem Designed to raise/The *Poet's,* not the Person's praise," but there was little anyone could do. In spite of pretensions to the contrary, Puritanism was dying, for the very heart of it, piety, had, as everyone knew, declined severely. This was a sensitive issue, especially to the clerical and political guardians of New England's piety and morality. Cotton Mather could joke and pun in elegies and call attention to himself at the expense of his subject; he could reject the representation of grief in an elegy because, as he said, *"Grief never made a good Poet"*;[54] yet he and his colleagues resented being told that the elegies themselves betrayed the failure of the ministerial and civil Establishments to keep New England religious and virtuous.

In the seventh Dogood letter Franklin shows that he was familiar with the tradition of Puritan funeral elegies and understood how and why they had changed. Mrs. Dogood is made to attack the elegies for their mere formulism, insincerity, and impiety as well as for their incompetence. The Widow's letter is prefaced by verses from Isaac Watts' "The Adventurous Muse." Watts was a popular poet at the time and one of Franklin's favorites all his life, and the lines he quotes are devastatingly appropriate to Mrs. Dogood's satire on the New England funeral elegies:

> Give me the Muse, whose generous Force,
>   Impatient of the Reins,
> Pursues an unattempted Course,
>   Breaks all the Criticks Iron Chains.

Watts calls for an inspired poetry that in breaking through traditional rules and in ignoring fashion uplifts us with its courage and originality.

The Widow adopts a mask appropriate to the lines as she ostensibly defends the New England poetic genius. To do so is to defend the elegies since, as she points out, New England "produces" almost no other kind of poetry. She is well aware of the bad reputation native poets have among foreigners and admits that most of the elegies have indeed been "Dull and Ridiculous," but there have always been some good elegies, she insists, and recently there appeared the best one ever done in New England. This, of course, is the anonymous *An Elegy upon the much Lamented Death of Mrs. Mehitabell Kitel, Wife of Mr. John Kitel of Salem, &c.*[55] Silence praises the poem for precisely those qualities it most seriously and obviously lacks: its "soft and Easy" language, "moving" and "pathetick" expressions, and, "above all," its "Verse and Numbers so Charming and Natural, that it is almost beyond Comparison." The irony becomes clear when we are treated to the opening lines:

> *Come let us mourn, for we have lost a Wife, a Daughter, and a Sister,*
> *Who has lately taken Flight, and greatly we have mist her.*

The mechanical injunction, *"Come let us mourn,"* the hackneyed *"taken Flight,"* and the forced rhyme are anything but "soft and Easy," "moving," "pathetick," or "Charming." More important, the perfunctoriness of the lines and the terribly forced rhyme are intended to indicate that the writers of such verse are so insincere that they are using the occasion of death to show off their talents, as such, and that they are also making a pro forma response to what is supposed to be a genuine loss. The original elegies, though generally failures as poetry, impressed one with their obvious sincerity, a quality which was more important to the early elegists than was artistry. The kind of piece the Widow discusses, then, is impious. The clergy, who were largely guilty of them, knew this to be true; many readers knew it to be true; and Silence knew it also.

The remaining lines of the tribute are of the same character:

> Some little Time *before she yielded up her Breath,*
> *She said, I Ne'er shall hear one Sermon more on Earth.*
> *She kist her Husband,* some little Time *before she expir'd,*
> *Then lean'd her Head the Pillow on, just out of Breath and tir'd.*

The second line is clearly absurd to us and would have been to the *Courant*'s increasingly secular readers as well. Fifty years had passed since Urian Oakes had bemoaned the fact that even church members had become so "Sermon proof" that the ministers might just as well have preached "to the Walls"[56] as to their flocks. The situation deteriorated with time, and so the dying words of Mrs. Kitel are actually a public joke at the expense of the clergy. Furthermore, her protracted death, which is made a point of in the first and third lines, places her final words within a comic framework and underscores both the sentimentality that had become fashionable in the elegies and the unreality of her concern over missing sermons. And again the mechanical language and deadly determination to rhyme in addition to the ridiculous syntactical inversion in the fourth line all call satiric attention to the fact that writers of such verse are far less concerned about the significance of death and piety than with gaining reputations as poets.

Silence goes on to say that the elegy on the late Mrs. Kitel is the best New England has ever "produced." The word "produced" was carefully chosen. Such poems, in effect, are production jobs and therefore can be turned out by anyone at any time, at least as long as he has the proper "RECEIPT" for producing elegies. Indeed, so insincere and mechanical are the elegies that all it takes is a formula for making one. Emphasizing these qualities for her satire, Silence points out that the first thing the elegist must do is compile a list of the deceased's virtues. Should this requirement strike terror in the breasts of poets, however, she goes on to tell them that in the event the subject is deficient in virtue the poets "may borrow some to make up a sufficient quantity." The Widow's point is obvious enough to have been understood by *Courant* readers, including the clergy. The casual manner in which she suggests padding the list of virtues indicates not only that New

England had changed considerably, but that there was a tradition of padding in the elegies. Gookin and Noyes had called for an end to the tradition, but they had little success. Furthermore, since they themselves were members of the clergy as well as elegists, no one had to be upset by their criticism. The creator of the Widow, though, was not a member of the religious or secular Establishments, and so her satire constituted an important part of the general social attack being conducted by the Couranteers, an attack from those on the lower end of the social structure against those at the top, as well as on many who were trying hard to regain a position near the top.

Continuing her satire, Silence cautions the elegists to pay particular attention to the dramatic elements in their poems. As anyone familiar with Puritan sermons and personal narratives, in addition to the elegies, would know, the "last Words, dying Expressions, &c" were very important and thoroughly predictable. To Mrs. Dogood they had also come to be insincere, a mere part of the "RECEIPT." She thereupon instructs the elegists that in making up a list of dying expressions, they must be sure to "*strain* them well," as they had been strained by numerous elegists before them. Then the poets had to "season all" with the expected sad words and finally add to them "a sufficient Quantity of double Rhimes." Since, the Widow is saying, true piety and virtue, once so central to New England life, had become impossible in seventeenth-century terms in modern New England, and since the clergy in particular had not adjusted to modern conditions, insisting instead on attitudes that even they no longer found viable—whether they were aware of the fact or not—present expressions of the older perceptions had to be insincere and manifest both decline and stagnation. Automatically pious elegies were fit only for automatically pious mourners. This was Mrs. Dogood's message in her seventh letter to the other good, average people, and it fit in well with the other *Courant* attacks. It also revealed Franklin's antipathy toward a group whom he considered dangerously irrelevant and authoritarian. The chief difference, perhaps, between the *Dogood Papers* and the other anti-ministerial pieces in the *Courant* was that Benjamin's biting humor and effective persona made his contributions superior and more insulting to those in power. Whether in individual letters Franklin had the Widow attack the clergy, the secular Establishment, or both, he normally did a better job of it than his allies, who lacked his skill.

In her eighth letter Silence gets back at the "Rulers" for imprisoning James Franklin for a month. The editors of the Franklin *Papers* correctly identify this and the following letter as two of the apprentice's "Rubs" against those in and out of government who were responsible for the act. Most of the pieces can be so classified, however, and none is more biting than the Widow's farewell piece. Moreover, all of the rubs seem to have been prompted as much by Franklin's general hostility to the Establishments as by James' misfortune.

The eighth letter is an abstract from the *London Journal* and deals with the necessity of the freedoms of thought and speech in a good and peaceful government.[57] Since it appeared in the *Courant* immediately after the authorities locked up James, the implication of the piece is clear: the government of Massachusetts and its ministerial allies do not insure or even grant the "sacred Privilege" of freedom to its citizens; therefore the government is neither wise nor free.[58] Silence attacks the clergy for their role in stirring up anti-*Courant* sentiment! Following this bit of irony with another, she compares the New England clergy with the oppressive, corrupt, and "Wicked Ministry" of Charles I.[59] Having read Locke, the Widow declared that the "Administration of Government, is . . . nothing else but the Attendance of the *Trustees of the People* upon the Interest and Affairs of the People. . . . for whose Sake alone all public Matters are, or ought to be, transacted. . . ."[60] Governor Shute and his party had been having trouble enough from the people's Representatives, led by Elisha Cooke, to frown upon an additional expression of democratic sentiment from the *Courant*. Further, the eighth letter appeared at a bad time, for Shute and the Council had been fighting with the House of Representatives over its refusal to go along with the demands of the Governor and Council and suppress publication of their deliberations.[61] It is also important to keep in mind that since James' imprisonment for "High Affront"[62] to the authorities such an attack as this letter had to be looked upon as a direct challenge to the powers that had inflicted the punishment. Silence was treading on dangerous ground, but the stakes were high. She was trying to jar the civil and religious Establishments, hoping to make them less authoritarian and more responsive to the people and to new realities. The Widow also wanted to break the bond between the ministers and the Governor's party. Yet their mutual support was important to both of them, particularly to a clergy that sought government help in getting higher salaries from a reluctant people.

Mrs. Dogood's ninth letter also struck out at the Establishments. She poses the question, "Whether a Commonwealth suffers more by hypocritical Pretenders to Religion or by the openly Profane?"[63] Once more Silence is off on a course filled with danger, but she tells her readers that to her mind the hypocrite, "especially if he sustains a Post in the Government," is by far the more serious offender, for he betrays the public's trust. Obviously referring to New England, Mrs. Dogood goes on, with tongue in cheek, to remind her fellow citizens that the hypocrite has an easier time practicing his deceit in a religiously pure country. Once the people of such a place discover the truth, however, they will give vent to their disgust by fully exposing the deceiver.[64] They and their leaders must be very careful not to place too much trust in seeming sanctification, she warns, because *a little Religion, and a little honesty, goes a great way in Courts.*[65] Silence may have in mind Joseph Dudley, a hated former Governor,[66] but her letter also charges the Establishments with gullibility at best. That such people had a right to imprison an honest printer, or were proper guardians of the people, the Widow doubted. Furthermore, the incredible suggestion that one should be held suspect *because* of his evident sanctification must have come as a surprise to the clergy, who would have settled for any evidence of sanctification at all among the laity in or out of government. Given their desperate efforts to overcome what they themselves called the general anti-ministerial sentiment in New England and to reassert their eminence in secular affairs, they must have been angered by the charge that they are duped as easily as anyone else in identifying hypocrites. If the deceivers are a detriment to society, then so too are their highly placed but naïve judges who too readily allow a pretense to stand for the real thing. Just how valuable such judges of true piety and virtue are to society and how much of the people's hard-earned money they are entitled to for their salaries is clear to Silence: very little. In fact, contrary to the steady complaints of the ministers that they could not live on the miserable salaries they had bargained for, particularly during the present inflation, the Widow argues that the ministers usually fail to spot hypocrisy in the first place and then generally side with the hypocrite and unwittingly help him gain his ends because they are paid very well. Since the clergy "are honourably supported (as they ought to be) by their People," they "see nor feel nothing of the Oppression which is obvious and burdensome to everyone else."[67] The parenthetical comment is intentionally weak, weighted down as it is on either side by a stinging attack on the ministers. Not only are they being paid amply for their services, such as they are, but the clergy are perhaps receiving too much for the good of the common people! In a later piece Mrs. Dogood confesses that there are, unfortunately, some hard-pressed ministers, but they, like her late husband, are of the "Inferior" rank and live in the outlying districts of the country. Their condition is evidently quite different from that of their presumably comfortable brothers in and around the town.[68]

In later correspondence Silence tackles the problems of drunkenness, slander, and prostitution in Boston.[69] Yet righteous condemnation of these vices is couched in a humor that serves as a brash insult, if also to some as a welcome contrast to the usual homiletic treatment of these matters. Then too her frame of reference, though moral, does not take into account the special impiety of vice in a town that still made pretenses, at least, of being a covenanted community. The Widow also assumes that wickedness, if it is to be corrected, will be rectified not by the clergy, but by morally indignant lay people like herself. Her letters therefore contribute to the diminution of the role and importance of the ministers as well as the fragmentation and secularization of society. These sad events, however, were among the chief expressions of decay as far as the ministers were concerned.

Mrs. Dogood's final letter is one of her best. Her specific reference is ostensibly to the disaffection of three Connecticut ministers who created a sensation in Old and New England by renouncing their Congregationalist ordination and taking Anglican orders.[70] Some New England ministers feared that this rebellious act would presage the demise of Congregationalism and a reign of episcopal corruption and authoritarianism.[71] Cotton Mather offered *Hints of Counsel to the Chhs of Connecticut* on how to deal with the dangerous situation.[72] Worry and confusion were widespread and Silence, taking advantage of the situation, warned that such things were bound to occur when people became too "zealous Advocates for any Cause."[73] Such men are unable to cope with situations unless things go their way continually. When disappointed in something, they respond irrationally. They are extremists who, with characteristic naïveté, come by their initial beliefs too quickly and then abandon them with the same rapidity. The real culprit here, then, is religious advocacy or sectarian zeal. "All I would endeavour to shew is," Silence writes, "That an indiscreet zeal for spreading an Opinion, hurts the cause of the Zealot." Then in what is unmistakably a reference to the activities of the clergy in their war with the *Courant*, she points out that there are "too many blind Zealots among every Denomination of Christians."[74] A passage from *The Spectator* furnishes her with a parting shot at the ministers, especially Cotton Mather. Every zealot should " 'examine his Heart thoroughly, and, I believe he will often find that what he calls a zeal for his Religion, is either Pride, Interest or Ill-nature.' "[75] Pious effort in itself was suspect to Mrs. Dogood.

When James Franklin pretended to turn the *Courant* over to Benjamin, the apprentice promised an end to squabbling and abuse and ironically vowed that under his management the newspaper would henceforth include innocent pieces only, "designed purely for the Diversion and Merriment of the Reader."[76] This was on February 11, 1723. If the clergy and civil authorities felt they had won a significant victory, their joy was short-lived, for the next week saw the appearance of the *Courant* essay "On Titles of Honor." It is a clever if somewhat transparent parody on men who assert the "most absurd and ridiculous Opinions" without the "least colour" and yet think themselves "wiser ... than the rest of the World" and therefore condemn any "who dissent from the peculiar whims of their troubled Brains."[77] Considered in the context of all the strife and trouble with the religious and governmental Establishments, the piece appears to continue Benjamin's onslaught against them.

In fact the essay calls to mind the very second sentence she wrote for the *Courant*, declaring that most people did not come out in favor of or against a work until they knew about the status of the writer; for the remainder of the letter is based on an old piece of William Penn's which expresses an equalitarian contempt for titles of honor and such artificial distinctions.[78] With this attitude the apprentice heartily agreed. He had already acquired sufficient experience to learn that persons of elevated position and all sorts of titles could be as malicious and petty as anyone else. But so, too, could the untitled penmen for the *Courant*.

In the struggle over inoculation, James Franklin and his friends were wrong. In the struggle against excessive authority and prerogative and in fighting for a free press, however, the *Courant* played a significant and honorable role. It gained in subtlety and effectiveness not from the vituperative set of "ingenious Men," but from a seventeen-year-old penman whose pseudonymous letters demonstrated that argument and biting satire gained much from an exterior that was humorous, graceful, and charming. To be sure, the stings were still felt keenly, as Franklin intended them to be. He had, after all, attacked some of the most powerful men in New England. One must use the best ammunition he has against such opponents. His criticisms are as universal in their application as they are local. This quality, so apparent in his later work, he had learned while a boy. As the Widow Dogood he not only picked up themes that had already been crudely explored by the *Courant* group, but he made more of them. The smallpox controversy became, in the Dogood letters, the monumental problem of the will of the majority—right or wrong—against the will of the few, some hierarchy or Establishment. As he would do throughout his life, when events came to such a head, Franklin sided with the people, or what he conceived to be the majority of them.[79]

He also took on the sensitive problem of the separate functions of church and state, and he tried to curb the authoritarianism of both and to prevent any closer cooperation between the clergy and the Governor's party. It is clear that he and the other writers for the *Courant* had a fair amount of support for their efforts. In spite of the punishment meted out to James, the newspaper was not suppressed, and there were those in New England who liked the provincial attempts at Augustan urbanity and wit in the *Courant*. Establishments, though, change slowly. Cotton Mather expressed the sentiments of many influential people when he wrote in his *Diary* that "Warnings are to be given unto the wicked Printer, and his Accomplices, who every week publish a vile Paper to lessen and blacken the Ministers of the Town, and render their Ministry ineffectual." This was a "Wickedness never parallel'd any where upon the Face of the Earth!"[80] It is not surprising that both Franklins eventually found it wise and more profitable to leave Boston.

Franklin makes only the briefest allusion to the *Dogood Papers* in the *Autobiography*. He implies that no one other than the Couranteers ever knew he wrote these obscure pieces and is sure that after half a century they have been forgotten. He wanted to mention his first serious effort at authorship, but he did not want to recall the specifics about his satires on the clergy and the government. Nor did he wish to tell posterity about the bitterness and even violence that resulted during the smallpox epidemic in Boston. The *Autobiography* would do nothing to tarnish either his own image or that of his countrymen.

This concern leads him to offer some questionable history in his memoirs. He says that his reasons for leaving Boston were his youthful and unwise disquisitions in behalf of deism and James' cruelty to him. The connection between the Dogood letters and his running off to New York is thoroughly subsumed and, we are led to believe, had little to do with his decision. How worried the good people of Boston were about Benjamin's philosophical and religious speculations is a matter of conjecture, but everything we know about James suggests that he was anything but the cruel master he is made to seem. Judging from his courage in criticizing the Establishments and the humor with which he challenged them, there is little reason to believe him likely to take advantage of even as "saucy and provoking" a little brother as Benjamin may have been. Certainly there is no shred of evidence available today that corroborates the picture drawn of him in the memoirs.

Furthermore, the suggestion that the Dogood letters remained of unknown authorship for long is simply untrue. Unable to resist the temptation of declaring himself the author of the successful pieces, Benjamin "discovered" his secret.[81] Thus the insiders, at least, knew the true identity of Silence Dogood. Then, too, it is difficult to believe that a youngster indiscreet and vain enough to argue openly in favor of deism, one who loved to debate, regardless of the position he took, would keep from discussing the proceedings at the *Courant*, especially the Dogood letters, with his ready antagonist and friend, John Collins.[82]

Franklin himself admits that he had begun to be considered by many good people in Boston "in an unfavourable Light, as a young Genius that had a Turn for Libelling and Satyr."[83] This must be a reference not to the arguments on behalf of deism, which he said were rather formal disquisitions, but to written pieces on matters that lent themselves to vitriolic humor. Other than a couple of unexceptionable poems, the *Dogood Papers* are the first things Franklin wrote that could have reached a number of people and gained for him any sort of notoriety. The sentiments of the good people of Boston were shared by Josiah, Benjamin's father, who worried about his son's "lampooning and libelling to which he thought I had too much an Inclination." It would seem that the concerned father also knew who Silence Dogood was. In fact he may have been pressured because of the conduct of his sons. In the *Autobiography* we are told that the father "was never employed" in "publick Affairs" because he was always at his trade, trying to support his large family. The truth, however, is that he had been a Boston town official on at least five different occasions. The earliest record of his service to the community is for 1697, when he was a tithingman. Four years later he was clerk of the market, and in 1703 he served as a constable. He was twice more a tithingman, first in 1715. Curiously, he was made a tithingman for the last time in 1721, the year his sons were becoming notorious in Boston. After this time Josiah Franklin never held public office, though he lived for another twenty-four years.[84] Apparently the Establishments had their revenge not only on James and Benjamin, but on their father as well; for it seems that contrary to Benjamin's claim in the *Autobiography*—that his father was always held in high esteem by the "leading people" in public and local church affairs—he suffered in his own way for the activities of his sons.

On the whole, however, the Couranteers were victorious. Although James had been imprisoned and forced to begin in business again in Newport when he could no longer earn a living in Boston, and though Benjamin had to sneak out of town at night and make his way, finally, to religiously tolerant Philadelphia, they and their fellow writers had discredited the clergy and their political allies in the Governor's party and had insisted that secular and religious institutions had to be separate. They especially demanded that the ministers mind theology and keep their noses out of less godly matters. This call for further fragmentation of influence was detrimental to the Governor's party as well as to a clergy that wanted very much the prestige, influence, and power it once enjoyed, though it was increasingly incapable of dealing with changing secular conditions in viable ways. These groups needed each other's support, and the Couranteers tried to divide them.

Of all the pieces in the *Courant* the *Dogood Papers* are the most effective and damaging.[85] The youthful Franklin had already developed a comparatively urbane and charming style which caused his contributions to stand out among the others. Further, he had learned the advantages one gains from using a persona, and his mask of the Widow Dogood enabled him to ridicule his opponents in a manner so devastating as to bring joy to the hearts of the unregenerate. Silence, as the widow of a good country parson, the kind of minister whom she sets up as a contrast to the clergy she attacks, is a perfect foil. That she is portrayed as being as moralistic as the ministers and as concerned about public virtue as the civil officials gives her a presumed right to tread on their ground. When she discovers vice and corruption in the town and finds herself at odds with those who should have kept the community good, it is they who are at fault and open to attack. As a satirical observer and friend to good men, Silence has only to expose evil and to blame those in power. If they cannot do their jobs properly, then it is time for the decent, average people like herself to change things.

Franklin was dealing with extremely sensitive and important issues, and his position had been a radical one. He therefore mentions none of this in his memoirs or in any of his other writings. In 1771, when this early part of his life was being recorded, he did not have to present any evidence that he had been a radical and bigot or that New England had been a place of intolerance and authoritarianism. Franklin's enemies had been saying such things about him for years, and given the unflagging industry of hack writers for the English ministry, he did not want to help them in their efforts to undermine America in the eyes of the world. He therefore portrayed himself as the genial and benevolent deist of complete toleration; and he insisted that America had always been the Land of Opportunity for a good man of tolerable abilities and industry who wanted to get ahead in the world and could permit everyone else to do the same.

III

An Unorthodox Defense

It was nearly twelve years before Franklin again engaged in a full scale battle with a Calvinist Establishment, but in 1735 he fomented what proved to be the most open and prolonged attack to that time on any Christian group in Pennsylvania and launched a thirty-five year campaign against the Presbyterian Church. In 1735 Franklin was no longer a precocious, if indiscreet, youngster but a mature, respected, and responsible businessman in Philadelphia. Furthermore, the liberal religious tone of the city pleased him. Under the tolerant rule of the Quakers, the 11,000 inhabitants were free to get ahead in the world, and they enjoyed solid comfort. Their great concern for material gain, the absence of an established church, the scarcity of ministers, and the Friends' concern with moralism and personal virtue rather than with theology and institutional religion all contributed to the spirit of religious apathy and tolerance throughout the province.[1] In fact, there was enough good will, or indifference, so that even Catholics thrived.[2]

Franklin settled in this mild and growing city in 1723. The next year, hoping to be set up in business, he left for London with James Ralph to buy type. There he became increasingly familiar with the varying degrees of deism and learned more about Newton's harmonious, if mechanical, universe and the changes in philosophical perspective resulting from the great scientist's thinking. By 1725 the young printer had become sufficiently involved in the intellectual ferment of his time to compose his *Dissertation on Liberty and Necessity, Pleasure and Pain*. The following year he returned to Philadelphia with the Quaker merchant, Mr. Denham, for whom Franklin worked until 1727, when the older man died. Franklin then returned to Samuel Keimer's printing shop where he was employed until 1728, when he and Hugh Meredith formed the partnership that was to be dissolved two years later to Franklin's great advantage. By 1735, the time of the trial of the Reverend Samuel

Hemphill, Franklin was the most important member of the Junto club, which is depicted in the memoirs as a group of typical American tradesmen who made use of their many opportunities to improve others and themselves. Moreover, by this time Franklin was an experienced author, founder of the first subscription library in America, the Philadelphia Library Company, the owner of a successful newspaper, the *Pennsylvania Gazette,* and also of a very popular almanac, and was a partner in the *South Carolina Gazette.* To add to his prestige and comfort, he had been appointed Public Printer by the Quaker-controlled Pennsylvania Assembly and, finally, he had been honored among Masons by his election to the office of grand master.

Why should a young man, who was achieving success he would have never thought possible in Boston, bother with an obscure itinerant Presbyterian minister who was something of a charlatan? Franklin himself passes over the unpleasant incident lightly in the *Autobiography*, but this promotional piece is not always a reliable source for understanding its author's motivation and actions; nor does the persona, who moves gracefully through its pages from one success to another, loving or at least tolerating his fellows and beloved and respected by nearly all of them, including his opponents, represent the whole man and his experiences. To understand the significance of the trial and censure of Samuel Hemphill by the Presbyterian Church, and Franklin's spirited defense of the minister, we must consider this seemingly minor incident in light of both the development of the Church in the Middle Colonies, and of Franklin's thinking on philosophical and religious matters in 1735. It is against this background that we will be able to appreciate the relationship of the defense to Franklin's Boston experiences with the New England Calvinist Establishment and to his general involvement with American Calvinism before the Revolution. Such an understanding should help make clear the fact that the *Autobiography* is a very effective piece of personal and national propaganda designed to improve the images of the man and his country.

Although the Presbyterian Church in the Middle Colonies had to struggle mightily to grow, it fared much better than did most of the other denominations. Its success resulted from the monumental efforts of its clergy to keep all congregations supplied with at least a part-time ordained minister. One who reads the records of the young Church cannot help being impressed by the devotion of the men who traveled great distances over dangerous country to serve some nearly isolated congregations whose members, fearing a decline in Christian belief, pleaded for the Word and the sacraments.[3]

What caused the shortage of ministers was the great influx of Scotch-Irish

Presbyterians into the Middle Colonies and the addition of existing "Puritan" churches.[4] Even before this migration reached its peak, sensitive observers recognized that the area would be a center of strength for the Church in America. As early as 1716 it was decided that the Presbytery of Philadelphia had become so large as to make practical its division into four subordinate presbyteries which, beginning in 1717, made up the Synod of Philadelphia.[5] Before the middle of the century the Presbyterians were numerically the most powerful church in Philadelphia. The Friends controlled Pennsylvania politics, but their chief strength lay in the areas outside the city. Further, although the Church could not claim for members as many men of wealth and influence as the Quakers or Anglicans, it was gaining in this respect too.[6]

Success for the Presbyterians was won, however, in spite of serious obstacles within the Church itself, and these are relevant to the Hemphill trial. For one thing, as even a sampling of the cases will demonstrate, the moral level of some of the clergy was quite low. In 1720, James Morehead was refused admission to the Synod for a number of reasons, the chief being his "irregular and factious carriage in his own country," and "his scandalous and disorderly behavior since he came to America."[7] The same Synod heard Robert Cross, who was to be one of Hemphill's judges, confess to the sin of fornication. Yet the minister's serious and humble confession enabled him to get off much more easily than Hemphill would fifteen years later. Cross was merely forbidden to preach for four consecutive Sabbaths, after which time he resumed his regular duties.[8] Evidently the Church, needing clergy as much as it did, was forced to forgive immorality if it possibly could. As the events of 1735 would prove, though, it would be less lenient when confronted with heterodoxy: it could deal with and overcome vice, but the clergy felt that the greatest threat to the Church came from unorthodox ministers.[9]

Because of the shortage of ministers, the Synod was compelled to welcome applicants from Ireland, the country that was turning out many unorthodox clergymen, some of whom were also immoral.[10] The conservative members of the Philadelphia Synod felt that the American Church had to take steps to insure an orthodox moral ministry. The Reverend George Gillespie, who was another of Hemphill's judges, protested the general leniency of the Synod, and especially the easy punishment that was meted out to Cross. Twice Gillespie tried to get the Synod to invoke sterner measures, but he was defeated each time.[11] Eventually, as many of the clergy realized, the Church would have to take steps to insure a uniformly acceptable ministry. But unfortunately for Gillespie and his cause, the time was not yet right in 1720 or 1721 for such a move.

As the situation became more acute, it seemed to many that the American Church was in danger of becoming as plagued by irregular ministers as the Church in Ireland. The orthodox clergy believed that the Philadelphia Synod was being threatened by liberals, Arians, and deists.[12] Though the Synod had been divided over theological and administrative matters, all factions agreed that something had to be done to keep out heterodox clergy. These parties could not, however, agree on the proper course to follow. To orthodox or conservative clergymen, most of whom were Scotch-Irish and constituted a majority of the Synod, the Church had to become more thoroughly orthodox, in the Scottish manner. This meant that it had to insist that each minister or candidate and lay member subscribe to the Westminster Confession and to the creeds of Presbyterianism. The moderate group, Americans who were raised in the more liberal traditions of English Puritanism, were also concerned about the quality of the clergy, but they held that such a degree of conformity was unnecessary and a violation of the spirit of the Saybrook Platform.[13] They believed that although the Confession and creeds had to be upheld, the best way to insure a sound ministry was to insist that candidates be examined closely for evidence of a conversion experience.[14] This position is closer to that of the evangelical awakeners, later the third powerful group in the Church, who were led by William Tennent, Sr., and his sons, particularly Gilbert. These men cared very little about orthodoxy as such, which they considered a mere expression of self-defeating formalism. Going further than the moderate group, which was headed by Jonathan Dickinson, the evangelists demanded that all ministers give ample proof of conversion and dedicate their lives to awakening the spiritually dead—using any means necessary. These ministers, as the other factions in the Church later saw, thought it incumbent upon themselves, converted saints, to invade the territory of those apathetic or unconverted ministers and awaken their congregations even if they had to use terror to do so.[15] It also became obvious that the awakeners themselves were to be the final judges of the regenerate state of all in the Church, including their colleagues.

The signs of the divisions that would later create a schism were visible, then, even before 1730. Nevertheless, during the years before the Hemphill affair, most conservatives and moderates tried diligently to avoid any rupture, and the evangelists were not yet strong enough to have any great impact in the

Synod. The great majority of clergy realized that they would have to work out some reasonable compromise to help the struggling young church that was beset with such problems as servicing widely scattered congregations, growing religious apathy, and a dangerous decline in the morality and orthodoxy of an imported ministry.

The Presbytery of Donegal offered only one cogent example of what the lack of dignity and general cohesion meant to the Church. It was not unusual for the presbytery, much less individual congregations, to be treated contemptuously and have its authority challenged.[16] Some communicants thought little enough of their ministers to make unfounded, and eventually unproven, accusations of heterodoxy against them much too often for the well being of the Church. The most striking illustration of this lack of respect, but by no means the only one, concerns the troubles between the Reverend William Orr and an elder, John Kirkpatrick. The latter was constantly bringing charges against Orr, and when the minister was found innocent by the presbytery, Kirkpatrick took his complaints to the Synod. When this body also defended the minister, the persistent elder, still unsatisfied and showing no regard for the Synod's determination, prevented Orr from receiving his salary. The minister finally had to initiate a suit to get his pay.[17]

It was obvious to most people that such disorders had to cease and that the people had to be taught a dutiful regard for the clergy. Of course, as the Reverend Gillespie for one realized, the ministers would have to deserve the respect of the laity. In 1721 he therefore made another attempt to achieve an acceptable clergy by covertly preparing the way for a general subscription to orthodoxy.[18] Once more, however, the attempt was defeated, to the chagrin of conservatives. Dickinson, the most prominent intellectual in the Synod, had enough support from his fellow moderates to prevent subscriptionist measures from passing. Though feelings were strained between these opposing groups in the Synod, they were able to remain temperate and accept things as they were rather than push for a total victory that would cause grave disruptions and perhaps the dreaded schism which would make either side's victory a disaster for the Church.

Continuing peace enabled the ministers to effect a compromise in 1729 with the Adopting Act. All Church members were to adopt "the Confession of Faith, with the Larger and Shorter Catechisms of the Assembly of Divines at Westminister," and also were to declare "the said Confessions and Catechisms" to be the confession of their faith. It was further agreed that each present and future minister had either to subscribe to the Confession and Catechisms or give his verbal assent to them. Those who had reservations about any of the articles of the Confession or Catechism were to bring them before the presbytery or Synod. If one's scruples concerned nonessential points of doctrine, he would be considered in full communion and permitted, in the case of a clergyman, to perform all ministerial functions. If one, however, were found to disagree on fundamental points of doctrine and could not be persuaded to change his view, he could not, of course, be admitted to communion. Regular ministers already in communion, who were in disagreement, would unfortunately have to be excommunicated.[19] The Adopting Act was a compromise in every respect. Neither side was altogether happy with it, but both were determined to live with it for the good of the Church.[20]   This is not to say that tensions did not continue. Conservatives persisted in their efforts to win a less qualified adoption[21] against the opposition of the New England-bred moderates. A Dickinson supporter, Jedediah Andrews, one of the most active and elderly of Presbyterian ministers, thought that the Church would be well served if the moderates let the conservatives go their separate way rather than go along with the Scottish approach to church government.[22] It is interesting that Andrews, after his experience with Hemphill, became a subscriptionist.

Hemphill, though, gave conservatives as much cause to reconsider their thinking as he did the moderates. His name appears among the clergy in attendance at the Synod of 1734, which, ironically, made a special point of inquiring whether all new candidates admitted during the year had yet formally adopted the Confession and Catechisms.[23] He had done so twice, in Ireland as well as in America. Whether or not he realized it, in America he was entering a tense Synod whose welfare had long been in danger. The peace achieved by the compromise was incomplete and precarious. Any significant threat might easily set the different factions against each other in earnest and cause a schism. Such an environment was obviously a handicap to a minister coming in to preach morality and a rationalistic and loving God rather than predestination and God's absolute sovereignty.

The evangelists also helped to make Hemphill's situation difficult. Led in 1735 by Gilbert Tennent, his father, brothers, and their colleagues from the elder Tennent's Log College, the group had grown in size and was a significant factor in the Church. Staunch revivalists, who were often guilty of excessive zeal, undignified methods of gaining converts, and a denigration of learning in favor of the workings of the Spirit, the awakeners incurred the scorn and hostility of conservatives in the Church and of rationalists without.

The moderates, who could admire some of the evangelists' beliefs and results, nevertheless still had serious reservations about these "New Lights," as they eventually came to be called. Yet there was a real need for what they had to offer, and since they were clearly men of piety and great dedication, they became increasingly successful in inspiring others. And with their success came growing opposition from conservatives and thus greater strain in the Church.[24]

It was a tense Church, then, dangerously divided and, it seemed, lacking only the proper occasion to bring it to schism. The Commission of the Synod that judged Hemphill knew this, of course, and it is not surprising that they treated him harshly. In a sense the minister helped the Church remain undivided for a time, for all factions could agree that the doctrine he preached was inimical to Presbyterianism and even to Christianity. Though the clergy gave it different labels—deism, Socinianism, Arminianism, and Arianism—some were certain that they had come across Hemphill's words from notorious rationalist clergymen abroad. They could also agree that his beliefs had to be kept out of Presbyterian pulpits.

Many lay people, however, liked what the minister preached. To his enduring fame, Hemphill even made Franklin enjoy attending church. The printer was a contributor to the Philadelphia Presbyterian church and hoped that Hemphill would eventually succeed the aged Jedediah Andrews. Franklin tells us in the *Autobiography* of his dismay that charges were brought against the young minister. He believed Hemphill ill treated and therefore generously "lent him my Pen" in the minister's defense against the Church authorities. All this is true, but Franklin also feared the increasing strength of the Presbyterian Church in the Middle Colonies, thought its clergy as arbitrary and irrelevant as the Calvinist Establishment in New England, and therefore rushed into the fray with the vigor and relish he had displayed more than a decade earlier in Boston. The objects of his assault were once again Calvinism and its clergy. This is not to imply that he was merely engaging in sweet revenge for old wounds. His reading and general experience had confirmed him in his rationalism and in his belief that Calvinism, whether of the Congregationalist or Presbyterian variety, was absurd; and more important, when it became involved in matters that affected the community at large, it was an enemy—a dangerous one—to reason, liberty, and the virtue that sound religion should inculcate.

If evangelism appealed to the generally unsophisticated and emotionally demonstrative, rationalism, especially deism, gained the favor of colonial intellectuals. Less radical than their European counterparts, most native deists were content to espouse the commonsensical verities of natural religion, which derived its tenets from the idea of a First Cause, emphasized a life of virtue, and accepted the belief in a future state.[25] This was, indeed, the basic creed of rationalist ministers, except that they sought to prove the reasonableness of biblical revelation, as well as the religion of nature, whereas secular rationalists normally ignored the Bible.[26] All of them, however, rejected the doctrine of the Trinity and the tenets that were central to Calvinism. Like Franklin, they regarded as incredible the concepts of an arbitrary, vengeful God who has to be continually placated by mankind; that man was born depraved; and that most of the race, in fact all but a few, were to be eternally damned. The notion that all of this horror is foreknown and permitted by God was also thoroughly rejected by rationalists, who instead advocated a reasonable and benevolent God, who is one Being, and a creature, man, who is responsible for his own actions.[27]

The tolerant spirit in the Middle Colonies, especially in Philadelphia, provided a hospitable climate for new ideas. Consequently, rationalism flourished in the area, and Franklin was able to promote deism through his press. Although he read widely among rationalist authors, he was most influenced by Locke, who, in the *Essay Concerning Human Understanding*, argued that

> however faith be opposed to reason, faith is nothing but a firm assent of the mind: which if it be regulated, as is our duty, cannot be afforded to anything but upon good reason; and so cannot be opposite to it. He that believes, without having any reason for believing, may be in love with his own fancies; but neither seeks as he ought, nor pays the obedience due to his Maker, who would have him use those discerning faculties he has given him, to keep him out of mistake and error.[28]

With reason and faith thus separated, Locke asserted that one's reason is a surer guide to religious belief than revelation.[29]

This proved to be just the kind of intellectual verification the budding young deist needed and, while in England, he made use of this assurance when in 1725 he confidently set up the type for the a priori arguments of his *Dissertation on Liberty and Necessity*. He was moved to print the essay when, after helping with the third edition of William Wollaston's *The Religion of Nature Delineated,* he found himself in disagreement with some of the

Englishman's arguments, particularly Wollaston's contention that man is a free agent and therefore accountable for his actions.[30] Taking what he thought was a deistic position,[31] Franklin sought to prove from God's attributes— infinite wisdom, goodness and power—that "Evil is excluded . . . ."[32] What man, as a result of happy or bad experiences, calls good and evil are, as Locke would say, merely the impressions that sense has caused to register on his mind. It seemed to Franklin, then, that it was foolish to make moral distinctions about these experiences because God loves his creatures equally and so balances pleasure and pain, good and evil. What man does is irrelevant, for the balance can never be disturbed, God being infinitely powerful; therefore, along with good and evil, "Merit and Demerit" are also done away with.[33] Man has only a kind of Newtonian free will which allows him to act according to God's harmonious design.[34] The *Dissertation,* though Franklin counted it an erratum and tried to destroy it, was read not only in England but in Ireland, where a pirated edition was brought out in 1733.[35] It would be interesting to know if Samuel Hemphill had seen the pamphlet before he came to America and was defended by its author.

Franklin soon recognized that everyday experience was at least as significant a fact of life as logic and admitted in the *Autobiography* that theoretical truth did not always work well in the marketplace. By the time of his return voyage home in 1726, he had decided that man did have free will and began thinking of regulating "my future Conduct in Life" along more manageable lines. He would strive to live frugally, to speak the truth, "the most amiable excellence in a rational being," to be industrious, and to treat others with charity.[36] This plan is obviously limited in vision, but unlike the *Dissertation* at least it has the virtues of being sensible and harmless. The plan also contains the basic principles which the Junto[37] members would employ to improve themselves and their city. Franklin organized the club the year after his return to Philadelphia, and in developing its practical morality expressed the influence on him of Locke and the Quakers.

To these must be added the influence of other rationalist thinkers. From a translation of Lord Herbert of Cherbury's *De Religione Laici*, the young man found corroboration for his own negative feelings about religious denominations and ministers. Their chief purposes, the writer charged, were to make religion incomprehensible and to terrify and intimidate mankind.[38] An intelligent man, though, will use reason, faith, and prayer with "a painstaking search for truth" to attain virtue. The pursuit and consequent discovery of virtue, moreover, will be most pleasing to the benevolent and knowable "Father" of us all.[39]

Franklin complemented this commonsense approach to God with those of a number of other writers, including John Ray. In his substantial piece, *The Wisdom of God Manifested in the Works of the Creation*, Ray strives to demonstrate that the astronomical number of God's works bespeak not only an infinite power, but also unlimited "skill and the Foecundity of his Wisdom."[40] Riding the wave of Newtonian physics, Ray draws the analogy between our appreciation for God and for the inventor of an excellent machine or building. We pay due respect to the human artist and admire his intelligence and skill for his single or few creations. The magnificence and diversity of nature must imply, then, a vastly superior mind. Who but the greatest of Architects or Engineers could have developed "that excellent Contrivance for Beauty, Order [and] Use," observable in nature and kept all intact?[41]

Accepting a superbly ordered universe presided over by a kindly and rational Artist was easy for Franklin. But such acceptance implies a commitment to live accordingly, to fit into the divine harmony. For the young deist this meant developing a creed by which to live. If he was not religious in any conventional sense, he was at least very concerned about religious matters. In 1728 he formulated his *Articles of Belief and Acts of Religion*, a set of rules by which he could live usefully and happily and praise God for creating a world in which good deeds and a rational life led to expectations of rewards in the "here or hereafter."

The preface to the piece, taken from Addison's *Cato*, suggests the tenor of the whole:

> Here I will hold—If there is Pow'r above us
> (And that there is, all Nature cries aloud,
> Thro' all her Works), He must delight in Virtue
> And that which he delights in must be Happy.[42]

The importance assigned to virtuous behavior as the test of man's faith is interesting, for *Articles of Belief* is Franklin's first sustained rejection of his *Dissertation,* in which he did away with the idea of moral responsibility. Experience had taught him that a man must be held accountable and hold himself responsible for his own conduct. And the God who delights in virtue is different from the more mechanical and less personal God of the earlier work. He is a necessary moral guide to be discovered rationally through understanding the natural order of the universe. Reason makes man "capable of observing" God's "wisdom in the creation."[43] It presumably enabled

Franklin to conceive of many universes, each with its own God, who is in charge, and the *"Supremely Perfect"* God in control of all, including "that particular wise and good God, who is Author and Owner of our system."[44] In effect, this approach to an understanding of the cosmological order is based on the popular idea of the Great Chain of Being, with God in His proper place, below the Infinite, but "infinitely above" us and our progress. Yet Franklin held that man should worship God, though He does not require our prayers. Indeed, it is man who needs to express love and thanks. Although man is not an especially high link in the chain, God has been extraordinarily good to him in giving the creature one of God's very own "passions," reason.[45] Gentle and kind, this Being wants his children to be wise, virtuous, and happy (in some humanly recognizable sense of the word), and is Himself pleased with man's "pleasant exercises and innocent delights," in his "rational joy and pleasure." Franklin therefore loves Him "for his goodness" and adores Him "for his Wisdom."[46] This is the rational and kindly God loved by Franklin and Hemphill. He is not, however, the God of serious Presbyterians, who would rid themselves of the heterodox minister, and thus lay themselves open to the ready hostility of his anonymous penman.

Franklin's ideas about God and man seem also to have been influenced by the men who were instrumental in first causing him to doubt Calvinism: Anthony Ashley Cooper, third Earl of Shaftesbury, and Anthony Collins. Although he could not entirely accept Shaftesbury's sanguine view of man, Franklin found the Englishman's "An Inquiry Concerning Virtue," with its insistence on man's benevolent *"natural Temper,"* which leads him to moral conduct regardless of any system of rewards and punishment,[47] a necessary, accurate, and healthful qualification of Hobbes' unhappy notions of man. Further, to Shaftesbury and to Franklin after the *Dissertation,* man has free will and chooses how he lives. Man's kindly impulses, of course, will lead most people to strive for and eventually achieve moral excellence.[48]

Collins was influential in expanding and liberalizing Franklin's conception of God. His primary importance, though, probably lies in making God an advocate of skepticism. In his anonymously written *Free-Thinking,* for example, Collins engages in a long attack on the Bible as revelation as well as on the clergy of all faiths, who by endless doctrinal disputes and base threats have kept people ignorant and superstitious about religion.[49] In truth, God intended man to think freely; therefore, it behooves all reasonable people to reject the many "Crackbrain'd and Enthusiastical" clerics who use their position to advance their private ambition.[50] This negative view of the clergy was one which Franklin had held since his Boston days, contrary to what he says in the memoirs, and it was going to help determine his conduct during the Hemphill affair.

Armed, then, with convincing arguments from some of the outstanding men of his age, the young printer felt confident that he knew his mind on God, religion, and human responsibility. When he wrote his epitaph in 1728, sixty-two years before his death, he was certain that one who expressed his love of God in concrete acts of virtue would be rewarded by Him without the doubtful help of institutional religion or violent awakenings.

The next year, 1729, the spirit of Silence Dogood once more arose, this time in the male person of the Busy-Body. In his memoirs Franklin mentions the Busy-Body pieces, but he tells us nothing about them. Like his predecessor, this good common person sets himself up as a critic of human follies and delivers moral lectures.[51] In his first letter he announces that the reforming spirit lives on and is "properly the concern of every Man; that is, Every one ought to mend One."[52] How this reformation is to be accomplished is discussed in the next letter. Churches and ministers, he charges, have had their chance to improve the world but have failed because they always insist on the wrong things. Virtue is not gained by piety or grace, but by the constant exercise of practical morality, which is "alone sufficient to make *a Man Great, Glorious and Happy.*"[53] The combative tone of the piece suggests that the Busy-Body may well have recalled how petty and even vicious some of the most pious ministers of Boston became during the smallpox crisis.

His fifth letter appeared in the late winter of 1729, at the time when the Presbyterian Church was about to formulate the Adopting Act to strengthen its position by trying to insure an orthodox ministry. The Church's fear of heterodoxy was, of course, no secret, nor were its internal disturbances that threatened a schism. As an aggressive publisher eager for news, it is very likely that Franklin knew about these problems. Further, it seems probable that as a shrewd businessman determined to be successful and to play an active part in community life, he realized that by ridiculing Presbyterianism he would not hurt his chances of gaining government business from an anti-Presbyterian Quaker Assembly. Finally, his own antipathy toward Calvinist Establishments made him a concerned observer of their affairs when these seemed to bear on the secular life he found so congenial. It seems to be more than coincidence, then, that the Busy-Body's fifth letter satirized the pretentiousness of Calvinist saints. In his effort to reform as many people as he can, the Busy-Body warns that he is going to be helped by an "extraordinary Person," one who is capable of discovering "the most secret Iniquity." This person was born in Scotland and inherited from his father, a man who "delighted in the *Pilgrim's Progress,* and mountainous Places," the gift of *"Second Sight."* His peculiar virtue enables him to see what many people are doing in a variety of places, even while "I am sitting in my Closet." He is therefore a great discoverer of evil and, presumably, a perceptive judge of men. There is a problem, however, for the gift has created "too great a Burthen" for his mind and inclines this prodigy to solitude. Having debunked claims to speciality and the right to judge others because of claims of supernatural excellence, Franklin next has the Busy-Body discuss his unusual "Correspondent" and his gifts in connection "with my poor Monkey," who grinned and chattered at all girls and women. The monkey was thought to have a kind of second sight about females, and it was believed it "snarl'd by instinct at every Female who had lost her virginity. This was no sooner generally believ'd than ... he was assassinated in the Night."[54] Franklin, then, associates the unusual claims to special talent and virtue, asserted in this case by a Presbyterian zealot, with the unhappy monkey. Such a satire was found to appeal to many of Franklin's readers not only for literary reasons, but because they shared his antipathy toward zealots in general and Presbyterians in particular.

After Franklin assumed sole ownership of the *Gazette* in 1730, he continued his attacks on Presbyterianism. He obviously did not feel that his actions would cause him to lose the good will of the Quaker Assembly, since he had been satirizing them for some time and had already, while still Meredith's partner, been appointed Public Printer by that body. On October 22, 1730, he published his famous spoof, "A Witch Trial at Mount Holly," which reminded Pennsylvanians about the tragic affair at Salem. That the witch trials could have been a topic of much conversation after more than three decades seems unlikely. Yet Franklin insists on bringing up the event again and, in doing so, exposes the irrationality and narrow-mindedness he found in all Calvinists. The piece is a satire on the trial of some persons charged with bewitching a number of their neighbors' sheep. The accusers confidently and self-righteously demand that the accused take the scales test, but this method of convicting them proves unsatisfactory. The accused, on the one side, are pitted against the Bible on the other, the assumption being that the truth of the Bible will be too heavy for the presumed witches and will therefore weigh them down. Thus they would be convicted and the Bible and

God would triumph. Sadly, though, one of the witches proved heavier and the results of the test were puzzling to the faithful. Still, as true zealots, they were undeterred in their hope of gaining convictions in the end and, of course, they remained convinced of the reality of witches. They therefore demanded another absurd test, betraying to Franklin's readers their stupidity, arrogance, and bigotry. Franklin milks the hoax until all its potential for comedy is drained. He especially delights in mocking the irrationality of his characters.[55] Not only did they accept biblical revelation, which was contrary to reason, but they insisted that all people conform to their particular orthodoxy, ridiculous as it was. Yet it was just this kind of free-thinking irreverence, whether couched in a Christian vocabulary or not, that all factions in the Presbyterian Church were struggling to overcome by increasing demands for greater orthodoxy or regenerative piety. The state of mind represented by Franklin and Hemphill was clearly inimical to the most basic interests of the Church and, as the minister's trial would prove, the notions of religion held by the Church and by Franklin and Hemphill were also irreconcilable.

The "Witch Trial," though anonymous, may have been the printer's response to unkind letters he had received earlier that summer from orthodox citizens he had offended. The *Gazette* had carried three essays from the *London Journal*, all of them from a work entitled *Essays of Primitive Christianity*. Although the selections were "exceedingly acceptable to the generality of the newspaper's readers, some "worthy and learned men" (which is the manner of Franklin's tone referring sarcastically to ministers with whom he fought) called the piece "false, heretical and pernicious."[56] Franklin challenged these detractors to refute the essays, but apparently no one accepted the offer.[57]

In 1731 he wrote his *Observations on Reading History* which, as others have noted, is the "genesis" of his unrealized party of virtue.[58] The *Observations* draw on Franklin's New England background: he wanted the organization he had in mind in writing the piece to be comprised exclusively of all "the Virtuous and good men of all Nations." These leaders would govern in such a way as to provide an example of morality for men to follow.[59] The membership in the party was really an international group of thoroughly secular saints whose concern was practical virtue rather than piety or orthodoxy. Franklin always retained the Puritan notions of morality. What he rejected was its religious foundation.

It was in this year that Franklin joined the Masons, a group that taught its members morality rather than theology, and stressed fellowship and toleration. Moreover, it expressed belief in one God, who was discovered through reason, and preached that natural religion was universal.[60] That these doctrines appealed to Franklin is attested to by his very regular attendance at Masonic meetings[61] and his subsequent rise in the organization. Three times before 1735 he was honored with offices, and in the year of the Hemphill trial he was appointed Provincial Grand Master of Pennsylvania.[62]

One of the reasons for Franklin's success in the Masons is that he was sure of his beliefs and found them akin to those upheld by that organization. As Carl Van Doren observed, Franklin had reached intellectual maturity by 1732. He "had investigated his own mind till he knew it and was at home there."[63] It is certainly true that by this time he thought he knew what beliefs and modes of conduct would promote happiness. Though he himself, as he says, never attained perfection, he was confident that he knew what it consisted of and how one could become perfect. In his humorously treated but nevertheless serious effort to become perfect himself, he pointed the way for others to succeed where he had failed, or to at least improve as he had done. With a Lockean avoidance of abstraction, he listed his famous thirteen virtues: Temperance, Silence, Order, Resolution, Frugality, Industry, Sincerity, Justice, Moderation, Cleanliness, Tranquility, Chastity, and Humility.[64] After each of the virtues he added a short but specific notation indicating his meaning. In effect, the list inductively creates what Franklin considers to be the perfectly moral man, insofar as man can be perfected. And for the typical American living in a country free of oppressive laws, taxes, and an established church, such a plan and such a goal seemed possible to Franklin. The list of virtues is one that the most religious Puritan could accept, though he would be uncomfortable, to say the least, with the final definition, which makes Christ a man and the equal of Socrates! Further, the list of any religious person would include piety, whereas Franklin's contains nothing of the kind, and any strict Calvinist would be horrified by the framework of the project, the atomistic approach to reform, and by the assumption that man could achieve anything like perfection without having first undergone the conversion experience. Upon close examination, then, we see that the list constitutes a thorough rejection of the doctrines of predestination, irresistible grace, and salvation by faith, as well as of the Calvinist views of God and man.

Success in attaining perfection, or at least in achieving a very high level of morality, required only deliberation, practice, and time. Franklin amusingly allowed one week of concerted effort at each virtue, while still working at the other twelve. The special emphasis on a single virtue, he felt, would produce visible results quickly and thus provide additional incentive for continuing the project. Since one week was given to each virtue, he could go through an entire course every thirteen weeks and four courses in a year. Because he was a young man, he might have enough years ahead of him to become a perfect man. The attainment of the goal was for him essentially an act of will; therefore, it was possible for any good and conscientious person to undertake the task, in the Land of Opportunity at any rate. Franklin embraced the humanistic creed, developed in the memoirs and in other writings with propagandistic intent, that in America a man can become very largely what he believes he can become. Even the failure of his own attempt at becoming perfect did not shake this belief.[65]

Some of the pressures which consumed much of Franklin's time and made it impossible for him to continue this weekly regimen had themselves to do with promoting benevolent projects. His "Standing Queries for the Junto," written in 1732, is one of the works that reveal his concern for his fellow men. The "Queries" shows the influence of Cotton Mather's *Bonifacius: Essays to Do Good*. Although Franklin fought against Mather and his supporters, he still respected the minister's effort to improve the moral climate of New England. He therefore secularized what he thought practical in the *Essays* and formulated twenty-four questions for the Junto to consider. The Junto is depicted in the *Autobiography* as a group of average American tradesmen with a desire to better themselves and their community. Yet the "Queries," expressing as they do a Baconian interest in such diverse matters as "history, morality, poetry, physic, travels [and] mechanic arts," as well as a concern about the causes for failures and success in business, unusually "worthy" actions, or errors to be avoided, particularly those having to do with "intemperance," "imprudence" or "passion,"[66] belie Franklin's portrayal of the club. Most of the members were gifted and superior men who were well on their way to becoming successful. Making them typical Americans, however, suggests that all hard working and competent people can accomplish much for themselves and others in a country that is filled with opportunity and receptive to new ideas and to different kinds of ability. All Junto members were enjoined to emulate the lives of other successful Americans so that they could elevate themselves, and the "Queries" further called on the members to be diligent in promoting achievement and virtue wherever they could.[67] It was not in the least unreasonable to expect such things of Americans.

Another Junto piece of the same year indicates distrust of zealous converts. The "Proposals and Queries to be Asked the Junto" is even more hostile to those who switch denominations than "Silence Dogood, No. 14" had been. In his own person, Franklin calls converts renegades and says they are "worse than 10 Turks." If one arrived at his religious beliefs through the prudent exercise of reason, he would be unlikely to change them. Converts, therefore, seemed to him unsophisticated and irrational enthusiasts and inferiors.[68]

The queries in this work uphold views previously stated: that man can become as perfect "as his present Nature and Circumstances" allow;[69] and that "the Happiness of a rational Creature" lies in enjoying health, moderate prosperity, and the love of God and man.[70] It is clear that all four of these are within the control of the average American, and they are all equally necessary. Rather than wanting us to pursue some impossible state of perfection, Franklin's God wanted man to strive for attainable human perfection. In this effort He would freely give His help and love, for virtue is pleasing to God and the greatest love man can express for God is in being good, charitable, useful to mankind—and at least seemingly modest. Even salvation, then, for Americans, is achieved by the exercise of will and by the benevolence of an approving God. Such rational happiness on earth, and presumably in the hereafter, Franklin wrote just two months before the Hemphill trial, was to be learned as one learned a science.[71] Opportunity for self-improvement—moral as well as material—abounded. Given a general and rational belief in God and the precepts of good, useful teachers, Franklin's fellow Americans could become uniformly virtuous and perhaps even perfect.[72] Devout Calvinists, however, had no place in this pleasant landscape that was so central a part of the Land of Opportunity. Franklin's intellectual antipathy for Calvinist beliefs and his early experiences with the Congregational Establishment in Boston made him an enemy to the dominant religious groups of his time in America. The Hemphill affair would soon indicate the degree of hostility that had begun years before when he was a boy and was to continue to develop until the impending Revolutionary troubles made him feel that loyalty among all Americans was a necessity.

If in the 1730's Franklin sincerely respected any theologian, it was the liberal Anglican Archbishop Tillotson, some of whose works the printer read and enjoyed. Although there was much the Archbishop wrote that Franklin could not accept, he could agree with Tillotson that, for example, "peace and tranquility" spring up naturally "in the Mind of a good man,"[73] whose life will serve as a model for others and thus promote human happiness.[74] Both men further believed that prayer should be, as Tillotson says, "hearty" rather than formalistic and expressive of confidence that God is benevolent and "will hear us."[75] Finally, Franklin must have agreed with the Englishman's attack on pious hypocrites and ignorant zealots whose enthusiasm dishonors God and destroys the peace.[76] In other words, Franklin could go along with the clergyman's intellectual and moral precepts, though not with his theology. The Presbyterian Church in America, though, weak as it was, and in danger of being invaded by heterodox ministers from abroad, felt better able to suffer poor morality than theological error or dissent. The trial and the pamphlet war that were about to begin would test whether a staunch if secret enemy and a newly arrived rationalistic preacher could change the nature and course of American Presbyterianism.

The guiding force behind the Presbyterian church in Philadelphia was Jedediah Andrews, a Harvard graduate and follower of the Mathers, who devoted nearly an entire lifetime to helping the denomination prosper in the Middle Colonies.[77] Years of toil, however, had weakened him and at the Synod meeting of 1733 he asked for an assistant. Andrews was then fifty-nine years old and had served as a minister for the previous thirty-five of those years.[78]

His reward for this service, Samuel Hemphill, arrived in America in 1734 and was present at the Synod meeting of that year. Since he had brought with him recommendations from the Presbytery of Straban in Ireland, provided "satisfactory certificates . . . of his qualifications,"[79] and had accepted the Westminster Confession abroad and declared his willingness to sign the Adopting Act in America, he seemed a good choice to assist Andrews. Hemphill must have seemed an oratorical relief to some members of the Philadelphia church who had endured Andrews' dry fare. Franklin writes of both men as preachers, and it is well known that he gave up hope of ever being illuminated by the older minister, but thoroughly enjoyed the rationalistic morality and commonsensical Christianity preached by Hemphill.[80]

The younger minister may have been too good, though, for he was soon drawing large crowds, including those unorthodox citizens like Franklin, who Andrews later said made up the worst persons in his congregation. They and the rationalist Hemphill seemed meant for each other. Or so thought Andrews, for he found his assistant's liberal sermons heretical. When early in 1735 he could no longer stand by and see so many people for whom he had labored long being led into heterodoxy, he went to the Commission of the Synod with a complaint against Hemphill.[81] The story of the Hemphill trial is fairly well known.[82] Franklin and a number of other persons defended the minister against the Presbyterian Establishment. Taking the lead in the affair, the printer wrote pamphlets in Hemphill's behalf and used the *Gazette* to promote his cause. The Commission of the Synod found Hemphill guilty, and as a result incurred Franklin's wrath and abusive wit. The whole Synod nevertheless agreed with the judgment of its Commission. After the trial it was discovered that the minister had passed off as his own the sermons of others; therefore, most of his supporters deserted him, but not Franklin. Defeated, Hemphill disappeared into obscurity. A thorough analysis of the character of this controversy and its relation to the affairs of the Church in the Middle Colonies will be helpful here. A discussion of the pamphlet war that ensued, and particularly Franklin's role in events, will also be enlightening.

Hemphill's career was stormy from the beginning. Before he was ordained he had made an enemy in Ireland of another Presbyterian minister. For reasons that may have been petty, this preacher, named Vance, perhaps falsely accused Hemphill of heterodoxy. The young minister cleared himself before the Synod, was ordained, and then left for America. According to Franklin, Vance wrote to friends in America and continued to defame Hemphill. These people, clergymen as well as laymen, believed the charges without hesitation and without proof.[83] In one of his essays on the affair, Franklin, for rhetorical purposes, assumes naïveté. This was a device he was to use throughout his life to gain an advantage over an opponent. Here he expresses his utter amazement that there are so many American Presbyterians who would "not only venture to violate the peculiar duties of Christianity, but even everything . . . human." Using the name of Christ as an excuse, they sin against the principles of their calling and against their own humanity.[84] In assuming their calling for them and in charging them with sinning against their own natures and consciences, Franklin is adopting a stance only slightly less arbitrary than the one John Cotton took toward Roger Williams.

His affected innocence shattered, Franklin has to admit the sad fact that there are Presbyterians in America who do not live by the Golden Rule. One Kilpatrick had called Hemphill a "*New Light man*, a Deist, one who preached nothing but morality."[85] His detractors had not yet heard him preach, as Franklin notes, but they relied on the information furnished by Vance and accused him of being one of those ministers whom all factions in the Church saw as a threat. Hemphill was, however, admitted to the Synod and took his place in Andrews' church. Franklin's report of the affair indicates that the older man was at first pleased by his assistant's eloquence, and it was only his envy of the young preacher's popularity that prompted his charges of heterodoxy and the subsequent investigation.[86]

Just before the trial, the printer anonymously declared that he looked forward to the proceedings, confident that the Commission of the Synod would treat Hemphill justly.[87] For Franklin, of course, this meant that they would find the young preacher innocent. On the surface this seems an unusually optimistic position for Franklin to take considering the antagonism toward Calvinist clergy he had been harboring for thirteen years. Here as elsewhere, though, we cannot accept what he says at face value. He was undoubtedly hoping that an exonerated Hemphill would one day replace Andrews at the important Philadelphia church, a change that would surely alter the character of Philadelphia Presbyterianism and might even have far-reaching effects. It is also likely, however, that Franklin was setting up his readers and the Commission for the attack that would follow any conviction of the minister.

On April 7, 1735, at the Synod meeting in Philadelphia, Andrews formally brought charges against Hemphill, and a Commission was formed to examine the case.[88] In Franklin's opinion the elder clergy had no right to silence a man for preaching differently, especially if he was actively promoting virtue instead of harping on dull and irrelevant points of official doctrine. Even the Synod itself had no real right, in Franklin's mind, to question a minister who was cultivating morality. Assuming once again an innocence of which he was by no means guilty, he pretends to be unaware that a religious denomination, unlike a club for personal and civic improvement, might believe ardently in a particular theological interpretation as well as in secular virtue.

Three days after Andrews officially charged Hemphill with heterodoxy, the *Gazette* carried its owner's ostensibly hopeful "Dialogue between Two Presbyterians."[89] It is actually a Socratic dialogue, for Mr. S., the good, plain spokesman for the minister and writer, has all the better of Mr. T., the dupe. Mr. S., like Silence Dogood, is a lover of virtue who considers particular orthodoxies and religious enthusiasm irrelevant and potentially inimical to sound religion and human happiness. Moreover, like the Widow, Mr. S. has the good of the public at heart and therefore hopes to see the Church rectify itself by permitting Hemphill to continue his good work. There is no doubt in Mr. S.'s mind that the minister is a true Christian and will prove a great benefit to the Church and the community. Mr. T., who is an orthodox Presbyterian and as such represents the Establishment in the Church, dislikes Hemphill because he "talks of nothing but the duties of morality," a doctrine "not . . . fit to be preached in a Christian congregation."[90] The irony in this speech must have been clear to many readers of the *Gazette* when they were reminded by Mr. S. that morality was the "principal part" of the preaching of Christ and the apostles.[91] Mr. S. goes on to argue that faith is merely a "means of producing morality," and morality is the key to "salvation." Mr. S. follows his reversal of orthodox doctrine with this challenging assertion: "But that from such faith alone salvation may be expected, appears to me to be neither a Christian doctrine" nor, what is at least just as bad for Mr. S. and his creator, "a reasonable one."[92] By this time Mr. T. and the position he represents are thoroughly defeated. He is reduced to asking whether faith is not also "recommended" in the New Testament.[93] Franklin clearly strikes at what he feels is the ignorance and irrationality of Hemphill's opponents, for even after it is obvious that Mr. T.'s arguments will not stand up against those of Mr. S., the faithful Presbyterian maintains his position. He cannot believe that faith is necessary only for those who are deficient in it, namely "heathens," but insists that it is also required of Christians as well. Mr. S., confident of his rhetorical victory, notes with an ironic smile that Presbyterians have an "abundance" of faith. Their problem is that they are "evidently deficient" in morality,[94] and this situation is precisely what the young minister is trying to correct. Mr. S.'s wit, like his arguments, are lost on his opponent, who insists, in spite of all evidence in favor of Hemphill's preaching, that he does "not like" morality in church. Franklin's efforts, however, were not lost on his readers. Mr. T., after all, is a device intended to expose the banality and bigotry the printer had long believed to be characteristic of Calvinism. Mr. S.'s confidence in the "good sense" and "true piety" of the Commission thus seem only a ploy to force the Church into approving of Hemphill or of appearing to be an institution not only as ridiculous as Mr. T., but one actually hostile to virtue. Such an institution, of course, was fair game for assault in the public interest and in the name of the Reformation; for if the Commission should find Hemphill guilty, it would, in effect, be denying the right of later generations to interpret the Gospel in light of their own experience. What would happen, then, to the reform that is supposedly at the heart of the Reformation spirit?[95]

Unlike Mr. S. the Commission members were Presbyterian clergymen and so believed differently from deists and Christian rationalists. Regardless of the faction of the Church they belonged to, they all opposed the heresy of rationalism and morality at the expense of theology. It was a foregone conclusion that in addition to Andrews, James Anderson, John Thomson, George Gillespie, Robert Cross, Jonathan Dickinson, John Pierson, Thomas Craighead, and the moderator, Ebenezer Pemberton, were going to protect the Church from Hemphill by silencing him. They were hardly fair in their treatment of him, however, since the moderate Pemberton, as well as such conservatives as Gillespie and Cross, joined forces in preaching sermons against Hemphill before the Commission of which they were members completed its trial of the minister.[96]

After meeting for ten days, the Commission, on April 27, unanimously censured Hemphill and suspended him, claiming that his doctrines were "unsound and dangerous, contrary to the scriptures and our excellent Confession and catechism."[97] The decision shocked a good many people, and in the first week of May the judges felt compelled to defend their verdict in a pamphlet listing six points on which they believed the minister to be wrong. Although the pamphlet declared that Hemphill was given the opportunity to offer evidence of his innocence and have friends speak in his behalf, "it gave no hint of what he or his supporters said."[98] Franklin saw his chance to defend Hemphill and, more important, to attack the steadily growing Presbyterian Church. His anonymously written *Observations* on the affair were published July 17; because of the furor created over the trial and the sensational nature of the *Observations*, the piece went into a second edition by August.[99]

The tone of the pamphlet suggests a man far different from the kindly friend to all religions created in the *Autobiography*. Franklin's anger goes far beyond the "rubs" Silence Dogood gave the Boston Establishments. In the *Observations* he determined not only to clear Hemphill's character, as he says, but "to convince the world how unjustly some Men will act, when they have their own private Ends in View."[100] As the Widow Dogood had done earlier to good effect, Franklin enlarges the scope of his attack to include such nontheological matters as the ability, intelligence, and integrity of the clergy, thereby hoping to render them contemptible and impotent. Given the religiously apathetic and non-Calvinist tone of the Philadelphia area, Franklin's chances of success were greater than they had been in Boston. Throughout the *Observations* he struggles to show that one may uphold orthodoxy and spout pious sentiments and yet be immoral in his dealings with others. The judges provide him examples of such men. If they, respected ministers of the Presbyterian Church, are immoral, then, as Franklin's readers were likely to conclude, one should indeed be judged on his works. Franklin harps on the Commission's "unchristian treatment" of Hemphill and of its self-serving defense of Andrews and support of his "trifling" and "groundless" charges.[101] All of these things betray the lack of basic morality in the judges.

Not only did they support these charges, he says, but they positively denied

Hemphill a fair trial. There could be no other reason than a predetermination to find the minister guilty by hook or crook that prompted the Commission to renege on its promise to provide Hemphill a copy of the minutes of the proceedings in time for him to make use of it. Nor could anything other than desire to ruin the minister and protect Andrews and themselves have caused the judges to preach against Hemphill while the trial was in progress.[102] Yet such men see fit to interpret God and to exclude from their midst good ministers who preach virtue and are able to influence people positively. The matter of Hemphill's influence is important, Franklin charges, because Andrews was prompted to move against his assistant out of jealousy over the young man's popularity and effectiveness.[103] Though he offers no proof for this assertion, Franklin asks that it be accepted as fact and implies that such baseness is common among Presbyterian clergy. There is no doubt that his seething anger at what he saw as an unfair and irrelevant trial was genuine, and he responded accordingly. Whereas Mrs. Dogood had challenged the morality of the Boston area clergy with pleasant humor, Franklin was now, under the protection of a milder religious climate, emboldened to attack his enemies directly and brutally.

His extracts of the Commission's findings, in which he criticized its position and methods, gave him further opportunity to vilify that body, the Church in general, and particularly Calvinism. Andrews had accused Hemphill of calling Christianity largely a "new edition of nature's laws." The Commission, therefore, claimed that Hemphill was enjoining men to live according to their nature and to rely on reason in governing themselves. This belief was, the judges pointed out, contrary to the Gospel and the Confession.[104]

Franklin freely admits that Hemphill used such words; however, arguing theology in a way that would surprise the hero of the memoirs, who claims to dislike and avoid theological debates, he insists that the view expressed is entirely consistent with the Gospel and even with the Confession! What Hemphill meant, Franklin claims, was that Christ came to earth to help men return to their initial state of "perfection." To this end he gave men laws which are "agreeable" to the original law, "as having such a natural tendency to our present ease and quiet, that they carry their own reward,"[105] as if there were no reward or punishment after life. Franklin, arguing for a knowable and rational God that promotes morality and prosperity to average people, regardless of their religious affiliation, finds Hemphill's position consistent with the Gospel. Further, he charges, "the opposite opinion is de-

structive of both the Gospel, and all the notions we have of the moral perfec-
tions of God, and the disinterested love and benevolence which appear
throughout his whole conduct to mankind."[106] Having assumed the of-
fense, Franklin even boldly challenges the Commission's understanding of
the Confession.[107] This is done for effect only. His chief concern is to undermine the integrity of the judges and eventually of the Church. He therefore accuses the Commission of dishonesty and treachery, declaring that it had "perverted and altered the very words of Hemphill's sermon" in order to protect the jealous Andrews and to lend some air of credibility to its own
prejudiced decision.[108]

Andrews' second charge, that Hemphill did not uphold the need for conversion among people born in the Church and leading moral lives, was also
supported by the Commission. Once again Franklin tries to make the judges
objects of contempt. In coming to their decision, he writes, the Commissioners
sought "to amuse the world," for nothing but malice and envy could move
"them to act so unjustly as they have done."[109] They omitted from the extract
those parts that would have made Hemphill's meaning clear and have proved
him innocent of the accusation. Franklin supports his point by printing the
whole paragraph in question. He argues that the minister said that good Christians are not really converted or in need of conversion, because being brought
up in a Christian way, and leading moral lives, they have remained constant,
"except the progress and improvement which they daily make in
virtue."[110] They are different from those who do not know or do not
follow the teachings of Christ and in this sense are new creatures; however,
they are not different from what they have always been, if they have lived by
the Gospel.[111] To this rather specious argument, Franklin, perhaps striking at
the awakeners in the Synod, adds that ministers who insist on "spiritual pangs
and convulsions" rather than good works from those who have lived as
Christians make Christianity contemptible and altogether "unworthy of its
divine Author."[112] The Synod, then, since it supported the Commission, is
identified with enthusiasm, anti-intellectualism, and unsound Christianity.

In upholding Andrews' third charge, the Commission agreed that
Hemphill was preaching a doctrine "subversive to the true and proper satisfaction of Christ."[113] The young minister had declared that those who
work up audiences over the matter of Christ's satisfaction, far from
glorifying him, make a mere "charm" of him and seriously detract from his
goodness. The judges particularly attacked Hemphill's alleged contentions
that an explication of "the eternal laws of morality" is the most Christian

and most useful preaching, since God judges the inner man by his conduct.[114] Such doctrine, the Commission held, denigrated the satisfaction of Christ and had no place in a Presbyterian pulpit.

In defending Hemphill on this point, Franklin once again assaults his judges and their supporters. He treats the affair in surprisingly simplistic terms: Hemphill, a true follower of Christ, is being wronged by seemingly pious but bad Christians for whom religion is a matter of legalisms and meaningless holy expressions that are contradicted by their actions. The charge would be serious if it were true, Franklin admits, and this is precisely why the judges have invented the case on this matter against the minister. They have sought not the truth, but only ways in which to strip a respected and popular minister of his justly deserved following. They have thus not only injured Hemphill but everyone else, since they have had to resort to deceit in corroborating Andrews' complaints and in attempting to make credible their own prejudice.[115] Having attacked Hemphill on the grounds of the satisfaction of Christ, considering that they have the minister's sermons before them, only proves that the judges know that their case is inadequate.[116] Nothing else could account for such desperate action. They have determined to convict Hemphill regardless of the facts, and hope that by blackening his name the people will turn against him.

Stressing the dishonesty and deceit of the Commission, Franklin contends that when the paragraph in question is quoted in full, one sees immediately that Hemphill is really flaying the irrational Antinomians who "never look upon Christ as a Lawgiver, but only in their mistaken notion of a Saviour."[117] It is their doctrine that he was trying to "explode" in favor of the one of Christ as a teacher. Franklin himself was sympathetic to a view of Christ as a lover of practical virtue and giver of moral laws and so did not have to compromise his conscience to say this much. The Commission, and later the whole Synod, demanded that a Presbyterian minister preach Presbyterian doctrine, however, and not a generalized Christian rationalism and morality. Franklin must have understood that the institution had to protect its own beliefs to remain viable, but since he had long felt that any form of Calvinism, if powerful enough, was a threat to liberty, reason, and civic morality, he continued his assault. He contends that Hemphill properly preached a moral and rational Christ. Franklin, after all, had heard the minister's words and knew what he said. More important, Hemphill's conduct and his charitable behavior toward his accuser speak of his Christian bearing. Recognizing, however, that he has been unable to make much of a case for the preacher on the specific point raised, Franklin gropes for more evidence. He reminds his readers that the minister "constantly in his prayers" gave thanks for Christ.[118] This does not say a great deal, as Franklin knew, and so he again turned away from defending the minister to attack the judges. Regardless of the charges, he declared, Hemphill is certainly more of a Christian than the members of the Commission, who at the trial not only upheld the doctrine of predestination but its practice as well. Such an argument, of course, would appeal to the nonreligious and to many non-Presbyterians among his audience, just as the Dogood satires and other *Courant* pieces had been intended to appeal to those indifferent or hostile to the Boston area ministers. None of the Couranteers was hoping to change the clergy then, and Franklin was certainly not appealing to the Synod or to religious Presbyterians now. Rather, he was trying to work up a general resentment toward that body, the Church, and Calvinism.

The Commission also supported Andrews' next complaint, holding that Hemphill preached "too general a description of saving faith" and that he did not explicitly mention that one must receive Christ only "upon the terms of the Gospel." His preaching rendered the doctrine of faith ineffective and could therefore be misleading and dangerous.[119] Franklin hardly answers this charge at all, though the Commission offered a detailed explanation of its complaint. He simply accuses the judges of more vagueness than they attribute to the preacher and says that they use this point only to show off what they think is their learning. They succeed, however, merely in betraying their stupidity. Unprejudiced minds would see at once that since Hemphill's description of faith mentions good works, it cannot be a means of leading mankind away from good works.[120] In the course of arguing this point, Franklin shows himself quite capable of splitting theological hairs and, in spite of disclaimers in the memoirs and elsewhere, displays an appetite for theological disputation. The chief point, though, is that here, as elsewhere in his dealings with Calvinism, he is less concerned with arriving at truth than at making his opponents contemptible. By the time he finished defending Hemphill on this fourth accusation, he left his readers wondering whether the Commission was primarily ignorant or dishonest.

The judges also supported Andrews' fifth complaint, declaring that Hemphill denied the importance of divine revelation and believed that man could be saved by following the dictates of nature.[121] The Commission further accused the preacher of saying that the heathen Cornelius obeyed only his own reason and conscience and that he was *therefore* saved.[122] Franklin once more challenges the fundamental decency of the Commission. He charges it with intentionally falsifying Hemphill's meaning by omitting the final part of the paragraph under discussion and quotes the whole to show that all the minister was saying was that Cornelius' good works "disposed God to give him a miraculous revelation of the Gospel."[123] Franklin does not deny that his friend meant that Cornelius was ultimately saved by his virtue. Other than the benevolence of God, there was nothing else that would save a man. This was sound doctrine to both Franklin and Hemphill, doctrine which the Commissioners would do well to learn, for their "base Conduct" and "wicked Ends"[124] were awful evidence of their moral deficiencies. That the judges were little more than prosecutors from the outset is undeniable. They were determined to find Hemphill guilty and rid themselves of yet another problem in a Church beset by divisions. In fact, the image of conservative and moderate factions, Hemphill's judges, joining in condemning him while the trial was still in progress has the earmarks of a ritualistic sacrifice. The unfortunate minister was exploited as a means of uniting, no matter how fragilely and temporarily, a dangerously divided Church. He was certainly most unfairly treated. But even when his doctrines are taken in the context Franklin presented them, it is clear that the minister was heterodox from a Presbyterian point of view. This is why Franklin's reading of the minister's words is just as doubtful (and at times downright specious) as that of the Commissioners. They were both using Hemphill for their own ends: the judges to unite the Church, and the printer to attack it.

The Commission also agreed with Andrews that his assistant perverted the doctrine of justification by faith, a belief Franklin despised, by asserting that it " 'peculiarly belonged to the first Christians,' " but did not " 'concern' " persons born and educated in the Christian religion. If Christians expected to be saved only by " 'purity of Heart and a virtuous Life,' " they were doomed to disappointment.[125] So central a doctrine was, of course, crucial, and Franklin hastens to attack the judges for designing to misstate Hemphill's meaning, and for changing his own words again. What the minister really said was that wicked Christians, who expected to be saved by faith alone, though continuing in their wickedness, were deluding themselves.[126] So excellent a doctrine is this to Franklin, that he declares one can express genuine faith only in his "Obedience" to the moral laws of Christ. The Commission, judging from the conduct of its members, does not believe that morality is necessary to salvation.[127]

To lend weight to his attack on the judges, Franklin cites Thomas

Gordon,[128] a prolific English writer of well-known anti-ministerial sentiments. Another rationalist, he stressed the central role of reason in religion and insisted that faith had to be manifested in good works.[129] Gordon encouraged the laity to demand that the clergy respect the sanctity of an individual's conscience on all matters, including one's interpretation of the Bible and his judgment of the clergy themselves.[130] The laity, he insisted, should strive to "mortify" the clergy's "Pride"[131] and insatiable desire for wealth and power. This was especially important to Gordon, and he urged his readers and listeners to remember that "the clergy, whenever left to take as much Power and Wealth as they pleased, rarely thought the whole too much . . . ."[132] Furthermore, the ministers were generally guilty of a "furious" and therefore "false Zeal" which was nothing more than "miserable Bigotry and Prejudice"[133] normally used against the masses of men to make them slaves.[134] Such words as these were unlikely to convince the Commission or its supporters to reconsider Hemphill's case or to change their own views. This was not Franklin's intention. Another passage from Gordon not only expresses Franklin's sentiments, as well as the writer's, but indicates what he was doing in defending Hemphill. Focusing on Presbyterians, Gordon declared that there was never "a more bitter, untolerating Race, or more rigorous Exactors of Conformity."[135] Later in his life, a national hero and the most famous printer in the world, Franklin often appealed to his countrymen not to engage in writing or printing libels, for he felt it was an obnoxious practice and presented Americans in a bad light, giving ammunition to their enemies. As a young man, too, he generally tried to avoid printing and writing libels, realizing that as a printer and owner of a newspaper he had a decided advantage over others and might injure innocent people. His normally excellent standards in this and in other areas, however, did not apply when he was dealing with Calvinist Establishments.

That he kept a close watch on the affairs of the growing Church is certain. He even refers to its divisions, arguing that the judges who "are now so zealous for the Confession, that they seem to give it Preference to the Holy Scriptures, were of late Years more indifferent than Hemphill has yet appeared to be."[136] He seems to have in mind here the Adopting Act, which many conservatives felt did injustice to the Confession. The whole matter of the minister's alleged heterodoxy, then, is merely a convenient excuse for getting rid of him because he preached the Christian doctrine of virtue with great success. To the Commission's point that the censure of Hemphill was unanimous, Franklin responds pointedly: such a claim "will likewise prove that the

Spanish Inquisition is in the right, which is as unanimous."[137]

The psychological and rhetorical advantages gained by identifying the Commission with the Spanish Inquisition are too apparent to require comment. There are, though, two other items of special interest in his statement which should be explored. Franklin first derides the judges and, by extension, the Synod and the Church generally for laxity in defending the Confession they were supposedly so concerned about in the trial. Silence Dogood had also called down the Congregational clergy for not living up to the requirements of their denomination and for actually lifting their sermons from the liberal Anglican Archbishop Tillotson. In both cases Franklin not only ridiculed the beliefs in question, but attacked the clergy as unworthy of even those beliefs. The second matter worth mentioning in the statement is that it is possibly a reference to the increasing evangelism and small awakenings in the Church. These, of course, were initiated by the Tennent family and the other students from the elder William Tennent's Log College. Most of the clergy, to one degree or another, thought the activities of the evangelists unorthodox, and the conservatives believed them a threat to the Confession and order in the Church.

The *Observations* provoked a quick response. The anonymous author of *A Vindication of the Reverend Commission of the Synod,* presumed to be Jonathan Dickinson, held that Hemphill represented the "prodigious Growth of Error and Infidelity . . . in this unhappy Age" and that the minister sought only to undermine the Word of God.[138] The writer claims that Hemphill was guilty of heterodoxy, both in Ireland and in Philadelphia, and goes on to defend the actions of the Commission throughout the trial. It is evident, and significant, that the author of the *Vindication* believes Hemphill to have written the *Observations*.[139] By writing his abusive pamphlet anonymously, Franklin not only protected himself against the Presbyterian Establishment but actually worsened Hemphill's position. Franklin is the one who had everything to gain from the attack. Since it was Andrew Bradford who printed the clergy's Philadelphia pamphlets and sermons during the affair, the ministers might well have known that Franklin was, at least, actively supporting Hemphill. Anyone who had read the *Gazette* for a time knew of its satires on Presbyterianism. Yet it appears that the clergy did not know that the printer was Hemphill's penman. At the same time, however, other Philadelphians of Franklin's views, who at first supported the minister, certainly knew where Franklin stood with regard to Calvinism and deism. As an anonymous author, then, he was in the advantageous position of being able to vent his hostility against his opponents, do injury to the Church, promote deism, or a nondescript rationialistic Christianity, and still be looked upon by those who knew his mind on religious, social, and philosophical matters, as a friend to sound morality and a well-wisher to his country. Thus he was able to establish himself more firmly in Philadelphia as the kind of benevolent man he had on occasion created to excoriate Calvinism and protect the community from evil.

As for the unfortunate Hemphill and the Presbyterian Church, they were the losers. That the Church needed ministers desperately was no secret. Nor was the fact that it had been forced by circumstances to accept back into the fold grossly immoral clergymen after they had confessed their sins and seemed genuinely sorry for them. Hemphill, an excellent preacher, could likely have been reinstated if he were willing to retract what he had said and promised to be orthodox in the future. Had he been unable or unwilling to do so, he could have taken Anglican orders as other rebellious Calvinist ministers had done in New England and the Middle Colonies. Franklin himself must have remembered the famous case of the Connecticut clergymen who gave up the New England Way for the Church of England, since as Mrs. Dogood he had written about the event. Even had Hemphill decided against Anglicanism, he would have had little trouble settling with another denomination or sect, for many of them would have at least tolerated his religious views. But no group wanted a scoundrel, and this is exactly what Hemphill appeared to be by the time Franklin finished defending him. Franklin had kept his hands clean; yet it is worth noting that he was the first man in the Middle Colonies to carry on a sustained and open attack on Calvinism and the Presbyterian Establishment, just as he and his fellow Couranteers had been the first to perpetrate an open and sustained assault on New England Calvinism and its supporters. In the case of the Philadelphia attacks, the precedent established set the tone for future religious arguments in the newspapers and presses of the Middle Colonies; and, understandably, they were usually of low quality.

Franklin continued to flay the clergy in *A Letter to a Friend in the Country,*[140] which was advertised in the *Gazette* for September 9 as "just published." In this piece he boldly identifies himself with anti-Presbyterian forces, for *A Letter* contains a preface which, though signed simply "A Layman," is entitled "The Publisher to his Lay-Readers." This designation, however, in no way indicates that the "Publisher" wrote this or the previous attacks. The preface appeals, in the hostile manner of Thomas Gordon, to the laity to think and act "like men" and oppose the "sinister designs" of the Presbyterian clergy who strive to keep men ignorant and slavish.[141] The writer calls upon his readers in anger—as the Widow Dogood had done earlier with charm—to remember that the clergy have always been "too fond of Power to quit their Pretensions to it." They must therefore be defeated by the united opposition of a laity determined to preserve "The Glorious Cause of Christian Liberty."[142] The people must not be fooled by the clergy's assumption of piety and morality, for history has proved that they are base and ignorant. Moreover, they are nearly always in error, though they defend their positions with violent enthusiasm and slander any who disagree with them.[143] These are the men who have always made mankind miserable and, the author warns, they are trying to impose their will upon everyone nowadays, too. "Nothing . . . can prevent our being a very flourishing and happy People, but our suffering the Clergy to get upon our Backs, and ride us as they do their Horses, where they please."[144] The optimistic reference to America's prospects was one which Franklin was to use often later in calling for separation from England or for continuing the war. In 1735, though, the enemy, the only obstacle to the citizens' utopia, was the Presbyterian clergy.

The body of *A Letter*, which is signed "H--p--ll," largely goes over ground already covered. The author attacks authoritarian ministers and their "Priest-ridden" secular allies, who violate the principle of private judgment, the essence of true Protestantism, in their effort to impose their unscriptural creeds on Christians. One should need to believe only in the Bible, not in the Westminster Confession, to be a minister.[145] Everything other than the Word constitutes a perversion of the original church and opposes the spirit of Christian liberty.[146]

Jonathan Dickinson once again replied to his adversary, this time in *Remarks upon a Pamphlet, Entitled, A Letter to a Friend in the Country. . . .* Because he found himself in the difficult position of trying to preserve the dignity of his Church and of striving to keep intact its tenuous coalition, Dickinson had to argue both for individual liberty as well as for subscription. The authors of *A Letter,* he says, have misunderstood liberty or private judgment. What they mean by liberty is really license, which leads to infidelity. For the clergy to perform their duty and check such a tendency is no intrusion upon the liberty or conscience of an individual.[147] Arguing on commonsensical grounds, Dickinson points out that one must allow societies of believers, not just individuals, "to suppose themselves Right," for no one can be certain about doctrine.[148] If the Presbyterian Church, then, decides that according to the Bible certain things are necessary to be believed by all its clergy and laity, it has a right to avoid or withdraw communion from anyone who does not believe in these things. The ministers who decide what points are essential may be wrong, but a society as well as a single person has the right to follow the dictates of its collective conscience.[149] It is therefore necessary for all Presbyterians to subscribe to and uphold certain basic creeds and doctrines. Dickinson then picks up Franklin's argument in behalf of liberty and turns the tables on him. He agrees with his opponent that no church has the right to force its beliefs on an individual. But, as the minister dryly points out, this is not the case here: rather, Hemphill, in trying to impose his beliefs on the Church, is showing disrespect to liberty and private judgment.[150]

Franklin's anonymous rejoinder to the *Remarks,* entitled *A Defense of Mr. Hemphill's Observations . . . ,* was announced in the *Gazette* for October 30 as "just published."[151] It is the most unrestrained attack on a Calvinist Establishment he had ever written and seems intended to overcome Dickinson's cool and superior argument with vituperation quite out of character with the persona of the *Autobiography.* The authors of the *Vindication,* Franklin charges, are merely trying to "flatter and deceive their unthinking Readers into an Opinion of their honest Zeal and inflexible Justice."[152] Actually, he goes on, hoping to alienate the people from the clergy, the ministers have created chaos among the honest citizens of Philadelphia by attacking the soundness of the respected Mr. Hemphill's doctrines.[153] Perhaps recalling his own earlier difficulties in Boston, the printer declared that the conduct of the Commission was typical of orthodox ministers who generally slander "and let loose the popular Rage upon their Adversaries."[154] He accuses the judges of depriving the people of an excellent minister in order to protect Andrews' dubious virtue.[155] Worse yet, he continues, enlarging the scope of his assault, their silencing of Hemphill has social and political implications, for it constitutes a direct challenge to American liberty! The Presbyterian clergy have assumed the role of Spanish inquisitors in a "free Country."[156] Franklin accuses the Commission of behaving like Jesuits instead of arguing reasonably and fairly, and he quotes effectively from *Hudibras,* II.ii.262-66, to illuminate his point:

> And therefore topical Evasions
> Of subtil Turns and Shifts of Sense
> Serve best with th' Wicked for Pretence,
> Such as the learned Jesuits use,
> And Presbyterians, for Excuse.[157]

Indeed, Franklin criticizes the unethicality of one member of the Synod, whose identity his fellow clergy tried to conceal. The Reverend Nathaniel Hubbel's audacity and lack of principle led him to declare that it was proper for judges to lie to force a guilty person to confess the truth. This, the printer charges, generalizing with abandon, is the quality of the men who have permanently censured and suspended Hemphill and ruined his career.[158]

In the course of defending the minister and attacking his judges and the Synod, Franklin also accuses them of promoting "Enthusiasm, Demonism and Immorality,"[159] of failing to understand the goal of Christianity, which he then undertakes to explain to them,[160] and of being Antinomians.[161] It was clear to him that the ministers and their allies prefer their "darling Confession . . . [to] the Gospel of Christ."[162] Presbyterianism, then, is made the enemy of true Christianity! Franklin next stoops low for satire and adopts what he calls the logic of the Commission that found Hemphill guilty, discovering that

> Asses are grave and dull Animals
> Our Authors are grave and dull Animals; therefore
> Our Authors are grave, dull, or if you will, Rev. Asses.[163]

No reasonable group could rebuke a minister for preaching a merciful Christ. Yet the Commissioners, less concerned about a loving Christ than about upholding their stupid and cruel doctrine of original sin and their notion of an implacable God, did irrationally and unfairly condemn Hemphill. And behind their actions was their desire for power. They preach original sin and an eternally wrathful God to frighten "an unthinking Populace out of their Sense" so that the clergy can rule over them and go on to their selfish and miserable goal of complete control over the people.[164] In truth, however, it is Hemphill's views that are orthodox and those of the Commission that are heterodox.[165]

Franklin presents the minister's doctrines by quoting sparingly from his sermons. Hemphill believes it is the duty of the clergy to preach Christ as a rational teacher and giver of moral laws, not as a " 'Charm to work up the Hearers to a warm Pitch of Enthusiasm without any Foundation of Reason to support it.' " The Christ preached must be one that can be understood by common people, and the will of God should be treated in a similar manner. " 'Tis not to exalt his Glory as a kind condescending Saviour, to the dishonouring of the supreme and unlimited Goodness of the Creator and Father of the Universe, who is represented as stern and inexorable, as expressing no Indulgence to his guilty Creatures, but demanding full and rigorous Satisfaction for their Offences.' "[166]

These are a summary, we are told, of the minister's beliefs. Since they have been judged heterodox, the Presbyterian Establishment must, then, desire something like the following from its clergy:

> . . . to preach Christ . . . as a Charm, to work up the Hearers to a warm Pitch of Enthusiasm, without any Foundation of Reason to support it . . . to make his Person and Offices incomprehensible . . . to exalt his Glory as a kind, condescending Saviour, to the dishonouring of the supreme and unlimited Goodness of the Creator and Father of the Universe, who is really a stern and inexorable Being, expressing no Indulgence to his guilty Creatures but demanding full and rigorous Satisfaction for their Offences.

Franklin concludes this point by noting that "these are glorious Principles and a most excellent Method of Preaching Christ."[167]

By 1735 Franklin knew enough about the art of persuasion to realize that few people would accept this summary of presumed contradictory elements as a statement of Presbyterian orthodoxy. Moreover, the great majority of his readers, regardless of their religious opinions, knew the basic doctrines of the faith as well the writer himself did. Franklin was thus not advancing his friend's position in any way. What he was doing in this, as well as in the other pieces he wrote in his ostensible defense of Hemphill, was what he generally did when writing about Calvinism and its Establishments: he rendered the faith and its clergy contemptible and absurd, but also dangerous to a people who properly appreciate Christ, reason, justice, and liberty. To gain authority for his assertions, Franklin again turned to outside authority, irrelevantly quoting extensively from Joseph Boyse, an Irish Presbyterian minister, who preached morality and called for toleration for all Dissenters, and from James Foster, a nonsubscribing English Presbyterian of Arian views.[168]

The final ministerial reply came from one who called himself Obadiah Jenkins.[169] His *Remarks upon the Defence of the Reverend Mr. Hemphill's Observations* shows that the clergy were feeling the sting of Franklin's vicious pamphlets and were worried enough to reply in kind. Jenkins believes Hemphill to have authored the insulting *A Letter to a Friend* and calls him to task for the low level of his argument.[170] Once more Franklin's abuse of the Presbyterian Establishment had injured the preacher who, by this time, had no reputation left at all either as a minister or as a man.

The *Remarks* was dated at New York on November 24, 1735, and was published in Bradford's *American Weekly Mercury* on January 6, 1736, nine months after Hemphill's trial. Franklin had been successful in prolonging the affair and keeping the controversy alive—even after most people had lost regard for the minister and interest in the case.[171] The piece offers nothing new except that it emphasizes Hemphill's dishonesty. The Commission had discovered in the summer of 1735, before Franklin's *Defense* was ever published, that Hemphill had passed off as his own the sermons of "notorious Arians."[172] Jenkins named three such sources for the sermons: "Dr. Clarke, an open Arian" and "Head of the Arian Party in England," his assistant "Dr. Ibbots," and "Mr. Foster."[173]

Hemphill may have been influenced by Samuel Clarke or his brother John, who wrote the famous Boyle lecture for 1719, *An Enquiry into the Cause and Origin of Evil.* In this piece John argued for free will and attacked those who tried to "make God the Author and immediate Cause of all Evil and Wickedness, and Men to be mere Machines, not acting of themselves."[174] To believe differently, he said, was to destroy "the essential and eternal Difference of Good and Evil" and to remove "the Foundation of Rewards and Punishments."[175] The reason that religion and mankind have so long suffered under such false beliefs as natural depravity and man's complete dependence on God is that we have not approached religion as we would any other complex matter—in the spirit of rational inquiry rather than with blind faith.[176] One who brings reason to bear on belief comes to understand that religion and virtue are the same,[177] and that a wise and kind God wants man to live morally and harmoniously, thus becoming part of His perfectly regulated "*System.*"[178] It is conceivable that Franklin knew the origin of Hemphill's popular sermons before the Commission did. In the memoirs he tells us that the Boyle lectures helped turn him to deism. He had been reading some works against deism, and the pious authors, to refute the heresy, quoted at length from a number of Boyle lectures. Franklin found the excerpts more appealing than the attacks and soon became thoroughly deistic in his principles. Since we do not know which Boyle lectures Franklin read, it is impossible to say for certain that he recognized any of Hemphill's sources. Both he and the minister, though, considered the rationalistic Christianity offered in these sermons to be sound, and for Franklin it had the additional virtues of being rather bland and inimical to Calvinism.

That Hemphill preached such doctrine proves he was indeed heterodox, contrary to Franklin's claims. James Foster has already been discussed, but there remains to be said a few words about Benjamin Ibbot, the third of Hemphill's sources. His position is the same as Clarke's. Religious beliefs and doctrines, he says, must always be subjected to clear-headed scrutiny, or else we shall become enslaved to a mere set of creeds and in effect deny the true ongoing reformation.[179] God Himself demands the careful use of reason and the rejection of such absurdities as the Trinity and the resurrection.[180] The Commission and the Synod, to be sure, mistreated Hemphill. There can be no doubt, however, judging from his sources and from the "Extracts" of his sermons, that he was heterodox by Presbyterian standards. When Franklin tries to defend the minister as orthodox, he therefore fails. When he argues that the censured preacher presented sound morality to his audience,[181] he is on safe ground and is able to argue a good case for Hemphill, because he himself had already thought through the relative benefits of morality and theology.

The main point of the Hemphill affair, though, is that Franklin acted in a manner quite different from the benevolent deistic persona of the *Autobiography*. Contrary to many of Franklin's claims in the British press years later, and to the image of his country he created in the memoirs, there was a good deal of religious intolerance and hostility in America. He also engaged in the fussy nit-picking and long-winded logic-chopping he often claimed to despise and avoid because it created animosity and division and should have no place in his own life or in that of his country. Yet his diatribes against Calvinism did help to undermine Congregational and Presbyterian Establishments—and this, to Franklin, was all to the good.

In fact, before politics forced him to change his mind, he saved his most obviously vicious pamphlets for Calvinists, and time seemed only to make him more of an enemy. Other than the satiric "Dialogue," which had been written before Hemphill's trial and conviction, the pieces are not only hard-hitting, but almost vulgar. In dealing with Calvinists, Franklin's tone is quite uncharacteristic of him. Normally he could ridicule and demean an opponent without becoming obnoxious himself, or make the presumed author of an anonymous piece seem odious. In a Revolutionary War paper of 1777, the "Comparison of Great Britain and the United States in Regard to the Basis of Credit in the Two Countries," a piece obviously intended to wreck the English funds, and one written after Franklin had suffered great indignity at the hands of Tories, he was able to declare England a bad debtor, relatively unindustrious, wasteful, imprudent, and tyrannical; yet he did so without name-calling, or evident rancor, and even without direct attack. Four years earlier he had scored the King and Parliament in his "Rules by Which a Great Empire May Be Reduced to a Small One." The biting satire here is sustained brilliantly, and by the end of the piece the satirized objects are made to appear ridiculous and even more dangerous than any of Pope's dunces. Franklin, however, came away from his attack with clean hands, never having stooped to conquer. His use of the fictive satiric frame and of the effective persona ("I, a modern simpleton") achieve the distance which prevents him from becoming dirtied by his own assault. Further, these devices enable him to gain sympathy for the American cause as well as to belittle the King and Parliament.

Certainly Franklin did not develop a literary mental block and write without control when he dealt with Calvinists. On the contrary, as a writer Franklin knew what he was about. Shortly before he left Philadelphia in 1764 as agent for the province in the tax troubles with the proprietor, he responded perfectly to the rancor of nearly all Presbyterians who, with their political allies, turned him out of the Assembly for the year. Franklin first defended himself with sound arguments and restraint against a host of slanderous charges. This approach in itself is winning, as he well knew, and it also enabled him to portray himself, in his *Remarks on a Late Protest Against the Appointment of Mr. Franklin as Agent for this Province,* as a terribly wronged patriot and friend to his fellow Pennsylvanians. Confident of having won the hearts and minds of fair men, he concluded his defense by saying: "I am now to take Leave (perhaps a last Leave) of the Country I love, and in which I have spent the greatest Part of my life. *Esto Perpetua.* I wish every kind of Prosperity to my Friends, and I forgive my Enemies." This final rapier-like thrust is ideal because it disarms his opponents and leaves them helplessly besmirched in their own dirt.

The difference between the *Remarks* and the Hemphill pamphlets, especially the *Defense,* is the difference between the graceful thrust and the bludgeoning onslaught. The controversy over the minister and the Commission and Synod had afforded Franklin his best opportunity to lash out at Calvinists. The Couranteers had made much of the inoculation dispute. Here, though, was concrete evidence that Presbyterianism was authoritarian and inimical to practical morality and liberty. Also, whereas the *Remarks* identified Franklin as the author, he did not have to fear for his reputation in the anonymously written Hemphill pieces. Moreover, the dispute over Franklin's agency had been effectively settled by the time he answered his detractors, since he was on his way to England as agent and had the utmost interest in ending debate over the issue. In the Hemphill case, he was trying to keep the controversy alive and heated. Then, too, since he was to be agent for Pennsylvania in England, any intemperate acts or words of his would surely be used by his enemies to undermine his position. He did not have this worry in 1735. Instead of having to be reasonably fair and prudent, he could—and did—air his hostilities against the Church to make it hated and feared. He had nothing to lose in attacking it, since none of the clergy could prove he wrote the abusive pieces. He had much to lose in 1764. He already enjoyed great power in America and was gaining more, though voted out of office for the year. As leader of the Assembly and the chief architect of its plans for the province, he must be able to deal with enemies in a more sophisticated and efficient manner than had been the case in 1735, for he now had a vested interest in doing so. It cannot be argued that Franklin had not learned by the time of the Hemphill affair what he would learn thirty or forty years later. Such early works as the Busy-Body letters, "A Witch Trial at Mount Holly," the spoof on Titan Leeds' death, the Dogood letters, and other lampoons show that even when very young, he could be charming while on the offensive, thanks to the distance he achieved through his use of satire and clever personae.

He did not attempt to create any distance between author and subject in the Hemphill pamphlets. He was concerned only with injuring the Calvinist Establishment. Hemphill was a mere tool that Franklin used to vilify his enemies. Using the minister as a buffer, he appealed to the anti-Presbyterianism in the area and gave free rein to his animosity. Hemphill and the Church lost. The preacher received all the return blows; and the judges, after seeing themselves, their faith, and their institution defamed, were in the untenable position of perhaps lending credibility to the attacks by their silence, or, like the Congregational clergy during the dispute with the Couranteers, losing dignity by responding. Only Franklin won in the battle. That his friends knew his sympathy for Hemphill's cause and his antipathy for the Presbyterian Establishment was also of benefit to him, so long as he did not disgrace himself publicly. Although by 1735 the Presbyterian Church was numerically the largest in Philadelphia, the Quakers still controlled the province and, along with Anglicans, claimed as members most of the wealthy and influential citizens.[182] Franklin was an enterprising young printer who admired the broad morality and tolerance of the Friends. Furthermore, he knew that the Quaker Assembly feared the increasing Presbyterian strength in the province and might be pleased by efforts to check Presbyterianism. It seems significant that Franklin's business with the province of Pennsylvania was nearly twice as great in 1735-36 as it had been in 1733-34.[183] Moreover, the year after he defended Hemphill and excoriated the Church, Franklin was appointed clerk of the Assembly.[184] Another factor that may have encouraged Franklin to lend the itinerant minister his pen had to do with his competitor in the Philadelphia printing trade. Andrew Bradford reaped significant benefits from the wide circulation of his *American Weekly Mercury,* and the newspaper was taken regularly by many of the city's most prominent citizens.[185] During the time of the Hemphill furor it was the Anglican Bradford,[186] rather than the nominally Presbyterian Franklin, who printed most of the Commission's pamphlets and sermons. Bradford was therefore identified with the Church's cause in the affair. Though speculative, it seems likely that Franklin hoped to ingratiate himself to the anti-Presbyterian elements in the province by his identification as Hemphill's printer and supporter (though not as his pen), and in this way draw to himself some of Bradford's more rationalistic, liberal, and anti-Presbyterian subscribers.

There were many who feared the success of the Church, including people in high places outside of Pennsylvania. It is worth remembering that when Franklin succeeded Bradford as Postmaster of Philadelphia, he had to thank the Anglican Alexander Spotswood. Two things need to be said at the outset. Bradford's efforts failed to please Spotswood and he would have been replaced by someone else, if not by Franklin. Second, Spotswood was no bigot. He had, however, as his biographer notes, "inherited a tradition" of extremely hostile feelings toward Presbyterians because in 1646 his Anglican grandfather had been executed by them in England.[187] He too, then, might look favorably on an energetic young man of ability who was evidently no friend to Presbyterianism. There is little doubt, then, it might have been profitable as well as intellectually and morally honest for Franklin to become friendly with the anti-Presbyterian forces in the colonies.

In summary, Franklin used his *Gazette* to attack the growing Presbyterian Church and thereby to curb its influence. He found its doctrines and, to his mind, authoritarianism, repulsive and threatening. The clergy seemed to him like those he knew in Boston, for he made no distinction between Congregationalism and Presbyterianism and saw both groups as enemies to rational religion, morality, and personal liberty.

Franklin defended Hemphill because he believed in his cause and thought his theology generally sound. Nevertheless, Hemphill's conviction offered him an opportunity to test the strength of the Church which, though increasing in numbers, was nevertheless beset by problems and strife, and to wage a full scale verbal war against it. Ignorant of the preacher's hypocrisy, Franklin felt confident that a group gathered in Hemphill's behalf would enjoy a good deal of popular support. Further, any showdown between the Church and its opposition, especially during this period of internal strife, was bound to weaken Presbyterianism. Franklin therefore welcomed the confrontation as an excuse to condemn the Church in the most abusive, even disgraceful, terms. Though Hemphill himself might be ruined, the effort to denigrate the Church would grow. By keeping the controversy alive and dragging the Commission, the Church, and Presbyterianism itself through the mud for nine months, Franklin achieved what he most desired: the integrity and competence of the clergy had been impugned and the credibility and usefulness of Presbyterianism had successfully been brought into question.

Franklin deals neither with his own antagonisms nor with the patent unfairness of the Commission in the *Autobiography*. British writers, during the turbulent years between the Stamp Act and the Revolution, had joined his American enemies in accusing him of being, among other things, a deceitful and self-serving politician whose highly publicized moral pronouncements did not express the real man behind the public mask. And as for the Calvinists, with whom he had aligned himself before 1771, they were being attacked incessantly in the British press; therefore, Franklin neither could nor would, at this time, give the Ministry writers any more weapons to use against himself and his countrymen.

IV

The Spirit and the Press

Franklin's next significant involvement with the Presbyterian Church occurred during the fiery era known as the Great Awakening, another event in which his hostility toward Calvinist success led him to work against it. On this occasion he used his press in ways that would not easily identify him as an enemy. In light of later political and social changes surrounding the Revolution and its aftermath, his caution proved fortunate for him and for his country.

Although the Great Awakening in the Middle Colonies has had its historians,[1] it will be necessary to discuss the most important matters that eventually led to the schism in the Church so that Franklin's role in its troubles can be determined with some clarity. The delicate peace within the Church was periodically disrupted by tensions between conservatives, who thought of Christianity in terms of strict adherence to creeds, and evangelists, who held that the institution had become apathetic, carnal, and damnably secure and therefore needed to be revitalized by the life-giving breath of soul-searching preaching. Jonathan Dickinson led the moderate group in the Synod, and it tried to act as a buffer between the two extreme factions. Although in 1735 all sides joined in ridding the Church of Hemphill and in condemning heterodoxy, their unity was but a fleeting moment in what proved to be a generation of discord and strife.

On the surface, it would seem that the subscriptions were a clear majority, with seventeen members in the Synod. The evangelists had only four sure votes and three others they could possibly swing in their favor. Three other members were apparently independent.[2] The moderates, however, numbered fourteen, and while they were sympathetic to the principle of revivalism, believing the Church too formalistic, they nevertheless rejected the terror tactics of the evangelists. It was therefore dangerous for either of the extreme groups to look upon itself as in control of the Synod, though they persisted in their power struggle. As events later turned out, both of these groups lost. The conservatives lost most of the laity as well as Dickinson and his followers. But these moderates joined no one until after the schism. Then, with the seemingly victorious radicals on the verge of chaos due to the lack of an organization that could control their agitated supporters, Gilbert Tennent turned to Dickinson with compromise on his mind. They were able to effect a coalition which rejected the excesses of the Awakening and left Dickinson the leader of the new organization.

In the important years before the Awakening, though, both evangelists and subscriptionists came to think of true compromise as an ungodly retreat to be resisted. To the Log College men, uninspired, formalistic preaching was a more serious problem in the Church than even the difficulty of supplying ministers for all congregations. The people, especially those on settlements, needed and longed for a more demonstrative approach toward religion that would be emotionally satisfying, one that would make them see vividly their present awful state, show them the way to the Kingdom, offer them the incentive to embark on the arduous journey there, and assure them that with God as their constant guide, they would be successful.

Conservatives, however, were just as certain that Tennent and his kind were wandering down the dark road of mysticism by emphasizing profound convictions and assurance. Moreover, by the standards the awakeners demanded, subscriptionists were unconverted, much less fit ministers. There was no doubt in the mind of the majority that the Log College men were tainted by Antinomianism and, if successful, would destroy the rational bases of Christianity.[3]

But Tennent, aroused by the affecting preaching of a zealous itinerant, Jacobus Theodorous Frelinghuysen,[4] was committed to revivalism. In 1735 he published four of his own sermons. Along with those of his brother John, to which Gilbert added an "Epostulatory Address," they popularized the Tennents' efforts and gained for them much notoriety. Gilbert's *The Danger of Forgetting God* was delivered in March of that year, just before the Synod judged Hemphill guilty. Tennent published the piece so that objective readers could determine for themselves whether it should have provoked "so much Flame and Noise."[5] Taking for his text Psalm 50.22, *"Now Consider this, ye that forget God, lest I tear you in Pieces and there be none to deliver,"* he warns that men must make God the center of their consciences and perform their duties toward him *"Now;* now, this Day, this Moment," for "to

Morrow may be too late, and you torn in Pieces." The unconverted, who take comfort in their false security, are reminded that God is merely for a time "upon a Treaty of Peace" with them. But this will soon end and they will then discover not the gentle God, but one who is "as a Bear that is bereaved of her Whelps, and he will rent the Caul of your Heart."[6]

Inspired by the "Flame and Noise" his sermon caused, Tennent published three more sermons in 1735: *The Espousals or A Passionate Perswasive to a Marriage with the Lamb of God . . . , The Necessity of Religious Violence*, and *A Solemn Warning to the Secure World. . . .* The first of these contains early suggestions of Tennent's hostility toward the conservatives. Christians, he says, have a duty to follow only godly ministers, those who are not "satisfy'd with the Performance of Preaching as a Task," but rather look for "some Signs of the Effects of their preaching, some Signs of Sinners consenting to embrace the Redeemer." Only such ministers can drive men to repent.[7]

Tennent did not care that sermons of this kind would be divisive, for the things at stake were too great. Besides, as he said, religion was not a genteel affair, but one of godly violence that came from a "thorowly and perpetually broken" heart and drove one to any godly lengths to seek grace.[8] The violent seekers were constantly battling against the forces of Satan, "subtil, Spirits" among whom were "unconverted Ministers" and the preachers of free will, universal salvation, and other pernicious errors that would lead many down to hell.[9] The battle lines between piety and particularly orthodoxy were here drawn clearly, and Tennent called for support from those who longed for salvation.[10]

In effect, he told his followers that they could be useful instruments in their own salvation, a point which appealed to his self-reliant audiences who, living as they so often did in remote places, had long been responsible for their own spiritual lives. Although he tried not to make them believe they could actually save themselves, he did offer them hope that they could struggle to prepare themselves for grace from a watchful and waiting God who would not disappoint them. And when he preached in New York, Perth Amboy, and other places, he spoke as a former unregenerate, who himself had gone through the terror and ecstasy of conversion.[11]

There is no one better able to convert men than a former sinner who is able to move them because he is living proof of what he says. Tennent, and later the great English evangelist George Whitefield, had this advantage over their opponents: disgusted with rationalism and creeds and unafraid of emotionalism, they convinced many that they could sympathize with them in their terrible wanderings through the woods of sin and help direct them on the straight and narrow road to the Kingdom, for they too had taken the journey. They had hacked their way out of the woods, with God's help, and were now on the right path, calling for all to join them. Those who heeded the call and were truly repentant, though living in the midst of great diversity of religious and sectarian persuasions, or in lonely frontier settlements, would transcend all obstacles and become a community of the gracious. The conversion experience created spiritual uniformity amid great heterogeneity. This feeling of union, spreading as a result of the labors of the evangelists, did, however, cause subscriptionists to renew efforts to preserve what they believed was the proper character of the Church.

The Synod catered to the extreme formalists in Jedediah Andrews' Philadelphia congregation by allowing them to break off from the less conservative members and be served by ministers more to their liking, though Andrews himself was now a subscriptionist.[12] Although Franklin, who still paid his share of support for Andrews' church, may have been gratified by his discomfort and the obvious divisions in the Presbyterian Church, he could have no more regard for Robert Cross, another of Hemphill's former judges, than he had for Andrews.

Of greater ultimate importance than the split in the Philadelphia church was a conservative move in the Synod of 1736. With nearly all revivalists and moderates absent from the meeting, the majority encountered little opposition in declaring that the Synod accepted fully, and without modification, the Westminster Confession, Catechism and Directories and that it had, in fact, accepted these things completely in 1729.[13] This pronouncement changed the agreement of that year in favor of strict subscription and thus augmented the power of the conservatives to thwart revivalism.[14] Their success, however, was costly. Although Poor Richard remained happily unaffected by the awakeners and in 1736 said that "None preaches better than the ant, and she says nothing,"[15] the Dickinson group recoiled from conservative measures and became increasingly sympathetic to the Log College men.[16]

Tensions within the Church continued to mount the following year. Samuel Blair published an awakening sermon in Philadelphia, and Tennent, on his way to the Synod meeting, stopped off at the vacant congregation at Maidenhead and blew additional life into the revival there with one of his most terrifying sermons, "The Solemn Scene of the Last Judgment."[17] Here he warned sinners that "God's stern Justice and almighty Power, will," on the last day, "be glorified, in your utter and eternal Ruin!" Soon after Tennent's preaching of this sermon came to its attention, the Synod insisted that no minister supply a vacant congregation unless called by its presbytery, and without the agreement of his own presbytery; that probationers not be allowed to fill vacant posts unless they produce satisfactory credentials from their own presbytery, even if they were requested by a vacant congregation; and that no minister invite any other minister on probation from another presbytery to supply a congregation "without the advice and Concurrence of the brethren of his own Presbytery."[18]

Franklin still remained uninvolved in Presbyterian troubles, though these were becoming increasingly public; however, he continued to promote deism in the *Gazette*. Soon he would become involved in Presbyterian affairs for, as the Synod of 1738 proved, the factions in the Church were heading for a direct confrontation. For one thing, appointing Cross the assistant to Andrews in the Philadelphia church pleased no one but conservatives. The moderate group wanted Dickinson to succeed the old man and were disappointed at the selection of Cross. This was yet another factor in their moving closer to the Log College group.

The second conservative response to the revivals also indicated that schism might not be far off. The majority tried to crush the source of their difficulties, which, as they saw it, was the elder William Tennent's Log College. Though the Synod granted permission for the evangelists to form their own presbytery, the Presbytery of New Brunswick, subscriptionists made certain that Tennent and his allies would not be able to supply it with ministers from Log College. The Presbytery of Lewes proposed that candidates from other than European or New England colleges be required to "apply" themselves to the Synod, or a committee appointed by it, for examination before they could preach.[19] Moreover, the Synod reaffirmed its position against itinerancy and declared that "no Minister belonging to this Synod" could disobey its order.[20] The evangelists must have felt that their subscriptionist brethren, instead of issuing edicts intended to halt a good work, should have used some of their energy to make certain that ministers were pious and moral as well as orthodox and learned. George Gillespie, at this time independent although later a conservative, complained bitterly of the plagiarism and general dishonesty of two candidates from the ultra-conservative Donegal presbytery. He also criticized the presbytery sharply for its disgracefully inadequate punishment of the offenders and insisted that the Synod right matters. But the majority were once again more concerned with keeping their plurality, and thus controlling the Synod, than with the integrity of their clergy, even if the conduct of some of them was at times embarrassing. They therefore conveniently ignored the moral issue—one of the Synod's post facto rationales in defending itself against charges of unfairness to Hemphill—and let the matter drop.[21]

Subscriptionists looked upon the 1738 meeting as a victory. They controlled the Philadelphia church and, they thought, had neutralized Log College and the revivals. What they did not realize was that their actions that year had sealed their fate. The Tennent party, committed as they were, could not back down. In fact, they intensified the stirrings at Maidenhead and Hopewell and generated new revivals wherever they could. It also seems that the conservatives were unaware of how much support the itinerants had among the laity and the moderates. Yet one of Dickinson's followers, Ebenezer Pemberton of New York, delivered and published awakening sermons throughout the winter of 1737 and spring of 1738,[22] and the evangelists were meeting with increasing success among Presbyterians.

Although the revivals had not yet spread to Philadelphia, knowledge of them was common. Early in 1738 Franklin devoted a substantial part of the *Gazette* to reprinting the "Declaration and Protestation" of Thomas Nairn, a Presbyterian minister in Edinburgh. The piece had obvious significance for the beleaguered Church in America, particularly for the evangelists. Nairn, like Tennent in America, insisted that the Church in Scotland had degenerated, and that the causes of its problems were the spiritual ungodliness and general immorality of the great majority of its ministers. He therefore seceded from his "Presbytery and all superior Judicatures of this Church" while defiantly declaring himself still a Presbyterian minister with full rights and privileges.[23] In light of the traditional negative feeling toward clergy in the Middle Colonies and the growing strife within the Presbyterian Church, with its frequent charges of spiritual lifelessness and countercharges of enthusiasm, the *Gazette* piece both discredits Presbyterianism in general and provides additional ammunition for the awakeners to attack their kirk-oriented opponents.

Franklin did not align himself with any side, however, and in the late autumn reprinted a gibe from Edinburgh on the awakening field preaching of two ministers who, like Nairn, had seceded from the Church and tried to reform it and Scotland by following the dictates of Christ rather than those of sinful men and a corrupt institution.[24] It seems clear that Franklin at this time was happy to print whatever Presbyterian material he came across, as long as it showed the faith and its clergy in a bad light and served to intensify hostilities within the American Church.[25] Poor Richard expressed his creator's feelings about most of the pious when he rebuked those who merely make a big noise about virtue but proved to be sinners themselves. Indeed, there had been too much haranguing for the peace of this scholar, and he declared that "Great talkers should be cropt, for they've no need of ears."[26]

Franklin was seriously concerned about political and religious power struggles in Pennsylvania and their possible implications for the freedoms he and others enjoyed in the colony. In a major *Gazette* piece he therefore attacks those who, he feared, would sacrifice the colony's civil and religious liberties and particularly warns against a tyranny effected by a coalition of powerful civil officials and "an ignorant vicious Clergy," who would insure political and religious conformity. He goes on to insist on the individual's right to make up his own mind about politics and religion and declares that the exercise of reason on all matters is pleasing to God and that any attempt to thwart its use "is, if not Blasphemy, at least something very near a-kin to it."[27] This article refers to all churches equally, but Franklin's greatest interest up to this time was with Calvinist Establishments in America, and he was particularly concerned about the growing Presbyterian Church. That the Church was being steadily augmented by immigrants from the north of Ireland, a group for whom Franklin felt only disgust, and that the itinerants were arousing zeal in those who were formerly indifferent were also causes for worry; for, as he knew, in numbers there was also religious and social power.

The subscriptionists knew this too and in 1739 again took advantage of the absence of nearly all moderates to pass anti-revival measures. It was discovered upon examining its records that the New Brunswick presbytery had licensed John Rowland in defiance of the Synod's act and permitted him to preach at Maidenhead and Hopewell when he was called there.[28] Rowland stirred up even greater revival activity to the consternation of subscriptionists. Anticipating trouble at the Synod of 1739, the Tennent party argued "against the acts of last year" regarding itinerancy.[29] The Synod offered to have the "whole Synod or its Commission" examine and pass on candidates. Those from other than European or New England colleges, if they passed, would be given "a Certificate" of acceptance.[30] The new act, of course, was still intended to crush the revival by rendering Log College ineffective and by requiring compliance with conservative ideas of orthodoxy. After Tennent again protested, the Synod, as a useless consolation, revoked its unenforceable itinerancy act. Instead it declared that any minister who preached out of his bounds and caused "Division" in a congregation could be brought before the presbytery whose congregation he had disrupted and be tried before it. If he were found guilty, the injured presbytery might prohibit him from preaching in its bounds until either it or the Synod lifted the ban.[31]

With respect to the Rowland affair, the Synod accused the New Brunswick presbytery of acting "very disorderly," admonished the itinerants, refused to admit Rowland as a member, and also warned "our people" against allowing him to preach until he was properly examined and approved. As for the awakened at Maidenhead and Hopewell, they were charged with "great Indecency" toward the Philadelphia presbytery, which they rejected in favor of the one at New Brunswick.[32] Finally, as if to throw the last shovel of dirt over what they hoped had been the burial of Log College, the Synod appointed a committee to study the possibility of creating a Presbyterian seminary. This group—Dickinson, Pemberton, Robert Cross, and James Anderson—were to meet later in the summer to discuss plans for the school. Significantly, there were no Log College men on the committee. Conservatives had reason to feel that although revivals properly conducted could be godly and saving, they frequently led to chaos, and the majority in the Synod believed that the Church was in serious trouble because of them and the bitterness they elicited. The evangelists, however, were also justified in diagnosing the sickness in the Church as atrophy rather than convulsion, and they determined that their opponents would not prevent them from dispensing the necessary potion to save the patient.

Still prospects looked very bleak for the Tennent party before the arrival of Whitefield. Even sympathetic moderates, by not showing up in force at recent Synod meetings, had left conservatives in control. The frequent absences of the Dickinson group were caused partly by the great distances they had to travel to reach Philadelphia, but it is also true that they looked with considerable disfavor on the methods of the awakeners as well as on the views of subscriptionists.

In a sermon preached in October 1739, Dickinson expressed his deep concern about the factiousness that attended the revivals. There had been much disaffection on the part of the laity toward individual ministers when Dickinson preached on *The Danger of Schisms and Contentions* . . . at his friend John Pierson's congregation in Woodbridge, New Jersey, not far from New Brunswick. Pierson had been accused of lacking zeal by some of the aroused in his congregation.[33] Dickinson warned them that "a factious setting up and preferring one faithful minister of the Gospel above another, is an Argument of a carnal Mind." Truly converted Christians, he said, will appreciate a devout minister for whatever gifts he does have and will not sow the seeds of discord in their congregations.[34] It is clear that although Dickinson was sympathetic to the evangelical sentiments of the Tennent party and was later to welcome Whitefield and strive to awaken his own congregation, he insisted on a greater degree of order and stability than at this time seemed important to the itinerants.

Undaunted by the lack of sufficient moderate support and by conservative hostility, the evangelists pressed forward to expand the revivals in New Jersey and Pennsylvania and met with increasing success. Moreover, Tennent collected seven of his own sermons and one each by his brother William and Samuel Blair and published them in 1739 as *Sermons on Sacramental Occasions.* In general they are penetrating pieces which call for experimental religion, emphasize man's infinite sinfulness, and insist on a truly humbled and broken heart as a prerequisite for salvation. In spite of the normally strict Calvinism of these men, especially Gilbert Tennent, here and elsewhere he goes quite far in making man at least the initiator of his own salvation. He therefore achieved wide success and his efforts were later praised by Whitefield, who noted the great decline in religious fervor in areas not visited by Tennent and his followers. In comparison to other places, Pennsylvania seemed to Whitefield the spiritual "garden of America." There the people had been blessed with "faithful ministers such as the Messrs. Tennents, Cross" and other evangelists. Only Northampton, in Massachusetts, seemed as godly a place to the great orator.[35] Yet before he threw himself into the Presbyterian struggle on the side of the revivalists, they seemed in danger of being thwarted by the subscriptionists.

Early in the year Poor Richard came before the public for the seventh time. Just as earlier Franklin personae used to attack opponents, he announced that he would begin "scattering here and there some instructive Hints in Matters of Morality and Religion."[36] Unlike the Widow Dogood and the Busy-Body, however, whose lessons often enough were colored by anti-Congregationalist or anti-Presbyterian sentiments, Poor Richard seldom openly expressed hostility to Calvinism. Nevertheless, he did serve as a spokesman for rational religion. In his most important theological pronouncement for the year he declares, "Sin is not hurtful because it is forbidden but it is forbidden because it is hurtful."[37] This position is arrived at by moving outward and upward from common sense and experience rather than by moving down from prescribed biblical or church law or by relying on the unusual insights of a converted conscience. Franklin thought so well of this view that he used it himself years later in his memoirs.[38] It was a sentiment far more conformable to his beliefs than any he had discovered in the preachings of Calvinist clergymen. In fact, just before closing for the year, Poor Richard spoke for his creator in warning of a "universal Droughth this year through all the Northern Colonies." The rice would be dry in Carolina, the bread dry in Pennsylvania and New York, and New England would suffer from "*dry* Fish and *dry* Doctrine."[39] Dry doctrine is not what people heard from the evangelists, especially not from the greatest of all of them, George Whitefield.

Although he had the Tennent party to thank for much of his success outside of Philadelphia, there were other important factors that helped Whitefield in his work throughout the Middle Colonies and other parts of America. The dreary sermons of formalistic ministers had failed to satisfy the emotional needs of Presbyterian masses. Further, the low caliber of many Presbyterian clergymen was another factor aiding Whitefield, as it had aided the Log College men. Then, too, the Englishman's abilities and good works were well publicized in America, and he seemed to thousands of the dismayed and disaffected the embodiment of a newfound hope that religion could be different. The *Gazette* was printing notices about him even in the early summer of 1737, and in the winter of that year subscribers to the paper read: "We hear that the Rev. Mr. Whitefield, a young Gentleman of distinguish'd piety, very eminent in his Profession, and a considerable Fortune, will go voluntarily to preach the Gospel in Georgia."[40] In all, Franklin printed eight Whitefield items before the evangelist began his second tour of America on October 30, 1739.[41]

Whitefield benefited from a magnificently theatrical voice and delivery, both of which were acclaimed by no less an authority on such matters than David Garrick, as well as by the staunch Puritan Paul Dudley.[42] But there was more to the preacher than show. Like Tennent, he won converts because when he spoke passionately of the New Birth, he spoke as one whose own soul had gone through hellish torments until, eventually, it discovered God. Finally, Whitefield, at least during his first tour of the Middle Colonies, had the advantage over the Tennent group in that his theology was much more broadly Christian than theirs. He was an ordained Anglican minister with evangelical leanings until he came under the influence of the Log College group and thereafter became increasingly Calvinistic in his theology. Even then, however, his doctrine retained the qualities of universality and personal involvement that for years won the hearts of great numbers of people.

One cannot read his journals without being impressed with the minister's sincerity and zeal. He preached on board the sloop that carried him and his party to Lewis Town and effected "strong convictions" among many. Arriving in Philadelphia on November 3, he was received kindly by Commissary Cummings of Christ Church and by other citizens. By the next day, the Sabbath, he was busily reading prayers, assisting at the Anglican communion service in the morning, preaching in the afternoon "to a large congregation," and attending a Quaker meeting that evening.[43] During the remainder of the week he preached every day to growing numbers—by Thursday, the most "numerous" he had "yet seen here"—and found that his hearers still multiplied. Soon there were too many for the church, and so he preached from the Court House steps. They did not want to let him go even after he had spoken for an hour, and he "began to pray afresh" to crowds swelling from 6,000 to 8,000 people and more. His house was filled with visitors who had come to be told what some of them had never been told before in affecting terms of the New Birth and of the religion that "does not consist in outward things, but in righteousness, peace and joy in the Holy Ghost." Joy—emotional, even mystical, according to Whitefield's detractors—but joy nonetheless, a quality that had been missing from the lives of many, filled the very beings of his followers. When some cried out during the service, he knew that "the Divine Presence was manifest among us" and that many had been roused out of their carnal, damning security.[44]

It did not take him long to win the hearts of thousands; however, he also revealed signs of the forthrightness, or arrogance, depending on one's views, that was to make him as loved and hated in the colonies as he was in England. While preaching to a packed Christ Church which included three of his "reverend brethren," the evangelist castigated them and other Anglican ministers for lacking piety. He did not know, he said, whether the men were offended by his words, but the fact is that he did not care. Though he professed to recognize that he was no scholar, his total confidence in his spiritual condition usually made him certain of his stand on theological matters. To those like the Tennents, with whom he felt spiritual kinship,[45] he was gracious and humble; however, he judged quickly all who opposed his views about the fundamentals of Christianity. Such people were more than wrong—they were ungodly.

Franklin feared and deplored this attitude, which he found a hallmark of the Congregationalist and Presbyterian clergy in New England and in Pennsylvania. Yet the *Gazette* proved during Whitefield's early tours in the Middle Colonies to be one of his most ardent supporters and promoters. The issue for November 8 announced his arrival and published an account of his plans. Then, following his activities closely in Philadelphia, Burlington, Trenton, New Brunswick, Maidenhead, Neshaminy, Abingdon, and Philadelphia again, Franklin printed glowing reports of the minister's successes. The evangelist planned to preach in every English colony in America before returning to England, and the printer of the *Gazette* received from "Mr. Whitefield . . . Copies of his Journals and Sermons" with permission to print them all, and Franklin planned to do just that if he found "sufficient Encouragement." The *Gazette* carried additional reports of Whitefield's achievements in Pennsylvania and even in England. Poetry exalting him, reports and letters doing the same and vilifying his opponents all appeared in the newspaper. Just three issues, for November 15, 22, and 29, carried a dozen items, all praising or promoting the orator. The issue of November 22 included an article which not only glorified Whitefield but rebuked the Anglican clergy in England for its hostility to this godly man. Such publicity obviously had the effect of gaining new support for the minister and his cause which, as conservative Presbyterians, Anglicans, and nearly everyone else came to realize later, was akin to that of the Log College group.

In the meantime, Whitefield continued his first journey in the area, confident that "a good work [had been] begun in many hearts." At New Brunswick on November 13, he commended Gilbert Tennent and his allies as "the burning and shining lights of this part of America," and the Anglican joyfully preached to the Presbyterian congregation.[46] Tennent joined his new friend the following day and at New York delivered the most searching sermon Whitefield had ever heard. Very moved, he was beginning to come under the influence of the Presbyterian minister.[47]

Most of Whitefield's experiences during his first tour of the Middle Colonies were happy. Fellow Anglicans in New York and Elizabethtown accused him of creating divisions and denied him the use of their pulpits, but to Whitefield the Church of England clergy had fallen away "sadly" from true Christianity and, undaunted by their rejection, he preached against the corruption of the Anglican clergy to a large and responsive audience in New York.[48] At Elizabethtown Dickinson offered the orator his pulpit and Whitefield used it to chastise "both ministers and people among the Dissenters" who contented themselves with a mere "speculative" understanding of grace.[49]

Returning to New Brunswick on his way back to Philadelphia, he preached three times at Tennent's church, baptized two children, and met, among others, the evangelical preachers Frelinghuysen and John Cross, both of whom impressed him as worthy servants of God.[50] The following day found Whitefield and Tennent at John Rowland's congregation at Maidenhead, where the Englishman preached effectively. Later in the day Whitefield and Tennent brought the Word to 3,000 people at Neshaminy,[51] and in the evening they spent a period of "sweet communion" with the elder William Tennent whom Whitefield likened to "one of the ancient patriarchs" of biblical times. In his journal for this day, November 22, Whitefield established himself definitely on the side of the Log College men in their struggle with the "Carnal ministers" in the Synod. When he took leave of his friends, they exchanged promises "to remember each other *publicly* in our prayers."[52]

After preaching at Abingdon to more than 2,000 people,[53] the orator returned to Philadelphia. His continuing efforts aroused ever growing numbers out of their complacency, but the enmity of his brethren in the Church of England also increased. Richard Peters, an Anglican clergyman but now secretary to the proprietor, Thomas Penn, accused Whitefield of demeaning morality and good works. The minister defended his insistence on imputed righteousness to a packed church and declared that Peters' position was nothing more than "reasoning infidelity."[54] Though Whitefield was himself involved in many good works, such as the orphanage at Bethesda and a proposed sanctuary and school for poor Negroes and for Methodists who were being persecuted in England, he divorced such deeds, and morality in general, from salvation. Christ had to impute his righteousness to the sinner or all was lost.

The hostility of the Anglican clergy served only to augment his esteem and reputation among many of the non-Anglicans in the area. The "People now apply to me so fast for advice under convictions, and so continually crowd in upon me," he noted, "that I have not enough time to write to my English friends." In Philadelphia he left large numbers under convictions, and at Germantown many of his 6,000 auditors broke down.[55] Word came from Pemberton in the meantime congratulating him on having left New York "under a deep and universal concern."[56] On the day of his departure from Philadelphia, November 29, the people thronged around the door to Whitefield's house and wept. He was followed out of town by 70 men on horseback and this number soon swelled to 200. Worried men, women, and children ran from their houses to get a final word—perhaps *the* word needed—from the man who had made Christianity an affair of the heart for them. At Chester, fifteen miles away, he preached to about 5,000 persons, a fifth of whom had come from Philadelphia to hear him. It was court day, but the justices volunteered to defer their proceedings until Whitefield had finished.[57] Theirs was a fitting tribute to the achievements of this indefatigable evangelist during his first tour of the area.

While he moved into less receptive areas to the south,[58] the Log College group, inspired by Whitefield, put forth even greater efforts to intensify existing revivals and create new ones. In the six months between Whitefield's visits to the Middle Colonies, fully developed revivals spread over much of Pennsylvania, New Jersey, and New York, the most famous of which, so far, was conducted by the fiery Samuel Blair at Faggs Manor, Pennsylvania.

This minister was a participant in the affair which reached its peak with Tennent's notorious sermon, *The Danger of an Unconverted Ministry*. Blair had been asked to preach at the long vacant congregation at Nottingham, not far from Faggs Manor. By doing so, he disobeyed the Synod's rule about itinerancy. Blair knew that he would be punished by the Synod and by his own presbytery, New Castle, at the request of the conservative Donegal presbytery which had charge of the Nottingham church. Tennent realized this fact also, and thus when, on March 8, 1740, he too complied with the congregation's request that he preach there, he delivered the sermon which indicates that he and his allies were determined not to go down to defeat at the hands of conservatives.

Tennent makes it very clear in his dedication to the people at Nottingham that he intends his sermon to influence their choice of a permanent minister. They must, he pleads, make certain for their own sakes that they avoid the many unconverted clergy who, themselves damned, cannot be instruments of salvation[59] and will therefore drag their congregations to hell along with them. To those in the vacant congregation who are perhaps ready to accept any seemingly orthodox preacher, Tennent says that a congregation is at least as bad off with an unconverted minister, one who lacks strong evidences "of experimental Religion," as with none at all.[60] Indeed, he boldly asserts, it is both "law and expedient" and of the greatest importance to one's soul to leave unconverted ministers and attend the preaching only of "Godly Persons."[61] Tennent was clearly appealing to an awakened and worked up laity to join him and his fellows against their opponents. In this way he hoped to gain enough strength to offset the numerical advantage enjoyed by subscriptionists in the Synod. It was a daring plan, fraught with the elements of disunion and chaos, and it worked.

About a month after the Nottingham sermon Whitefield noted "how mightily the Word of God had prevailed" in Pennsylvania since he was last there. The Awakening was nearing its peak. As he moved closer to Philadelphia, he preached to crowds that increased in numbers as they did in responsiveness: 3,000 in Wilmington, 4,000 at Germantown, and 10,000 at Philadelphia.[62] Even more ardently than before, his followers mobbed him, and he gathered in not only souls for the Lord, but copper, silver, and gold for the orphanage. He was seriously offending Satan, however, and so began to feel the opposition of his emissaries. Many complained of his growing Calvinism and denigration of morality. Yet Whitefield himself was sure that his detractors, now including Archibald Cummings of Christ Church, were doing him and the cause of revivalism much good by their opposition.[63] There had been a "glorious stir" of God in Pennsylvania, the orator wrote a friend. If many of the clergy and the Quakers were "greatly offended" by his general castigation of them, as well as by his Calvinism, the common people and many ministers hung on his every word and loved him almost idolatrously.[64]

The intensified revivalist spirit also made a greater impact among Presbyterian moderates. Dickinson, for example, striving to awaken his apathetic congregation, delivered in 1740 a very warm, powerful sermon in which he insisted strongly on a thoroughly humbled heart and on the recognition of man's complete dependence on Christ for salvation.[65] He also significantly took sides in the Synodical debate by condemning formalism and warned of the "Endless despair" that awaited the lukewarm.[66]

During the period between Whitefield's first and second tours of the area, Franklin manifested a zeal that the persona of the *Autobiography* never betrays. He repeatedly used the *Gazette* to report the young minister's activities and print laudatory accounts of Whitefield's travels and success in America as an extraordinary preacher and as the founder of the orphanage in Bethesda. Moreover, *Gazette* readers, just nine days before the orator's return to the area, read his vindication of an earlier assertion that "Archbishop *Tillotson* knew no more of Christianity than Mahomet," and that he was "but Deism refined." The liberal Tillotson was the theologian that Franklin most admired during his teens and young manhood, and he held him in high regard later. Yet, for the present, the printer not only published Whitefield's intemperate letters against Tillotson and the defense of them, but followed up by printing nearly a dozen and a half more pro-Whitefield items in the *Gazette* between the minister's visits. All of them present his views, praise him without restraint, and thus add to his already great popularity, to his effectiveness, as well as to that of the other itinerants, and consequently to the turmoil of the Awakening. Franklin did not exhibit such obvious favoritism and print a scandalous piece against Tillotson merely to satisfy the desires of his readers or to make money. In fact, though Whitefield's popularity was mounting, so, too, was hostility toward him and the revival. Further, among the considerable number of antagonists toward Whitefield and the revival were most of the men of wealth and influence. Franklin could easily have endeared himself to Quakers, Anglicans, and inadvertently to conservative Presbyterians, who were the more prominent group in the Church, by making the *Gazette* an anti-Awakening newspaper. Or he could have remained neutral and presented a more balanced picture of events, thus alienating no one and still being able to profit from the Awakening and Whitefield's popularity. But he did not. *Gazette* readers were offered a one-sided view which omitted even the unlovely hysteria and fierce hatreds generated by the warring factions in the area.

It was during this enormously successful second tour of the Middle Colonies that Whitefield publicly cemented his alliance with the Log College men. At Elizabethtown God gave him "much freedom of speech," and noticing ten dissenting conservative ministers present for his sermon, Whitefield "dealt very plainly with the Presbyterian clergy,"[67] accusing most of their faction of being immoral and unconverted. He also expressed his certainty that Jenkins Jones, the Philadelphia Baptist minister who favored the Awakening, was the only preacher in the city who was himself converted. He finally called on the laity to join with the evangelists who were by far the "most worthy preachers" in Pennsylvania.[68] In appreciation of his efforts and as tribute to his success, Whitefield's followers began to erect a tabernacle for him and like-minded preachers in Philadelphia.

Spurred on by him, Tennent and his followers labored diligently in Pennsylvania, New Jersey, and New York with encouraging results.[69] Moreover, Dickinson spoke of the need to revitalize the Presbyterian Church and conveyed his general sympathy with the principle of revivalism (though still not with the techniques of all the evangelists) by delivering another awakening sermon before Whitefield left the Middle Colonies.[70]

Franklin and the orator became friendly during this second visit. So good a press had Andrew Bradford, and especially Franklin, given Whitefield that they incurred the hostility of the unawakened. The *Gazette* for May 1, 1740, had carried a statement by William Seward, Whitefield's companion and promoter, declaring that because of the evangelist's preaching in Philadelphia "the Dancing School, Assembly and Concert Room have been shut up, as inconsistent with the Doctrine of the Gospel . . . ." A number of gentlemen, disregarding Whitefield's frequent pronouncements against dancing and music, had rented the hall for their final weekly entertainment and resented Seward's having caused it to be locked. They broke down the door and held a dance there on April 22. There was no dance held the following week, and Seward, perhaps not knowing that the meetings had been concluded for the season, issued the statement which attributed the closing of the hall to his friend's efforts. The gentlemen who had opposed Seward replied angrily in the *Gazette* for May 8, and, in effect, challenged Franklin to publish their complaint. He had to do so because the men charged that the Philadelphia printers had been "engag'd" in Whitefield's behalf, and because the men, who styled themselves "the better Sort of people in Pennsylvania," honestly felt themselves injured. Yet he printed their letter, the first negative piece on Whitefield or the revivals to appear in the *Gazette*, only with the greatest reluctance. Further, even under such pressure for justice, he prefaced the attack with a piece of his own apologizing for having to print the letter and criticizing the minister's enemies. For the next three weeks the *Gazette* printed Obadiah Plainman's praises of Whitefield and vilifications of his opponents, while Tom Trueman, spokesman for the gentlemen, saw fit to publish his letters in Bradford's *American Mercury*.[71]

The June 12 issue of the *Gazette* is memorable. After reporting that the itinerants, taking up where Whitefield had left off, preached at least fourteen sermons "on *Society-Hill* to large Audiences," the man whose self-drawn image as the imperturbable common-sense deist has become ingrained in the national psyche, waxes very enthusiastic indeed. "The Alteration in the Face of Religion here," he writes admiringly of the changes brought about in Philadelphia, "is altogether surprising. Never did the People show so great a Willingness to attend Sermons, nor the Preachers greater Zeal and Diligence in performing the Duties of their Function." Franklin himself had been moved probably for a variety of reasons to attend Whitefield's sermons and seems for a time to have been sincerely caught up in the excitement of the Awakening. Stirred by its success, he continued: "Religion is become the Subject of most Conversations. No Books are in Request but those of Piety and Devotion"; and as a bookseller, Franklin certainly knew the facts about demand and sales. The people, instead of singing "idle Songs and Ballads," perhaps like those he himself wrote on occasion, "are everywhere entertaining themselves with Psalms, Hymns and Spiritual Songs." Then, though somewhat narrow in his attribution, this long-time enemy of Calvinism and religious enthusiasm exclaims piously and warmly that the splendid events are all, "under God . . . owing to the successful Labours of the Reverend Mr. *Whitefield*." If the great preacher deserved fame for no other reason, he would have been entitled to a niche in history as one who had moved the younger Franklin to rhapsodic praise in behalf of religious effort.

It was a tense Synod that met amid the excitement of the Awakening. Conservatives were, of course, aware of the Tennent group's plan to win over the laity. The evangelists preached stirring sermons from Whitefield's new tabernacle and denied its use to moderates and subscriptionists alike.[72] It will be recalled that while the Synod repealed the unenforceable itinerancy act of 1739,[73] it refused to alter its position on examining all ministers who had only a "private education." Evangelists realized that the Synod's plan was to place them in an inferior position and make certain that their number would not increase;[74] therefore, the only hope the Log College group had was to win the laity through the pulpit and press, institutions which they used widely and effectively.

Attempting to offset the effects of the many works that issued from the itinerants, including Whitefield, subscriptionists also began using the press. Among their more notable contributions are the series of pamphlets written by some members of the New Castle presbytery entitled *The Querists,* which, strange as it seems, attempted to prove Whitefield to be sometimes an Antinomian and at other times an Arminian and even a papist![75] The authors, however, also struck at their opponents and the awakened where they were quite vulnerable: they were completely uncharitable toward those who disagreed with them and showed a marked tendency to rush to condemnation. All who resisted their methods or questioned their results were, at best, "blind."[76]

This restricted, indeed parochial, mentality Franklin despised. Yet the *Gazette* carried Charles Tennent's defense of Whitefield on October 16, 1740, and Whitefield himself replied two weeks later.[77] The journalistic struggle in the Presbyterian Church, which at the outset showed some restraint on the part of conservatives, was rapidly becoming a no-holds-barred fight to the finish that seemed hardly any longer in the control of the participants. Before it was over both sides would be considerably bloodied and look rather unlovely in the eyes of more dispassionate persons who either were never drawn into the Awakening or who, moved for a time, pulled out when the affair came to seem less an effort to improve behavior than merely another ecclesiastical donnybrook staged with carnival trappings, but ultimately expressing little of practical moral significance.

A number of men, moderate or independent in spirit, tried to restore peace and order in the Church. George Gillespie, for example, who had long desired a reformation of conduct and a revitalization of the Church but was nevertheless shocked by the Nottingham sermon and dismayed at the course of the Awakening, pleaded for the factions to strive for unity. Fearing a schism, he warned that all divisions proceed from Satan with the help of men eager for popular applause. God established love and order, not hatred, delusion, or chaos. What the Church now required was peace and understanding.[78]

Still the revivals and their attending emotionalism and hostility grew. In June 1740 Dickinson finally achieved a revival at Elizabethtown,[79] and non-Presbyterian ministers were now feeling the effects of the itinerants' efforts. Ebenezer Kinnersley, a Baptist lay preacher, attacked Whitefield as an enthusiast and Jenkins Jones, the regular Baptist minister, for supporting the Englishman and other awakeners. Kinnersley in turn was denounced by the converted in the congregation and denied further use of the pulpit. Franklin, again under pressure from anti-revivalists, published Kinnersley's defense, and the debate between him and his alienated brethren in the congregation grew hotter through the summer months.[80]

William Currie, Anglican minister at Radnor, Pennsylvania, worried about the effect of the revivals on the Church of England. He complained on July 7 that Whitefield had made "a great rent in all the congregations belonging to the Church of England."[81] This was also the experience of Alexander Howie of Oxford, Pennsylvania, whose congregation at Trinity Church had dwindled to a fraction of its former size because of the severely critical sermons of Whitefield and the Tennent party.[82] At least a couple of Anglican ministers, though, fared better in the summer of 1740. George Ross of Newcastle said that most of his congregation (unlike Franklin) turned against the orator because of his attacks on Tillotson and the author of *The Whole Duty of Man*.[83] At the time these Anglican ministers were surely far more fortunate than their Presbyterian counterparts, according to Richard Backhouse of Chester, Delaware. He wrote that the Dissenters had particularly been driven "to the wildest extravagancies," though his own Anglican congregation had remained temperate.[84] Nevertheless, Archibald Cummings was less sanguine and feared that Whitefield might establish his own sect and destroy the Church of England,[85] and even all concern for reason and good works in Christianity.[86]

In the period between Whitefield's second and third tours of the area, Franklin continued to lionize him. The only negative items to appear in the *Gazette* were by Tom Trueman, spokesman for the Philadelphia gentlemen, and one by Kinnersley, printed to offset charges leveled against Franklin and Bradford of being "engag'd" to promote Whitefield. All other *Gazette* items popularized the evangelist, and Franklin himself wrote quite uncharacteristically emotional and even rhapsodic pieces extolling Whitefield and his achievements. After months of waiting and anticipation in the area, Franklin announced on November 6, 1740, that "WHITEFIELD" would soon be arriving in Philadelphia from his tour of the South and New England and that Franklin would publish the preacher's reply to the Querists.

In spite of mounting hostility,[87] Whitefield's final efforts in the Middle Colonies before the schism were at least as successful as his previous attempts had been. On November 9 he began preaching in Philadelphia, where he had enjoyed his most spectacular results, and wrote to a London acquaintance the next day that once again in the city "the word runs very swiftly."[88] He converted an "eminent" deist and brought the newly convicted to see Christ and cry out his presence. Many fainted, and one woman, in a state of shock, had to be carried home, where she remained "almost speechless" for some time.[89] There was "such a universal commotion in the congregation, as I never saw in Philadelphia before."[90] Silence Dogood had attacked overzealousness, and so did Hemphill's anonymous defender. Franklin had before the Awakening always scorned such behavior, as he had arrogance and bigotry, and Whitefield certainly was guilty of these things and of creating them in others. Yet the printer continued his ardent support of his friend. By the conclusion of his third visit, Whitefield had intensified the Awakening, played an instrumental role in achieving a tremendous revival at Cohansie, where Tennent had been laboring, condemned "reasoning unbelievers" and the skeptical, helped organize religious societies among both sexes, and collected more than £700 in money and provisions for the orphans.[91]

Franklin, who had helped in the erection of Whitefield's New Building, continued to promote the preacher's efforts. *Gazette* readers were informed of Whitefield's every move, of his heavy schedule, and of his immediate and longer range plans in very detailed, vivid reports and itineraries. Franklin also announced new Whitefield items soon to come off his press, as well as others recently published, and still others that had gone into new printings. The many conversions, the general reformation, and the numerous letters and poems praising the orator and, on one occasion, condemning "haughty Deists," continued to appear in the *Gazette* throughout the autumn and even after Whitefield left the country. Moreover, Franklin told of the minister's charitable act of purchasing 5,000 acres of land on the Forks of

Delaware "in order to erect a Negroe School there, and to settle a Town thereon with his Friends." Throughout the winter and spring, as the revivals grew and spread, and as animosities mounted dangerously, the *Gazette* continued to offer many pieces on the Awakening. This publicity was to the immediate advantage of the itinerants, who became steadily more popular and effectual among throngs in the Middle Colonies, but it brought the Presbyterian Church to grief. The conservatives in the Synod had to take action in the next Synod; indeed, everyone expected them to do so. In desperation they moved to assert themselves once and for all, and the *Gazette* for June 11, 1741, in addition to carrying a notice of Whitefield's preaching in London, told of the schism that was to wrack the Presbyterian Church officially for seventeen years. In fact, however, the factions plotted against each other and perpetuated old quarrels through the mid-1760's.[92]

Before the Synod met, Tennent announced that the New Brunswick presbytery rejected the Synod's laws concerning both itinerancy and the examination of privately educated candidates.[93] When that body met, therefore, the conservatives (known after the schism as the Old Side) had the choice of either excluding the evangelists (New Side) or of capitulating to them. With the entire moderate group absent, and some ministers in neither camp, subscriptionists constituted the majority of the Synod, twelve to ten. Robert Cross, spokesman for the majority, read a Protestation which declared that because the New Brunswick prebytery had failed to adhere to the subscription standards of 1736, its members were guilty of "heterodox and anarchical principles," "opposition," and generally divisive practices and had forfeited their right to sit and vote in the Synod.[94] The protest was hurriedly signed, and Tennent and his allies were excluded from the Synod. When they left, however, they took with them a majority of the laity.

The ensuing events are not of great concern to the present discussion[95] and so will be mentioned only briefly. In spite of great effort, the factions in the Church could not be reunited. For a time after the schism it seemed that both Old and New Sides would collapse, as difficulties and animosities increased too rapidly for either group to control them. Conservatives had lost popular support and were soon officially to lose the Dickinson party also. The Log College group, though quite effective as a godly minority in the Synod, were unprepared to take upon themselves the responsibility of becoming the founders of a new institution. In fact, their enmity toward opposing presbyteries and the Synod encouraged their followers among the laity to insist on a degree of individual freedom and spontaneity that made order very difficult. Tennent could not handle the situation, and in 1743 it became apparent that Dickinson was emerging as the single most influential figure in the Church. The Log College men, to avoid being destroyed by their own flank forces, withdrew to Dickinson's better fortified positions on theology and government,[96] and two years later the New York presbytery joined with that of New Brunswick to form the Conjunct Presbyteries of New Brunswick and Londonderry and the Synod of New York. The union, however, was too late to save the revival, which by 1745 had largely been consumed in its own flames. Even a year earlier Tennent reported sadly that there had been an obvious decline "in the liveliness of the religious feeling of the people." But there was one hopeful sign: if the people were now less pious, Tennent wrote, "they were becoming more humble and merciful."[97]

Much has been made of the impact of the Awakening on other than Presbyterian groups, and Whitefield's widely publicized catholicity has long been considered an important factor in his ability to convert people of all persuasions and stations.[98] This view, however, does not seem correct. Undoubtedly he did *move* a wide cross section of people, some of whom converted. It appears, though, that he had very little long-term effect on any English-speaking groups other than Presbyterians, and these he inadvertently led to a level of individualism that was easily taken for Antinomianism. Many of the awakened proved unwilling to accept any institution for fear it would interfere with the vital immediacy of true religious experience.

Other groups fared better, according to available evidence. John Pugh, Anglican minister of St. Anne's Church at Apoquinimink, Delaware, his nearby colleague, George Ross of New Castle, Robert Jenney of Christ Church in Philadelphia, and Richard Peters all reported that the Church of England had either remained unaffected by the Awakening or had returned to normal. But as some of these men reported, the Presbyterians were being driven "mad" by the evangelists, who had "almost broken [the Presbyterian Church] to pieces."[99]

The Friends were even more aloof from the zeal of the revivals than the Anglicans. Their leading position in colonial Pennsylvania society caused them to reject enthusiasm many years earlier in favor of a quietism that was more suitable to their prestigious rank.[100] Although Whitefield claimed to have won over a number of Quakers and was expecting new converts, James Pemberton, a leading member of the Society of Friends, said that the orator appealed only to some "of our curious youth of rash judgment, who look more at words than substance."[101] Most other Quakers, though, including

Franklin's admired friend, James Logan, were hostile to Whitefield's methods and to the revivals.[102] The available information seems to indicate, then, that the evangelists left almost no enduring mark on English-speaking Christians in the Middle Colonies, other than Presbyterians.

It is proper now to focus our attention on Franklin's relationship with Whitefield. The nature of their friendship has been misunderstood because we have allowed Franklin's account of it in the *Autobiography* to determine for us its true character. Again, however, when we take at face value what he says in his memoirs, we wind up with a protective and intentionally simplistic view of events. The section of the *Autobiography* dealing with Whitefield and the Awakening takes up six pages of the Yale-American Philosophical Society edition of the work, a substantial amount of space considering all that Franklin had experienced by 1788 when he wrote these pages. Yet the orator and his cause are both slighted by virtue of the way in which Franklin treats them, making them less important than they were for national and personal reasons. Writers for the British Ministry had countless times represented Congregationalists and Presbyterians as a horde of wild and ranting enthusiasts with whom no sane man would voluntarily choose to live. What the new nation needed, in Franklin's mind, however, were large numbers of settlers from Europe: honest, industrious, and frugal men of skill, such as the hero-tradesman of the memoirs. Franklin therefore altered the truth about the past by subsuming the impact of the Awakening on the American people by ignoring the excesses of the event in his account. Neither enemies nor potential settlers would be told of the hysteria and bitterness of the exciting years when the country was engulfed in spiritual fires and bigoted hostility.

Moreover, just as he protected the image of his countrymen, he protected his own. One must wonder, in fact, if it were even possible for Franklin to treat his actual response to the Awakening in a straightforward manner. After all, by 1788 we have Dr. Benjamin Franklin, who is the sage of sages, the man who ripped lightning down from the sky and toppled a monarch from his throne, the honest man for whom Diogenes had been searching, the First Civilized American, the patron saint of practical virtue and possibility, whose likeness appeared on snuff boxes, music boxes, and plaques, the representative of the New Man, finally enjoying what had to be a brief retirement—and this Benjamin Franklin almost necessarily had to look upon himself as his own ancestor for whom he had nothing but the kindest feelings. Naturally, when he sat down to write about Whitefield, the orator seemed a minor figure from the distant past, and for this reason, too, he is treated as something of an amusing oddity.

The truth, though, is that during the years of the Awakening this was not the case. Destroyer of false confidence and carnal apathy, challenger of all who opposed the ways of the Lord as he understood them, and magnificent speaker who made tens of thousands *feel* their sinfulness and *see* the alternatives before them, Whitefield was by far the greater man, loved and reviled, a household word on two continents, a manifestation of the anger, power, and love of God. Further, when we compare the statements concerning Whitefield in the memoirs with those written by the printer of the *Gazette,* we discover that the former are detached, humorous, and designed to make the evangelist seem less than he was, whereas the promotional pieces in the newspaper show that the younger Franklin was, for a time, not only a sincere admirer of Whitefield's but quite enthusiastic about his great abilities and success. This, in spite of the fact that the two men, though both humanitarians, lived according to irreconcilably opposed conceptions of God, man, faith, and works. To argue, however, as has often been done, that Franklin publicized Whitefield because their humanitarianism bridged the wide intellectual chasm between them[103] is to tell only a very incomplete story.

Whitefield was a fundamentalist who was influenced first by Methodism and later by Calvinism. He insisted, for one thing, on the doctrine of original sin. We are, he said, fallen men, and as such are "a motley mixture of the beast and devil."[104] It must have been some such statement that caused Franklin, in his memoirs, to express wonder that Whitefield's auditors continued to love and respect him, in spite of "his common Abuse of them, by assuring them that they were naturally half Beasts and half Devils."[105] Franklin, a poor speaker, admired Whitefield the orator. But he undoubtedly heard the evangelist assert many things that galled him intellectually and morally. One of the minister's proofs of original sin may have been particularly obnoxious to the man whose four-year-old son died in 1736 and who, as late as 1772, could not think of him without real sadness. Whitefield was absolutely certain that the sickness or death of a child was obvious proof of man's natural depravity.[106]

He further believed that as a result of original sin, man was completely incapable of aiding in his own salvation; he was instead completely dependent on the imputed righteousness of Christ, which would be granted only to the elect.[107] His insistence on these doctrines caused Ralph Erskine, the Scottish Presbyterian evangelist, to think of Whitefield as very nearly a Presbyterian by 1739,[108] and it is fair to say that although his Calvinism was broader than that of the Tennents, it came to be as central to his faith as to theirs. He may not have realized, though, that his association with them had confirmed his

Calvinism, for in a letter of 1740 he attributed it solely to Christ who had "taught it to me."[109] Yet it was shortly after he met the American evangelists that he did battle with his good friend John Wesley, who opposed Calvin's theology.[110]

Franklin, of course, had rejected this theology before he was sixteen years old. Moreover, his deistic beliefs and temperament made him look upon the preaching of terror as unreasonable and repugnant as the rest of Calvinism. Whitefield, however, pictured hell and the torments of the damned in vivid terms. It is interesting to speculate on what the printer thought as he set the type in 1740 for a volume of his new friend's sermons and read that people who do not attend sermons frequently and give them their undivided attention actually "crucify the Son of God afresh" and shame him. Such people are "cast into hell, lifting up their eyes" pleadingly from the "burning fiery Tophet" that is "kindled by the fury of God's eternal wrath,"[111] but to no avail. Sinners invariably discover not the compassionate, understanding, rational, and forgiving God of Franklin, but a "righteous Judge," leader of the "dreadful tribunal," whose fury would have to be satisfied.[112] This is one of the positions, the image of God described, that Franklin attacked viciously in defending Hemphill. It was, the printer felt, repugnant both to reason and to God.

The two men were equally far apart on the matter of becoming acceptable to God. For Franklin, a kind God would judge man on how virtuously he had lived, but for the minister the ultimate judgment hinged entirely on the matter of conversion. And conversion to Whitefield was not to be confused with "mere morality," which by itself was actually damning.[113] On the other hand, his auditors might be the "murderers of fathers, and mothers . . . ; yet if you believe on Jesus Christ," and while dying cry out to him, Whitefield was willing to "pawn my eternal salvation upon it, if he does not shortly translate you to his heavenly paradise."[114] This belief, too, Franklin had long despised as completely unworthy of God and man.

Whitefield also declared that the activities Franklin, in his "Articles of Belief," had referred to as "pleasant Exercises and innocent Delights"[115] were in fact devilish, damning devices that served only to distract one from thinking about Christ.[116] Further, the minister's staunch and frequent defenses of enthusiasm,[117] regardless of how many converts it appeared to make, could not be acceptable to Franklin for very long, any more than could his incessant condemnation of all rationalists.[118] The truly godly did not reason about God; indeed, they were so enthusiastic as to be considered mad by the mere reasoners who were unconverted.[119] As we shall see below, the time came when Franklin could no longer tolerate such views, even from Whitefield.

Another factor that caused him to change toward the minister eventually was Whitefield's personality. His certainty as a man of God bred in him an arrogance that was expressed in his Olympian unconcern for the feelings of those who could not agree with him on religious matters. Franklin was also occasionally guilty of a smug pride, which he learned to tolerate as well as conceal, but he found the fault obnoxious in others, at least when they made no effort to disguise it. It is true that the preacher was less interested in winning friends than in saving souls, but one nevertheless feels uneasy when, for example, he scolds a backsliding friend to whom he writes: "Did I not forwarn you of this? Permit me to pray for you. Though you are now dead comparatively, yet, I trust, you will be alive." He hopes that another correspondent will, with God's help, triumph over his "carnal reasonings" and "depraved heart" by confessing to his utter corruption.[120]

These are extracts from Whitefield's letters, and it can perhaps be argued that they were intended only for the recipients; however, no such case can be made for his journals and sermons, and in these he lashes out at all who disagree with him, especially the clergy. He considered the great majority of them on both sides of the Atlantic to be ignorant of true Christianity, and he did not scruple to let them and their congregations know how he felt.[121] When he was caught in theological errors, as he was by the Querists, he smugly dismissed their corrections as trivial.[122] Whitefield thought all his errors were trifling and all his opponents damned because he sincerely believed himself to have "received the Spirit of adoption before I had conversed with one man, or read a single book" on theology.[123] Here, then, we have the man. Franklin liked the benevolent and indefatigable doer of good deeds, and admired the wonderfully successful speaker, but he became disgusted with the overbearing, thoroughly Calvinistic minister who enjoyed a special relationship with God and pronounced His sentence on rationalists and all others who rejected Whitefield's notions of Christianity and a good life. Nor was Franklin by any means alone in objecting to these characteristics. Others in the Middle Colonies, including the governor of Pennsylvania, and many in New England, the South, and abroad, were all put off by the evangelist.[124]

How, then, can we account for Franklin's earlier extremely partisan treatment of Whitefield and the Awakening in the *Gazette*? It will be recalled that he did not print any anti-Whitefield items until absolutely forced to do so, and even afterward he offered only a few scattered criticisms in the *Gazette* until the winter of 1740-41. There is enough evidence to make plausible reasons for his actions seem more consistent with his deistic views and twenty-year hatred of Calvinism and Calvinist Establishments than claims that his love of Whitefield's humanitarianism caused him to ignore his doctrine, or that he wanted only to profit financially from the orator's popularity. Franklin could certainly be moved by benevolence, and like most men he sought to improve his financial state. But at least insofar as available evidence indicates, there was enough opposition, especially among wealthier and prominent people, to have enabled Franklin to make a handsome profit either from attacking Whitefield and the Awakening or from offering his readers a more balanced picture of events without alienating any group. Yet, contrary to frequent claims, Franklin, discounting the *Gazette* and all other newspapers for the moment, published more items favoring Whitefield and his efforts than any other printer in America.[125] Even if we dismiss as a purely economic venture his printing of fifteen works by the evangelist from 1739 to 1741, more than any other colonial printer and five times as many as his competitor, Bradford, we are still faced with other facts difficult to account for in the traditional ways of judging Franklin's relationship with Whitefield. From the beginning of 1740 to June 1741, he published four times as many pieces defending and praising the orator as those attacking him. Bradford, though, expressed no partisanship at all during this period, presenting three items favoring the minister and three against him. Bradford, it should be noted, unlike Franklin, remained a supporter of the preacher and his efforts.

Comparing Franklin with all other colonial newspaper printers except Bradford, we find that the *Gazette* carried more than six times as many pro-Whitefield items as any other newspaper in America for this period. But from the time after June 1741, through the summer of 1743, when the Old Side was defeated and the Log College men were floundering and about ready to renounce extremism and join the moderates in the hope of salvaging something from the Awakening, Bradford was far more sympathetic to Whitefield and the revivals than Franklin. During this time, in fact, Bradford printed twenty-seven revival items, eighteen of them favoring Whitefield and nine opposing him. Franklin's activities during this period present an interesting problem. Although he had printed works written by the orator himself, he came out with no new ones or reprints after 1741, though Whitefield's popularity remained great in the Middle Colonies. Moreover, from 1742 through 1745 he printed twice as many pieces against his friend and revivalism as for them. As if acknowledging this change in support, the Old Side gave Franklin the job of printing the eleven parts of the Westminster Confession of Faith.

These activities seem to reflect Franklin's changed attitude toward Whitefield and his efforts. A study of pertinent material published in newspapers of the day will show that the percentage of pro-Whitefield and revival pieces printed by Franklin, ninety percent, was exceeded only by the ninety-six percent of the *New England Weekly Journal*, which printed only about forty percent as many pieces about the minister and the Awakening as the *Gazette*. Yet every newspaper in the colonies for which it is possible to accumulate data continued its support of Whitefield and his work except two: Franklin's *Gazette* and the *South Carolina Gazette*, in which he had been a partner and was still influential. In terms of percentages, Franklin switched from ninety percent support for Whitefield and the Awakening before the schism to sixty-seven percent opposition afterward. Peter Timothy, son of Franklin's late partner in the *South Carolina Gazette*, received copies of the *Pennsylvania Gazette* and appears to have picked up the fact of Franklin's shift and changed from seventy percent support before the schism to fifty-nine percent opposition thereafter.

Other facts about the *Pennsylvania Gazette* are also revealing. Between 1739 and 1743 it carried more items about Whitefield, the Tennent party, and the revival than any other secular newspaper in America. Franklin published 223 items, which is nearly three times as many as the average of all other colonial newspapers in America operating during approximately the same period. This ratio still holds true when we make allowances for the unhappy condition in which many of the newspapers survive today and adjust the dates of the *Gazette* so that it can be compared fairly with other newspapers, including those that are far less complete. Before the schism the *Gazette* carried 141 items, more than one and one-half times as many as the second most involved newspaper, the *Boston Evening-Post*, which carried 87. After the schism, however, the *Gazette* carried only 82 pieces for the next twenty-six months. Yet the period from June 1741 to 1743, with all its excitement, would seem to be one that should have been of great popular interest. The percentage of this decline in involvement, moreover, is greater than that of any other newspaper in America for this period. The *Post*, in fact, carried twelve more Whitefield and Awakening pieces after the schism than it had for the earlier period.

Of the 141 items the *Gazette* carried before the schism, 127, or ninety percent of them, were favorable to Whitefield, the other itinerants, and the

Awakening. The 82 pieces published afterward, however, tell a different story. Of these, 27 are favorable and 55, or nearly two-thirds, are opposed to the orator, his allies, and the revival. Moreover, of those 27 commending evangelism, more than half are advertisements for books, usually Whitefield's, and nearly all the others are brief articles which offer a qualified defense of Gilbert Tennent and the Awakening, while they condemn the unstable itinerant, James Davenport, and enthusiasm. Of the 55 pieces negative to the evangelists and their work, 10 are stinging and often vicious attacks, and most are much longer than articles on the other side. A number of hostile articles run nearly 2,000 words, and some are about 2,500 words long. This change takes on added significance when we remember that Franklin published 46 items in favor of Whitefield and the Awakening before he reluctantly, and under pressure, published one against him and his work. No other newspaper in America waited so long or showed such imbalance. In general, the first attack appeared as the sixth item, although the *Boston Evening-Post* launched an immediate attack on Whitefield and revivalism, and the *Boston Weekly Post-Boy* waited only until its second item to offer opposition.[126]

It is perhaps especially illuminating to further compare the *Gazette* with its competitor, Bradford's *American Weekly Mercury,* since the two printers were presumably subject to the same experiences and pressures, working as they did in the same city. If the printers were merely catering to the tastes of their readers and trying to sell newspapers by pleasing them, their newspapers should reflect the fact by similar reporting and emphasis. In fact, one might expect Bradford, who, though Anglican, was quite responsive to the Awakening and was also religious, to have gone beyond his deist competitor in promoting the efforts of Whitefield and the other evangelists. Yet the *Gazette* carried half again as many items about the revivals as did the *Mercury.* Of the 151 pieces the *Mercury* did carry between May 17, 1739, and August 11, 1743, slightly more than sixty percent are advertisements promoting the works of either side that was willing to pay for space. Only about twenty-one percent of the *Gazette's* material, however, are advertisements. In other words, Bradford devoted only about forty percent of his material to *discussions* of the Awakening and the itinerants, whereas Franklin presented nearly twice as great a percentage, including pieces he had written himself. Furthermore, Franklin carried about three times as many major articles as did Bradford.

Statistics, though, do not tell the full story about the treatment of the evangelists and the revivals. One must read and evaluate how colonial printers dealt with these men and the movement. The results will impress upon him the degree of Franklin's partisanship before the schism, especially prior to the winter of 1740-41. The *Gazette* devoted far more space to the Awakening and its preachers than did any other secular newspaper in America. Before that winter when Franklin began to recoil from Whitefield and the Awakening, he thus led all other printers in the number of favorable items about the revivals and the evangelists, and he also offered the greatest number of discussions of them and their work, filling pages of the *Gazette* with items concerning the exciting events that led many to believe a new and better day was at hand. Bradford did print 122 pieces favoring the itinerants, particularly Whitefield, and only 29 opposing them; however, just 17 of the 122 are articles. The rest are very brief notices of two or three lines, poems, and advertisements. Moreover, 3 of the favorable articles are lukewarm in their support and could fairly be called neutral.

Bradford, though, was far more consistent than Franklin in his allegiance. The affairs in the Presbyterian Church did not influence the *Mercury*. It printed its first anti-Whitefield piece after nineteen in favor of him and his work had appeared in its pages. Before the schism Bradford printed only four articles opposing the itinerants, exclusive of advertisements; and after June 4, 1741, he, and later his wife, printed only five such articles during the next twenty-six months. These figures show that Franklin, living in the same city as Bradford and dealing with the same audience, was much more of a promoter of Whitefield, his allies, and their work before the schism and far more of an opponent afterward, once the Presbyterian Church was divided by the tensions resulting from the revivals. Further, the results of this comparison between Franklin and Bradford hold true when we measure the deist against any other colonial printer.[127]

Franklin, then, was not pandering to the tastes of his readers, for Whitefield had many enemies before the schism and a great many friends afterward, especially among the Presbyterian laity. When we consider Franklin's activities in light of his long-nourished, deep hostility toward Presbyterianism, we can conclude that he was motivated to support evangelism not only because he admired many things about Whitefield and was, for a time, moved by him, but because, at least beginning with the winter of 1740-41, he sought to encourage the dangerous animosities in the Presbyterian Church. Everyone knew that the strife within the Church could easily cause a serious rupture and that some way had to be found to end the awful war between its factions. As involved as he was in events, Franklin certainly realized this too. It seems that the hard winter of 1740-41, which forced the Awakening indoors and found Whitefield away and not likely to return soon, signaled the change in Franklin's attitude and in his support. The excitement had abated considerably and Franklin could no longer be affected by Whitefield. Gradually, he recoiled from his earlier partisanship and decided to use the furor of the Awakening and Whitefield's popularity, as well as conservative opposition, to keep the flames of strife smoldering.

It should be remembered that while Franklin was apparently not much influenced by the Log College men, he was more moved by Whitefield than he cared to admit when, as a great and internationally famous man, he wrote the section of his memoirs dealing with the orator. He therefore protected his carefully wrought image as the generally unflappable man of reason by playing down Whitefield's impact on him. This is, in effect, what he did for his countrymen as well. Instead of the chaos of the time, we are presented with a picture, a thoroughly idealized one, of the awakened sweetly singing psalms and behaving like the best of Christians. Franklin would not permit enemies to use his memoirs to accuse Americans of fanaticism, bigotry, and riot, or to learn from his story just how influenced he was by Whitefield and the revivals. And, of course, he would not reveal his own role as a partisan first and a troublemaker later. Everything is therefore relegated to the charmingly trivial by Franklin's humorous and condescending treatment of the great preacher and by his distorted picture of the Awakening, including Franklin's own activities in the affair. For the same propagandistic reasons he had minimized the importance of his brother's newspaper in the life of Boston and his own significant impact on the town. He had also deemphasized the importance of his role in the Hemphill affair to the point of inaccuracy by neglecting to mention his sharp and even vicious attacks on the clergy and their faith. As an old man he was no longer at war with Calvinist Establishments. In fact, by 1788, the time he wrote the part of his memoirs dealing with Whitefield, Congregationalists and Presbyterians had already been ardent patriots and his staunch allies in the Revolution, and there was no danger that any Church would become *the* Church of the United States. And, again, Franklin would not permit his *Autobiography* to become a source of embarrassment to either his country or himself.

These are the reasons that made him disguise or ignore the realities of many events, including that of the Awakening and of Whitefield's central role in it, his influence on his printer-friend, and Franklin's involvement in the turmoil. The memoirs do not mention the *Gazette*'s partisanship or Franklin's change of heart that led him to play the factions of the Presbyterian Church against each other and then, increasingly, to use his newspaper to attack the evangelists.

It is impossible, of course, to specify a date on which Franklin changed his mind about Whitefield and the revivals. Nevertheless, it is possible to focus more closely on his attitudes. Franklin reached the peak of his enthusiasm for the orator and his efforts during the period of the late spring of 1740 to the late autumn or very early winter of that year. This period found power in the Presbyterian Church shifting from the mere Synodical majority enjoyed by conservatives to the more significant winning over of the laity by the evangelists. From May 15, the week after he had been forced to publish his first item against Whitefield, through September 25, 1740, for example, the *Gazette* carried twenty-seven items about the preacher and the revivals. Twenty-four of them were favorable, often full of praise and designed to generate excitement and to gain support for him and his cause. Of the three negative items, one was an advertisement and two were continuations of the earlier debates concerning Kinnersley and the Baptist congregation, and the gentlemen of Philadelphia who felt that they had been wronged by the *Gazette*. It was also during this time that Franklin wrote the most moving account of the Awakening that had yet appeared in the secular American press, in which he attributed the remarkable rise in piety and morality solely, "under God . . . to the successful Labours of the Reverend Mr. *Whitefield*." This laudatory article contrasts sharply with the unemotional and abbreviated version in the *Autobiography*.

Franklin's treatment remained constant through the autumn of 1740, but when we examine the *Gazette* and the printer's new venture, the *General Magazine*, from the beginning of the winter to the schism, we can detect a real change. Of the 109 items published in both publications during this period, 66 oppose Whitefield and the revivals and many of these are very hostile articles of substantial length. Of the 43 pieces on the other side, only one, a poem, actually praises Whitefield even slightly; 2 articles defend him from attack and 2 others tell of Tennent's successful New England tour. With a few exceptions the remaining 38 items are generally neutral commentaries on the activities of the itinerants and advertisements. The pro-Whitefield and Awakening material in the *Gazette* and *General Magazine* was far too flimsy and lukewarm to offset the more significant negative pieces that Franklin printed and wrote.[128] Anyone who reads the colonial press will discover that this change was quite uncharacteristic of all other Whitefield supporters among printers, except for Timothy of the *South Carolina Gazette*. Since there is no evidence to suggest that any of the itinerants other than Whitefield could arouse Franklin, it seems clear that the absence of the orator, even more than the severe winter of 1740-41 which drove the revivals off the streets and into the churches, precipitated Franklin's change of heart and support and thereby augmented hostilities within the Presbyterian Church before the crucial Synod meeting in June 1741.

That Franklin had second thoughts about Whitefield and his work is corroborated by their correspondence. In the autumn of 1740, just after the evangelist's third visit to the Philadelphia area, he wrote the following to his friend: "I do not despair of your seeing the reasonableness of christianity; Apply to God; be willing to do the divine will, and you shall know it."[129] It appears that although he still found Christianity unreasonable, Franklin nevertheless had become concerned enough about the efficacy of his deistic beliefs to have discussed the matter with the minister, a matter which he normally considered his business alone. Indeed, he could hardly tolerate any interference or even questioning about his beliefs. He had earlier written so sharp a letter to his parents, who had called into question his religious sentiments, that he had to tone it down before mailing it. Even the revised letter, however, let them know that in 1738 he was old enough to have developed his own beliefs and did not take kindly to advice, even from them.[130] Moreover, Whitefield was condescending to Franklin, who was always proud enough to resent being treated as an inferior, and he received the letter shortly before he turned away from Whitefield and the Awakening.

Franklin also came to be angered by the orator's implacable bigotry concerning anyone who did not accept his notions of Christianity, and Whitefield was especially hard on deists. In a later defense of deism, Franklin insists that it be distinguished from atheism "because I think they are diametrically opposite and not near of kin, as Mr. Whitefield seems to suppose where (in his journal) he tells us, *Mr. B. was a Deist, I had almost said an Atheist*. That is, Chalk, I had almost said Charcoal."[131] This disenchantment grew over the years and was expressed in different ways. The preacher and two of his most ardent supporters in the Awakening, Samuel Moody and William Pepperrell, were involved in the Louisbourg expedition. Pepperrell had commanded the colonial force and the others preached to the troops and prayed for victory. In a letter to his brother John about the expedition, Franklin satirized Whitefield as well as Presbyterianism. The Presbyterian ministers, troops, and their supporters had been praying for about five months, thereby sending some

45,000,000 prayers to heaven. These "which, set against the prayers of a few priests in the garrison, to the Virgin Mary, give a vast balance in your favor." If, in spite of this advantage, the attack failed, he said: "I fear I shall have but an indifferent opinion of Presbyterian prayers in such cases, as long as I live." He was unable to resist suggesting that the pious Presbyterians might have more success by relying on works rather than faith in the battle.[132] The letter was written in 1745, years after Franklin's involvement in the Awakening, and therefore his tone and attitude are much closer to that of the memoirs than of the contemporary accounts in the *Gazette.*

Only two of Franklin's letters to Whitefield survive, and both are sarcastic. In one of 1764, after Doctor Franklin had been widely honored in his own country as well as in England and Scotland, he replied to the evangelist who had with his customary forwardness expressed his concern for Franklin's eternal and earthly happiness. Whitefield also let his friend know that he was praying he would one day see the light. Franklin thanked the preacher for his efforts and then turned the tables on him by offering his own deistic prayers in Whitefield's behalf. He also expressed his confidence that the "Being" who had been so kind to him for nearly sixty years looked as favorably on deists as he did on devout Christians. "This to some," he wrote, perhaps anticipating the minister's response, "may seem Presumption; to me it appears the best grounded Hope," which he declared was not Christian faith but "Hope for the Future, built on Experience of the Past."[133]

Another letter, written in 1749, is plainly insulting. At this time Franklin had been retired from business a year and a half and was becoming increasingly aware of his growing importance in Pennsylvania. The Awakening was dead, the Presbyterian Church still split and replete with hatred and intrigue. As for Whitefield, he was already by this time little more than a remarkable curiosity out of the recent past. Therefore, when the minister proudly wrote to Franklin to let his American friend know that he too was gaining in influence—among the great people of England, no less—Franklin replied cuttingly. "If," he chided, "you can gain them to a good and exemplary life, wonderful changes will follow in the manner of the lower ranks . . . ." This was the wise principle behind the practice of Confucius, who was much wiser, then, than European reformers, who normally tried to begin "with the ignorant mob" and work up to reforming the great. Then Franklin, realizing that Whitefield himself had commented on the sharp decline in piety in the colonies, wrote in as artificial rhetoric as he ever employed, perhaps parodying the orator: "O that some method could be found to make them lasting! He that shall discover that, will, in my opinion, deserve more, ten thousand times, than the inventor of longitude." Whitefield had been reminded that his tireless efforts had failed to produce lasting results. Since he knew this to be the case, the remark had to have hurt.[135] In asserting that reformers, including Whitefield, chiefly influenced "the ignorant mob," Franklin seriously distorts the impact of the orator and the Log College men—so much so, in fact, that one is forced to wonder whether Franklin, more than eight years after he changed his mind about the evangelist, was still embarrassed by his earlier partisanship.

Whitefield finally began to realize that he was not going to make Franklin a Christian. He complained that the plans developed by Franklin for the Academy of Philadelphia slighted Christianity. He expressed some understandable anger himself when he slightingly pointed out that the school would be "well calculated to promote polite literature," but that it lacked what was most essential, "*aliquid Christi*," without which it would not be very useful.[136] In a letter written in August 1752, Whitefield resorted to sarcasm, inspired perhaps by envy of the recognition Franklin received for mere secular dabbling. Declaring that promotion sometimes turns people from their proper concerns, "true religion and virtue," he addressed his American friend directly and deprecatingly:

> I find that you grow more and more famous in the learned world. As you have made pretty considerable progress in the mysteries of electricity, I would now humbly recommend to your diligent unprejudiced pursuit and study the mystery of the new-birth. It is a most important, interesting study, and when mastered, will richly answer and repay you for all your pains. One at whose bar we are shortly to appear, hath solemnly declared, that without it, "we cannot enter the kingdom of heaven."[137]

It seems clear from the letters between the two men that Franklin privately became cool toward Whitefield because of his opinions and personal faults. After a time the minister recognized the change and responded accordingly. Once the deist ceased to be a partisan of the evangelist, the alteration was inevitable and general. Long before it showed up in their correspondence, it was revealed in ways that were important and damaging to the Presbyterian Church in America.

In his struggles with Calvinist ministers in Boston and Pennsylvania, Franklin always used the same tactic: siding with the underdog against the more powerful group. In Boston this technique found him aligned with the secular interests, and to a degree with liberal Anglicans, against the ministerial Establishments and its supporters in the Governor's party. Later, in the Hemphill affair, the same approach caused him to join forces with a rationalist minister and other like-minded secular persons against the Presbyterian Establishment. When Whitefield and the revivals seemed to swing the Presbyterian laity into the evangelical camp, and when Franklin rejected the orator and his cause, he used the minister and the rampant enthusiasm to create additional hostility in the Church by reversing his position on the awakeners. A Presbyterian power structure was a threat, whether it was Old Side or New.

In fact, the one time Gilbert Tennent appealed to Franklin for help in raising funds to build a new church, the professional man of good works, though he gave the minister £5 for public relations purposes, "absolutely refus'd" to aid Tennent with support or even a list of names of generous people. Instead he ineffectually advised Tennent to ask everyone for money.[138] The minister's request was concrete testimony to the schism in the Presbyterian Church, which was to plague it officially until 1758 and actually for at least another decade afterward.[139]

Franklin, though, revealed nothing of his role in the Awakening or in the difficulties of the Church in the *Autobiography* or in any of his other writings. In 1782, as a great man and venerable patriot with a relatively short time to live, he appealed to Francis Hopkinson "to avoid being concern'd in the Pieces of Personal Abuse, so scandalously common in our Newspapers" that he found it impossible to show any of them to Europeans for fear of what they would think of his countrymen. To the old printer, the owner of a newspaper had to "consider himself in some degree the Guardian of his Country's reputation, and refuse to insert such writings as may hurt it."[140] He knew that the British press, as he wrote in the summer of 1784, was filled with "fictitious Accounts of Distractions in America" that were intended to console Englishmen and "to discourage Emigrations,"[141] and he was worried that the kind of people he wanted to see come to the new nation would stay home. He wrote to his friend Jan Ingenhousz that if the "very improbable Stories" about America were believed, "all Strangers would avoid" it, and "foreign Merchants would as soon carry their Goods to sell in Newgate . . . ."[142] And just two years before his death, and only a few months before writing the part of the memoirs dealing with Whitefield and the Awakening, he pleaded with newspaper editors to avoid the "Spirit of Rancour, Malice, and Hatred"[143] so common in Philadelphia newspapers, since these would create very negative images abroad of Pennsylvanians and Americans generally. This was the work being done by the enemies of America, and Franklin hoped his countrymen would not help them in any way. And when he wrote the *Autobiography*, he followed his own advice and protected both his own image and that of his "Virgin State."[144]

V

Religion in the Schools

Just a few years after the Great Awakening ceased to be a living force and became a lingering memory whose vitality was expressed chiefly in the new Church order and in continuing bitterness among Presbyterians, Franklin realized a long cherished dream: he took in a partner, his former apprentice, David Hall, and retired from business in 1748. At the age of forty-two the exile from Boston had become prosperous enough to enjoy life as a man of leisure. We can forgive him the pride he felt in his accomplishment, for retirement to him meant, as he often told his friends, the opportunity to further his intellectual life and enlarge his horizons.

As early as 1743 he had tried to create a dialogue among thinking men, and his *Proposal for Promoting Useful Knowledge* did indeed give rise to the American Philosophical Society. When he would be "quite a Master of my own Time,"[1] he said, he would continue his experiments in electricity for, as he wrote to the British businessman-scientist Peter Collinson, "I was never before engaged in any study that so totally engrossed my attention and my time . . . ."[2] A few months after his retirement he wrote to another scientific correspondent, Cadwallader Colden, that his sole purpose in quitting business was to "obtain some Leisure"[3] to pursue his philosophical studies. He was dismayed when he found himself embroiled in local politics and with having to organize an association for the defense of his city. He determined, however, that he would soon rid himself of such bothersome and time-consuming, albeit necessary, affairs. Years later, he often wrote from abroad to his wife Deborah that he longed to retire from public life and devote his remaining years to his family and to his long-neglected experiments. No doubt he was sincere. He was often discouraged by the political machinations that occupied so much of his time, and surely one of the reasons he tolerated such a life was his profound sense of duty. It is also true, however, that Franklin's work in electricity had made him famous. The applause and degrees he had received from his countrymen were no doubt pleasing, and the Harvard degree probably had special significance to Silence Dogood. But the praise and honors from England and the Continent had to be even more gratifying. They had assured his reputation as a scholar and Franklin knew he could therefore, if necessary, afford to ignore or politely reject the many requests from England and Europe that he retire from public life and return to his laboratory. Or he could promise his correspondents, as he often did, that soon—very soon—he would be free of all public obligations and settle down finally to his scientific work.

But he did not retire until it was too late, even for so remarkable a man, to engage in any serious experimentation. Of the many factors that worked against his retirement, the chief one seems to be that after a time he came to find the power he had gained in politics irresistible and impossible to relinquish. Even a decade before the Revolution, he was one of the most influential men in America and looked forward to a time when, moving beyond the sphere of local politics, he would be in a position to use his fertile mind for the benefit of a more closely united America led by moral and benevolent men not unlike the persona of his memoirs. Such hopes are not at all surprising or vain on the part of the one who thought possible the formation of a United Party for Virtue made up of "the Virtuous and good Men of all Nations into a regular Body, to be govern'd by suitable good and wise Rules."[4] In the practicability of this plan, he never lost faith.

By the time he retired, Franklin had proved himself to be a very able promoter of useful projects, and one that he particularly cherished was the establishment of a first-rate school which would teach a variety of useful and moral things to the local youth. In fact, it was only a year after his election to the Philadelphia Common Council that he published his *Proposals Relating to the Education of Youth in Pennsylvania.* If he could be helpful in initiating good causes as a private citizen, he could undoubtedly be even more influential as a public man in contact with the most important and wealthiest citizens in Philadelphia. Franklin had some such scheme in mind when he entered politics. For a dozen years he had been the clerk of the Assembly and learned that men with connections found it easier to carry out plans than ordinary citizens. He did not foresee a time when his public activities would force him to give up serious experimentation and even thwart him in promoting what he was certain were very useful projects. Nor could he imagine that one day politics would force him out of a position of importance in the school he would help found.

Although he learned to adjust to a life essentially removed from scientific research, he was often frustrated and angry when his plans for the benefit of his province were interfered with by political foes; and to his dismay, if not to his surprise, among his chief opponents were, once again, the Presbyterians. Franklin found himself locked in bitter struggles with them through the middle 1760's. The first of these concerns the relationship of Franklin and his son William, Royal Governor of New Jersey, with the colleges of Philadelphia and New Jersey. The final battle deals with the Paxton massacre and Franklin's efforts to make Pennsylvania a Crown colony. A continuous thread that runs through these affairs is the benevolent philosopher's enmity toward Presbyterianism. It is, however, a thread that is never woven into the carefully wrought tapestry of the *Autobiography*. The work ends with the year 1758, before the Franklins' involvement with the College of New Jersey and the father's attempt to bring Pennsylvania under the Crown. Nevertheless, Franklin's very full outline of his memoirs does not mention the Jersey school, so the intrigues against it would probably not have been mentioned. He did intend to discuss the Paxton affair and his efforts to make the province a royal colony, but, judging from his handling of the memoirs, one is forced to believe that he would not have told us the role his anti-Presbyterianism played in his schemes. The College of Philadelphia he does discuss, but nowhere does he suggest that he ever had any difficulties in the institution, and he does not even bring up the name of one of his chief enemies, Provost William Smith. The reasons for the omissions and consequent distortion of events, of course, are Franklin's great desire to present positive images of himself and his country and thus make his memoirs a personal and national propaganda piece.

Especially trying to his moderate disposition and philosophical detachment was the tampering by his enemies with his brainchild, the Academy of Philadelphia. As early as 1743 he had proposed that an academy be established in Pennsylvania.[5] Unfortunately, nothing came of his suggestion at this time. Six years later, in the *Proposals Relating to the Education of Youth in Pennsylvania*, Franklin tried again to get his province busy doing something constructive about its inadequate educational opportunities. Though the education he envisioned leaned heavily toward what would be useful to men of business—"*Arithmetick, Accounts* . . . some of the first Principles of *Geometry*," mechanical drawing, English, and penmanship—Franklin had to compromise with his fellow promoters who desired a more classical education for the young. Indeed, the spirit of a rather reluctant acquiescence pervades the following:

> As to their Studies, it would be well if they could be taught every *Thing* that is useful, and *every Thing* that is ornamental: But Art is long, and their Time is short. It is therefore propos'd that they learn those things that are likely to be *most useful* and *most ornamental,* Regard being had to the several Professions for which they are intended.[6]

The italics tell an interesting story of what must have transpired in the committee room. The compromise they worked out called for two equal departments in the Academy—Franklin's practical English school and a classical school. There was also included a Charity school to teach poor children "Reading, Writing and Arithmetick."

The most important point was to interest the public in the Academy; and there were also some things on which nearly all concerned parties could agree. The institution was not to become the educational training ground of any particular church. Franklin could never be happy with such a situation. Moreover, a religiously affiliated school would be certain to create hostility in a colony like Pennsylvania, with its many denominations and sects, and with its large body of unchurched citizens. Rather than cater to any specific group, Franklin wanted the school to teach basic morality. His associates, however, were not deists and so it was finally agreed that students would be taught, through a moralistic approach to history, "the Necessity of a *Publick Religion,*" especially of Christianity.[7] Franklin and the other founders, in taking over Whitefield's New Building for the Academy, had to satisfy the demands of its trustees that basic Protestantism be taught. Franklin accepted what he could not change. He was determined, however, that the school would never suffer from denominationalism and sought out a rector who was an educator and moralist rather than a religious partisan.

Franklin's search for a rector belies the widely held belief, which he himself fostered, concerning his alleged regard for all religious persuasions. The truth is that until about 1770 he identified liberal, sophisticated, and intellectual Christianity almost exclusively with Anglicanism. This feeling is reflected in his choices of men to head the Academy.[8] His first selection was his old chess opponent, David Martin, who served the institution for eleven months until his death. Since he was interred in the Christ Church burying ground, he was almost certainly a member of the Church of England.[9]

Martin's appointment had always been considered temporary. Franklin had earlier asked Samuel Johnson, Anglican minister and scholar, to accept the position, and after Martin's death Franklin reopened discussions with the man Silence Dogood had once attacked as irrational because he left one religious order for another. The years proved to Franklin, however, that, as with the case of Archbishop Tillotson, he could agree with Johnson on many matters and genuinely respect his moral views. He had almost never given himself the chance to achieve this kind of relationship with an American Calvinist minister or scholar. He might respect a few orthodox Dissenters as men, but since he found the central tenets of their belief incredible, he was' unable to have much regard for them as thinkers.

When he read Johnson's works he discovered that at the heart of the minister's Christianity were morality and good works. God created man, he wrote in his *Elementa Philosophica*, to be happy, and happiness consists of a religious faith expressed in a moral life.[10] In his *Ethices Elementa*, which was reprinted by Franklin and Hall, Johnson rejects the basic tenets of Calvinism and treats Christianity as a moral system. In doing so he engages in what had become an important part of his life—attacking Presbyterians,[11] this time concentrating on the awakened who had been disparaging morality.[12] One did not glorify God by making professions of piety, but in using his reason to understand God's great law of nature, which leads him to avoid sin and to do good to his fellow creatures.[13] Johnson's rational Christianity was an important factor in Franklin's efforts to win him for the Academy.

There were other scholars in America who could have led the school, and one of them was much closer to Philadelphia. Francis Alison, Old Side Presbyterian minister, who later served a long and useful career as Vice Provost at the institution, was an excellent scholar and teacher and, as Franklin knew, was an experienced and able administrator. Alison had been quite successful in establishing and keeping up a Presbyterian grammar school in New London, Pennsylvania, in spite of serious financial difficulties. It is true that he was a traditionalist and thought education synonymous with classical learning, which he fortified with Calvinist theology. But Johnson was also a thorough classicist, who insisted on religious as well as secular knowledge,[14] and as events later proved, he demanded that any school he led have an Anglican atmosphere.[15] Moreover, there were rumors circulating as far away as Princeton, New Jersey, that Johnson was a poor teacher, writer of English, and thinker.[16]

Had Franklin taken the trouble to inquire into Alison's beliefs he would have discovered they were, in a number of important ways, much like his own. The minister followed Locke in rejecting the notion of innate ideas, insisted on the necessity of reason, moralism, and charity in religion, and demanded that religion and government address themselves to the common good. Alison, indeed, speaks in the tradition of two of his American near-contemporaries—John Wise and Jefferson—by arguing, as Franklin argued, that "Ye end of all civil power is ye publick happiness, & any power not conducive to this is unjust & ye people who gave it may Justly abolish it."[17] Franklin himself respected Alison, at least before they became political opponents, and thought him a genuinely *"Honest Man"* as well as "A Person of Great Ingenuity and Learning" and "a catholic Divine."[18] Nevertheless, the philosopher did not consider him the man to assume control of the Academy. Alison was therefore insultingly offered the rectorship only after Johnson had refused it repeatedly and Franklin and his associates, for a time, had no one else in mind. Recognizing the sentiments of the founder and the other trustees, Alison understandably rejected the honor. The chief difference between the two ministers was their denomination, and whereas Johnson's Church of England status made him desired, Alison's Presbyterianism made him an unhappy choice.[19]

Indeed, the Anglican's widely known hostility toward Calvinism probably made him an even more desirable candidate to Franklin. Johnson and the New England Dissenters had been engaged in their own Thirty Years' War, since the prodigal son had returned home an unrepentant Anglican. His enemies soon convinced him, he warned the Bishop of London, that they were trying "To keep our church under"[20] and that they would never cease in their efforts.[21] He therefore longed for an American bishopric[22] and for the importation of more Anglican ministers who could take measures to "stop their [Congregationalists' and Presbyterians'] progress."[23] As he made clear in numerous writings, Johnson identified Calvinism with arrogance, deceit, bigotry, and persecution;[24] and he especially hated what he considered to be his foes' smug assurance that theirs was the "established church" in America.[25] As an avid reader, a man interested in church affairs, and as a printer, Franklin had ready access to many of Johnson's pronouncements. He may also have learned about the minister's views from Cadwallader Colden, who was friendly with both men. Further, it is not unlikely that Johnson discussed his feelings when Franklin and the Anglican politician Tench Francis visited him in the early summer of 1750, hoping to get him to take the position at the Academy. It is certain that Franklin would hasten to learn as much as he could about one to whom he was going to entrust a long held and cherished dream: and he discovered enough to cause him to spend a

frustrating year trying to win Johnson over. He offered him every encouragement—improved financial prospects, status, authority, and gifts. He even undertook to gratify Johnson's scholarly vanity—at a considerable financial
loss to himself—by reprinting the *Elementa Philosophica* and advertising it
with an eye to pleasing its author.[26] He argued charmingly, in terms familiar
to both of them, that as a scholar and a clergyman Johnson had a moral
obligation to use his God-given talents in behalf of the Academy to which he
was being "strongly *called* as if . . . from heaven."[27] By January 1752,
however, even the indefatigable and persuasive Franklin had to admit defeat.
Dr. Johnson was not going to leave his old home in Connecticut and take
charge of the school at distant Philadelphia. Two years later, though, he found
himself able to accept another call, this one as President of King's College
(Columbia).[28]

Franklin once more, then, had to seek a man to run the Academy, and for a
third time he turned to an Anglican. He soon thought he had found in William
Smith a better choice than Johnson, for Smith was much younger, more
religiously liberal, and a budding scholar with his most productive years ahead
of him. Then, too, Smith was more likely to have wider appeal in Pennsylvania than Johnson because the younger man had not at this time taken
orders. Yet he was doubtless a good Anglican and could even claim the patronage of the Archbishop of Canterbury.[29] He would certainly be acceptable
to the trustees, three-fourths of whom were members of the Church of
England. To Franklin, Smith seemed a worthy product of Anglican education.
His intellectual curiosity, general competence, and sincere interest in education made him an ostensibly happy choice for the Academy position and
Franklin tried to bring him to the school.

Smith had come from Scotland to New York in 1752 and soon began writing pieces for the press, including several on education. Franklin had read one
of them, *Some Thoughts on Education*, which was published in 1752. A year
later, hoping to get a college started in New York, Smith wrote *A General
Idea of the College of Mirania* and sent a copy of it to Franklin. In it Franklin
read that the ideal college would turn out "a succession of sober, virtuous, industrious citizens"[30] and also check "the course of growing luxury."[31]
Such views naturally appealed to the tradesman-trustee, and although Smith
was a classicist, like Franklin he believed that education had to be useful
rather than merely decorative.[32] Finally, Smith's religious views were not at
all incompatible with Franklin's, for the young man, at least theoretically,
leaned in the direction of Christian deism with its emphasis on reason and

practical benevolence.[33] It is not surprising that he was an active Mason and became one of Franklin's lodge brothers.[34]

The two men opened a correspondence and Franklin, though disturbed by Smith's tendency toward censoriousness, chose to overlook the fault and expressed "great Esteem" for him.[35] When he visited Franklin, Smith told him of his intention to return to England and settle there, but the philosopher was confident that Smith would accept the Academy position if it could be made more profitable.[36] He therefore worked through English connections to get Thomas Penn to endow a chair for the young man,[37] and the proprietor responded generously.[38] Franklin was disappointed when he discovered that his friend had decided to be ordained in England, for this act was likely to alienate non-Anglicans, including the Quaker Assembly.[39] He had a generally high regard for bright Churchmen, however, and so reasoned himself into a cheerful humor. If the change "should prejudice the main design with some," he said, "it might perhaps advantage it as much with others."[40] Then, too, until 1756, Franklin felt sure that he would be able to guide his young friend and keep a benevolent but firm hand on the reins that would give direction to the Academy. After all, he was only half joking when he referred to Smith as "my Pupil" to whom he had been endeavoring to teach his "Philosophy."[41]

Any master-pupil relationship, however, existed entirely in the mind of the older man. In fact, politics and religious squabbles, which should have been irrelevant to school affairs, were almost synonymous with it, and nearly everyone of importance from Thomas Penn[42] on down hoped to make use of the school to further specific political or religious ends. Unfortunately, such matters caused Franklin and Smith to become life-long enemies and the school to lose the support of its most able founder. Franklin became the leader of the reorganized Quaker party in the Assembly, a group of men who, unlike Israel Pemberton and the pacifists he led, were willing to sacrifice the sacred principle of nonviolence to retain political power.

Smith, an inveterate politician, became the ruthless, deceitful but competent penman for the Proprietary Party, which included about half the Anglican population and virtually all of the Presbyterians.[43] His natural conservatism and his gratitude to Thomas Penn logically placed him in the proprietary camp. Further, Penn had become a member of the Church of England, and Smith hoped to use this situation and his friendship with the Archbishop of Canterbury to improve his secular and Church positions. From Penn, Smith looked forward to financial gain and political power. From Canterbury, he longed for the pair of "lawn Sleeves" that would proclaim him the first Bishop of America.[44] The best of both worlds is what he wanted, and it is not without reason that his Quaker detractors referred to him as the "Pope."

Smith's ambition was evident from the first. His vanity required a more prestigious position than the rectorship of the Academy offered and so in 1755, just a year after he arrived, he pushed through a new charter that made him the Provost of the College of Philadelphia, a degree-granting institution. Although he did not oppose this change, Franklin did resent the efforts of the trustees, and especially Smith, to make the classical school more important than the English school. Once the former tradesman was forced out of the school, however, his enemies let this branch of the institution decline miserably.[45] Franklin's resentment endured, and shortly before his death he chastised the trustees severely for betraying their trust by ignoring the stated wishes of the founders.[46] But though there were many guilty parties over the years, Franklin was certain that Smith had been chiefly responsible for the disgraceful condition of the English school.[47] This was an especially galling situation, since Franklin had selected the Provost carefully and in light of some of his most cherished preconceptions. Had extraneous matters not interfered, Franklin would have been of help to the schools even when abroad. But this was not to be. Politics did interfere, and in Pennsylvania, as in all colonial America, politics was normally inseparable from religion.

Penn looked upon the proprietary family as the owners of Pennsylvania and sought to reestablish their position, which had been lost through its own financial incapacity and indifference, and through the Quakers' seizure of power.[48] He gained the support of about half the Anglican population, but, at first, only the wealthier among the Presbyterians. This coalition lacked the strength to wrest political control from the Friends and their German allies, whose past sufferings taught them to fear proprietors. The Penn faction therefore tried especially hard to win the loyalty of the numerous Presbyterians in the back counties and they eventually succeeded. The frontier Presbyterians and the Quakers were enemies on religious and social grounds. The wealthy and status-conscious members of the Proprietary Party had little more use for the uncouth frontiersmen than did the Friends, but the Penn group put aside its prejudices and courted the settlers with demands for equitable representation and protection for the back areas. They and their frontier allies charged the Quaker Assembly with retaining power by underhanded means in denying truly representative government for non-Quakers. Furthermore, they complained, the Friends were unfit to rule because their principles prevented them from protecting the people against the merciless attacks from the papist French and their savage Indian allies.

The position of the Quakers was becoming less and less tenable when Smith's anonymously written piece, *A Brief State of the Province of Pennsylvania* (1755), brought matters to a head. The pamphlet was an obvious attempt to seize political power from the Quaker Assembly by uniting the Crown and Parliament with the Proprietary Party. Appealing to their prejudice and fear, Smith warns the King and Parliament that the Quaker-dominated Assembly, in trying to gain and keep popular support, have reduced the colony to "a pure Republic."[49] Their greed for power is thus leading the province to ruin, and their pacifist principle has rendered Pennsylvania defenseless against any foe. The poor settlers in the back counties particularly have suffered at the hands of the savages and the French. Nevertheless, the Assembly is deaf to their numerous pleas for protection and insensitive to their murders; moreover, the Friends neither protect the frontiersmen nor provide them with the means to protect themselves. And so the innocent groan and die because men that are unfit to rule are concerned only with maintaining both their principle and their power.[50]

Smith points out that the settlers, a great many of whom are Germans and Presbyterians, far outnumber the Quakers. Yet the Assembly makes certain that they have no political power. By creating unfair representation of counties and by working on the fears of the ignorant Germans, the Friends turn them against the benevolent Penn family and are thus assured of German support and a clear majority in all elections. Smith calls upon Germans to unite with their Presbyterian neighbors and fellow sufferers against the Assembly, their common enemy. The pamphlet created a sensation on both sides of the Atlantic. Although Smith was suspected by some of having written the piece, Franklin could not bring himself to believe that his "Pupil" could have done so.[51]

The following year, however, soon after he offered to become Penn's propagandist,[52] Smith unleashed his second vicious attack, *A Brief View of the Conduct of Pennsylvania*, which was for sale in Philadelphia in the spring of 1756. He carries out the logic inherent in his earlier work, calling the Quakers "Infatuated Enthusiasts"[53] whose politics are religiously motivated.[54] In the case of refusing to defend the five back counties, Smith implies, the Quaker Assembly would rather see the settlers die than protect them; for the Friends know that these people constitute a great majority and are largely "*Presbyterians* from the North of Ireland."[55] Smith diminishes the German population for the sake of appeal in this second pamphlet. Earlier he had called the Germans to rebel against their allies, and now he was summoning the Presbyterians to unity and battle. Further, he again tries to enlist the support of the King and Parliament on the side of the proprietor by repeating his charges against the Friends and by accusing them of following a policy which actually promotes the French interest in America.[56]

Smith's attacks had come at a very sensitive and unfortunate time for the Quakers. About four months before the *Brief State* appeared, John Pemberton, a member of the eminent Quaker family and a preacher in the Society of Friends, expressed widespread Quaker fears that the Society was in a sadly declining condition. He grew terribly discouraged when he considered "how unpromising the prospect is of a right Succession among us."[57] Like other members of the Society, Pemberton feared more than anything being overwhelmed by the rapidly increasing Presbyterian population in the area. Small wonder, then, that the Quaker meeting of 1755, taking official notice of the decline, insisted on the necessity of the principle of nonviolence and expressed its grave concern about the widespread "wavering" from Quaker tenets.[58]

Threatened even further by Smith's polemic, Friends in England as well as in America responded. Henton Brown in England warned James Pemberton that the "Scandalous pamphlet" had "poisen'd the minds of many & with too great success has begot An Opinion that a parliamentary enquiry must ensue." Although, as Brown noted, English Friends were working up immediate replies to the anonymous author of the attack, he feared that their defenses lacked adequate clarity and power and appealed to Pemberton to have the Assembly appoint "with all possible Speed . . . some Able penn" to respond. Though the manuscript of Brown's letter is torn, it appears that he also thought the Assembly should send a capable person to England to neutralize the effects of the pamphlet.[59] William Logan, writing to his cousin Israel Pemberton, later thought it essential that Quakers find out for certain the identity of the author of the *Brief State* and *Brief View*, and suggested that some member of the Society bribe "one of the Printers Boys" to discover the truth.[60]

Once the strict pacifists in the Society quit the Assembly for the sake of their principle, their proprietary opponents hoped to take over power in the legislature.[61] But more flexible Quakers, such as the speaker of the Assembly, Isaac Norris, remained on and were determined both to keep control of the province and to gain revenge on the author of the pamphlets.[62] British and

American Friends spread the word that Smith was "a Man of Infamos Character" and that his attacks were not to be believed.[63] So great was the furor caused by the Society that Richard Peters, who had approved of Smith's pieces while their author remained unknown, feared that the "intestine Broils" in Pennsylvania were a greater danger than the French and Indians. He tried in vain to deny that Smith wrote the pamphlets, but even such enemies to Quakers as the Reverend Samuel Chandler, influential Dissenting minister of Old Jewry, who was a friend to the proprietor, Smith, and the College of Philadelphia, thought that the Provost had done all branches of the institution a disservice by involving himself in political controversy.[64]

It took Franklin some time to join the Friends in their antipathy to Smith even after it seemed clear to many that he had written the anti-Quaker pieces. Although he became the Provost's archenemy, Franklin at first discounted the mounting evidence that he had so seriously misjudged Smith and that his preconceptions about bright, cultivated Anglicans were not always reliable. Just as he was certain that no Presbyterian, regardless of his intellectual abilities, would be a proper choice to run the school, he was sure that a seemingly liberal-minded Anglican would be the man for the job. Smith may have recognized something of Franklin's prejudice, for when he first arrived in Philadelphia he was confident that he would win the philosopher over to the proprietary faction, or "Presbyterian Party" as the group was frequently called. By the autumn of 1755 he was less certain,[65] however, and soon the two men were bitter foes who lost few opportunities to attack each other. Smith came to accuse Franklin of taking credit for electrical experiments that were first conducted by Ebenezer Kinnersley. Kinnersley himself defended his old neighbor,[66] but Smith, as was often the case with him, relied on the fact that an exoneration never completely removed the stain from a man who had been thoroughly slandered, even if he had been awarded an Oxford doctorate.[67]

The Quakers and Franklin enjoyed some revenge.[68] Isaac Norris, second-in-command of the reorganized Quaker party, informed Franklin, who was in England as agent for the province, that "Our old Inviterate Scribbler has at length wrote himself into a Jail." By not informing Smith of the charges to be brought against him when he appeared before the Assembly, that body treated him the way the Synod had dealt with Hemphill twenty-five years earlier. One observer thought the later proceedings in England also cruel, reporting that Franklin took particular pleasure in making Smith suffer during the trial.[69] Franklin himself had the opportunity of defending the Assembly's

Benjamin Franklin of Philadelphia, L.L.D. F.R.S., by Edward Fisher.
Courtesy of the Philadelphia Museum of Art, photograph by A. J. Wyatt, staff photographer.

The Reverend William Smith.
Courtesy of the Historical Society of Pennsylvania.

James Pemberton.
Courtesy of the Friends Historical Library-Swarthmore College.

Francis Alison.
Courtesy of the Presbyterian Ministers' Fund Life Insurance.

actions when Smith's request for a hearing in England was granted. Yet more than mere revenge was involved in the matter. After all, the situation of the Assembly was very delicate, and the imprisonment of a man who had connections with the Archbishop of Canterbury and Thomas Penn was a very dangerous move—especially since Smith's case marked the first time that any Assembly had ever tried a citizen for libel.[70] Considering that the Quakers, who were skillful politicians, took the chance and that the very cautious and shrewd Franklin supported the action, they must have considered the risk of hostility from King and Parliament worth taking. And it was. As Norris said, Smith, in his effort to win support for the Proprietary Party, "had been made a Tool to narrow Presbyterian Politicks."[71] Although the Provost, like most Anglicans, disliked and even opposed Presbyterianism, he found himself in a strong political alliance with the Dissenters. To defeat the Assembly, he called for fair representation and thus greater power for the numerous Presbyterians in the colony. The proprietary allies proved to be able politicians who could work against each other along denominational lines while representing a united front against Franklin and the Quakers and their supporters.[72] Smith and the other proprietary Anglicans were confident that the Church of England would benefit most from a Quaker defeat. Thomas Penn was, after all, a High Churchman and considered the College of Philadelphia an Anglican seminary.[73] But the Presbyterians, relying on their far superior numbers, were equally sure that the defeat of the Quakers would put them in political and religious power.

Though Smith and the trustees of the College of Philadelphia who stripped Franklin of influence in the school were mostly Anglicans, they were expressing a political policy that catered especially to the bulk of his opponents, who, once again, were Presbyterians. One knowledgeable Dissenter, and an ardent enemy to Franklin, claimed that the Presbyterians were unanimous in working against him and the Assembly.[74] The leader of the Proprietary Party in Pennsylvania, and the man who freed Smith from jail, was, significantly, Chief Justice William Allen, the wealthy and prominent Old Side Presbyterian. More than any other man, he mapped out the proprietary war strategy against Franklin and his supporters. Franklin, the trustee, was a casualty in a political war with religious undercurrents, and so too, as things turned out, was the College. The Friends had suspected that the school would become embroiled in religion and politics, and they were right. It made matters even more dismaying to them and to Franklin that the power behind their political opposition—which ultimately turned Franklin and the other trustees into enemies—was Presbyterian. The Dissenters within the Proprietary Party itself and the great many effectively disenfranchised frontiersmen were, to complicate the difficulties for Franklin and his allies, growing angrier at the seemingly insensitive, do-nothing political-religious Establishment in the secure areas of Pennsylvania. One Assembly supporter tried to break up the Proprietary Party by dividing Smith and his fellow Anglicans from their Presbyterian support, accusing the Provost of being an enemy to all Dissenters.[75] This came as a surprise to no one, and Smith's denial of the charge was more a matter of form than a true defense.[76] The Quaker writer, though, had wasted his shot. The Proprietary Party would remain intact to work against the Assembly and Franklin in every way possible.

Richard Peters, Penn's secretary and the new President of the Board of Trustees of the school, admitted privately that Franklin had been squeezed out of the school for political reasons.[77] Franklin, of course, was understandably bitter and, writing from London to Kinnersley, who was master of the declining English school, he complained that the "Trustees had reap'd the full Advantage of my Head, Hands, Heart and Purse, in getting through the first Difficulties" and then they "laid me aside." He exaggerated the openness of his purse, his contributions being less than the average, and after resigning as President of the Trustees he neither gave nor raised money for the institution. He was angry and disgusted that "before I left Philadelphia, everything to be done in the Academy was privately preconcerted in a Cabal without my Knowledge or Participation and carried into Execution. The Schemes of Public Parties made it seem requisite to lessen my Influence wherever it could be lessened."[78] The letter, written more than three years after his resignation, during which time he had been abroad and involved in complex provincial matters, clearly indicates the depth of his resentment that his political enemies among the trustees, members of the Presbyterian-dominated Proprietary Party, were to blame for this personal tragedy. Franklin's hurt was well known to his foes. One of them, expressing the sentiments of those who became Tories, thought the best way of getting Franklin out of politics even as late as 1774 was to promise him an active and leading role again in the College of Philadelphia if he returned to his philosophical pursuits full time.[79]

Franklin was also obviously bitter that Smith and the trustees, contrary to the original plan, were striving to make the school a breeding ground for Anglican ministers, thus causing antagonism with the school's Presbyterians. In this he was correct. Smith had taken Anglican orders under the direction of the Archbishop of Canterbury, and the two men discussed plans for the College with respect to the Church of England.[80] This deceit created problems in the school and, to Franklin's dismay, plunged it into a religious battle for supremacy between Anglicans and Old Side Presbyterians. Smith denied the fact, and even his recent apologist has insisted that he was above such betrayal,[81] but Peters knew differently, as did Smith himself. Peters wrote to the Archbishop of Canterbury, who feared that the Presbyterians might become too powerful in the institution, that it was the unstated intention and practice of the Provost and the trustees to hire Dissenters as faculty *only* when there was a desperate need to fill a position and no Churchman applied for it.[82] Peters had earlier written to Smith, who was in England raising money for the school, about the same matter: "I blush to tell you that we have not one Church Tutor in all our Academy. There is not a Churchman upon the Continent as I can hear of that is fit to make a Tutor: and it is from downright necessity that we are obliged to take such as offer."[83] Smith, however, was confident that no part of the school would fall into Presbyterian hands. Trying to allay Anglican fears, he said that under his leadership, "the Church by soft and easy Means," would continue to gain influence in all branches of the school. He reminded his correspondent, the Reverend Philip Bearcroft, Secretary of the Venerable Society for the Propagation of the Gospel in Foreign Parts, that with the Provost and nearly all the trustees Anglicans,[84] there was little chance that the Dissenters would progress far in the school. Moreover, twice each day the students were required to read the set prayers of the Church of England and were instructed solely from its catechism.[85] Smith, who upset Thomas Penn by his heavy-handed efforts to promote the Church of England through the College, knew better than Bearcroft or other nervous partisans how thoroughly Anglican he was trying to make the school.[86] Alison, who had hoped to fashion Old Side Dissenting ministers at the institution and had been confident that he could bring the College under the influence of Old Side Presbyterianism, was later so frustrated in his efforts that he was "ready to resign my place in the College and retire to the country meerly thro chagrine." In 1752 the Synod of Philadelphia, unable to begin a major seminary of its own to offset New Side numerical superiority, appealed to Alison to use his new position in Philadelphia "not only to promote the good of the public, but also of the church"[87] by turning out Old Side ministers. By 1766 the chagrined Alison wrote to Ezra Stiles that the "Episcopal Trustees" controlled the College and actually were getting Presbyterian youth to take Anglican orders! This was being accomplished by acquainting the students with the "high life" they might expect as Anglican clergymen as well as by exploiting the lingering hostility between the nominally reunited Presbyterian parties.[88] Smith and the trustees did indeed try to make the school an Anglican breeding ground (if not a seminary), and during the Revolution they suffered for their close connection with England and its Established Church by being forced out of the school.

For years before this event the air was filled with charges that the institution was Presbyterian or, more commonly, that it was Anglican. The fear on both sides, even within the Proprietary Party, was so great that the Archbishop of Canterbury, Samuel Chandler, and the proprietors, Thomas and Richard Penn, jointly put on a show of unity and called on the trustees to guarantee the equal treatment of all denominations.[89] Thomas Penn made a similar demand on his own, feeling that the Quakers might be further alienated by denominational power struggles in the school.[90]

By the time of the plea for fairness (1764), however, secular and church politics were already a major part of the Philadelphia institution, as they were in the other Middle Colonies schools. In spite of their political alliance, the proprietary Anglicans and the Presbyterians carried on a religious struggle for dominance that seriously affected the affairs of the colleges in Pennsylvania and New Jersey. Peters once more expressed the sentiments of the Proprietary Party Anglican trustees toward Presbyterians in a letter to Thomas Penn. The trustees, he wrote, did not want Alison on the faculty because he was a "Dissenter," and it was only his "uncommon Talents" that overcame the bigotry, if not the resentment, of his employers.[91] And Peters himself, for religious as well as social reasons, referred to the frontier Presbyterians, for whom he had sympathy when it was politically expedient, as "the very Scum of the Earth."[92] Smith, who was the chief promoter of fair representation and adequate defense for Dissenters, plotted with Peters to secure a quick and secret ordination for an Anglican minister, a graduate of the College of Philadelphia, who would be sent to an area as yet unserviced by the Church of England. As Smith notes, the minister would actually be used as a bulwark against the Dissenters in "Gloster" and Egg Harbor, in which places Smith said that the people were degenerating and "the Presbyterians will soon get them all."[93]

On their part, the Presbyterians of both factions made life miserable for Anglicans. The Reverend Thomas Barton complained bitterly of constant persecution by New Side "Bigots and Enthusiasts" who insulted "both the Church & I" and prevented him from carrying on the Anglican service.[94]

The Dissenters, including those in the Proprietary Party, expressed their profound fear and hatred of the Church of England by their ardent opposition to an American bishopric. Peters, angered by their unrelenting hostility toward tne idea, wrote to the Archbishop of Canterbury that the Presbyterians were "fond to a madness" of popular government "and would dislike Bishops on any footing."[95] This was written just a year before the election of 1764 in which the Presbyterians "to a Man" would turn out and vote for the proprietary interest and defeat Franklin. The political coalition itself was nearly destroyed when the Presbyterians discovered that Smith had tried to sabotage the Reverend Charles Beatty's efforts to raise money in England. The fund was ostensibly for the relief of widows and orphans of Presbyterian ministers, but Smith told wealthy Anglicans, who might otherwise have given something, that the money was actually being used to propagate the Presbyterian faith. Word of Smith's actions got back to America and, although he was able to mend some fences, the Provost lost the friendship of William Allen and other influential Dissenters.[96] Smith justified his efforts against Beatty privately to other Anglicans by accusing the Presbyterian of trying to thwart the fund-raising campaign for the College of Philadelphia.[97]

These machinations, however, are relatively minor when compared with the intrigues concerning the schools in Philadelphia and New Jersey. The records of the Synod of Philadelphia clearly show that the New Side had long flaunted their College of New Jersey in the face of their Old Side opponents. To the New Side the outcome of this intra-denominational struggle was certain, for their seminary would turn out more ministers than the Synod of Philadelphia could import or than Alison could prepare at his small New London school.[98] Recognizing this problem, the conservatives therefore encouraged Alison to use his new position in the Academy of Philadelphia to train Old Side ministers.[99] Both the Old Side and the Anglicans wanted the Academy to become a college so that it could grant degrees and thereby compete with the New Jersey college. Peters explained to Penn that unless a new charter were granted, the Philadelphia school would be "like to suffer much by the Neighbourhood of the Jersey College to which abundance of People send their sons for no other reason than because they can there take Degrees."[100] Many of these young men, of course, became New Side ministers, and Peters reminded Penn that he had previously expressed his "apprehensions and Fears" that the Presbyterian institution would become a very powerful factor in America and render the Academy powerless as a bulwark against it.[101] Peters had formerly opposed the change and Penn also had doubts as to

its wisdom; however, Smith changed their minds.[102] Shortly thereafter Smith
himself was able to thank the proprietor for the new charter, telling him that it
came none too soon.[103] The Old Side could agree wholeheartedly, for almost
immediately after the College of Philadelphia was established, it presented a
formal proposal asking permission to "ingraft a seminary upon the
Philadelphia College." The plan was to have a minimum of six students
following the course of study there while reading divinity under Alison.[104]
Eventually these students would be graduated as ministers who would be able
to offer competition to the Jersey graduates. The Old Side was undoubtedly
confident that the trustees and Smith, who were political allies, would encourage the plan. Smith, after all, was known to be contemptuous of the New Side
and had already done a good deal to discredit Gilbert Tennent while he was in
England trying to raise money for the College of New Jersey.[105] So intensive
were Smith's efforts that, to the delight of conservatives and Anglicans, he
turned the Reverend Samuel Chandler against the school for a time.[106] The
Provost was willing to let a seminary under Alison be engrafted, hoping to
gain influence among his political friends and also weaken the New Side's
position.[107] But as Alison and other Old Side members would discover, the
trustees and the Provost, in spite of alliances, hated all Presbyterians. The
feeling, of course, was mutual. Anglicans and Presbyterian political allies used
each other to further private as well as common ends. When the Presbyterians,
because of their numerical superiority on the faculty and because Smith had
indeed become the tool of the party which they dominated, seemed about to
take over, Smith and his fellow Anglicans stopped them, as they had promised
the Archbishop of Canterbury they would.[108]

Convinced that they would never get far in what they were sure now was an
Anglican school, the Old Side clergy in 1766 were desperate for any
compromise with their brethren. Their effort to achieve one involved Presbyterians throughout the Middle Colonies, for they all feared their common
enemies, Smith, the Anglican trustees, and their school. Old Side sympathizers
therefore proposed a coalition between conservative and New Side ministers
and teachers in the College of New Jersey. They felt that either Alison or John
Ewing, professor of natural philosophy in the College of Philadelphia and an
important Old Side leader, should be president.[109] This plan was unacceptable
to the New Side and failed. It did have much to recommend it to many Dissenters, however, who looked upon the College of Philadelphia as an Anglican
institution. Samuel Purviance, Jr., who knew all Presbyterian matters and sentiments, expressed the feelings of many of his brethren in a letter to Stiles
written just before the New Side rejected the plan. Full of anticipation, he

explained to Stiles that the departure of Alison and Ewing "will certainly ruin Phila. College."[110] Though one of Smith's chief proprietary allies against the Quakers and Franklin, Purviance hoped that the plan would not only give the Old Side control over the Jersey school but also defeat the Anglicans and their school. The Provost, he knew, like most Anglicans, took pleasure in the division in the Presbyterian Church, confident that the long struggle would weaken both sides enough to permit the Church of England to establish an American bishopric. Along with many other informed persons, Purviance was certain that Smith had long been angling for the position himself. The best way to prevent a bishopric, to retaliate against Smith, and to weaken Anglican interest, Purviance felt, was to unite all Dissenters and "ruin" the College of Philadelphia.[111] Once the plan had been rejected by the New Side, he lapsed into despair. He was positive that the Church of England was an even greater threat to Presbyterians than the Quakers because it controlled a school to turn out ministers. The conservatives would especially suffer, he feared, for their young men would most probably have to be educated in Philadelphia, where each day they would be "perverted by the Intrigue of that designing subtile Mortal Dr. Smith."[112] Although the numerically superior Dissenters continued trying to make headway in the College of Philadelphia, the trustees and the Provost were too much for them, and by 1769 Alison, who was still at his post, was desperate. "Our Jersey College," he wrote, "is now talking as if she was soon to be the bulwark against Episcopacy: I should rejoice to see her Pistols, like honest Teagues, grown up into great guns."[113] While looking forward to the growth of the College of New Jersey, though, Alison remained active in the Old Side seminary at New London[114] and continued to do his best for his faction at the College of Philadelphia.

In spite of financial and other difficulties, the College of New Jersey had been doing well. It was founded for several reasons. The New Side, perhaps influenced by the Dickinson group, grew to recognize the crucial importance of an educated ministry.[115] It had been blamed, with only partial justification, for even the worst excesses of the Awakening and so had to change the direction Tennent and other radicals had taken in the heat of battle. Rather than condemning college-educated ministers, the New Side would establish its own seminary to teach its youth the ways of God. These young men would then fill the many vacant congregations that the Old Side failed to supply, and New Side Presbyterianism, as it had been reorganized, would become American Presbyterianism.

About the time that William Tennent, Sr., died, in 1746, a group of New

Side laymen of the New York presbytery secured a charter for the school from Governor James Hamilton. The New Side had been suffering since the closing of Log College in about 1744, so the faction wasted no time and in 1747 opened its seminary. That it was able to survive its financial troubles and the loss of five presidents in twenty years is a testimony to the dedication of its supporters and to the need for the school. To make survival even more difficult, the Old Side and Anglicans offered it nothing but hostility. Finally, like the rival College of Philadelphia, the New Jersey school was faced with the concealed but nevertheless real opposition of Franklin and his son William.

In fact, both institutions, as set up, were inimical either to the political interests of Franklin and the Assembly or to the religious security of Quakers in Pennsylvania and New Jersey. The College of Philadelphia was dangerous because of its Presbyterian-dominated proprietary politics, and the College of New Jersey because it promised to spread anti-Quaker Presbyterian ministers throughout the Middle Colonies. Given such circumstances and the fact of especially the elder Franklin's anti-Presbyterian sentiments,[116] it is understandable that he and his son, who shared his father's feelings, worked against both schools. Their appraisal of the situation was accurate. The Reverend John Ewing, for example, had plans whereby the Presbyterian Church, controlling the Philadelphia and New Jersey schools, could graduate enough ministers to dominate religion in America.[117]

Opposing them, however, was not easy for Franklin, since he was abroad for nearly the entire period with which the remainder of this discussion deals. He left for England in the summer of 1757, about a year after resigning as President of the Board of Trustees of the College of Philadelphia, and did not return home until the autumn of 1762. Yet even while in England, engaged in the most important matters of his public life, he once again demonstrated his continuing fear of power in the hands of Presbyterians and his hostility toward the denomination. Unfortunately, the school also suffered from Franklin's animosity. Although it benefited from a lottery conducted in its behalf each year from 1757 to 1764, thus raising more than £9,000,[118] the institution was still on shaky ground. Matters became so strained that in 1761 Smith was sent to England and Scotland to raise money.[119] He succeeded admirably, eventually raising more than £7,000 in Pennsylvania currency. In 1762, however, all branches of the institution were still in grave financial trouble.[120] Throughout this continuing crisis, when many people of small means gave what little they could to the struggling school, the affluent Franklin gave nothing at all. Moreover, it had been the fervent hope and even expectation of the trustees and other concerned parties that Franklin, while still in Philadelphia, would have persuaded the Assembly to grant money to the school, just as he had for the Pennsylvania Hospital in 1752. Though he had far more weight in the Assembly in 1756, he made no attempt to do so because of the political and religious hostilities within the school and between the Assembly and the Proprietary Party.[121] His bitterness is also in part indicated by the fact that in making up a will before leaving for England, he left his "Electrical Apparatus" to Yale.[122] It is true that Yale enjoyed a scientific tradition and doubtless made good use of the equipment, but the College of Philadelphia with Smith, and especially Kinnersley, was by no means backward in electrical experimentation, as Franklin knew. Furthermore, President Clap of Yale had earlier ignored or rejected Franklin's urgent request that the school raise money for a "compleat Apparatus for Natural Philosophy" even after he generously offered to donate "the Electrical Part"[123] in the interest of science. Franklin made no such offer to the College of Philadelphia, and he did not mention it, the charity school, or even the Academy in his will.

Moreover, Franklin went along with, and even encouraged, the Assembly's efforts to outlaw lotteries, which in Pennsylvania were most frequently run for the benefit of the College and its affiliated schools. A battle raged in the press between those who were certain that the lotteries were *"ensnaring and delusive* Practices"[124] that were robbing the people of their money and corrupting the morals of the province,[125] and those who defended them. Thomas Penn and others charged the Assembly immediately with using the lotteries merely as an excuse for trying to ruin the schools, the College in particular, which the Assembly felt was sectarian and political. It was an opponent of the lotteries, however, who stressed the political and religious struggle underlying the dispute. Eventually the King repealed the Assembly's law and the school raised money through lotteries until 1764.[126]

Franklin was no enemy to lotteries on moral grounds, for he had made good use of them himself and, indeed, had begun the first one ever conducted in Philadelphia. A letter written by William Franklin, who served as his father's secretary, confidant, and fellow schemer in England, however, makes it clear that Franklin not only knew about the Assembly's actions but had a hand in directing them. The letter, which was intended for Joseph Galloway, Franklin's young political ally and William's friend, further makes it clear that the attacks on lotteries were indeed designed "to prevent the ill Effects to the Province that [were] likely to proceed from the present Management of the College."[127] The Assembly and others of the popular party had kept

Franklin abreast of the various aspects of their political struggle and so he knew all about the "Scheme on foot" to hit at the Proprietary Party through the school. William slyly reports that "Parson Duché," a graduate of the College of Philadelphia and one of Smith's defenders who was in England for the Provost's trial, came up to William Franklin and, in effect, blamed his father for being in back of the trouble over the lotteries and with spreading the "many abominable Lies" concerning the efforts of the trustees to make the institution a political and religious instrument.[128] Duché would not have charged Franklin had he not been certain of his facts, for his father and Franklin were old friends and such political compatriots that a disgusted Richard Peters referred to the elder Duché as one of the "meer Franklinists" among the Anglicans.[129] That the son was correct in his accusations is confirmed not only by William's letter but by Franklin's later actions toward the College of Philadelphia.

When Smith left for England to raise money for the school, he received explicit orders from the trustees to gain the influential Franklin's aid in soliciting funds and in meeting the many wealthy people he knew.[130] The trustees assumed that the two enemies would be able to put aside personal bitterness to help the struggling institution that the one had founded and the other was leading. Things did not, however, work out this way. Franklin at first claimed that he regretfully would be unable to help Smith much because he was preparing to return to Philadelphia. But knowing about the plans to raise money in England and Scotland, he did find time to discredit the school and thereby undermine the collection. Smith indeed complained of opposition from Franklin's friends among the fellows at St. John's and Balliol colleges, where he had comparatively little success in collecting funds.[131]

The Provost's complaints seem justified. His *Collection Books* show that although he raised more than £12 on the average from each of the other Oxford and Cambridge colleges in 1762 and 1763, he collected nothing from either St. John's or Balliol.[132] Franklin did, indeed, have friends at both colleges and they knew of Smith's efforts to prevent him from receiving a degree. In fact, the Provost had written to the President of St. John's in an attempt to blacken Franklin's character. The whole affair was well known at Oxford, and so it is understandable that those sympathetic to Franklin would have nothing to do with Smith or his school. When Smith reported his side of the case to Richard Peters on March 22, 1762, he merely noted that Franklin had "readily offered his assistance" but doubted that he could be of any help because he expected to leave England "in about six weeks."[133] Although he does not mention his own schemes, neither does he criticize his adversary. In fact, there is a complete absence of rancor in the letter, which indicates, I believe, that the Provost took Franklin at his word and was completely unprepared for what he later discovered.

Nearly five months later Smith wrote once more to Peters, and this letter shows that he still had no idea that Franklin was an enemy to the school. To Smith, he and the founder parted on neither "the best Terms, nor the worst." He encouraged Peters to suspend judgment of Franklin until it was clear "what Part he takes in our Academy." Though advising caution, the Provost thought it possible that Franklin might once again be allowed to assume a position of leadership in the institution.[134]

Three weeks changed the complexion of everything. Smith's later letters to Peters, two of them in particular, are worth careful consideration. The first of these is undated but is marked by Peters "rec'd $2^{n}8^{ber}$ 1762" (October 2, 1762), and in it Smith claims that "one Mr. Hanna, a very benevolent and wealthy gentleman of Barbadoes," told him that "he had enquired about the College of some Gentlemen from Philda. & was informed it was 'an Instrument of Dissension. . . .' " Smith offered to disprove the charge but Hanna refused to become involved in the matter, "and then gave me £25 intimating that it was not near so much as he intended, and that he did not give it freely." Smith soon discovered "that Mr Hanna had his information from an intimate Friend of His Mr T. Allen, who had it from young Franklin, who is continually after Miss Downs, Allen's Sister in Law." Determined to test his conclusion that the Franklins were trying to injure the school, Smith continues, he asked one Mr. Sargent for money. This gentleman, "who had large Dealings" in Philadelphia, "told me he would consult his Friend Dr Franklin to know what was proper to be done. . . ." Franklin's advice was shocking. He asked Sargent not to give money, for he thought the campaign a mere nuisance and that Smith "ought to apply" to the Quaker Assembly for funds: Sargent therefore refused to give money but did "give two Gold medals annually £5 Value, to some of the best Scholars, and had given his Directions about the Matter to Dr Franklin."[135]

Smith here seems to be reporting the matter accurately. As his *Collection Books* note, Mr. Hanna is George Hanna who, on April 22, 1762, did give £25.[136] Moreover, his friend Mr. T. Allen was the brother-in-law of Elizabeth Downes, whom William Franklin was courting and soon after married.[137] The "Mr. Sergant" to whom Smith refers is John Sargent of Sargent Aufere & Co., one of the firms that had been appointed recipient of Pennsylvania's share of the parliamentary grant for the 1759 campaign against the French.[138] Sargent did give medals instead of money and in August of 1762 sent the "Trifles" to Franklin. As he carefully notes, they cost him "5 Guineas each." His donation was actually larger than the average one that Smith collected in 1762-63, but, though the Provost accepted the offer, he privately scorned it. Smith, of course, was collecting primarily for the College, and what it needed was money, not medals. Franklin knew that all branches of the institution were very short of funds. He realized, however, that the lion's share of whatever Smith collected would be used for the College; and Franklin's hostility was always directed against the College alone, for this was the branch that had become the prize over which Anglicans and Presbyterians were battling, and it was the students of the College whom Smith taught, and tried to make loyal to the Proprietary Party rather than the Assembly. Convinced that the Academy was lost anyway, Franklin was willing to sacrifice what remained of it in order to make certain that the College would not prosper. Angry as he was at being excluded from the school, he was especially fearful that Smith's political activities, together with the complex religious intrigues in the area, might eventually cause the institution to fall into Presbyterian hands. The Old Side was desperate for ministers and, after all, the entire faculty was Presbyterian and Alison was Vice Provost. While Franklin surely did not want the school to be an Anglican seminary, he dreaded what might happen if the Presbyterians took control and graduated numerous ministers. New Side and Old Side distinctions mattered little. Presbyterianism might soon be the clearly dominant power in Pennsylvania and New Jersey, as it was in other parts of America. John Ewing, a College of New Jersey graduate and later Provost of the Philadelphia school, eagerly anticipated such control of Pennsylvania and New Jersey as a prelude to Presbyterian preeminence throughout the country.[139] A compromise which would permit both groups to graduate preachers was no more appealing to Franklin, for the gloomy consequences remained the same.

He could not reject Sargent's gift, though, for the man believed he was showing his appreciation for handling the province's financial business. What Franklin could and did do was make sure that the gift would not be cash. Years before, when he first recognized what was happening to the Academy and to the College, he tried to do exactly the same thing. He had been given £20 for the College and told to put the money to the best use. He did nothing for a time, but when he was about to embark for England he turned the money over to his friend William Coleman, treasurer of the Academy, explaining that he was asked by the benefactor to determine its use. Franklin insisted that the money be "put to Interest, and that three Prizes [be] purchas'd with the yearly Produce, to be distributed yearly for the three best Pieces of Writing" done by Academy students.[140] It is no coincidence that Sargent's medals were to be awarded for excellence in writing. One was to be awarded "for some Classical Exercises" that seemed useful, and the other was to be given to the Academy student that wrote the best English essay "on the reciprocal Advantages arising from a perpetual Union between Great Britain and her American Colonies."[141]

A final word should be devoted to the subject of the English piece. Although Sargent had much to gain from "a perpetual Union," and though the topic was a familiar one on both sides of the Atlantic, it was an obsession with Franklin. His idealization of the glorious and monolithic British Empire was reaching its peak in these years before his attempt to make Pennsylvania a Crown colony. Furthermore, his years in an England that had honored him and given him good and cultivated friends caused him to fall almost blindly in love with the land and its people. He wished for nothing more, he said, than to leave America and settle there permanently.[142] The subject of the discourse, the fact that Sargent donated medals rather than money, and Franklin's feelings toward the school leave little doubt, I believe, that he tried to prevent Smith's success in raising funds.

Just as pertinent is the role the Provost attributed to William Franklin in thwarting the campaign. The father, perhaps because he felt guilt concerning his son's illegitimacy, developed a very close relationship with the young man and made certain that he would grow up a proper British gentleman. Because Franklin was never able to associate with the good Boston families at Harvard, he determined, having always been an unloyal Bostonian, that William would get even better than Harvard could offer, and the son was accordingly educated at the Middle Temple. Franklin carved out for his son a career not unlike his own after retirement. He earlier had William succeed him as clerk of the Assembly and as postmaster of Philadelphia. His legal training in England, Franklin knew, would help his son's political career. Like his father, who worked behind the scenes in the business, William, in 1762, was also awarded a Crown position, as Royal Governor of New Jersey. Franklin instilled in the young man his own veneration for the Empire and for all things English. Part of the son's training in becoming an influential English gentleman was handled by Franklin himself, for he had William accompany him to England in 1757 not only to study but to gain political experience. The son therefore served as his father's secretary, confidant, and, under direction, as a competent propagandist for his father's causes. He knew the elder Franklin's schemes and evidently gave his full assent to all of them. In fact, until just before the Revolution, when the father was to discover that he had made his less pragmatic son too English, there is no evidence to indicate that William ever disagreed seriously with Franklin's views and policies. That the young man was an enemy to Smith and the Proprietary Party is made clear by abundant evidence. That he was involved in schemes to injure the College of Philadelphia is shown by his letter to Galloway. There seems little doubt, then, that Smith was again reporting the matter honestly in accusing the son, along with the father, of trying to damage the school.

Smith's second letter to Peters, dated "7ber 14th 1762" (September 14, 1762), is of the same nature and also apparently true. It should be kept in mind, moreover, that Smith could not gain political revenge for old wounds from lying to Peters, since there was little Peters could do to injure Franklin. Earlier in the year he had resigned as Penn's secretary and in May succeeded the Reverend Jenney as rector of Christ Church. This church was still suffering the effects of political and religious divisions, and so the position was bound to occupy most of Peters' time, leaving him little opportunity to discredit Franklin and thereby enhance Smith's position in the Proprietary Party. Then, too, as Smith and other key persons in Pennsylvania knew, Peters was not the man, either mentally or physically, that he had been in earlier years and could not be expected to confront the powerful Franklin and his allies. It seems clear that Smith's compelling reason for writing to Peters was to protect the College by advertising Franklin's conduct.[143]

An unnamed "eminent Dissenter called on me," the Provost wrote, to inform him that "Dr. Franklin took uncommon Pains to misrepresent our Academy before he went away and to sundry of their People; saying that it was a narrow bigotted Institution, got into the Hands of Proprietary Party as an Engine of Government and that Dissenters had no Chance in it. . . ." According to Smith, Franklin said that were it not for these faults the Assembly would support the school and that Smith and the trustees had no need "to beg," seeing that they had only to right matters to get sufficient funds. But, the letter continues, Franklin made himself disgusting to the Dissenter and once Smith proved to his satisfaction that Francis Alison supported the collection, the man promised "40 Guineas to the Design."[144] Although Smith claims a victory here, he nevertheless betrays his guilt and his deep nonprofessional concern in the matter by pleading with Peters not only to deny

Franklin's charges, but also those of the Reverend Charles Beatty, whose efforts to raise money, ostensibly for the widows and orphans of Presbyterian ministers, the Provost sought to undermine.[145]

Franklin was well aware of the lingering and only partly submerged hostility between Anglicans and Presbyterians. Moreover, he knew well what few people in England were likely to know—that the College was involved in proprietary politics.[146] Smith's earlier trial in Pennsylvania and his appeal in England, after all, had on the surface nothing to do with politics. The legal issue concerned the alleged libel on the Assembly and their right to imprison him as they did. Further, the school appeared to be a catholic institution. Though Smith and most of the trustees were Anglicans, nearly all the faculty were Presbyterians, and one of its most distinguished members, Kinnersley, was a Baptist. Only someone intimately familiar with the school could know of the religious infighting, and Franklin had even earlier made just such charges of which Smith accused him. For example, in 1756, after he lost influence in the school, Franklin wrote to Peter Collinson that the College had been declining seriously because of Smith's intrigues. The Provost, he claimed, was now disliked by everyone except the Proprietary Party and its supporters, who alone would benefit from his schemes.[147] Then, in the previously quoted letter to Kinnersley, the disgusted Franklin, three years after he resigned as President of the Board of Trustees, accused his political enemies of having betrayed him and the school for the sake of proprietary politics.[148] It was widely known that Franklin was hurt deeply by being forced out of the school, and Richard Peters thought that the personal issue was a very important factor in Franklin's implacable hatred of Smith and in his efforts against the College.[149] Smith's charges against Franklin, then, are also entirely consistent with those made by the Reverend Duché to William Franklin and which he in turn was pleased to report to Galloway, his friend and his father's political ally.

Smith was representing matters accurately in these and other letters. No one knew better than Franklin that the stated intention of the original trustees was to keep the institution free of sectarian and, consequently, political disputes. No one knew better than its disenchanted and angry founder that the school desperately needed the support of people of different denominations who would give money to a truly catholic institution. No one knew better how to get back, through the school, at the Presbyterian-dominated Proprietary Party that seemed to the Assembly and its leader to threaten Pennsylvania's cherished liberties and even to supplant Quaker-Franklin rule by that of some

Anglicans and a horde of Presbyterians. Because he dreaded the consequences of a proprietary victory, and because he believed that the College had been made an instrument of this group's politics, Franklin used his intimate knowledge to injure the school of which he had once been the very "Soul."

In cultivating William's Anglophilia[150] and his anti-Presbyterianism, Franklin played a major role in the alienation and grief that both men were to suffer a decade later when the son became a loyalist and went to England to spend the remainder of his long life. Colonial politics did nothing to change William's views. At least as much as "that miscreant Parson Smith," he hated William Allen, the leader and chief strategist of the Proprietary Party, as well as one of the most prominent Old Side Presbyterians in the Middle Colonies.[151] They and other foes working for Thomas Penn kept up a steady barrage of abuse against both Franklins. Angered, William betrayed the common prejudice of an English gentleman against Scottish opponents, complaining bitterly of "the Vanity and Self-sufficiency which so particularly distinguishes the lower class of the Scottish Nation."[152] Religious matters were indeed an important factor behind William's antipathy toward Dissenters. Writing to Ezra Stiles, Alison urged "a Union among all ye anti-Episcopal churches" in America to block an expected Anglican move to establish an American bishopric and thereby add to the strength and prestige of the Church of England in America. Elsewhere he tried desperately to foment such a union, at least between the Presbyterian factions. In fact, as if to show how compliant—and worried—he was, he adopted the old extreme evangelical positions on Church order and learning, arguing that both were far less important than piety and affecting preaching.[153] Although William did not know of Alison's letter, he did know of the overt hostilities of Dissenters to a bishopric, an institution he much desired. When he assumed office as Royal Governor of New Jersey, he therefore determined to promote the Church of England in his province, as he was obligated to do, and also to upset the fortunes of Presbyterianism, which was not a requirement of his commission.

In New Jersey the two largest groups were the Dissenters and the Quakers, and, according to a contemporary history, the Presbyterians had about twenty percent more houses of worship than the Quakers and more than twice as many as the Anglicans. The history, written by Samuel Smith in 1765, showed the Presbyterians as having forty-six churches, the Friends thirty-eight houses, the Anglicans twenty-one, the same number for the Dutch Calvinists, nineteen for the Baptists, seven for the Dutch Lutherans, two for Seventh-day Baptists, and one for the Moravians.[154] As was the case in Pennsylvania, although the

Presbyterians were more numerous, the Quakers in New Jersey controlled the Assembly and, as Aaron Burr, President of the College of New Jersey, said, in 1751, without intended irony, were "no Friends" to the College.[155]

Governor Franklin worked within this framework to prevent the mounting religious and political influence of Presbyterians in the Middle Colonies by striking at the College of New Jersey.[156] He knew that caution was necessary, though, for he had already made enemies with such prominent Dissenters as Allen, Purviance, and the Shippen family. Moreover, he was aware that another royal governor, Sir Francis Bernard, having earlier tried to work Anglicans into the College, failed miserably when a great furor broke out from the Jersey Presbyterians.[157] Not wanting to make the same fatal mistake and incur the wrath of the whole denomination, the new governor waited for the right time.

It came in 1766. Samuel Finley, the beloved and respected president of the College, died. The New Side was thrown into gloom and confusion. Hostility between Presbyterian factions expressed itself in the Old Side's frustrated attempt to take over the Jersey school with either Alison or Ewing as president. The New Side looked frantically for a new head who would represent its particular views and yet unite the Church against Anglicans and Quakers. Benjamin Rush, by turns, became charming and hysterical in his efforts to convince Dr. John Witherspoon and his wife to come to Princeton. To make matters even worse the Anglicans—with help from Governor Franklin, the Dissenters charged—[158] openly renewed their attempt to get an American bishopric, an office the elder Franklin thought necessary[159] and the younger desired.[160]

In the midst of the turmoil Presbyterians discovered that the governor was trying to take advantage of the harried trustees. The College had always suffered from a lack of funds, and in 1766 William Franklin moved quickly to have approved a change in the school's charter. He promised to improve the College's financial situation if the trustees would merely consent to a revision in their charter which, in effect, would turn the seminary over to the royal governor.[161] The College of New Jersey was the most important Presbyterian institution in the Middle Colonies, for it was the source of most Dissenting ministers. What Franklin was aiming at is clear. Had he been able to control the school, it would have become an Anglican seminary in short order, and the tasks of creating an American bishopric and of thwarting the growing Presbyterian Church—now without its chief native source of supply—would be wonderfully simplified. As local Presbyterians saw matters, the Jersey school was the one orthodox and pious Presbyterian, or even Calvinist, school in America. Harvard and Yale, they felt, had become genteel and were poor bulwarks against episcopacy, and the other colleges were Anglican. Squeezed between the Anglican institutions in Philadelphia and New York, and besieged by hostility from within its own denomination, the College of New Jersey was in a dangerous position. William Franklin, having learned lessons from his father, made matters still more difficult, and he had ample help from the Quaker New Jersey Assembly, which had feared the school from the outset and offered steady opposition to it.[162] Further, Rush, studying medicine in Edinburgh, informed his friends that Governor Franklin was trying to undermine the College by working for an Anglican bishopric in America, and John Ewing made the same charge.[163]

The New Side Presbyterians knew their enemies and throughout America, and even in Scotland, they responded to what Rush called "the schemes of Governor Franklin, Dr. Alison, &c with regard to the College."[164] Rush had been informed of these schemes by his Philadelphia friend, Jonathan Bayard Smith, and in turn alerted Witherspoon as well as Richard Stockton, who was in London.[165] Even the Old Side worried that the College would be wrested from all Presbyterians. Purviance had evidence, he said, that the Franklins and William Smith, a traitor of the first order, had worked out a deal whereby both the proprietor and the Presbyterians would be wrecked by making Pennsylvania a Crown colony and establishing an American bishopric.[166] The New Side, as John Read reported to Benjamin Franklin, responded to Smith's treachery by nominating "some Wits . . . to handle him"[167] and his cause. Nor was the Old Side slow in retaliating against the scheme. William Allen, in the autumn of 1766, informed Thomas Penn of it himself,[168] certain that the proprietor was more loyal to his investment than to the Church of England and would work in England to defeat the move.

Both this plan and the governor's attempt to take over the College of New Jersey eventually failed. But even as Allen was expressing his fear to Penn, William Franklin was preparing a new scheme which, if nothing else worked out, would, he believed, prevent the school from realizing its potential. The Jersey College now needed a president to replace Finley, money, and the freedom to grow. The governor could do nothing about a president, for the trustees meant to keep the school under their control. The Quaker Assembly, however, made certain that the seminary received no public funds, and William undertook the task of stifling its growth insofar as he could by granting a charter for a competing school only fifteen miles from Princeton. This was Queen's College (Rutgers).

The trustees of this institution were warm in their thanks to the young governor, for they had been trying unsuccessfully since 1761 to get a charter. Understandably, they felt it unnecessary to inquire into Franklin's motives, but the Presbyterians saw behind his generosity both in November of 1766 and again in the spring of 1770 when he granted an even more advantageous charter for the Dutch seminary.

Queen's was born in turmoil. One faction of the Dutch Church threw in its lot with King's College and opposed the New Brunswick school which, unlike its rival, sought to educate and ordain its ministers in America rather than in Holland. Although neither faction wanted to give up its identity, both had good relationships with the Anglican churches in America.[169] Neither Dutch group was hostile to the Presbyterian Church, but each had long been holding out, especially against the New Side's attempts to win them over and unite them in the College of New Jersey.[170] The Dutch, as one of the larger groups in the Middle Colonies, would have added to the Presbyterians' strength. Realizing this, the Anglicans also courted their favor, and it is to their credit that the Frelinghuysen faction, at least, resisted all enticements and held out for its own school.

William Franklin avoided any effort to get the Dutch to unite with the Church of England, for they were weary of attempts to Anglicize them. Furthermore, the governor wanted their political support for his father and himself against the Proprietary Party.[171] The chief reasons he granted the charter, however, were to prevent the Presbyterians from swallowing up the Dutch— Witherspoon had pleaded for a union between them and the Presbyterians in the Jersey College[172]— and to give competition to the Presbyterian school.[173]

William's was a shrewd move and the Presbyterians recognized immediately what he had in mind, for they also used the threat of Anglican and Dutch competition to raise money for the College.[174] In 1753 William Livingston of New York, fearful that the competition of King's College would be detrimental to the Presbyterian school, attacked King's as an Anglican effort to ruin the College of New Jersey by drawing away students who would likely go there. That William knew of the charge, made in Livingston's *Independent Reflector*, is almost certain, for the elder Franklin was a subscriber.[175] What the governor actually tried to do surprised the Presbyterians, but his antipathy to them and the New Side school did not, for as an early president of the College of New Jersey bitterly complained, the Church of England and its supporters had always opposed the Presbyterian school.[176]

John Wallace, an important man in Presbyterian affairs, and the Reverend

Johannes Ritzema, whose Dutch faction was loyal to King's College, both recognized William's anti-Presbyterianism and his desire either to take over the College of New Jersey or to ruin it.[177] As might be expected, the tireless Purviance also concerned himself about the establishment of Queen's College and looked upon it as an anti-Presbyterian move.[178] There was no doubt in his mind that Governor Franklin granted the charter "with ye most unfriendly Intentions agst. the present College & the Interest of Presbyterians in general on Accot. of our Opposn to his Father's Polliticks."[179]

As matters turned out, Witherspoon and time solved all problems. The College of New Jersey flourished in spite of Queen's, which did not open its doors until the autumn of 1771. But Governor Franklin showed his hatred at least once more for the denomination that was rapidly becoming the backbone of the political resistance to Parliament. In 1772 he refused the Presbyterians a charter which would permit them to raise funds for the widows and orphans of Dissenting ministers. When representatives of the denomination argued that the Anglican clergy had been enjoying such a charter for some time, Franklin bid them to take their case before the King, who, just four years before the Revolution, had few generous sympathies for the rioting Dissenters. Taking no chances, though, William guarded against their possible success by reminding Lord Hillsborough that in a similar situation Pennsylvania Presbyterians had, once they had been granted a charter, used the funds "to propagate and support the Presbyterian Religion among the new Settlers."[180]

The years as his father's protégé had not been wasted. William Franklin had become a thoroughly conservative gentleman who viewed Presbyterians with a mixture of contempt and fear. One lesson, however, he did not learn. Unlike his father, he could never learn to be pragmatic. He never became the friend of Presbyterians and the opponent of old Anglican and Quaker Tories. Therefore, the time came when the royal governor was deposed by a provincial council made up essentially of Presbyterians, including Witherspoon of the College of New Jersey;[181] and neither this rugged Scotsman nor his brethren forgot what William Franklin had tried to do to Dissenters. Had the council been less rushed, its members might have pondered for a moment the source of the governor's attitudes, but they had more important matters to consider at the time, and besides, Benjamin Franklin was now publicly defending and promoting policies that were given direction by Dissenters.

VI

On Using a Massacre

Franklin's last assault on American Presbyterianism occurred a decade
before the Revolution. The story centers on the Paxton massacres of 1763 and
the use he made of them. Though Franklin was unable to bring his memoirs
up to this time, his outline suggests that the events and his role in them were
going to be distorted and made far less important than they actually were.
Once more his desire to protect his own image and that of his country was
evidently going to lead him to violate historical accuracy. To have revealed
the truth when he and the new nation had so many enemies would have done a
disservice to both.

The story actually begins much earlier than 1763, with the concerted efforts
of Thomas Penn to reestablish what he felt were his legitimate rights in Pennsylvania. In addition to having lost power to the Assembly, he was angered
because many Scotch-Irish frontiersmen had been squatting on his lands. He
ordered his secretary, Richard Peters, to handle the squatters directly and
Peters, accompanied by magistrates, drove them off the land, in some cases
burning their homes. They had to be treated in this way, he wrote, for they
were uncivilized "rabble."[1] Later the proprietor and his friends would
court the westerners and treat them, if not more humanely, at least with
greater sophistication. A few years after Peters had burned their cabins, the
Proprietary Party called on the frontiersmen to join Penn's supporters by
running for political office against those sympathetic to Franklin and the
Quakers.[2] Penn believed that since many of his chief allies were eastern Presbyterians, he would be able to work with and use the numerous Scotch-Irish
on the frontier as well.

The settlers had no love for Friends. Besides the old religious antagonisms,
there was the matter of defense for the western counties. The suffering frontiersmen cared little about the political and economic squabbles between the

proprietor and the Assembly that made defense inadequate, and they attributed their grief to Quaker nonviolence and trade with the Indians. As later became clear, there were also those in the province who believed that the Friends let the settlers die because they hated them. The French and Indian War understandably heightened the bitterness toward the secure and comfortable Quakers, and eventually strict pacifists in the Society of Friends became convinced that Quakers had no business ruling in time of war.

It was difficult for Quakers to relinquish power. Minority that they were and, as they felt, surrounded by enemies, they feared being overwhelmed. Then too they had long been in power and many of them, taking for granted their control of the Assembly, were also psychologically unprepared to step down.[3] Though Israel Pemberton, leader of the pacifists, had left the Assembly in 1751 and hoped all Friends would join him in paying more regard to their peaceful testimony than to power, he was serenely confident of Quaker rule in the province. When his brother John had expressed concern over political affairs, Israel assured him that the Society ran Pennsylvania politics.[4] And there was more than just a trace of smugness in the comment of Speaker of the Assembly Isaac Norris, a nominal Quaker, who wrote that although "there are Scarcely One Hundred" Friends in Lancaster County, they were still chosen to represent the area.[5] As late as 1755 the Yearly Meeting of Ministers and Elders in Philadelphia claimed that there was general "Love and Unity" among members of the Society. The Meeting made the same claim the following year, but this was wishful thinking, for it also noted that "many of the Representatives have absented themselves without giving notice to this meeting particularly several of Philada. . . ."[6] The absenteeism reflected tensions within the Society between pacifists and those Quakers who were willing to provide funds for a defensive war and, under the particular direction of Franklin, work out a militia bill to pay for a volunteer army. The bill excluded Friends from supporting the war effort and so was despised in America and England, yet the Quakers who supported the measure were still violating the sacred pacifist principle to the distress of their more sober brethren.

Even before the French and Indian War some Friends realized that they would one day have to choose between political power and pacifism. One anonymous writer in 1752 left no doubt where he stood on this matter, declaring: "A fighting Quaker's no true Christian. . . ."[7] Two years later a worried John Pemberton took a similar stance, complaining that too many members of the Society had become Quakers in name and speech only and lacked spirit.[8] Friends in England, apprised of this deteriorating situation, sent Samuel Fothergill to America on a religious visit. He too was "painfully disappointed" at the decline in spirituality. "I have been led since we parted," he later wrote to Israel Pemberton, "into a frequent and Deep Suffering in the view & feeling sense of the suffering state of the Church all along, which sitts in the dust, & has on her Mourning weeds. . . ." He sadly reported that he anticipated only a bleak future for the sect unless things changed.[9] In the autumn of 1755, in the midst of frontier troubles and the added problems caused by William Smith's *A Brief State of the Province of Pennsylvania,* James Pemberton wrote to Dr. John Fothergill that this was indeed a time of crisis for Friends. In his letter we can see the motivation behind Pemberton's decision to resign his Assembly seat the following June. While there were still a decent number of the orthodox left in the Society, something dramatic had to be done to call attention to the crucial importance of "the peaceable Testimony, we have long made profession of." To wait out events and hope for the best was to invite ruin. Already many Quakers in the Assembly had proved themselves willing to sacrifice their testimony for power, and as influential men they would surely have a negative influence on others "who may pay more deference than is due to their Judgement."[10]

As far as the Pembertons and their allies were concerned, the non-Quakers in the Assembly deserved little enough respect from Friends. James charged them with deceitfully undermining Quakers by leading them "step by step" along the path to war "much farther than they would formerly have gone." Now those Friends who remained in the Assembly had no opportunity to pull back "with any degree of reputation."[11] The situation of the orthodox was difficult, for they felt themselves surrounded on all sides by obvious enemies, disloyal members of their own sect, and unsympathetic politicians like Franklin.

Yet it is also true that the prospect of a test of strength between Quaker factions, however fraught with danger, was eagerly anticipated by those pacifists who saw the salvation of the Society depending on the willingness of the orthodox "to Suffer for our Testimony" and thereby bring the misguided back into the fold.[12] More practical members among pacifists tried instead to remain in the Assembly for another year and so ran in the elections of October 1755. Though they were reluctant to serve in such perilous times, they were prompted to do so because they were unhappy with the politics of Speaker Isaac Norris and especially of Franklin.[13] In fact, many Friends realized that Franklin was, by 1756, the chief power in the Assembly. It was he alone, after all, who had drafted the militia bill. This was most unusual, since bills were normally drawn up in committee.[14] Small wonder that the strict Quakers were disheartened over their situation. They could not afford to attack and therefore alienate the non-Quakers and militant Quakers in the Assembly, but they had to make certain everyone knew that the Society as a religious body did not support warlike measures.[15]

It was a mistake for the pacifists to run in 1755, for the war seriously increased antipathy toward them in America and England. Men of means and influence reported that they were ready to give up all and flee to England with their families because of the threat of the French and Indians. An angry Pennsylvanian blamed all the problems on "our Damnable Quaker Principal [sic] of non Resistance." He demanded that Parliament take back the province's charter and take full control of the government immediately or, he warned, the French would within eighteen months.[16] He wrote to another correspondent that one of the first things necessary to save the colony was to rid it of Quaker government and influence. All members of the Society, he insisted, had to be ordered out of office and forbidden to treat with Indians.[17] Such measures would have seemed extreme to most Friends, but Samuel Fothergill, writing from England, warned them that Quaker stock had fallen drastically there. The havoc on the frontier and the lack of defense appalled Englishmen, and Smith's "Scurrilous pamphlets" had worked up great anti-Quaker sentiment. It was clear to Fothergill that the Society in Pennsylvania was in grave danger.[18]

While Smith was doubtless a force to be contended with, the Quakers and the Assembly knew that the most persistent clamors were coming from eastern Presbyterians whose natural sympathy for their frontier brethren enhanced their enmity to the Society and the legislature. The Reverend Francis Alison castigated Quakers as traitors to their country.[19] The powerful Old Side leader, Chief Justice William Allen, charged that Franklin and his Quaker allies would enable the French and Indians to conquer Pennsylvania or at the very least to cause a civil war. He foresaw a time in the near future when thousands of frontiersmen, "chiefly Scotch-Irish, will be driven from their Habitations, & . . . come down among Germans & Quakers."[20] As a city man of means Allen also feared such an invasion, but he knew that its threat would be greater to the Friends and Assembly than to local Presbyterians or other members of the Proprietary Party. Thus Allen, like Smith, emphasized the religious issues involved in the matter of defense. Smith, in striving to unite the Presbyterians against the Assembly, accused Friends and their allies of leaving the frontier undefended so that Presbyterians would be killed. He repeated this charge in the late spring of 1756, declaring that Nathaniel Grubb, an assemblyman from Chester County, said that nothing had to be done about defense because "only some Scotch-Irish" were being "killed."[21]

Such charges, of course, made their way back to England. Dr. Fothergill warned that English Presbyterians were cooperating actively with their colonial brethren in trying "to exclude us altogether from legislation, I mean in Pennsylvania." This is something that even Penn did not want to see happen, for he looked with fear on a "Presbyterian Assembly."[22] Still, the attacks on Quakers continued from Presbyterians and their allies. Allen had at first been more circumspect than Smith, but as the tempo of the struggle picked up, he too made very damaging accusations. To the Reverend Samuel Chandler, he wrote that Franklin, the legislature, and the Friends were in league to keep the West unprotected so that Presbyterians would continue to be massacred and thus the denomination kept down.[23] Elsewhere he pleaded with Chandler to persuade the King and Ministry to take immediate action, and he tried to ruin Franklin's effectiveness by charging him falsely with misappropriating public funds and with a general dishonesty.[24] One of Franklin's oldest and closest friends cautioned him rather unnecessarily that his chief enemies and the power behind the Proprietary Party were "the Scots Clan" who wanted to rule the province.[25]

In 1756, however, the religious and political tensions in Pennsylvania were more of a strain on Quakers than on Franklin, for he was in favor of defense. The Meeting of Ministers and Elders in Philadelphia bewailed the great decline in faith and discipline among Friends that year. It was a dark day when respected members of the Society defended those Quaker assemblymen who voted money for war. Pacifists disavowed any connection with the Assembly's action, but feared that the Society would be shattered by political divisions. It even seemed possible to them that serious Quakers would be forced to serve in the militia and pay for defense, thus destroying the credibility of their nonviolent testimony. They therefore hoped that through their allies in England they could reach an agreement with the proprietor which would guarantee their liberties and privileges and preserve the Society.[26] This failing, the pacifists had to remain on good terms with the Assembly, including those of their brethren who voted in conscience for defense. Only the Quakers who actually bore arms in the militia were disowned. With all others there existed an uneasy but necessary communion.[27]

In June 1756, six Friends resigned their Assembly seats and four others refused reelection. On the surface Quaker political power had seriously diminished. Yet the Society knew that it was not quite throwing itself to the wolves.[28] The old members were being replaced by friendly Anglicans who would vote for the Quaker interest on most matters; moreover, even the strictest pacifists looked upon their resignations as a temporary move. Once the war was over they or others like them would return to power. In the meantime, their sacrifice was not only necessary, but it was good public relations as well, both in America and in England.[29] Enemies who saw their resignations as an opportunity to change the political, religious, and social power structure in the province were disappointed.[30]

Nevertheless, the pacifists were worried, and another reason for their concern was the fact that Franklin increasingly controlled the Assembly. James Pemberton angrily declared of him that the "Great Patriot . . . hath discovered little regard to Tender Consciences." Pemberton, in fact, told Samuel Fothergill that it was Franklin who was responsible for many of the Society's problems, for he did not really understand serious Quakers and therefore did not believe them as dedicated to nonviolence as they were. This failure, Pemberton wrote, led Franklin to be "Exceedingly Studious of propagating a martial Spirit."[31] Many Friends shared Pemberton's feeling and anger, and Franklin later discovered that while Quakers in America and England could like and respect him as a man, few trusted him.

In 1757 Franklin was sent to England to defend the Assembly's position on the taxation of the proprietor's lands. The pacifists, who supported the legislature's stand on fair taxation, also hoped the agent would succeed in "removing some Difficulties" English Friends had been experiencing in explaining and defending the conduct of Pennsylvania Quakers with respect to military measures. Half a year later, though, Israel Pemberton had concluded that "as a religious Society we can expect little more from him than a . . . candid representation" of that conduct.[32] Franklin did that much but nothing more; thus it is not surprising that Quakers on both sides of the ocean looked at him with suspicion and fear.[33] Their feelings were widely known, and Penn felt this situation would help him in his battle with the Assembly.[34] Indeed, Penn and his allies may have learned of pacifist distrust of Franklin from such English Friends as John Hunt who complained bitterly that the agent and the Assembly he led were enemies to the Society.[35] Hunt warned that American Quakers had better initiate their own defense and not rely on Franklin at all. Israel Pemberton and other pacifists took his advice, and within a few years succeeded in removing most of the animosity in England against strict Friends.[36]

The pacifists had misunderstood for a time the degree to which their less scrupulous brethren supported Franklin's measures. But there was little that either they or more militant Quakers could do about the political situation. The possibility of an open schism in their ranks was repugnant to all of them,[37] and they carefully avoided encouraging one. At times their desire led them to wishful thinking. The Yearly Meeting for Sufferings in 1756 declared that even those Friends who had remained in the Assembly would gladly relinquish power if the Society had assurances that its religious and civil privileges would be preserved.[38] Various Quaker meetings made numerous such statements, and they were intended as signals to the proprietor that the time was ripe for some kind of accommodation. Neither of them, after all, looked forward to a Presbyterian take over of the colony.

Penn failed to act positively in response to these messages, and the situation of the pacifists became worse. Such Quaker allies of Franklin as Hugh Roberts expressed their support of him by failing to show up at the important yearly meetings without offering any excuse for their absence.[39] There was little hope of trying to work on Speaker Norris, for his position was the same as Franklin's on defense, and he had declared his independence from the Society.[40] Further, Norris was furious with Provost Smith for his anti-Quaker pamphlets and was seeking ways to use his political power to punish him.

Though the Society still enjoyed considerable political influence,[41] all Friends knew that their disunity made them vulnerable to the intrigues of their enemies. They could make a show of accord at home and try to win back friends in England, but they realized that they needed Franklin's help to achieve their ends.[42] In spite of repeated assurances from his allies, the pacifists were still convinced that their agent would not permit Quaker scruples to interfere with his plans for the province. Even so prominent and moderate a Friend as William Logan reported that Franklin had no inclination to help the Society.[43] Indeed, the relationship between the agent and Hunt, an ardent pacifist, deteriorated so badly that they broke off all communications for months.[44]

Proprietary Party members saw what was happening and concluded that Franklin not only ran Pennsylvania politics but that he had "made tools" of his Quaker supporters to gain virtually undisputed authority. At first Penn could not believe that Franklin really enjoyed such power, but his allies, as well as his experience, finally convinced him.[45] Even William Franklin admitted that there had been a struggle for power in the Assembly between his father and Speaker Norris,[46] and that the elder Franklin had emerged the victor. William's confident tone bespoke not only victory but the fact that he knew the Quakers needed his father too much to antagonize him seriously. A decade later, though, when Franklin threatened to bring Pennsylvania under the Crown, showing little concern for Quaker privileges, many Friends openly united to oppose him while others worked behind the scenes.

It was William Penn himself who initially began the sale of the province to the Crown in 1712, and over the years there had been expressions of concern by the Proprietary Party that the King might assume control of the colony.[47] One of the weapons the Assembly occasionally brandished to frighten the proprietor in later years was the request for Pennsylvania to be made a royal colony. English and American Friends, particularly among strict Quakers, assured Thomas Penn that the threat of such a move was just a threat.[48] History had taught them better than to trust their religious and civil freedoms, which were guaranteed by proprietary government, to the uncertain generosity and good will of the Crown and, inevitably, it was believed, to the Church of England. Nonetheless, Franklin later gave the proprietor—and many Quakers as well—genuine cause for worry when he tried to effect just such a change in government. He had long thought about it and ardently desired it. No doubt his hatred for Penn was a major factor in his effort, and so too was his lack of interest in Quaker scruples. At least as important as these matters, however, was his hostility toward and fear of the great mass of Presbyterians in the province. They eventually made up the bulk of the Proprietary Party and became a dangerously potent force for change in Pennsylvania. Although a great many people looked with dismay upon growing Presbyterian influence—most of the Assembly, all the Quakers and the Anglicans, including those within the Proprietary Party—it was Franklin who spearheaded the drive for royal government. Yet in this drive, which at times bordered on the hysterical, he had relatively few behind him. That his efforts were even successfully launched can be attributed to two factors: the terribly strained relations between the Assembly and the proprietor over taxation, which reached a peak in March 1764, and the Paxton massacres which helped unite Presbyterians in the colony and gave those on the frontier a taste of power. Though the tax issue was very important in creating such support as there was for royal government, Franklin's efforts to use the murders and their implications in trying to drum up enthusiasm for the change preceded the revived tax dispute by two months.[49]

The Paxton affairs were the murders of apparently peaceful Christian Indians by Presbyterian frontiersmen,[50] who were tragic sufferers of Indian attacks but also frequent inciters of trouble. The defeat of the British under Braddock in 1755 had emboldened the Indians to undertake widespread warfare on the frontier. The settlers were bitter not only toward the Indians but toward the Assembly that seemed unable or unwilling to protect them. Understandably, some of them made no distinctions among Indians, believing the worst of all of them. The converted Moravian Indians in the Paxton area seemed in danger, but no one did anything to protect them or the frontier. On December 14, 1763, a group of Scotch-Irish Presbyterians from Paxton rode to nearby Conestoga Manor and killed half a dozen Indians who were living there under the protection of the government. Fourteen members of the tribe, who were away at the time of the massacre, were placed in the workhouse at Lancaster for their protection. On December 27, however, the Paxton Boys invaded it and killed the remaining Indians.

The murders caused the predictable outcry from outraged but secure citizens of the Philadelphia area and from both factions of government. Demands were made that the killers be apprehended, but the settlers, either because they feared or they sympathized with those responsible, ignored the government. Flushed by their success, the Paxton Boys and their followers decided to carry their war east and kill the Indians under government protection at Province Island just at the mouth of the Schuylkill. Clearly, the entire government and the city were threatened by the challenge of the frontiersmen. Though they claimed not to mean harm to whites who did not interfere with their design, rumor had it that they also intended to kill Quakers. Israel Pemberton had enough faith in the credibility of this story to leave Philadelphia when the Paxton Boys marched on the city.

By the time some 250 of them reached Germantown, they discovered that the frightened Philadelphians had been organized by Franklin and, with cannon loaded, were ready. The marchers, stopping at Germantown, waited for delegates from the city to come to them. Governor John Penn sent a politically and religiously mixed delegation, including Franklin, to confer with representatives of the settlers, Matthew Smith and James Gibson. After several hours of discussion it was agreed that the frontiersmen would return home and their representatives would remain behind to draw up a statement of the settlers' grievances for the immediate consideration of the governor and the Assembly.[51]

Amid the confusion of events, several things became apparent. There were

Quakers who, to the dismay of the Society, were willing to bear arms to defend their lives and property.[52] More significant were the effects of the march on eastern Presbyterians and the Proprietary Party in general. The settlers discovered that they had supporters in the East,[53] and that the Presbyterian ministers in the Philadelphia area sympathized with them for a variety of reasons, not all of them purely humane. When the clergy erroneously believed that the Paxton Boys were to arrive in Philadelphia about eleven o'clock on Sunday morning, they decided to close their churches and dispense with services for the time. Thus city Presbyterians who were so inclined could join with their brethren against their common enemies, who some thought wore feathers and others were sure wore flat hats. A number of the ministers wanted to use the crisis to gain political and religious advantages for their denomination and suggested sending agents to England to insist on greater representation for the frontier.[54] They claimed to be convinced that the condition of Presbyterians throughout the colony would not improve until they could send more of their number to the Assembly. Although eastern Presbyterians were not about to relinquish control to the West, they recognized in the frontier Presbyterians a source of great strength against Franklin and his allies. Governor Penn, it was therefore commonly alleged, did next to nothing about bringing the murderers to justice, though he made pious noises about the integrity of government and the horror of anarchy. Nor did he do anything to help the westerners. Instead, he merely used their votes in the election of 1764 and left them to try and survive on vague promises of equitable representation in the near future.

The massacres and governmental inefficiency did not set well in England. Not long after the killings, the governor received an angry letter from the King's secretary, the Earl of Halifax, rebuking the government for not defending the frontier and demanding that all its inhabitants be protected at once.[55] This chastisement, once the threat to the city had passed, may have prompted the governor to strengthen his alliance with the frontier speedily, to the disadvantage of Franklin, the Assembly, and their followers. According to one account, as soon as the delegates who had been sent by Governor Penn to meet with the Paxton Boys reported to him that the marchers were returning home, Penn dismissed them, saying that the settlers had been misrepresented and maligned by hostile elements.[56] Although there is no concrete evidence to substantiate the charge, many people, including Franklin, believed that the Proprietary Party also embraced the frontiersmen to use them as a threat against the Assembly to force it to accept the proprietor's position on taxation.

With Philadelphia once more safe, the time was ripe for a pamphlet war. And it is a significant fact that among the most virulent attackers of the Quakers, the Assembly, and Franklin were the eastern Presbyterians who, along with other of Thomas Penn's allies, seemed now to appreciate fully the problems of the westerners and sought to compensate for a lack of tangible help with a flood of billingsgate. The tragedy, almost as terrible as the slaughter of Indians and settlers, which the rhetoric of the pieces at times forces to be subsumed, lies in the cynicism or blindness that makes human beings become less important than principle, prerogative, or wealth; for after all, everyone had long known that the frontiersmen were suffering terribly and that even peaceful Indians were unsafe in difficult times. This was certainly true in 1764, and it should have come as no surprise to the politicians that the Conestoga Indians were in danger. Reliable reporters from former Governor James Hamilton down to ordinary people had informed those in power of the situation.[57] Unfortunately, it proved easier to write diatribes than to take more suitable action.

On the whole the Paxton pamphlets are vulgar religious-political attacks intended to vilify rather than persuade. One anti-Quaker author charges that the Friends' widely publicized virtue is actually a cover-up which enabled them to secretly encourage their Indian allies to kill the Scotch-Irish and still remain above reproach. According to this author, the Quakers want the Presbyterians dead so that they "may lord it o'er the Land,/And have the sole command."[58] This was a charge that was repeated by the representatives of the marchers and probably by James Dove, the famous Philadelphia schoolmaster, as well as by Hugh Williamson, the distinguished Presbyterian mathematics teacher at the College of Philadelphia.[59] Such attacks became an art in the eighteenth century, and one must not usually put much faith in them. But what is most awful and shocking about these accusations is that there is a fair amount of truth in them.

At times the Quakers did express concern for the Scotch-Irish and other settlers on the frontier, and no doubt there were Friends who genuinely grieved for their plight. Nevertheless, most influential Quakers cared only about protecting members of their own Society and the Indians. The evidence for this claim is considerable and antedates the Paxton affair by many years.

Israel Pemberton was furious that, after Braddock's defeat precipitated widespread violence on the frontier, the government should offer a reward for scalps. While his sensitive nature may have been appalled by the notion of bounties, it is also true that he believed "the bloodthirsty Presbyterians" would leap at the chance to make money by killing all Indians, friendly or otherwise.[60] He correctly pointed out that the natives had been grossly mistreated, but it was mere bias that led him to declare that the majority of them were "Innocent" of any wrongdoing. And his attitude is more than a predisposition in favor of Indians and against Presbyterians, for he also defended the savages since they "might be useful" to the Quaker interest.[61]

During Pontiac's rebellion in 1763, many Friends, at least among those out of the Assembly, shared Pemberton's feelings. John Hunt cared nothing about the settlers and worried only about frontier Quakers and Indians.[62] It was the rare Quaker who questioned the conduct of the supposedly converted redmen. Israel Pemberton severely rebuked one such member of the Society for even bringing up the matter.[63] It was far more common and safer to berate the settlers as a parcel of riotous and naturally vicious Presbyterians who had to be stopped from working up and attacking Indians.[64] To James Pemberton the Paxton Boys were simply murderers. He ignored their suffering and attributed their actions solely to the "old Envious persecuting Spirit" of Presbyterianism from which Friends had also suffered.[65] He was convinced that the frontiersmen exaggerated their plight and said that the massacres and other Indian troubles were part of a Presbyterian design to seize control of Pennsylvania.[66]

Quaker fears of a Presbyterian take over were common. George Churchman, a Friend who was closer to the Paxton situation than most, claimed that the Lancaster officials knew beforehand that the Indians were to be slaughtered but did nothing to save them, believing that the Assembly and the Friendly Association would be put in jeopardy because of the killings.[67] To another Quaker who used the same rhetoric as some of those who supported the Paxton Boys, the critical struggle in Pennsylvania, manifested by the slaughter of the Indians, was between the Friends, God's "chosen Children," and the Presbyterian emissaries of darkness who were enemies of God Himself as well as to Quakers.[68] The writer, who lived on the frontier, may have learned that the Presbyterians were determined to get Friends as well as Indians. This, at least, was the fear of frontier Quakers.[69]

Although there are admirable reasons for the sympathy the Society felt for the Indians, their relationship is hardly above suspicion. Not only was there an extensive trade between them, but the Indians did not as a rule attack Quakers, even those who lived in dangerous areas. Samuel Wyly was certain that "there is some thing Providential that they [Indians] Should Notwithstanding their savage Nature Spare friends."[70] The faithful Wyly may not have known that even the strictest Quakers had been making the Lord's work their own.

At a conference in the spring of 1756, when the French and their Indian allies were creating havoc on the frontier, a number of Quakers, including Israel, James, and John Pemberton, Anthony Benezet, John Reynell, and William Logan, met with the "Red Indians" who were led by Scarroydo, the chieftain and spokesman for the Six Nations. The Friends appealed to the Indians to realize that members of the Society had always lived in peace with them and treated them fairly and generously and sympathized with them in their disputes with the land-greedy proprietor and his supporters. Israel Pemberton pleaded with Scarroydo to keep in mind that

> Although we have Long lain hidden and almost Bury'd by the great Numbers of Other People who are come into this Province many of them [whom?] are Men of Different Principles from us, Yet We can inform you that there is a great number in this Citty & other Parts of the Province and Some Even on the Frontiers where a great deal of Blood had been Shedd Who are the Children of William Penn & First Settlers that are Men of the same Peaceable Principles, and who have you as our Brethren[.] We shall now arise and show ourselves unto you, for as We are sorrowfull that Differences between Your Cousins the Delawares and our People we are desirous of using our Endeavour to restore Peace, & if they will stop from doing further Mischief We shall be ready to stand between Them and the Government that They may be forgiven. . . .

Pemberton continued:

> Brethren, As you are Wise Men we desire you to consider in what manner We may soonest be Able to put a Stop to the Shedding for as many of our Friends of the same Peaceable Principles with us for whom you Express so much regard Live in different Parts of the Province & Some on the very Frontiers without something be done soon they may be destroyed among others. Therefore for Their Sakes in particular as well as of our Countrymen in General we are Concerned to have some speedy stop put to the Shedding of Blood[.][71]

Pemberton and his fellows effectively separated Friends from the other endangered settlers. Not that the Quakers wanted Scottish and German frontiersmen murdered, but rather they were trying to protect members of their own sect and leave non-Quakers to fend for themselves. Only the barest effort is made to encourage Scarroydo to intervene in behalf of the vast majority of westerners. These are generalized into the rhetorical abstraction, "our Countrymen in General." Much more concrete, specific, and effective is the attempt to make the frontier Quakers a central part of the Indians' consciousness. Moreover, Pemberton represents the Friends as unanimously adhering to pacifist principles, which was not true. Some of them thought, with Franklin and Norris, that defensive measures were necessary. Unlike the pacifists who left the Assembly for a time, more militant Quakers kept their seats and otherwise supported programs for defense.

Further, in his desire to protect the Society, Pemberton and the others clearly blame the killing on the white non-Quaker population, those who have "almost Bury'd" the "Children of William Penn," whom the Indians justly loved. Pemberton stresses the point that the people who make up the majority of settlers "are Men of Different Principles from us," non-pacifists who, unlike the Friends, do not consider Indians "Brethren." This is his chief and most revealing point. In effect, the Quakers are presenting a mild request for an end to all killing, but they are much more forcefully pleading to the Indians: If the wrongs you have suffered from men whose principles are different from ours necessitate war, please intervene in behalf of Quakers, for they have always been your brothers. Such a statement as this is strongly indicated, and the message was understood by Scarroydo who tried to put the whites at ease by informing them that the warring Indians "would not hurt any of you if They knew you as Such."

The relationship between Friends and Indians was exploited by the Proprietary Party. Provost Smith was an unrelenting enemy to Quakers, the Assembly, and Franklin and on many occasions used his acid pen to attack them. He nevertheless realized that these were powerful opponents, for he had once been jailed when the Assembly used a slanderous piece of his as the opportunity rather than the reason for imprisoning him. He therefore had to exercise some caution in what he wrote. Still, as early as 1756, the year of the conference between the Quakers and Scarroydo, he boldly accused the Society, the Assembly, and Franklin of keeping the frontier undefended and of aligning themselves with the Indians because they wanted the Germans and especially the Scotch-Irish Presbyterians dead.[72] His charge is too strong to be fair, but there is enough truth in it to have caused fear and consternation in the accused and to have been repeated in one way or another later by supporters of the Paxton Boys.[73]

During the pamphleteering that followed the Paxton murders the anti-Quaker and Assembly writers vilified their opponents on religious, moral, and political grounds. The Friends responded in kind, charging the Presbyterians with being barbarians who provoked the Indians whom they repeatedly robbed, debauched, and murdered in the name of Christ.[74] Samuel Foulke, a Quaker assemblyman from Bucks County, saw no difference between the Paxton killers and all other Pennsylvania Presbyterians. They were all, he said, "tainted with ye same bloody principles to ye Indians & of disaffection to ye Government."[75] Foulke's opinion was shared by another Quaker author who publicly included the Presbyterian clergy in his attack. He warned Friends that the Paxton affair was religious as well as political, and that the Society had determined enemies in the pulpit as well as in the fields. It was clear, the author said, that the marchers and other Dissenters really wanted to kill the Quakers as well as the Indians, but he warned that many of the Society were no longer strict pacifists and would fight to protect themselves.[76] Both the murderers and the threat to the city, charged another anonymous writer, were instigated by the Presbyterian ministers who hoped that such violent measures would "promote the advantage and good of the K_____k."[77] Another author sought to render the frontiersmen completely odious by ridiculing their Scotch dialect and by emphasizing their atrocities. "Thomas Zealot," who is supposed to represent the Paxton Boys, is made to boast about the massacre of the Indians: "we shot six and a wee ane, that was in the Sqaw's Belly; we sculped three; we tomhawked three; we roasted three and a wee ane; and three and a wee ane we gave to the Hogs." Now he and his fellows were ready to "foucht the *Quakers*" as well as the remaining Indians.[78] At this point the writer hits at what had long been a vulnerable spot for Dissenters—their certainty that God was on their side. Thomas asserts that the killings were absolutely justified because the men "were aw Presbyterians," fighting a holy war for the Lord.[79]

Franklin was both reviled[80] and praised[81] in the Paxton pamphlets. While the Dissenters were fired up at his vicious aspersions on their character as a religious body, even more disturbing to them, because it was far more dangerous, was his use of the Paxton riots and their frightening aftermath to take the colony out of the hands of Thomas Penn and put it under the direct control of the King. Just as the governor used the sad affair to effect an alliance with the frontier against the Assembly, so too did Franklin try to use the trouble to bring about a change he ardently desired. He launched his drive for royal government with his *Narrative of the Late Massacres.*

Although it is not the first of the Paxton pamphlets, the *Narrative* is one of the earliest and by far the most influential, for not only is it a very persuasive piece in itself, but everyone knew who had written the unsigned work. It is fair to say, then, that this piece set the tone for the other pro-Quaker and Assembly pamphlets that followed it. For example, Franklin's cohorts took his cue and conveniently ignored the fact that the marchers included a number of Lutherans. This maneuver was intended to avoid alienating the Germans and to make the Presbyterians alone seem responsible for the recent chaos. In trying to make Crown government seem the only safeguard against Presbyterian lawlessness, Franklin exploits the common belief that "To be govern'd is absolutely repugnant to the avowed principle of *Pr____ns*."[82]

One has to go back to some of his journalistic efforts on behalf of George Whitefield to discover pieces so charged with emotion as this one. But there is a crucial difference. Franklin had, for a time, been an ardent supporter of Whitefield. The *Narrative* is sympathetic and moving when it deals with the Indians, but when it deals with the Presbyterians, it becomes the most vindictive piece Franklin had written in the nearly thirty years since he published *A Defense of Mr. Hemphill's Observations*, another anti-Presbyterian diatribe.

Franklin disarms the reader with a startlingly direct and seemingly matter-of-fact first sentence: "These Indians were the Remains of a Tribe of the Six Nations, settled at Conestogoe, and thence called Conestogoe Indians."[83] What Franklin does here is to set up the reader for the still subdued but intensely sympathetic historical account of the relationship between the Six Nations and the white men down to the time of the massacre. The Indians are shown to have been gracious and generous to the whites and always to have honored the treaty of friendship made with William Penn, "which was to last 'as long as the Sun should shine, or the Waters run in the Rivers.' "[84] That the Indians were true to their word is attested to by their having "lived many years in Friendship with their white Neighbours, who loved them for their peaceable inoffensive Behaviour."[85] The attack on them by the Paxton Boys was, then, the first violence on either side, and it was conducted when the Conestoga Indians had diminished to only twenty people, "7 Men, 5 Women and 8 Children, Boys and Girls." These were the "Remains." The word placed carefully in the opening sentence becomes very poignant. Only about one-third of the group were men, the rest women and children, the latter of whom made up forty percent of the whole tribe. In murdering the "Boys and Girls" the frontiersmen ended the history of the whole tribe!

By associating the Indians with such Christian and universal values as benevolence, meekness, loyalty, and honor, Franklin, of course, attributes to their murderers the opposite qualities. Having appealed to the reader on these grounds, he now carefully sets out to personalize the Indians, to make them sympathetic and, insofar as he can, white and English.

He did not know much about them personally. All he had to work with were accounts of them and the massacre given by friends of his and a list of the Indians' original and English names followed by such descriptions as—"a Boy," "a little Girl," "his wife," and "Capt. John's Son."[86] All twenty of the Indians are listed, but Franklin, selecting for effect, chooses twelve for portrayal. The first whom he mentions is Shehaes, "a very old Man." This information Franklin did not learn from the list made up by sheriff John Hay of Lancaster, for he merely noted the Indian's name. Franklin, however, took the trouble to find out that Shehaes had "assisted at the second Treaty held with them by Mr. Penn, in 1701." Shehaes is made venerable because of his age and because of his association with the beloved first proprietor. The murder of a very old man who had treated with William Penn was a piece of evidence that had to work against the Paxton Boys among many in the province. Moreover, Shehaes never violated the treaty, for he had always, we are told, been "a faithful and affectionate Friend to the English," and was well known to be "an exceeding good Man, considering his Education, being naturally of a most kind benevolent Temper."[87] Shehaes is akin to the noble savage, an appealing figure to the eighteenth-century imagination. His virtue is intuitive, for after all, as Franklin tells us, the old man did not have much of an education, which is to say, he did not have the benefits of a Christian education. But the Paxton Boys did. Franklin himself did not have great regard for Indians. He is here merely using them to make the point that goodness is a matter of conduct rather than religious affiliation or presumptions of rectitude and superiority. Shehaes, whose Christianity is not mentioned, is then naturally good, and his Presbyterian murderers are vile.

The second Indian described is the old man's daughter, Peggy. Here two things are worth noting. First, whereas sheriff Hay initially listed the Indians according to where they were killed and then arranged some husbands and wives together, Franklin carefully places them in tight family groups at once, from the grandfather down to the granddaughter, thus making them even more sympathetic and their murderers even more inhuman. Second, wherever Hay provided an English as well as an Indian name for the victims, Franklin sought to gain sympathy for them by using their English names either instead of or in addition to the Indian name. Shehaes had no English name, but old and venerable as he was, Franklin wanted to use him.

His daughter Peggy—a name more likely to arouse pity than Chee-na-wan—is praised for her "filial Duty and Tenderness," an important virtue to parents who would read the *Narrative*. Although she had a family of her own to care for, she was constant in her service to her aged father.[88] Her husband, John Smith, "a valuable young Man," had courted her successfully and then settled with her and Shehaes. The couple "had one child, about three years old."[89] Hay did not identify which children and parents belonged together, but Franklin skillfully handles the problem by using the neutral yet personal word, "child." Since Hay did not mention the ages of anyone either, Franklin had to find out how old the child was himself. And the thought of a three year old being murdered is horrifying. So too is the idea of an entire family, three generations, being butchered.

There are also other Indians mentioned. But they are hardly Indians any longer, at least on an emotional level. Franklin has made certain that his readers will be able to identify with them as human beings not essentially different from Englishmen. Indeed, he emphasizes their connection with the English through their loyalty and other qualities and by virtue of their names. There is another Indian named John, "a good old man," his son Harry, who supported him, George and Will Soc, Betty, "a harmless old Woman," her son, Peter, whom Franklin describes in familiar terms as "a likely young Lad," and "Sally, whose Indian name was Wyanjoy," a devoted and "truly good" woman, who, having no children herself, raised the child of a dead relative, bringing it up "as her own" and performing "towards it all the Duties of an affectionate Parent."[90] Franklin uses only two Indian names. In one case he has no choice, and in the other, Wyanjoy, by virtue of her devotion, is clearly made to be Sally in the minds of readers of the *Narrative*. Even those who could not identify well with Indians would nevertheless be likely to appreciate such "white" virtues as Franklin cites. Moreover, the fact that so many of these Indians took English names, we are told, is significant, for they "give themselves, and their Children the Names of such English Persons as they particularly esteem."[91] That this "little Society" which had just welcomed Governor Penn and promised him their fidelity and asked for his protection should have been killed is horrible. Franklin calls attention to the bitter irony of the situation: their address of welcome had hardly been delivered when they fell victims to the "Catastrophe."[92]

The raiders, stripped of every possible excuse for their actions, are made to seem a vicious group of wanton killers. Their crime, as described in the *Narrative*, is not at all a passionate, irrational response to the savagery of warring Indians and the understandable fear and distrust of all of them, but a senseless, carefully premeditated, and cowardly slaughter.[93] The killers did not merely shoot their innocent victims but, surprising them and finding them unarmed (they expected no violence at the hands of their brothers), also "stabbed and hatcheted [them] to Death. The good Shehaes, among the rest, cut to Pieces in his Bed. All of them were scalped, and otherwise horribly mangled. Then their Huts were set on Fire, and most of them burnt down."[94] Franklin imagines for us in vivid terms the satisfied killers going home anticipating laurels from an appreciative mob, congratulating themselves on their deed, and sorry only that fourteen of the tribe were away at the time of the attack. Their cold-bloodedness is contrasted sharply with the "universal Concern" of the Indians' neighbors, who knew them to be good and peaceful, and with the grief of the survivors "when they returned and saw the Desolation, and the butchered half-burnt Bodies of their murdered Parents."[95]

Having made the Indians objects of pity and the Paxton Boys and their followers appear beastly, Franklin next repeats the process in describing the second massacre. The Indians were on their knees protesting their innocence and faithfulness to their white brothers, and in this position they were hacked to death. "Men, Women and little Children—were every one inhumanly murdered!—in cold Blood!"[96] An awful picture, indeed; and one designed to inspire hate as well as sympathy.

Franklin continues by interpreting the violence and the immunity of the killers from justice as both an attack on and a threat to government and order.[97] In doing so he was playing on the old prejudice that Presbyterians could not, or would not, abide by any government. Further, he was challenging a thoroughly incompetent governor and weakened government to do what he knew they could not likely do: bring the killers to justice and rule the inhabitants effectively. Even at this early point, just after the massacres and the threat to the city ended, he was already engaged in embarrassing the government and the Proprietary Party to enlist support for an appeal to the King to take control of the province. He therefore, perhaps remembering some New England sermons, puts on the mask of Jeremiah and prophesies that unless the men are caught and punished, unless the West is controlled, "the Guilt will lie on the whole Land" and "The Blood of the Innocent will cry to Heaven for Vengeance."[98]

Franklin goes on to consider the chief excuse made for the frontiersmen, their repeated suffering at the hands of hostile Indians, and demolishes it. The settlers should have had the courage to strike back at the warring Indians and not vent their hatred on the innocent.[99] This would have been reasonable and honorable; but these murderers—and here Franklin is reminding his readers that the self-styled saints have always assumed special prerogatives—did not feel the need to handle matters reasonably or honorably. They are positive "they have better Justification," which is "nothing less than the *Word of God.*" They can ignore the biblical injunction against killing and, spouting Scripture to suit their purposes, "justify their Wickedness, by the Command given to Joshua to destroy the Heathen." But the settlers are not the Hebrews, who were more merciful, and so such a defense is a "Horrid Perversion of Scripture and of Religion!"[100] The "Horrid Perversion" is typical of Presbyterian arrogance that, to Franklin, prompts them to crush the head of the serpent no matter when, where, or in what form it appears. It is clear that he is here attacking the Paxton Boys and their supporters as Presbyterians, which for him had long meant irrational, desperate, and degenerate bigots, most of whom were a danger to peace, government, and good men of all persuasions.

The final part of the *Narrative* consists of a historical summary showing that the poor Indians would have been safe among "Heathens, Turks, Saracens, Moors, Negroes" and other Indians—safe even among Spanish Catholics! None of them would have violated the universal laws of hospitality.[101] In fact, Franklin lashes out, the tribe would have been safe anywhere in the world "except in the Neighbourhood of the Christians[102] White Savages of Peckstang and Donegall!"[103] Once more the attack has been on the murderers and their friends who protect them as Presbyterians. Franklin ignores the fact that among those friends were Germans. It was the Scotch-Irish who were the most hated and feared group by him and numerous other Pennsylvanians, and he therefore played upon the common prejudice to make them odious, thereby diminishing their support in the province. It was a technique he had used long before against his enemies in Boston, and he had used it often enough afterward to become a master at abusing all those he lumped together as Presbyterians.

He was worried about the threat they posed to the Assembly and to the character of life in Pennsylvania. It was, then, not enough to show the Paxton Boys, somewhat unfairly, to be inexcusable villains; their villainy must be related to their religion. Presbyterianism is made the antithesis of morality and true Christianity. After the *Narrative* appeared it became substantially easier and even respectable to vilify the murderers and the marchers as Presbyterians. One writer, perhaps Isaac Hunt, following Franklin's lead, felt comfortable explaining that, as everyone had always known, "Presbyterianism and Rebellion were twin-Sisters,"[104] and that the Dissenters learned "from Mahomet to propagate ther [sic] Religion with the Sword."[105] And as for that religion, it was obvious that it was based not on a veneration of God, but only of "the Presbytery."[106]

One of the most significant accomplishments of the *Narrative* was that it unmistakably brought out into the open the political implications of the whole affair: the Presbyterians on the frontier were challenging a government which neither represented nor protected them effectively. As things turned out, once Governor Penn apparently worked out a political alliance with the marchers through their representatives, the Quakers and the Assembly came to be engaged in what seemed a life or death struggle with a coalition of proprietary Anglicans and virtually all the Presbyterians in the province. Franklin saw immediately that he and the Assembly stood a fair chance of having the reins of power snatched from them by a party dominated by Presbyterians. The prospect horrified him, but how could it be prevented? By ending proprietary rule and putting the province under the protection of the Crown. Such a change would likely bring to bear also the Church of England, and it was no secret that Anglicans longed for an American bishop. The influence of the Crown and its Church would, among other things, surely stifle the ambitions of Presbyterians and also repay Thomas Penn for his handling of the colony.

Nearly everyone of importance recognized early what Franklin was planning. Not long after the *Narrative* appeared Hugh Williamson charged Franklin and his lieutenant and chief political ally, Joseph Galloway, with trying to bring about royal government. Considerably worried, Williamson warned his fellow Presbyterians of the scheme, and in Great Britain as well as in America they responded actively to protect themselves. William Allen, in England, showed the proprietor a letter sent to him and to Dr. Samuel Chandler expressing opposition to the change. Three of the most influential Presbyterians in the colony signed a circular letter that was intended to make all members of their denomination realize that Franklin's plan was really an attempt to have the privileges of all Presbyterians "greatly *Abridged*." Samuel Purviance later appealed with Presbyterians to forget their factional differences and defeat Franklin politically, for he was defaming them.[107]

The plan to change the government did have some support. Disgust with

Penn and especially the pervasive fear of Presbyterian ascendancy brought Franklin allies. One writer flatly declared that if the Presbyterians gained control of the province, all other groups would lose their religious and civil liberties.[108] Another spokesman for the change argued that "we ought all to be alarm'd, and try to stem the Torrent of Presbyterianism, which is pouring down upon us . . . and if not timely prevented will, with more than *vandalic* Barbarity, bury us, our Religion and Liberties, in one general Inundation."[109] Still another writer agreed and said that the only hope decent people had, indeed the cure for all the colony's ills, was Crown government.[110] So intense was the hostility of some Friends that one of them wrote: "had I any number of children, I would sooner bring them up to the implicit belief of the Alcoran, than to make them Pennsylvania Presbyterians. . . ."[111]

Yet it would be a serious mistake to think that Quakers in general supported Franklin's plan.[112] In fact, it is far nearer to the truth to say that a great many pacifists were joined by their less scrupulous brethren in opposition to royal government. Their animosity toward Presbyterians and their concern about Presbyterian control in the province, even when taken with their genuine disgust with proprietary politics, were still not enough to overcome their fear of what Crown government would mean for their religious and civil liberties. Proprietary government, bad as it was, still protected their freedom and the special privileges which Friends had long enjoyed in Pennsylvania. Few were as confident as Franklin that these would be retained under the King.

James Pemberton, who was an experienced politician, refused to sign Franklin's petition for royal government and called upon other Quakers to recognize the danger in his scheme. He understood what had prompted Franklin and others to sign and work for the change: they were not only fed up with Penn, but had "dreadful apprehensions" of the Presbyterians. They worried that the denomination might one day get "the Legislative as well as the Executive part of Government into their hands, the latter of which they already possess in some Counties, & appear determined" to use "mob" force and "abuse to carry their points." Still, Pemberton had no more trust in the Crown or in Franklin's concern for Quaker privileges than he had of Presbyterians.[113]

Such Friends as Israel and John Pemberton, Hannah Pemberton, Mary Pemberton, John Griffith, Thomas Crosby, and John Hunt, dedicated members of the Society and persons who had long thought the proprietor wrong and utterly penurious in his disputes with the Assembly, nevertheless opposed Franklin's efforts.[114] The great majority of all persuasions in the province agreed. Franklin and his allies waged an intense campaign to promote royal government and to solicit signatures in its behalf. Yet they were able to produce only 3,500 signatures. The Proprietary Party, however, spearheaded by Presbyterians, clergy as well as laity, claimed to have gathered 15,000 signatures opposing the change.[115] It is interesting to note, too, that many of those who signed in behalf of Crown government were Philadelphia Quakers. But judging from reports among Friends, this group was a decided minority of the Society, and it is probable that all of them were doing little more than trying to frighten the proprietor once again. Further, the petitions were not all the same, and some were so cautious in behalf of preserving all liberties and privileges as to permit even strict Quakers to sign them.

Pacifists had long been afraid that, as one of them said, the "unhappy Conduct of our Representatives" led by Franklin would force "an irreparable break" with Penn and pave the way for royal government.[116] In spite of the troubles with the proprietor, it therefore seemed essential to Quaker interest not to effect such a change. The Proprietary Party, well aware of widespread concern among Friends that the political situation might, to their detriment, get out of hand, thought that any serious move for Crown government would be initiated by Franklin. A decade before the campaign, Governor Robert H. Morris had warned that Franklin was capable of the most extreme political measures against the proprietor and his allies.[117] Ferdinand John Paris, Penn's able solicitor and ally, in drawing up the battle lines between the political parties in the colony, was nevertheless confident that Franklin and the Assembly would not have enough support among Quakers or Anglicans to offset Penn's vast margin among Presbyterians. Consequently, as early as 1756 he predicted that the proprietor would never lose the province.[118] Paris had overestimated Penn's support among Anglicans and underestimated Franklin's following with Friends, yet in general his appraisal of the situation was sound. The later opposition of many Quakers and the resignation from the Assembly of the popular and respected Speaker Norris, who did not want the government changed, attest to Paris' foresight.

While Franklin was in England in 1758 pressing the Assembly's claims against Penn, John Hunt and other English Quakers were working with the American pacifists to bring about "an Amicable accommodation of the differences" between the contending parties.[119] Three years later William Logan reported that he, Hunt, and Dr. Fothergill were still working to make peace between Penn and at least strict Quakers.[120] Because the hatred between

Franklin and the proprietor retarded their efforts, English Friends were angry especially at Franklin and wanted him recalled and out of the political picture. It was a serious mistake and a grave danger to the Society, one of them complained, to look upon the agent "as a Second Sir William Pit," for he had never cared much about Quaker concerns and prevented reconciliation with Penn. The writer hoped that all of Franklin's followers in the Society would soon have their eyes opened so that "they may see clearer" for their own benefit. Like his brethren, however, this writer feared making an enemy of the agent, and so added to his correspondent, "Pray, let these Hints of him be to thyself."[121]

When in 1764 Franklin moved forcefully to change the government, Quaker opposition and hostility became more intense and at times more open. Their anxiety over his scheme exceeded their disgust with Penn,[122] and they were further angered by the way Franklin and his allies had crushed Norris and forced his resignation. James Pemberton reported to an English correspondent that he and Norris were both relieved when Franklin had been defeated in the election of that year.[123] James Logan and his family determined that even though Franklin had himself appointed agent to England again, he would not succeed in wresting the government from Penn. He knew, too, that American Friends could rely on a general effort among English Quakers to block all efforts at making Pennsylvania a Crown colony.[124] David Barclay, Sr., an old and prominent English Friend, who despised Franklin as a man and as a politician, refused to allow William Allen to bring him into the proprietary camp.[125] Yet he called Franklin one of those "evil designing selfish Men" who would sell the very freedom of Quakers to gain their private ends. Although the press of business prevented him from being as politically active as other Friends, Barclay also realized that the agent was prompted in his plan by more than an insensitivity to Quaker well being. He was sympathetic, he said, to Franklin's fear of Presbyterians and knew he intended to stop them by bringing the province under the Crown;[126] however, he joined with those Quakers, he said, who took great "Labour and Pains" to bring the Assembly and the proprietor together and thereby defeat Franklin and his supporters.[127]

Dr. Fothergill also worried about the growth of Presbyterian influence in the province and requested that James Pemberton tell him

> By what means can the increase of P.b.t.n. power in America be most effectually chequed consistently with liberty of conscience and the genius of British freedom? I see that sometime—America will be

P.b.t.n⌈,⌉ a persuasion altogether intolerant, and I could wish to re-
tard it, as long as possible.[128]

But Fothergill also eventually gave his wholehearted support to efforts in
behalf of keeping Pennsylvania a proprietary colony[129] and even suggested
that American Friends show their good will to Penn by working through Richard Peters to block Franklin.[130] Fothergill's suggestion was shrewd. Should
Quakers succeed in reaching Penn through Peters, who was now the rector of
Christ Church and no friend to Presbyterianism, the Society might be able to
check both the agent and Presbyterian influence at the same time. James Pemberton thought the plan a good one, for he said that most of Franklin's support for the change of government came from those who believed with him
that it was the only way of "curbing the Insolence of Presbyterian
Cabals."[131] Even the Assembly asserted enough independence to issue cautious instructions to its agent and actual leader, requesting that he do nothing
which would abridge the liberties of the people, and that he gain the approval
of that body before doing anything by way of effecting the change in government.[132] The instructions did little to allay James Pemberton's fears, though,
and in 1765 he decided to return to the Assembly and take an active part in
protecting the Society from Presbyterian attempts to take over the government
and from Franklin's desire to hand it over to the King.[133]

It is to be expected that Penn's allies worked against Franklin. The elder
Edward Shippen praised John Dickinson's speech against Franklin's appointment as agent,[134] and Shippen's nephew, Edward Burd, joined in a
campaign to ruin the career of this "worthless Politician."[135] It is no
surprise either to discover that Allen, Smith, Purviance, Governor Penn,
and others dedicated themselves to protecting the proprietor's interests.[136]
What is more revealing about the hostility which Franklin's scheme
provoked is that so old a friend and associate as David Hall, the former jour-
neyman-printer who became Franklin's partner, turned against his former
master once he was in sole control of the *Pennsylvania Gazette*. Another
friend, the province's highly regarded English agent, Richard Jackson, tried
hard to persuade Franklin to give up his plan for the sake of the people's
rights, but he was unable to deter him. There was little that Franklin or any of
his allies could do about Jackson's opposition, but Hall complained that
Galloway and William Franklin tried to ruin him financially by setting up and
encouraging a new newspaper, the *Pennsylvania Chronicle*, and using it as
their political organ.[137]

That they resorted to such tactics in trying to push through their policies suggests the intensity of the struggle rather than an absence of support. Though those favoring proprietary government greatly outnumbered them, the Franklin forces claimed many of the most eminent Pennsylvanians as allies. Henry Drinker, the wealthy Quaker merchant, his partner and Franklin's friend, Abel James, Thomas Wharton, another prominent Quaker merchant, Hugh Roberts, John Baynton, Philip Syng, Daniel Roberdeau, and many others had signed the petitions in favor of the change. Of course, at least one of the petitions that was eventually submitted was cautious enough to permit even James Pemberton to sign it, for it placed great emphasis on the absolute protection "of those inestimable religious and civil liberties and privileges, which encouraged our forefathers at their own expence, to settle and improve this colony . . . ."[138]

The moderate petitions which were drawn up and passed around by Quakers were, in part, an attempt to ease tensions in the Society between those lending their support to Franklin and those against his plan. But as John Reynell told two English Quakers, the Society in Pennsylvania was suffering great strain. Those who wanted the government changed had given "their Brethren . . . much Pain & uneasiness & made it difficult for ym to know how to act, so as to preserve Peace & concord in the society."[139] Indeed the controversy bred a degree of discord among Friends that few had ever experienced before. Two of Franklin's allies among Quakers, John Drinker and Stephen Collins, charged Israel Pemberton with trying to garner support for the Presbyterians and the Proprietary Party they now controlled to prevent the colony from being brought under the Crown. After reminding Pemberton that it was the Presbyterians who had butchered the innocent Indians at Paxton and had always been enemies to Friends, they warned him to quit politicking "before we join in condemning thee" as others were already doing.[140]

Franklin was the chief architect and most zealous advocate of the scheme. The *Autobiography*, of course, ends its narrative before these events occurred, but previous experience indicates that its author would not have placed his desire for royal government in the context of his fear of and hostility toward Presbyterians. Nevertheless, his vindictiveness toward the denomination and his more or less clandestine struggles against its influence in secular life, though of nearly half a century duration, had not lessened. It was, in fact, the chief consideration in his long and frustrating effort to make Pennsylvania a Crown colony, an effort he stubbornly continued in spite of the will of his countrymen and the growing tensions between America and England.

The Presbyterians understood Franklin's motivation and attacked him savagely. James Pemberton delightedly reported that the Presbyterian effort against Franklin was so uppermost in their minds that they left off abusing Friends. Even the most worried Quakers, he wrote, had to admit that the campaign for royal government was "a great means of Stopping the Progress of ye tumultuous proceeding of the Pr___tns who appear greatly alarmed."[141] James Burd joined the effort of all Presbyterians, of whom his family were leading members, in destroying Franklin's career once and for all before he did permanent injury to the denomination.[142] The anti-Presbyterian thrust of the movement for Crown government forced Thomas Penn, in spite of his inclinations to the contrary, to make the Presbyterians even more certainly the backbone of his party. When problems developed between his nephew, the governor, and leading Presbyterians, he warned John Penn not to forget who their chief allies were. And after Franklin had been defeated in the election of 1764 the proprietor confessed that he was not surprised, having been "assured" of total Presbyterian support.[143]

This much Franklin had anticipated well before the election. In a letter to Richard Jackson he bemoaned the fact that the Presbyterian mob enjoyed a wide following among "the common people" of the province, including Philadelphians.[144] There was, he felt certain, grave danger in such a union, and after the Paxton marchers returned home he harped on the matter for all its worth. Working on Jackson again, who as the colony's agent in England was a key figure in gaining royal government, he warned that the hostilities between Presbyterians and Quakers had become acute. Slighting his own leading and very partisan position in government and in the campaign, he adopted the stance of a benevolent and neutral observer and predicted serious trouble unless the change were made soon. No wonder, he wrote with little concern for accuracy, "All Parties begin now to wish for a King's Government." The present administration is not only incapable of protecting its people from the "armed Mob in the Country," but since the march on Philadelphia has "privately encourag'd" it.[145]

Franklin next worked on convincing eminent Quakers to promote royal government. To Dr. Fothergill he wrote that Pennsylvania Friends had actually been charged with encouraging Indians to kill the Scotch-Irish settlers. What is more incredible, he continued, "thousands" believed the story. Obviously, the belief of such tales speaks not only of credulity, but of a desire to believe them, and their circulation put Quakers in real danger. "Would you imagine that innocent Quakers, Men of Fortune and Character, should think it necessary to fly for Safety out of Philadelphia into the Jersies, fearing the Violence of such armed Mobs, and confiding little in the Power or *Inclination* of the Government to protect them?" The italics brought home the point forcibly, yet he continued to press the matter: "And would you imagine that Strong Suspicions now prevail that those Mobs, after committing 20 barbarous Murders, hitherto unpunish'd, are privately tamper'd with to be made Instruments of Government, to awe the Assembly into Proprietary Measures?" In brief, as Franklin expressed it, all evidence pointed to the inescapable fact that if the King did not assume control of the province quickly there would be anarchy, for "we shall soon have no Government at all."[146]

Such accounts of the situation in Pennsylvania were clearly designed to be read nervously as well as sympathetically, and Franklin sent off many of them. Peter Collinson, another prominent Quaker, was also an object of the scare campaign. Franklin told him that the Paxton pamphlets were part of the Presbyterian plan "to excite a mad armed Mob to massacre" the Friends. If this seemed farfetched to Collinson, especially in light of the fact that many Quakers opposed royal government, Franklin warns him that "it is my Opinion they are still in some Danger, more than they themselves seem to apprehend, as our Government has neither Goodwill nor Authority enough to protect them."[147] Those Friends who wanted to remain under a proprietary government were blind to their own danger; however, as an outsider who wished well to the Society, Franklin had a more accurate understanding of the situation. There is no hint in these letters that Franklin is himself an interested party. Instead, he presents himself as the disinterested good man who wants to do what is best for his country and for his friends. The picture is not unlike the one he paints in his memoirs, but truth demands that it be retouched considerably.

He expected that his correspondents would be concerned, and he spread the word in England to other potentially sympathetic persons and, in doing so, helped prepare the way for royal government. But he did not rely on letters alone. In the early spring of 1764 he published his *Cool Thoughts on the Present Situation of Our Public Affairs*. Ostensibly, the piece is intended to overcome the bitterness in the province and present rational reasons in behalf of Crown government. He therefore tries to reduce tensions by removing the conflict from the very personal and charged matter of religion: "Religion has happily nothing to do with our present Differences, tho' great Pains is taken to lug it into the Squabble."[148] The statement is absurd, as he knew, but Franklin is here trying to negate one of the points he realized his adversaries would exploit. He himself, in fact, deals with the religious issue at length. To placate Dissenters, including Quakers, he presents a long historical argument which is intended to prove that the Crown is the true protector of the rights and liberties of all Dissenters. Further, to those who fear that a royal government will cause an American bishopric to be established and therefore disadvantage other sects and denominations, Franklin says that they are surely wrong and unduly nervous. Moreover, he points out blandly, it is senseless to complain about the bishopric, for necessity makes one inevitable. It is simply too expensive and inconvenient for one to have to go to England for ordination. The crucial matter is one of liberty, and he is certain that non-Anglicans would never be injured by the Church of England or an American bishop.[149]

Franklin's efforts to pacify Dissenters on the matter of the bishopric are transparent. In other ways he deals more insidiously with Quakers and Presbyterians. He had to be careful to avoid charges of bigotry, and so on the pretense of defending the Friends from accusations of hatred to the proprietor because he left the Society and became an Anglican, Franklin says that this situation has nothing to do with any of the difficulties in the province.[150] This was hardly true, but the fact is that it is Franklin himself who brings up the matter and hits a very sensitive Quaker nerve. Everyone knew the facts, and fair-minded people realized that while many members of the Society resented Penn's act, there were other causes for the displeasure with him. The reason Franklin brought up the matter was to work on Quaker resentment and thereby gain additional support for the change in government.

Further on he discusses the Paxton affair and once more plays on fear and hatred. "Mobs assemble and kill (we scarce dare say murder) Numbers of innocent People in cold Blood, who were under the Protection of the Government," and yet that government only "truckles" to them. Since *Cool Thoughts*, which is dated April 12, 1764, appeared not long after the Paxton murders and frightening march on Philadelphia, Franklin did not have to specify what mobs he meant. Nor did he have to identify them as Presbyterians, since he and others had already attacked them as such. Moreover, he had made the same point numerous times: the proprietor's chief support is Presbyterian, and the government will do nothing to alienate the denomination, not even apprehend murderers and protect innocent people. Consequently, "honest Citizens, threatened in their Lives and Fortunes, flie the Province, as having no Confidence in Publick Protection." The Friends did not have to be reminded which "honest Citizens" Franklin had in mind, and he warned them that they could expect "more of these Tumults" daily.[151]

Continuing his determined efforts through the summer, Franklin bombarded correspondents with letters pleading for the change.[152] In addition, he wrote a "Preface" to Galloway's speech in support of the measure. Although the speech was lengthy, the half-desperate "Preface" was even longer. Franklin again and again repeats the points he had made numerous times before,[153] and they all lead to one conclusion: either the Crown or chaos. The only thing new in the "Preface" is his open attack on "the Presbyterian Clergy of Philadelphia" and their brethren in "every Congregation in the County" who, as proprietary "Allies," opposed Crown government.[154]

As the heat of the campaign increased, Franklin relentlessly appealed to anti-Presbyterian sentiments and betrayed his own hatred of the denomination. The "Mobs" that were terrorizing the West were bestial, he wrote Jackson, "And I am sorry to tell you, that . . . being Presbyterians, the whole Posse of that Sect, Priests and People, have foolishly thought themselves under a Necessity of justifying . . . their mad and bloody Brethren. . . ."[155] He knew that his words condemned the innocent along with the guilty and painted a very slanted picture of the situation, but this was his customary rhetoric for Presbyterians, developed over years of struggle against them. And now they seemed to him on the verge of seizing the province.[156] He confessed to his old friend Strahan a month before the election of 1764 that the denomination and he were "bitter Enemies." If he should fail and they succeed, he wrote with more truth than jest, "Behold me a Londoner for the rest of my Days."[157]

The politically experienced eastern Presbyterians were no more happy than Franklin over the Paxton murders. John Ewing, a distinguished member of the denomination, thought the settlers justified, but he nonetheless bewailed the fact that their actions gave Franklin the excuse he needed to injure the denomination with the campaign for royal government.[158] After Franklin, having lost the election, had himself sent to England as agent for the province to oppose the Stamp Act and to work for the change, Presbyterians led the effort at having him recalled. Purviance worked furiously to effect a coalition between members of his denomination and Quakers in Chester County, realizing that many of the Friends opposed Franklin's scheme. He joined this effort with a drive for "a general confederacy" among Presbyterians, Germans, and Baptists aimed at having the agent brought home.[159] After the Stamp Act was passed, Presbyterians were in the forefront of the attempt to destroy Franklin's reputation by spreading the rumor that he had tried to ingratiate himself to America's enemies by supporting the tax. The story was believed by many in Pennsylvania, as Joseph Shippen informed the proprietor, and

Franklin had little support left in the province. He hoped, he continued, that with all the effort being expended in Pennsylvania and England, the plan to bring the colony under the Crown would fail, reunite the proprietor with the people, and wreck Franklin's political career.[160]

The attempts to vilify the agent's character were so frequent and common that even James Pemberton, who was glad Franklin had lost the election, was thoroughly disgusted by them.[161] Still, as he wrote Dr. Fothergill, more and worse could be expected, since the Presbyterians all realized that the campaign for royal government was directed at neutralizing them as a political and social force in the province.[162]

Continuing their vigorous opposition to the measure, a number of Philadelphians, claiming that their views represented those of three-fourths of the people, issued a "Remonstrance" against the appointment of Franklin as agent in England,[163] and John Dickinson led a group of Assemblymen in protesting the appointment.[164] The protesters were certain that Franklin, caring little about the welfare of the province, sought to go to England only to change the government. Hoping to stop him, Allen and Governor Penn released information they had known for months but had withheld: the proprietor had yielded to the more equitable taxation of his lands. The news, coming at this late date, in any case, failed to produce the desired effect, and Franklin was appointed agent on October 24, 1764.

His enemies responded in an angry *Protest* which dredged up many of the scandalous charges that had recently helped turn him out of the Assembly.[165] As far as Franklin was concerned the attack was another in a long series of difficulties he had encountered at the hands of Presbyterians and their allies. He had had too much of them in battles that had gone back more than forty years. Furious, therefore, in a manner and to a degree that is entirely inconsistent with the persona of the memoirs and with the popular picture of him, he responded viciously in his *Remarks on a Late Protest*. He lashed out at and condemned the intrigues of his enemies in the past election and clearly identified them with the Paxton "Murderers" and their brethren, "those religious Bigots, who are of all Savages the most brutish."[166] The *Remarks* was published on November 5, two days before he set out for England. Little more than a month later he settled back comfortably in his old Craven Street lodgings among friends and admirers. He let the Presbyterians worry about what would come next.

He had ended his *Remarks* by donning a mask he would wear often in his personal and political writings in the years ahead; a mask designed to create an image of himself as the aging and benevolent philosopher, saying that he was now taking "Leave (perhaps a last Leave)" of his country. "I wish," he continued, "every kind of Prosperity to my Friends, and I forgive my Enemies." Franklin may have wished well to his friends, but he was not to forgive the Presbyterians and other enemies for some years yet.

Though Allen struck back at him for his animosity to Presbyterians,[167] Franklin learned that his *Remarks* had left the denomination in great fear of what he would attempt against it in England. Led by their ministers, Presbyterians therefore redoubled their efforts to foil his schemes.[168] The situation in the province became so tense that Thomas Wharton, a loyal Franklin supporter, feared that his friend might have gone too far in displaying his hostility toward the denomination. Many of them told him, Wharton wrote, "that had their Society been left unnoticed by thee—it might be well enough."[169]

As matters stood the Proprietary Party had trust in its ability to block Franklin in England and his allies in the colony. The governor ruffled the Assembly by replacing their men with loyal Presbyterians in provincial offices. Joseph Galloway and others feared the beginning of a political catastrophe.[170] Wharton forgot his other concerns and pleaded with Franklin to push through the change immediately.[171] The agent agreed that things had reached a very serious stage. Pennsylvania, he wrote in the winter, could not be left to fall "totally under the domination of Presbyterians."[172]

Purviance, by his relentless efforts to unite his denomination and all others who would join against Franklin, proved that Assembly and Quaker worries did little to put Presbyterians at ease. Writing to James Burd in the autumn of 1765, Purviance claimed to have proof that the agent was discrediting "our Society" in England and was plotting against it. There could be no rest, he warned, as long as "our dangerous enemy" had any power anywhere.[173] This feeling was shared by Presbyterians generally and largely accounts for their intensified smear campaign against Franklin, which sank to the level of accusations that he had betrayed his country by privately supporting the Stamp Act.[174]

The desperation of Presbyterians is easily understood, for the effort to gain royal government had come at an especially bad time for them. By the middle of the 1760's the Anglican clergy in America had begun once more an energetic campaign for an American bishopric. Indeed, Franklin had tried to allay widespread fears of the bishopric in his *Cool Thoughts*. It is doubtful, to say the least, that anyone could have had much success in convincing Dissenters generally that they had nothing to fear from the Church of England. Always hostile to the idea of a bishop in America, they at times seemed to forget their vastly superior numbers and organization in the colonies and acted as if they were a defenseless minority about to be swallowed up whole to appease an insatiable Anglican appetite for power. Now, however, the separate efforts of Franklin and the Anglican clergy created real problems for at least Presbyterians in Pennsylvania, though there were many Quakers who also looked with disfavor on the idea of a bishopric.

Presbyterians had long felt, however, that it was they who stood to lose most at the hands of Anglicans. Ezra Stiles had warned them in 1760 that the once insignificant Anglican population, as he wrote in *A Discourse on the Christian Union* . . . , had grown to 12,600, a number to be reckoned with. The Church of England clergy added to Presbyterian fears by their frequent appeals to those in power at "Home" for an American bishop.[175] It had been generally believed, moreover, that certain men, Provost Smith for one, were prime candidates for the honor. To Churchmen and Dissenters alike the bishopric seemed imminent in 1765, and Franklin's activities in England, many felt, aided the Anglican cause.

Pennsylvania Presbyterians, in particular, then, were beset by problems. Further, their task of blocking Franklin and the drive for the bishopric was complicated by the continuing struggle within their own ranks between Old and New sides. William Atlee, for example, thought the election of 1765 critical and called upon all Presbyterians to join forces against their enemies. Yet Atlee worked privately for the denominational supremacy of the New Side over their conservative brethren.[176] The battle between Presbyterian factions was, again, carried on in the colleges as well, at least until John Witherspoon took command and the politics of Empire became more important than intradenominational hostilities. In the meantime, with the elder Franklin working against Presbyterians in England and the younger one against them in New Jersey, they had a difficult time.[177]

Francis Alison had reliable information and good insights into the activities of the Franklins and Anglicans, and he was clearly worried. His welcoming of Witherspoon, in fact, was significant in at least reducing tensions between Presbyterian groups. He correctly saw that members of his denomination had more to fear from efforts to make Pennsylvania a royal colony and to promote the bishopric than from each other. Indeed, he saw these two threats as having the same dangerous end: "an English American Pope."[178] In 1767 he took comfort in the growing political crisis, since he knew that it would thwart the schemes of enemies to Presbyterian influence.[179]

Their strength, however, was a mixed blessing. Not only did Quakers reject a coalition between Friends and Presbyterians, but some of them hoped for the bishopric that would check the rising power of their old enemies while still resisting Crown government.[180] This was by no means an unorthodox view, and James Pemberton, writing to Dr. Fothergill, said that the bishopric seemed the Society's best hope of putting Presbyterians in their place.[181]

Thomas Penn, who was closer than the Quakers or most American Anglicans to those who decided about such matters as bishops, declared as early as 1767 that the argument in the colonies was futile. England was not about to make the colonists even more independent than they were proving themselves to be by providing them the means of ordaining ministers in America.[182] Still Anglican ministers continued to hope. Just two years before the Revolution, the Reverend Jacob Duché called for a bishop and, incredibly, charged his Presbyterian opponents with bigotry for suggesting that so laudable an institution as the Church of England would even consider lording it over Dissenters or interfering with their progress in any way.[183]

Duché's lack of realism is merely amusing. Franklin's is not. Resistance to his scheme at home and the worsening political situation did not deter him from desiring the change in government and pressing for it whenever he could. The proprietor was astounded that the normally realistic and pragmatic agent hung on so tenaciously to his plan. With an optimism that can be described as micawberish, he deluded himself, Galloway, William Franklin, and many others as well. He wrote with nearly complete inaccuracy, that "there is scarce a Man in or out of the Ministry that has not now a favourable Opinion of the propos'd Change of governmt.," and that it was only the "present violent Heats" that retarded his efforts to bring Pennsylvania under the King. Even after the Privy Council refused to consider the petitions for change, Franklin remained hopeful and determined. He tried to enlist general Anglican support behind him by an utterly bigoted, anti-Presbyterian argument which insisted that the success of the Church of England in America, and the consequent diminution of Dissenters, depended on its ability and willingness to establish itself in America. He left no doubt in his correspondent's mind that the Church of England could gain only if the government in England overcame its reluctance to excite Dissenters and asserted itself in America as it had in England, where the Church was prospering and "Dissenters are continually Diminishing, & tis thought will be all in the Church in less than another Century."[184] That Franklin could still be thinking along these lines measures less his enchantment with the British Empire than it gauges his hostility toward Presbyterians;[185] for he was steadily becoming less an Anglophile, and the letter was written in the spring of 1768, when he had already rebuked England severely for its treatment of America. Even after he wrote despairingly to Galloway in the late summer of that year that the change seemed impossible under the antagonistic administration of Hillsborough, he persisted in vain and foolish efforts in behalf of royal government until at least the winter of 1769.[186]

Events, however, conspired against Franklin and forced him to unite with his Congregationalist and Presbyterian adversaries. A new common enemy was emerging and old hatreds would have to be pushed aside as best they could. Almost as soon as he arrived in England, Franklin became so immersed in the affairs of the Stamp Act that he had less opportunity than he would have liked to effect the change. As his loyalty to America became clear even to his enemies, he along with his countrymen were scored repeatedly in the British press. Such treatment of Americans and himself, along with his eye-opening experiences of the political and moral corruption in England, which he had so long idealized, caused him to change his mind about royal government. He therefore wisely dropped the matter during 1769. Years later he admitted that he had been "fond to a Folly of our British Connections."[187] He learned slowly that his dream of a British Empire influenced by good men like himself, his United Party for Virtue, would not be realized in Great Britain.

Epilogue

Franklin's animosity toward Presbyterians, and theirs toward him, continued for a time even after he gave up his plan for Crown government. Yet by the autumn of 1768 the antagonistic parties in Pennsylvania had temporarily, at least, put aside personal quarrels and tried to decide what to do about British colonial policy.[1] Franklin, moreover, had been working to make peace for himself and his son with those Presbyterians—clergy as well as laity—who were coming to the forefront of patriotic resistance.[2] By the next year he was expressing his keen resentment that hack writers for the Ministry were condemning Bostonians, ridiculing them as lawless Puritans, for "a trifling Riot" when there were so many "mischievious Mobs and murderous Riots" in England involving John Wilkes and his followers.[3] As he lost respect for much of the Establishment in England, Franklin found himself defending the quality of his countrymen more and more, particularly Calvinists, who were the most savagely attacked. Eventually their cause became unmistakably and unreservedly his own, and by the time he returned to Philadelphia in 1775 they were firm allies. For the rest of his life, partly for propaganda reasons, but often with complete seriousness, he glorified and sentimentalized the infant nation and its limitless prospects far more than he had done for England. He no longer feared or hated his former enemies. They were patriots and heroes together in a magnificent, world-changing, providential struggle for mankind.

Writing to his daughter Sally in 1779, the seventy-three-year-old Franklin pointed out that he had definite plans for her son, who was with him in France. "Ben, if I should live long enough to want it, is like to be another comfort to me. . . ." He therefore planned for the boy the best education possible for an American of the future: "As I intend him for a Presbyterian as well as a republican, I have sent him to finish his education at Geneva."[4]

Franklin had come a long way since his days as Silence Dogood and perhaps an even longer way since his *Narrative* of 1764 and his efforts to bring Pennsylvania under the Crown. His plans for his grandson undoubtedly reflect his enthusiasm for his country's cause. Nevertheless, it seems that they also indicate that he was in part making amends for half a century of hostility, vilification and, often enough, bigotry. His old hatred was irrevelant and harmful in 1779. If discovered, it could then or later injure his country and tarnish his own reputation seriously. He therefore presented instead to the world images that would serve national as well as personal goals. The persona, though Benjamin Franklin, was also a typical American whose life was proof for Americans and foreigners alike that opportunity abounded in the young country. Franklin said nothing in his *Autobiography* or his other late writings to mar such a picture, least of all of the animosities and schemes that by the time he began his life story had become unimportant and disgusting as well as potentially dangerous. If the persona of the memoirs is, as has often been charged, a rather bland, emotionless, reasoning machine that grinds out one success after another with regularity, and if the nation depicted offers too few challenges and seems a trifle dull to some modern readers, both were still quite useful and their creator's intention was at best noble and at least completely human. These are not minor achievements, and Franklin would have been content with them.

Notes

Abbreviations

The following abbreviations are used in the Notes to this book.

Aldridge, *Nature's God*	Alfred Owen Aldridge, *Benjamin Franklin and Nature's God* (Durham, N.C., 1967)
APS	American Philosophical Society
Autobiography	*The Autobiography of Benjamin Franklin,* ed. Leonard W. Labaree et al. (New Haven, 1964)
Courant	*The New England Courant*
CR	*Critical Review*
[Duché], *Observations*	[Jacob Duché, Jr.], *Observations on a Variety of Subjects, Literary, Moral, and Religious. In a series of Original Letters* . . . (Philadelphia, 1774)
Ecclesiastical Records . . . New York	*Ecclesiastical Records of the State of New York,* 7 vols. (Albany, 1901-16)
FHLS	Friends Historical Library, Swarthmore
Gazette	*Pennsylvania Gazette*
GNDA	*Gazetteer and New Daily Advertiser*
Hanna	William S. Hanna, *Benjamin Franklin and Pennsylvania Politics* (Stanford, 1964)

Historical Collections	*Historical Collections Relating to the American Colonial Church*, ed. William S. Perry, 5 vols. II: *Pennsylvania* (Hartford, 1871)
HSP	Historical Society of Pennsylvania
Hutson, *Pennsylvania Politics*	James H. Hutson, *Pennsylvania Politics, 1746-1770* (Princeton, 1972)
Journals	*George Whitefield's Journals,* ed. William Wale, London, [1905]
LC	*London Chronicle*
Letterbooks	Letterbooks of Thomas Penn
Letters of Benjamin Rush	*Letters of Benjamin Rush*, ed. L.H. Butterfield, 2 vols. (Princeton, 1951)
Maxson	Charles H. Maxson, *The Great Awakening in the Middle Colonies* (Chicago, 1920)
MHS	Massachusetts Historical Society
Papers	*The Papers of Benjamin Franklin*, ed. Leonard W. Labaree et al., 17 vols. (New Haven, 1959-)
PHS	Presbyterian Historical Society
POC	Penn Official Correspondence
Records	*Records of the Presbyterian Church in the United States*, ed. William H. Roberts, enlarged ed. (Philadelphia, 1904)
[Smith], *Brief State*	[William Smith], *A Brief State of the Province of Pennsylvania . . .* (London, 1755)
[Smith], *Brief View*	[William Smith], *A Brief View of the Conduct of Pennsylvania, for the Year 1755* (London, 1756)

Stiles, ed. Dexter

Extracts from the Itineraries and Other Miscellanies of Ezra Stiles, 1755-1794, with a Selection from his Correspondence, ed. Franklin B. Dexter (New Haven, 1916)

Trinterud

Leonard J. Trinterud, *The Forming of an American Tradition* (Philadelphia, 1949)

Writings

The Writings of Benjamin Franklin, ed. Albert H. Smyth, 10 vols. (New York, 1905-7)

Notes   Chapter I

1. Aldridge, *Nature's God*, pp. 9-10.

2. For Adams' criticism of Franklin see Charles F. Adams, *The Life and Works of John Adams*, 10 vols. (Boston, 1850-56), I, 659-64. Van Doren's view of Adams' attack is expressed in his *Benjamin Franklin* (New York, 1938), p. 600.

3. Charles Angoff, *A Literary History of the American People* (New York, 1931), pp. 296, 299-300, 302-10.

4. Frank Davidson, "Three Patterns of Living," *Bulletin*, American Association of University Professors, 34 (Summer 1948), 368-70.

5. D.H. Lawrence, *Studies in Classic American Literature* (London, 1924), pp. 15-16.

6. Lawrence, p. 26.

7. Another student of Franklin has argued very convincingly that William probably did not know of his father's memoirs until after the elder Franklin had died in 1790. See Jack C. Barnes, "Benjamin Franklin and His Memoirs," Diss., University of Maryland, 1954, pp. 5-7. The letter form to William thus seems to be only a device and, I believe, one designed to disguise Franklin's real intention in his memoirs: the creation of favorable images of himself and of America. Further, as others, including Barnes, have noted (pp. 6-7), Franklin used the same device in 1775 in another work. On his way back from England to Philadelphia he composed "An Account of the Negotiations in London for Effecting a Reconciliation Between Great Britain and the American Colonies." This 33,000 word piece is clearly a public document which bears no signature or closing statement. There is nothing of personal warmth here between father and son; nor is there any reference to William's Tory sentiments that were leading to estrangement and total alienation later. Yet this document also begins with the salutation, "Dear Son," indicating that Franklin was here too using a convenient tool for helping him say what he wanted. Barnes has pointed out, too, that in addressing his memoirs to his son, Franklin was following an established literary tradition, for the salutation to one's son was a device commonly used in memoirs and conduct books throughout the seventeenth and eighteenth centuries. Many of these works were also replete with moral advice and moralistic in tone (p. 6). This last point fits in well with Barnes' view of the memoirs as a moral guide for young readers (pp. 27-28).

8. In addition to Barnes' excellent dissertation, another of the best commentaries on the *Autobiography* is the study by David Levin of its persona: "The Autobiography of Benjamin Franklin: The Puritan Experimenter in Life and Art," *Yale Review*, 53 (1963/64), 258-75. Levin recognizes, as do others, that Franklin thought of the hero of his story as the prototypical American. Yet Levin, Lawrence, and other critics do not see the relationship between this persona and the political and social situation in America between 1771 and 1790; the situation that, along with Franklin's desire to offset negative images of himself and his country, prompted him to conceive of his memoirs as a personal and national public relations piece. Another student, missing what I take to be Franklin's chief intentions in the memoirs, complains that the *Autobiography* fails to "give form" to its author's deism. Instead it expresses his pluralism, for Franklin failed to achieve a consistent picture of himself or, consequently, a clear design for his memoirs. See Robert F. Sayre, *The Examined Self: Benjamin Franklin, Henry Adams, Henry James* (Princeton, 1964), pp. 3-43. John G. Cawelti, though, is among those who contend that the *Autobiography* does have a central plan, and for Cawelti it is Franklin's portrayal of himself as the new man who is to be judged by his usefulness to society rather than by his rank in life. See *Apostles of the Self-Made Man* (Chicago, 1965), pp. 11-12. Richard Amacher finds it difficult to treat the memoirs as an important literary work. Interestingly, Amacher offers excellent insights into a number of Franklin's political masks, but he does not concern himself much with the persona of the *Autobiography*. See *Benjamin Franklin* (New York, 1962), pp. 38-50, 68-72, 78-89. Unfortunately, Bruce I. Granger's *Ben-*

jamin Franklin: An American Man of Letters (Ithaca, N.Y., 1964), though the best book on Franklin as a writer, offers little that is new on the memoirs. In a summary of Franklin scholarship, J. A. Leo Lemay notes that in the *Autobiography* Franklin portrayed himself as "an example of the American Dream." See "Franklin and the *Autobiography:* An Essay on Recent Scholarship," *Eighteenth Century Studies,* 1, (1967), 201.

9. *Autobiography,* pp. 69-71.

10. The author, perhaps Hugh Williamson, well-known Presbyterian and professor in the College of Philadelphia, included a note which explained what he meant by the "Great Doctor's *Triming.*" Franklin had, he charged, given vent to his hostility against Germans by supporting measures which prevented them from having just representation in the province, and on another occasion complained of the "*Palatine Boors.*" This is the same man, the author reminds his readers, who has claimed "to be the Friend and Patron of those people." Even the Quakers were not immune to his hatred, for he once proposed that he and a "very considerable Gentleman in this City ... should Unite in Order to demolish the Quakers entirely.... Even when last in *England,* tho' supported by the Influence of those very People, He privately made Merit of it, That he had effectually put an end to their growth in this province." *Papers,* XI, 382.

11. *Papers,* XI, 381-84.

12. *Papers,* XI, 408-12.

13. *Papers,* XII, 259, 267, 273-74, 312-13, 315-16, 320-30, 374; James H. Hutson, "An Investigation of the Inarticulate: Philadelphia's White Oaks," *William and Mary Quarterly,* Third Series, 28 (1971), 3-25.

14. *Papers,* XIII, 268, 273, 285, 313, 397.

15. *Papers,* XII, 240, 259, 274, 312n., 315-23, 329-30, 360.

16. *Papers,* XIII, 177-78.

17. *Papers,* XV, 14-16.

18. *Writings,* VI, 213-14.

19. Franklin was especially sensitive on this matter after he had been charged repeatedly with secretly supporting the Stamp Act. Though the accusation was false, he was reviled both in England and America. See *Papers,* XI, 267, 365, 366, 387-88, 406-7; Verner W. Crane, *Benjamin Franklin's Letters to the Press, 1758-1775* (Chapel Hill, N.C., 1950), pp. 73-75.

20. See, for example, Crane, pp. 102, 108, 153-55; *GNDA,* 17 January 1769.

21. *Writings,* IX, 151.

22. *Writings,* X, 252.

23. *Writings,* VI, 213-14. On the date of this piece, "Rodrigue and Fell," see also Crane, p. 153.

24. *Papers,* XVII, 314.

25. *Writings,* V, 298.

26. *Writings,* VI, 137, 145.

27. *Writings,* VI, 190-91.

28. Crane, pp. 240-44.

29. Crane, p. 249.

30. *Writings,* VI, 258-89; Crane, pp. 253-54.

31. *Writings,* VII, 10, 26.

32. *Writings,* VII, 347.

33. *Writings,* VII, 47-52.

34. The importance of personal matters in Franklin's public business with these men has been discussed by the following authors: Hanna, pp. 83-87; Ralph Ketcham, "Benjamin Franklin and William Smith: New Light on an Old Philadelphia Quarrel," *Pennsylvania Magazine of History and Biography,* 88 (1964), 142-63; James H. Hutson, "Benjamin Franklin and William Smith: More Light on an Old Philadelphia Quarrel," *Pennsylvania Magazine of History and Biography,* 93 (1969), 109-13. Also see the present author's articles on Franklin and Smith: "Franklin Looks for a Rector," *Journal of Presbyterian History,* 48 (1970), 176-88; "Benjamin Franklin and William Smith: Their School and Their Dispute," *Historical Magazine of the Protestant Episcopal Church,* 39 (1970), 361-82. One need not go as far as Professor Hanna in attributing the political split between Franklin and Penn to personal pique rather than to principles to realize that Franklin was human enough to permit private affairs to influence his thinking on politics and on his opponents generally.

35. *Writings,* VI, 176.

36. *Writings*, VI, 179-80, 190, 191.
37. *Writings*, VI, 214-18, 223-36, 228-30, 231-33; Crane, pp. 240-44, 245-46.
38. *Writings*, IX, 180.
39. *Writings*, IX, 644.
40. *Writings*, X, 84-85.
41. *Autobiography*, p. 192.
42. *Autobiography*, pp. 246-48. Franklin's enemies began creating the image of him as a self-serving, unprincipled politician early in his career. Governor Robert H. Morris, a Penn supporter, believed that Franklin used the turmoil in Pennsylvania politics to get himself sent over to England and established there at public expense. He knew that Franklin was sure of a great welcome among the learned in England and planned never to return to America. See Robert H. Morris to Richard Peters, June 26, 1757, Peters Papers. HSP.
43. *Autobiography*, pp. 238-39.
44. *Papers*, X, 210, 236; XI, 370n., 373-74, 383, 411-12, 438-41, 498, 501-2.
45. On his frugality see *Autobiography*, pp. 63, 79, 83, 125-26, 144, 145, 149, 151, 157, 163, 164.
46. *Autobiography*, p. 145.
47. *Autobiography*, p. 128.
48. Roy Pascal notes that Franklin treats his faults "with the same simplicity and ironical equanimity as he does . . . his achievements and wisdom." See *Design and Truth in Autobiography* (Cambridge, 1960), p. 37. Another Franklin student has pointed out that the image he created of himself in the memoirs was so powerful that it "overshadowed the repeated attempts of later writers to complete the story," at least before the Civil War. One of the reasons for this problem is that Franklin permits us only to "half see what happened during his early life." What we do get from the *Autobiography* is a picture of the "self-made man" who inevitably overcomes obstacles and gets on well in life. See Richard D. Miles, "The American Image of Benjamin Franklin," *American Quarterly*, 9 (1957), 117-43.
49. *Autobiography*, pp. 98-99.
50. *Autobiography*, pp. 99-102.
51. *Autobiography*, pp. 204-7.

52. *Autobiography*, pp. 172-73, 208.
53. *Autobiography*, pp. 185, 197.
54. *Papers*, IV, 234.
55. *Papers*, XI, 328, 376, 381.
56. Aldridge, *Nature's God*, pp. 222-24.
57. *Papers*, II, 54, 64.
58. *Autobiography*, p. 146.
59. *Autobiography*, p. 194.
60. Two students of autobiography in general have called Franklin's memoirs one of the basic types of autobiography: that of the Hero who, having understood the values implicit in the myth of his country, seeks to make his life correspond to the promise of that myth. The autobiography of such a figure will, then, be a fulfillment of the prophecy implicit in the national myth. There is no evidence that Franklin saw America in mythic terms or that he so constructed his life very long before he began thinking of himself as a national representative who could be of service to himself and to his country. See William C. Spengemann and L. R. Lundquist, "Autobiography and the American Myth," *American Quarterly*, 17 (1965), 509-10.
61. Crane, pp. 30-35; *Writings*, VI, 246-47.
62. *GNDA*, 14 May 1764.
63. *GNDA*, 23 October 1765.
64. *GNDA*, 3 January 1766.
65. *LC*, 11-13 February 1766.
66. *GNDA*, 7 January 1766.
67. *GNDA*, 21 January 1766.
68. *GNDA*, 4 February 1766.
69. *GNDA*, 11 February 1766.
70. Honorius in *GNDA*, 31 March 1766.
71. [John Ewer], John Lord Bishop of Landaff, *A Sermon Preached before the Incorporated Society of the Propagation of the Gospel in Foreign Parts* . . . (London, 1767), p. 19.
72. *Sermon Preached at St. Mary le Bow, February 17, 1769* (London, 1769), pp. 26, 27.
73. *GNDA*, 16 January 1770.
74. *GNDA*, 17 February, 4 June, 15 June, 20 July, 9 November, 1770.
75. *GNDA*, 12 November 1770.
76. *GNDA*, 4 June 1770.
77. Crane, pp. 30-283, reprints many of the

letters, but suggests that there are probably others as yet unnoticed.

78. Whitefield J. Bell, Jr., "Scottish Emigration to America: A Letter of Dr. Charles Nisbet to Dr. John Witherspoon, 1784," *William and Mary Quarterly*, Third Series, 11 (1954), 276-87; Edward E. Proper, "Colonial Immigration Laws," *Columbia University Studies in Economics and Public Law* (New York, 1900), XII, 75-76; *The Literary Diary of Ezra Stiles*, ed. Franklin B. Dexter, 2 vols. (New York, 1901), I, 192, 219, 404, 410, 417, 425, 428, 453, 615; *Writings*, VI, 10, 11, 20, 34, 35, 291-99.

79. *Writings*, VI, 2-3, 10-11, 20, 34, 35, 105-6, 291-99, 432, VII, 56, 108-9, 371-72; VIII, 354-55; 603-14; IX, 90, 91, 149-50, 256, 318-19, 347, 472-73, 489-90, 493, 495.

80. *Writings*, VIII, 647; IX, 627, 640-42.

81. Benjamin Franklin to John Witherspoon, April 5, 1784. PHS.

82. *Papers*, I, 9-45. The Dogood letters are discussed in the following chapter, but see especially, Nos. 4, 5, 6, 7, 8, 9, 12, and 13.

83. Dogood letters 5, 6, 11, and 13 in particular. For the criticisms of Martha Careful and Caelia Shortface, see *Papers*, I, 111-13.

84. *Papers*, I, 114-16.

85. For the Casuist letters, see *Papers*, I, 163, 221-26, 235-37; Franklin's writings in behalf of Hemphill are in *Papers*, II, 28-33, 37-65, 66-88, 90-126.

86. *Papers*, II, 384-85; IX, 17-18.

87. *Papers*, II, 411.

88. *Papers*, VII, 13.

89. *Papers*, IX, 17-18, 80-81, 90-91, 229-30; X, 102, 167-68, 169, 173, 209, 232-33, 320; XI, 19, 47-69, 77, 102-4, 107, 150-51, 158, 160, 180-81, 185-86, 189, 199-200, 239, 277-311; XII, 234-35; XIII, 416.

90. See, for example, Franklin's letter of February 17, 1758, to his friend and political ally, Joseph Galloway, *Papers*, VII, 375.

91. *Papers*, VIII, 340-41.

92. *Autobiography*, pp. 134-35.

93. *Autobiography*, pp. 43, 157.

94. Examples of this concern appear, for example, in *Papers*, XII, 244-46, 253-55, 406-7, 410-13, 413-16; XIII, 23-26, 26-28, 38-39, 52-54, 54-58, 63-66; XV, 48-50, 54-56, 63-67, 74-76, 111-12, 181-82, 220-22, 224, 239-41; Crane, pp. 169, 172, 195; Le Veillard's letter is in *Writings*, X, 463.

95. *Papers*, XIII, 4-6, 44-49, 54-58, 79-81; XV, 3-13, 63-67; XVI, 23-24.

96. *Papers*, I, 159-61.

97. *Papers*, X, 232-33.

98. *Papers*, X, 167-68, 320.

99. *Papers*, XI, 180-81.

100. *Papers*, XII, 206-8.

101. *Papers*, XIII, 168-70, 177-79, 186-87.

102. *Papers*, XIII, 186-87.

103. This matter is discussed in Chapter VI.

104. Crane, pp. 31-32. Reprinted in *Papers*, XII, 132-35.

105. Crane, pp. 55-57. Reprinted in *Papers*, XIII, 55-58.

106. *Papers*, XIII, 20, 47-48, 55-58; XIV, 64-71, 129-35, 228-32; XV, 81, 181-82.

107. *Papers*, XV, 81.

108. *Papers*, XV, 103-7.

109. *Papers*, XIII, 79-81.

110. Crane, p. 195.

111. Crane, pp. 212-13.

112. *Writings*, V, 362-63.

113. *Writings*, V, 399-405.

114. *Writings*, VI, 3.

115. *Writings*, VI, 78.

116. *Writings*, VI, 310.

117. *Writings*, VI, 312.

118. Crane, pp. 279-82.

119. *Writings*, VI, 409.

120. *Writings*, VI, 430.

121. *Writings*, VI, 431.

122. *Writings*, VII, 1-8.

123. *Writings*, VII, 56.

124. *Writings*, VII, 167.

125. *Writings*, VII, 289.

126. *Writings*, IX, 93.

127. *Writings*, VIII, 647; IX, 627, 640-42.

128. See, for example, *Papers*, XIV, 337-39.

129. *Writings*, VI, 20.

130. *Writings*, VI, 34.

131. *Writings*, VI, 291-99.

132. *Autobiography*, pp. 91-92, 107, 126.

133. *Writings*, VI, 432.

134. *Writings*, VII, 57.

135. *Writings*, VII, 109.

136. *Writings*, VIII, 354-55.

137. *Writings*, VIII, 603-14.

138. *Writings*, IX, 256, 260-64, 318-19, 347, 472-73, 489-90, 495, 530, 551.

139. Barnes, pp. 30-31. Barnes cites written and oral attacks on Franklin that were passed off as biographical information. See pp. 83-84, 171.

Notes   Chapter II

1. Samuel Sewall to Benjamin Colman, September 12, 1721. Colman Papers, I. MHS.

2. MHS, *Collections*, Seventh Series, VIII, *Diary of Cotton Mather, 1709-1724* (Boston, 1912), 639; G. B. Warden provides an excellent history of the town in *Boston, 1689-1776* (Boston, 1970), pp. 60-101.

3. John B. Blake, "The Inoculation Controversy in Boston: 1721-1722," *New England Quarterly*, 25 (1952), 489-506.

4. Warden, pp. 80-101.

5. *Courant*, 7 August 1721 (Boston, 1924-25).

6. Warden, pp. 85-86.

7. The piece is dated 10 August 1721; however, it appears immediately following *Courant*, No. 6.

8. *Courant*, 21 August 1721.

9. *Courant*, 28 August 1721.

10. Cotton Mather to Thomas Prince, June 18, 1723, and Jeremiah Dummer to Cotton Mather, May 1, 1722, Miscellaneous Bound Volume, IX. MHS.

11. [William Douglass], *Postscript to Abuses . . . Obviated* (Boston, 1722), pp. 3, 8.

12. [William Douglass], "Introduction" to *Inoculation as Practiced in Boston* (Boston, 1722).

13. [William Cooper], *A Letter to a Friend in the Country. Attempting a Solution of the Scruples of a . . . Religious Nature . . .* (Boston, 1721), pp. 5, 6.

14. [Cotton Mather], *A Pastoral Letter to Families . . .* (Boston, 1721), p. 15.

15. "A Journal of ye Inoculation at ye Hospital on Spectacle Island," by T. Robie, in "Recompense Wadsworth's Commonplace Book." MHS.

16. Increase Mather, *Advice to Children of Godly Ancestors* (Boston, 1721), p. 2.

17. John Webb, *A Sermon Preached . . . at the Time of the Session . . .* (Boston, 1722), p. 9.

18. *Courant*, 11 June 1722.

19. *Courant*, 8 December 1721.

20. *Autobiography*, pp. 114-15.

21. Franklin says he was born a Presbyterian, but he makes no distinctions between Congregationalists and Presbyterians, calling all Dissenters Presbyterians.

22. I am in debt to Professor Maynard Mack for a number of points he makes in his general discussion of rhetoric and satire. See. "The Muse of Satire," *Yale Review*, 41 (1951-52), 80-92.

23. Though the Widow comes to Boston from the country, her manner and style are decidedly those of a city dweller.

24. *Papers*, I, 9.

25. Perry Miller, *The New England Mind: The Seventeenth Century* (New York, 1939), pp. 66-108.

26. Warden, pp. 81-86.

27. *Papers*, I, 13.

28. *Papers*, I, 30.

29. *Papers*, I, 15-16.

30. "Notebook of John Leverett." Harvard Archives.

31. Seymour E. Harris, *Economics of Harvard* (New York, 1970), p. 100; but also see pp. 85-86, 91-92.

32. *Papers*, I, 17.

33. Relevant to this point is the struggle of three Harvard tutors, Henry Flynt, Nicholas Sever, and Thomas Robie with the Harvard Corporation. Among other things, the tutors complained that they could not live on their salaries. They insisted on more money and demanded that tutors be members of the Cor-

poration. In challenging the Corporation in 1721, they took their complaint all the way up to the governor, the Council, and the House. It is interesting that although the governor and Council supported the Corporation, the House backed the tutors, as it would later support James Franklin. See Harvard College Papers, Doc. 108; "The Memorial of Henry Flynt, Nicholas Sever & Tho. Robie . . . ," in Corporation Papers, 1715-1730, Folder No. 1; John Leverett's "Diary, 1707-1723," for January 4 and September 18, 1721. Harvard Archives. See also Josiah Quincy's *History of Harvard University*, 2 vols. (Boston, 1860), I, 265-321.

34. *Papers*, I, 17.

35. *Papers*, I, 17.

36. *Boston Gazette*, 28 May 1722; *Papers*, I, 18n.

37. Folder entitled "Joshua Gee, 1721-1722" in John Rogers, 1714—, Stephen Sewall, 1728, Librarian's Miscellaneous Records. Harvard Archives.

38. Samuel E. Morison, *Three Centuries of Harvard* (Cambridge, 1936), pp. 60-62, 63, 64, 65-75, 112-13; Leverett, "Diary," March 11, 1721.

39. Harvard College Papers, I, Docs. 115 and 129. Harvard Archives. Quincy, I. 221-23, 283-84.

40. Leverett, "Diary," March 11, 1721.

41. Harvard College Records, I, 139.

42. Mack, "The Muse of Satire," p. 85.

43. *Papers*, I, 21.

44. *Papers*, I, 21.

45. Warden, pp. 80-101.

46. *Papers*, I, 39-42.

47. For a different interpretation of the elegies, see *Colonial American Poetry*, ed. Kenneth Silverman (New York, 1968), pp. 121-31.

48. Nathaniel Morton, *New England's Memorial*, 5th ed. (Boston, 1826), pp. 238-39.

49. On the decline of piety in New England, see Miller, pp. 38, 47, 53, 55, 135, 183, 324-84, 401; Herbert Schneider, *The Puritan Mind* (New York, 1930), pp. 74-101, 153; Alan Simpson, *Puritanism in Old and New England* (Chicago, 1955), pp. 32-38.

50. Thomas C. Simonds, *History of South Boston* (Boston, 1857), p. 38.

51. Ibid., p. 37.

52. Harold S. Jantz, "The First Century of New England Verse," *Proceedings of the American Antiquarian Society*, 53 (1943), 376.

53. Howard S. Hall, *Benjamin Tompson, 1642-1714* (Boston, 1924), pp. 115-17.

54. [James F. Hunnewell], *Early American Poetry, Elegies and Epitaphs, 1677-1717*, The Club of Odd Volumes (Boston, 1896), III, [i]. Harrison T. Meserole, in his excellent edition, *Seventeenth-Century American Poetry* (New York, 1968), p. xxvii, cites Noyes to show the concern with the "excessive pride in poets who have lost sight of moral purpose and instead become enraptured by verbal fireworks," a sign of serious error. Professor Meserole sees wit not as a sign of decay, however, but as a central part of all Puritan poetry, including the elegies, pp. xxix-xxx.

55. Franklin apparently used the name of an actual resident of Salem who died in 1718. See *Papers*, I, 24n.

56. Urian Oakes, *New England Pleaded With . . .* (Cambridge, 1673), p. 25.

57. *Papers*, I, 27-30.

58. *Papers*, I, 27.

59. *Papers*, I, 27-28.

60. *Papers*, I, 28.

61. *Journals of the House of Representatives of Massachusetts*, IV, 10, 11, 12.

62. Ibid., p. 72.

63. *Papers*, I, 30.

64. *Papers*, I, 30.

65. *Papers*, I, 30.

66. *Papers*, I, 31n. The identification of Dudley by the editors of the *Papers* is doubtful, for Dudley had died in 1720.

67. *Papers*, I, 31.

68. *Papers*, I, 33.

69. *Papers*, I, 39-42.

70. Jeremiah Dummer to George Lucas, June 3, 1723, in H.H. Edes Papers, [n.d.]—766. MHS.

71. Letter of Joseph Webb, October 2, 1722, Miscellaneous Bound Volume, IX.

MHS.

72. John Davenport and S. Buckingham to Increase and Cotton Mather, September 25, 1727, Miscellaneous Bound Volume, IX. MHS.

73. *Papers*, I, 43.

74. *Papers*, I, 44.

75. *Papers*, I, 44.

76. *Papers*, I, 49.

77. *Papers*, I, 51.

78. *Papers*, I, 51-52.

79. It should be noted, however, that on December 2, 1722, when the epidemic was past, Cotton Mather preached from 2 Rev. 19 and raised £39, the largest amount ever to have been collected by a minister preaching before the Quarterly Charity Meeting. Three years later, before the same meeting, he set another record by raising £80.15. The Records of the Boston Quarterly Charity Lecture. MHS.

80. *Diary of Cotton Mather*, p. 663.

81. *Autobiography*, p. 68.

82. *Autobiography*, p. 61.

83. *Autobiography*, p. 69.

84. Robert F. Seybolt, *The Town Officials of Colonial Boston, 1634-1775* (Cambridge, 1939), pp. 95, 100, 105, 139, 155.

85. The editors of the *Papers* identify other *Courant* pieces that may have been by Benjamin, and in general these are also satires on the clergy and the secular Establishment in government for permitting the decline of New England's piety and morality (I, 53).

Notes   Chapter III

1. Carl and Jessica Bridenbaugh, *Rebels and Gentlemen: Philadelphia in the Age of Franklin* (New York, 1942), pp. 2, 16, point out the overriding concern for material prosperity of Pennsylvanians. The nonreligious tone of the colony pervaded the Middle Colonies generally, especially where the Quakers were influential. See *Life and Letters of the Reverend John Philip Boehm, Founder of the Reformed Church in Pennsylvania, 1683-1749*, ed. William J. Hinke (Philadelphia, 1916), pp. 83-84, 88, 243-44n., 254-55; Henry E. Jacobs, *A History of the Evangelical Lutheran Church in the United States*, 5th ed., "The American Church History Series" (New York, 1907), IV, 187-93; E.T. Corwin, J.H. Dubbs, and J.T. Hamilton, *A History of the Reformed Church, Dutch, the Reformed Church, German and the Moravian Church in the United States*, 2nd. ed., "The American Church History Series" (New York, 1902), VIII, 133, 134. Though many of the Presbyterian ministers worked prodigiously to promote the Church and piety, the Church had severe problems of many kinds. See *Records, passim.*

2. John T. Ellis, *Catholics in Colonial America* (Baltimore, 1965), p. 374.

3. *Records, passim.* Also see the minutes of the various presbyteries. The records of the Synod and presbyteries are in PHS.

4. Trinterud, p. 32.

5. These were the presbyteries of Philadelphia, New Castle, Long Island, and Snow Hill, the latter of which probably never met. See *Records*, pp. 45-56.

6. C. and J. Bridenbaugh, p. 17.

7. *Records*, p. 60.

8. *Records*, p. 65.

9. In 1722, however, the Synod did suspend Henry Hook for lying, misrepresenting facts, committing "folly and levity unbecoming a gospel minister," and for "obscene actions." *Records*, pp. 72-73.

10. Trinterud, p. 38.

11. *Records*, pp. 67, 68.

12. Trinterud, pp. 41-45. It should be pointed out that even in Scotland there were problems with heterodoxy, as influential Presbyterian ministers taught young divinity students Arminian and Pelagian doctrines. See E.H. Gillett, *History of the Presbyterian Church in the United States*, 2 vols. (Philadelphia, 1873), p. 50.

13. Gillett, p. 54; Maxson, p. 23.

14. Maxson, p. 23; Trinterud, p. 47.

15. The position of the evangelists is discussed in detail in Chapter IV.

16. MS records, Presbytery of Donegal, 1732-1750, pp. 2-3.

17. Ibid., pp. 2-3, 14, 21, 85-86, 112.

18. *Records*, p. 68; Trinterud, p. 39.

19. *Records*, p. 94.

20. There were minor exceptions to the general agreement, but they do not concern the present discussion.

21. *Records*, pp. 98, 173-74; MS records, Donegal, p. 2.

22. Trinterud, p. 47.

23. *Records*, p. 109.

24. MS records, Donegal, p. 12; Trinterud, p. 61; Maxson, p. 35; *Records*, p. 115.

25. Herbert M. Morais, *Deism in Eighteenth Century America* (New York, 1934), p. 15.

26. Morais, p. 15.

27. Morais, p. 60.

28. *The Works of John Locke*, 2 vols., 12th ed. (London, 1824), II, 262.

29. Ibid., pp. 262-65.

30. William Wollaston, *The Religion of Nature Delineated* (London, 1731), pp. 7-31, 167-219; *Papers*, I, 70.

31. Alfred Owen Aldridge correctly points out that Franklin's piece is actually atheistic in its "obliteration of the distinction between virtue and vice." See *Nature's God*, p. 17.

32. *Papers*, I, 70.

33. *Papers*, I, 70-71.

34. *Papers*, I, 70.

35. *Papers*, I, 57.

36. *Papers*, I, 99-100.

37. Pieces written for the Junto will be discussed in chronological order to show the development of Franklin's thinking up to the time of the Hemphill affair.

38. Lord Herbert of Cherbury, *De Religione Laici*, ed. and trans. Harold R. Hutcheson (New Haven, 1944), pp. 87, 89.

39. Ibid., pp. 89, 127, 133.

40. John Ray, *The Wisdom of God Manifested in the Works of the Creation* (London, 1717), p. 18. Franklin thought it "not improper" to read this work, among others, after reciting the prayers in "Articles of Belief." See *Papers*, I, 105.

41. Ray, p. 30.

42. *Papers*, I, 101.

43. *Papers*, I, 103. The views expressed in this piece are reaffirmed in a Junto essay Franklin wrote just three years before the Hemphill trial. See "On the Providence of God in the Government of the World," *Papers*, I, 264-69.

44. *Papers*, I, 102.

45. *Papers*, I, 103.

46. *Papers*, I, 103, 104.

47. Anthony A. Cooper, third Earl of Shaftesbury, "An Inquiry Concerning Virtue," *British Moralists*, ed., L. A. Selby-Bigge, I (Oxford, 1897), 7-10.

48. Ibid., p. 63.

49. [Anthony Collins], *A Discourse on Free-Thinking* (London, 1713), pp. 7, 35, 50-59, 98-99.

50. Ibid., pp. 177-78.

51. *Papers*, I, 116.

52. *Papers*, I, 115.

53. *Papers*, I, 119.

54. *Papers*, I, 127-30. The editors conjecture that Franklin may be satirizing Duncan Campbell, an Englishman who claimed to have second sight. Even if this is the case, the piece is certainly designed to ridicule Presbyterians.

55. *Papers*, I, 182-83.

56. *Papers*, I, 187.

57. *Papers*, I, 187n.

58. *Papers*, I, 192n.

59. *Papers*, I, 192-93. The organization was to be called the Society of the Free and Easy. Just two years before his death Franklin expressed his desire that the Society be deistic in principle and include as its moral and religious doctrines "the essentials of every known religion." These basic points, as he often said, were as follows: there is one God who is the creator of all; He rules providentially; man should worship Him with prayers and thanksgiving; man best serves God, however, by doing good unto other men; the soul is immortal; and, finally, there

is reward or punishment for man's actions "either here or hereafter." See *Autobiography*, p. 162.

60. *Benjamin Franklin: Representative Selections*, ed. Frank L. Mott and Chester E. Jorgenson, rev. ed. (New York, 1962), p. cxxix n.; Melvin M. Johnson, *The Beginnings of Freemasonry in America* (New York, 1924), p. 23. The year he was initiated Franklin wrote his "Doctrine to be Preached," a piece essentially like the "Articles of Belief," except that in the latter work he gave up polytheism.

61. *Papers*, I, 240n.

62. *Papers*, I, 373n., 375n.

63. Van Doren, *Benjamin Franklin*, p. 115.

64. *Papers*, I, 149.

65. *Papers*, I, 159-69.

66. *Papers*, I, 267.

67. *Papers*, I, 267.

68. *Papers*, I, 264-65.

69. *Papers*, I, 261-62.

70. *Papers*, I, 262.

71. *Papers*, II, 15-19.

72. *Papers*, II, 261-62, 264-65; *Autobiography*, pp. 149-50, 159-60.

73. John Tillotson, *Works*, 2 vols., 2nd ed. (London, 1717), I, 55.

74. Tillotson, I, 55.

75. Tillotson, II, 648.

76. Tillotson, II, 648; I, 200.

77. *Sibley's Harvard Graduates, 1690-1700*, ed. Clifford K. Shipton, IV (Cambridge, 1933), 219-20.

78. *Records*, pp. 104-5. Andrews later claimed that Hemphill had been forced upon him by some members of his congregation, a falsehood accepted without question and passed on as gospel to Hemphill's disadvantage by succeeding generations of church historians.

79. *Records*, p. 109.

80. *Autobiography*, pp. 147-48, 167.

81. The Commission was made up of Jonathan Dickinson, Robert Cross, George Gillespie, Alexander Craighead, John Pierson, John Thomson, James Anderson, the moderator, Ebenezer Pemberton, and, incredibly, Andrews himself.

82. Merton C. Christensen, "Franklin on the Hemphill Trial: Deism Versus Presbyterian Orthodoxy," *William and Mary Quarterly*, Third Series, 10 (July 1953), 422-40.

83. *Papers*, II, 38.

84. *Papers*, II, 38.

85. *Papers*, II, 39-40. This may be the ultraconservative Kirkpatrick who did battle with the Reverend Orr.

86. *Papers*, II, 40.

87. *Papers*, II, 32-33.

88. *Papers*, II, 28.

89. *Papers*, II, 27-33.

90. *Papers*, II, 28.

91. *Papers*, II, 28-29.

92. *Papers*, II, 29.

93. *Papers*, II, 29.

94. *Papers*, II, 31-32.

95. *Papers*, II, 31-32.

96. Ebenezer Pemberton, *A Sermon Preach'd before the Commission of the Synod at Philadelphia* (New York, 1735); George Gillespie, *A Treatise against the Deists or Free-Thinkers: Proving the Necessity of Revealed Religion* (Philadelphia, 1735); Robert Cross, *The Danger of Perverting the Gospel of Christ, Represented in a Sermon Preached before the Commission of the Synod at Philadelphia, April 20th, 1735* (New York, 1735). The sermon by Cross does not appear in either Sabin or Evans. It is in PHS.

97. *Papers*, II, 37.

98. *Papers*, II, 37.

99. *Papers*, II, 37.

100. *Papers*, II, 37-38.

101. *Papers*, II, 43.

102. *Papers*, II, 43.

103. *Papers*, II, 40.

104. *Papers*, II, 50-51.

105. *Papers*, II, 50-51.

106. *Papers*, II, 51.

107. *Papers*, II, 52.

108. *Papers*, II, 52-53.

109. *Papers*, II, 52-53.

110. *Papers*, II, 53.

111. *Papers*, II, 53.

112. *Papers*, II, 54.

113. *Papers*, II, 54-55.

114. *Papers*, II, 55.

115. *Papers*, II, 55.

116. *Papers*, II, 56.
117. *Papers*, II, 56.
118. *Papers*, II, 58.
119. *Papers*, II, 59-60.
120. *Papers*, II, 60.
121. *Papers*, II, 60-61.
122. *Papers*, II, 61.
123. *Papers*, II, 61.
124. *Papers*, II, 61.
125. *Papers*, II, 61-62.
126. *Papers*, II, 61-62.
127. *Papers*, II, 63.
128. *Papers*, II, 65.
129. [Thomas Gordon], *A Sermon Preached before the Learned Society of Lincoln's Inn, On January 30, 1732* (London, 1733), p. 2.
130. Ibid., pp. 2-3.
131. Ibid., p. 3.
132. Ibid., p. 11.
133. Ibid., p. 4.
134. Ibid., p. 13.
135. Ibid., p. 24.
136. *Papers*, II, 64.
137. *Papers*, II, 64.
138. *A Vindication of the Reverend Commission of the Synod: In Answer to Some Observations On their Proceedings against Mr. Samuel Hemphill* (Philadelphia, 1735), pp. 1, 2.
139. Ibid., p. 3.
140. The editors of the *Papers* say that although the printer "is probably" the author of the Preface, it is by no means certain that he wrote the body of the pamphlet. He may, they suggest, "have revised it" (*Papers*, II, 65n.). I find no appreciable differences in either the style or tone of *A Letter* from the *Observations* or *A Defense of the Observations*, both of which are Franklin's. It therefore seems likely that *A Letter* is either entirely or fundamentally and substantially his work. Further, Hemphill was not a good enough writer to pen his own sermons so it seems dubious that he did much of the writing of the pamphlets that followed the trial.
141. *Papers*, II, 66.
142. *Papers*, II, 66.
143. *Papers*, II, 66, 67.

144. *Papers*, II, 67.
145. *Papers*, II, 69-70.
146. *Papers*, II, 70, 71.
147. Jonathan Dickinson, *Remarks upon a Pamphlet, Entitled, A Letter to a Friend in the Country . . .* (Philadelphia, 1735), p. 2.
148. Dickinson, p. 4.
149. Dickinson, pp. 5, 6.
150. Dickinson, p. 15.
151. *Papers*, II, 90n.
152. *Papers*, II, 91.
153. *Papers*, II, 92.
154. *Papers*, II, 92.
155. *Papers*, II, 93.
156. *Papers*, II, 95.
157. *Papers*, II, 96-97.
158. *Papers*, II, 101.
159. *Papers*, II, 103.
160. *Papers*, II, 104-5.
161. *Papers*, II, 107.
162. *Papers*, II, 111.
163. *Papers*, II, 113.
164. *Papers*, II, 114.
165. *Papers*, II, 115.
166. *Papers*, II, 115.
167. *Papers*, II, 115.
168. *Papers*, II, 107-10, 120n.
169. The editors of the *Papers* suggest that the name is probably a pseudonym and that Jonathan Dickinson is the actual author of the *Remarks* (II, 91n.).
170. Obadiah Jenkins, *Remarks upon the Defence of the Reverend Mr. Hemphill's Observations . . .* (Philadelphia, 1735), pp. 2-3, 4.
171. *Papers*, II, 90n.
172. *Papers*, II, 90n.
173. Jenkins, p. 18.
174. John Clarke, *An Enquiry into the Cause and Origin of Evil* (London, 1720), pp. 25, 26.
175. Clarke, p. 25.
176. Clarke, pp. 27, 28.
177. Clarke, p. 35.
178. Clarke, pp. 67-68, 72, 296.
179. Benjamin Ibbot, *A Course of Sermons* (London, 1727), pp. 7-9.
180. Ibbot, pp. 165-67.
181. *Autobiography*, p. 167.
182. C. and J. Bridenbaugh, p. 17. The con-

servative party in the Presbyterian Church also could claim some persons of wealth, but not nearly as many as the Friends or the Anglicans of Christ Church.

183. *Account Books Kept by Benjamin Franklin*, 2 vols. (New York, [n.d.]), I, 26-28.

184. *Papers*, II, xxv.

185. Anna J. De Armond, *Andrew Bradford, Colonial Journalist* (Newark, Del., 1949), p. 44.

186. De Armond, p. 20.

187. Leonidas Dodson, *Alexander Spotswood: Governor of Colonial Virginia, 1710-1722* (Philadelphia, 1932), pp. 3-4.

Notes   Chapter IV

1. See, for example, Maxson, *passim*, and Trinterud, pp. 53-108. A more recent account appears in Martin E. Lodge, "The Great Awakening in the Middle Colonies," Diss. University of California, 1964.

2. Trinterud, pp. 65-66.

3. Trinterud, pp. 59, 60.

4. Lodge, pp. 135-36, offers convincing proof of this influence. Also see Peter A.B. Frelinghuysen, Jr., *Theodorous Jacobous Frelinghuysen* (Princeton, 1938), p. 49; *Ecclesiastical Records ... New York*, III, 2,275, IV, 2,466; *An Examination and Refutation of Mr. Gilbert Tennent's Remarks Upon the Protestation ...* (Philadelphia, 1742), p. 97.

5. Gilbert Tennent, "Preface," *The Danger of Forgetting God ...* (New York, 1735).

6. Ibid., pp. 7-8, 10, 18.

7. Gilbert Tennent, *The Espousals or A Passionate Perswasive to a Marriage with the Lamb of God ...* (New York, 1735), pp. 8, 12-13.

8. Gilbert Tennent, *The Necessity of Religious Violence* (New York, 1735), pp. 11, 12.

9. Gilbert Tennent, *A Solemn Warning to the Secure World, from The GOD of Terrible Majesty. Or, The Presumptuous Sinner Detected ...* (Boston, 1735), p. 97.

10. Tennent, *Violence*, pp. 32, 33.

11. Samuel Finley, *The Successful Minister* (Philadelphia, 1764), pp. ii, vi.

12. *Records*, pp. 122, 124-26, 129.

13. *Records*, pp. 126-27.

14. Trinterud, pp. 67-68.

15. *Papers*, II, 140.

16. Jonathan Dickinson, *The Vanity of Human Institutions in the Worship of God* (New York, 1736), p. 14.

17. "The Solemn Scene of the Last Judgment," in [Gilbert Tennent et al.], *Sermons on Sacramental Occasions by diverse ministers* (Boston, 1739), pp. 211-41. The quote appears on p. 239. See also Presbytery of Philadelphia Minutes, pp. 30-31; and Samuel Blair's *The Gospel-Method of Salvation* (Philadelphia, 1737).

18. *Records*, pp. 134-35.

19. *Records*, pp. 141-42.

20. *Records*, pp. 137-38.

21. *Records*, pp. 139-40.

22. Ebenezer Pemberton, *A Sermon Preach'd at the Ordination of Mr. Walter Wilmot ...* (Boston, 1738); and "The Certainty of a Future Judgment," *Sermons on Several Subjects* (Boston, 1738).

23. *Gazette*, 3 January 1738.

24. *Gazette*, 30 November 1738.

25. *Gazette*, 6 December 1738.

26. *Papers*, II, 192.

27. *Gazette*, 30 March 1738.

28. John Rowland, *A narrative of the revival and progress of religion in the towns of Hopewell, Amwell and Maidenhead ...*, appendix to Gilbert Tennent's *A Funeral Sermon occasion'd by the death of Mr. John Rowland ...* (Philadelphia, 1745).

29. *Records*, pp. 144, 145, 147-48.

30. *Records*, p. 146.

31. *Records*, pp. 146-47.

32. *Records*, pp. 147-48.

33. Trinterud, p. 83.

34. Jonathan Dickinson, *The Danger of Schisms and Contentions* . . . (New York, 1739), pp. 6, 9, 12, 14.

35. *Journals*, pp. 343, 362, 363, 374, 384, 387.

36. *Papers*, II, 218.

37. *Papers*, II, 224.

38. *Autobiography*, pp. 114-15, 158.

39. *Papers*, II, 227.

40. *Gazette*, 29 December 1737.

41. *Gazette*, 7 June, 5 July, 12 July, 23 August, 18 October 1739.

42. Elizabeth R. Charles, *Diary of Mrs. Kitty Trevylyan: A Story of the Time of Whitefield and the Wesleys* (New York, 1865), p. 107. Also see Stuart C. Henry, *George Whitefield: Wayfaring Witness* (New York, 1957), pp. 61-63, 177-78. Dudley, Chief Justice of Massachusetts and a Fellow of the Royal Society, claimed that the evangelist's success resulted less from "the matter of his Sermons" than from "the very Serious, Earnest and affectionate delivery of them & without notes." The quote appears in P[aul] Dudley, Commonplace Book kept on interleaves of Joseph Stafford's *Almanack For the Year of our Lord, 1740* (Boston, 1740). Harvard Archives.

43. *Journals*, pp. 335, 337.

44. *Journals*, pp. 338-41.

45. *Journals*, pp. 341, 342, 343.

46. *Journals*, p. 343.

47. *Journals*, p. 344.

48. *Journals*, pp. 344-47.

49. *Journals*, p. 348.

50. *Journals*, pp. 348-49.

51. *Journals*, p. 350.

52. *Journals*, p. 351.

53. *Journals*, p. 351.

54. *Journals*, pp. 352-53.

55. *Journals*, pp. 353, 354.

56. *Journals*, p. 356.

57. *Journals*, p. 358.

58. *Journals*, pp. 361-63.

59. Gilbert Tennent, *The Danger of an Unconverted Ministry* (Philadelphia, 1740), pp. 7, 8, 9, 10.

60. Ibid., p. 15.

61. Ibid., p. 18.

62. *Journals*, pp. 403, 406-7.

63. *Journals*, pp. 406-7.

64. *Journals*, pp. 165-68.

65. Jonathan Dickinson, *A Call to the Weary and Heavy Laden to come unto Christ for Rest* (New York, 1740), pp. 17-18.

66. Ibid., pp. 19-20, 26.

67. *Journals*, p. 412.

68. *Journals*, pp. 417, 419-20.

69. Luke Tyerman, *The Life of the Reverend George Whitefield*, 2 vols. (London, 1876), I, 477.

70. Jonathan Dickinson, *The Witness of the Spirit* (Boston, 1740), *passim*. Though Dickinson admired Whitefield, he was developing serious reservations about him and feared that the orator was a mystic. See Jonathan Dickinson to Thomas Foxcroft, May 24, 1740, Thomas Foxcroft Correspondence, 1740-1759. Princeton University.

71. In addition to the *Gazette* for 1 and 8 May, see Seward's *Journal of a Voyage from Savannah to Philadelphia, and from Philadelphia to England, MDCCXL* (London, 1740), pp. 6-7, 21-22, 61. Also see *Papers*, II, 257-58.

72. Robert Cross et al., *A Protestation to the Synod of Philadelphia, June 1, 1741* (Philadelphia, 1741), p. 3.

73. *Records*, pp. 153-54.

74. Trinterud, p. 97.

75. *The Querists, or An Extract of sundry Passages taken out of Mr. Whitefield's printed Sermons, Journals and Letters: Together with Some Scruples propos'd* . . . (Boston, 1740), p. iii.

76. Ibid., pp. 1-2, 9.

77. *The Works of the Reverend George Whitefield, M.A.*, 8 vols. (London, 1771), IV, 45-49.

78. George Gillespie, *A Sermon against Divisions in Christ's Churches* (Philadelphia, 1740), "Appendix," pp. ix-x, 3.

79. Charles Hodge, *The Constitutional History of the Presbyterian Church in the United States of America* (Philadelphia, 1851), Part II, p. 26; *The Christian History, Containing Accounts of the Revival and Propagation of Religion in Great-Britain & America, 1743,*

ed. Thomas Prince, Jr. (Boston, 1743), p. 255.

80. *Gazette*, 24 July, 14 August 1740. See also Kinnersley's *A Letter to the Rev. Jenkin Jones* . . . (Philadelphia, [1740]). The pro-Whitefield members of the congregation replied in *A Letter to Mr. Ebenezer Kinnersley from his Friend in the Country* . . . (Philadelphia, 1740).

81. *Historical Collections*, II, 208-9.

82. Ibid., p. 207.

83. Ibid., p. 204.

84. Ibid., p. 206.

85. Ibid., p. 203.

86. Archibald Cummings, *Faith absolutely necessary, but not sufficient to Salvation without good Works* (Philadelphia, 1740), pp. iii, vii, ix.

87. *Journals*, p. 486.

88. *Works*, I, 222.

89. *Journals*, pp. 492-93, 494.

90. *Journals*, p. 495.

91. *Journals*, pp. 492-97.

92. Hugh Williamson to Andrew Elliot [sic], May 29, 1762, Andrews-Eliot Papers. MHS; James Burd to Samuel Purviance, Jr., September 10, 1764, Shippen Papers, VI. HSP.

93. [Gilbert Tennent], "The Apology of the Presbytery of New Brunswick," *Remarks upon a Protestation* (Philadelphia, 1741), pp. 4, 47, 48.

94. *Records*, pp. 158-59.

95. Trinterud, pp. 109-10, offers an excellent summary.

96. In 1756, two years before the Church was reunited, Samuel Finley, New Side minister at Nottingham, expressed great concern for order in licensing ministers and thought that all candidates should be examined closely on "ye Confession of Faith" and be licensed "by ye Consociation to which they belong, or to where they design to Labour" rather than by "any 3 or 4 Minrs whom [the candidates choose] to pitch on." Such regulation, Finley held, would upgrade the quality of the ministry and keep it sound. See Samuel Finley to Joseph Bellamy, November 25, 1756, General Manuscript Collection. Princeton University.

97. Hodge, Part II, pp. 30-31.

98. See, for example: *Journals*, pp. 6-7, 8; Tyerman, I, 221-22; Trinterud, pp. 88-94; Henry, pp. 77-78, 151-53; Richard Webster, *A History of the Presbyterian Church in America* (Philadelphia, 1857), pp. 143-44; Frederick B. Tolles, *Quakers and the Atlantic Culture* (New York, 1960), p. 99.

99. *Historical Collections*, II, 214, 216, 230, 235. Peters noted, just five weeks before the schism, that although Whitefield had created "Distractions" among Anglicans, the situation for the Church of England in America was not critical. Richard Peters to Ferdinand John Paris, April 25, 1741, POC, III. HSP.

100. Tolles, pp. 91-92; Minutes of the Friends Yearly Meeting at Philadelphia, for 1740, 1741, and 1742, pp. 421-22, 425-26, 431. FHLS; Judah Foulke to John Smith, March 21, 1740, Correspondence of John Smith, 1740-1770. HSP.

101. Tolles, p. 98; The Philadelphia Yearly Meeting of 1740 wrote to London Friends that American Quakers were living in good Gospel order and unity, and a year later expressed their confidence that they would keep such order. Minutes of the . . . Yearly Meeting . . . for 1740, 1741 and 1742, pp. 421-22, 425-26. FHLS.

102. Tolles, pp. 100, 100-102; Deborah Logan, Extracts from "Selections" of James Logan, Logan Papers, p. 363. HSP.

103. *Papers*, II, 241n., 282n.; Tyerman, I, 338-39, 439; Henry, pp. 62, 163-64.

104. *Works*, V, 216, 341.

105. *Autobiography*, p. 175.

106. *Works*, V, 341.

107. *Works*, V, 95, 126, 300-301, 376-77, 379; VI, 172, 259.

108. Ralph Erskine, *A Letter . . . to the Reverend Mr. George Whitefield* (Philadelphia, 1741), p. 4. This was published by Franklin, though he certainly did not have to rely on the information of others to realize that Whitefield was becoming thoroughly Calvinistic.

109. *Works*, I, 205, 442.

110. *Works*, I, 181-82.

111. *Works*, V, 374, 420-21.

112. *Works*, V, 373.

113. *Works*, V, 228.

114. *Works*, V, 387.

115. *Papers*, I, 103.

116. *Works*, V, 128, 355.

117. *Works*, V, 13, 422; VI, 93, 94.

118. *Works*, V, 127.

119. *Works*, V, 354.

120. *Works*, I, 59-60.

121. *Works*, V, 53, 124, 356-57; VI, 11-12; *Journals*, pp. 342, 346.

122. *Works*, IV, 48, 49.

123. *Works*, IV, 45.

124. See *The Declaration of the Ministers in Barnstable County, relating to the late Practice of Itinerant Preaching* (Boston, 1745); *The Testimony of the President, Professors, Tutors and Hebrew Instructor of Harvard College ... Against the Reverend Mr. George Whitefield, And his Conduct* (Boston, 1744); *The State of Religion in New England, Since the Reverend Mr. George Whitefield's Arrival there* (Glasgow, 1742); George Gillespie, *Remarks upon Mr. George Whitefield, Proving Him a Man under Delusion* (Philadelphia, 1744); Alexander Garden, *Take Heed How Ye Hear* (Charleston, 1741). Even George Thomas, who usually tried to remain at least ostensibly neutral about religious disputes, since he was governor of Pennsylvania, called Whitefield an "Enemy" to the Church of England and to "Government." George Thomas to Edmond, Lord Bishop of London, May 14, 1741, and Richard Hockley to Thomas Penn, February 3, 1739 [1740], POC, III. HSP; Diary of Henry Flynt, 1707-1747, entry for October 12, 1740. Harvard Archives.

125. I have not included Thomas Prince's *Christian History* in any of the ensuing considerations, for these two volumes, published in 1744 and 1745, were written for the sole purpose of promoting revivalism. The volumes can therefore be excluded, for they neither present nor permit negative commentary or information about the revivals or any of the preachers.

126. The *New York Gazette* published its first anti-Whitefield and Awakening item on 20 August 1739; the *Boston Evening-Post* on 17 September 1739; and the *Boston Weekly Post-Boy* on 3 December 1739.

127. The statistics on page 239 are limited to the period of 1739-1743 to focus more closely on Franklin's role in the Awakening and because there were too few items published about the itinerants or the revivals after the summer of 1743 to change the results derived from the statistics.

The *Pennsylvania Gazette* published a total of 223 items about Whitefield (hereafter GW) and the Great Awakening (hereafter GA). Of these 141 were published prior to the end of December 1740. Of these 127 were for GW and GA, and 14 opposed. After this time 82 items were published, 27 for GW and GA and 55 opposed. Of the 141 items published before January 1741, nearly half were glowing reports of GW's success and almost one-third were 700-1,200-word articles of rhapsodic praise of GW and his efforts. Of the 14 items opposing GW and GA, only 2 are as long, and nearly all of the others are advertisements announcing the sale of pamphlets and sermons opposing GW and GA. Franklin did not publish his first item against GW until 46 in his favor had been printed. The first anti-GW piece in the *Gazette* appeared on 8 May 1740, only after Franklin and his competitive Philadelphia printer, Andrew Bradford (*American Weekly Mercury*), had been accused of being in Whitefield's employ. Of the 27 items favoring GW and GA published after the schism, 15 are advertisements announcing his or other evangelists' sermons and defenses of their actions and doctrines; 7 defend GW and *some* of the other evangelists, but deplore disunity and the fanaticism of the most extreme radicals; 5 are poems and articles (only one of which is long) praising GW and GA. Of the 55 items opposing GW and GA, more than half are very long (1,500-2,500 words), and are biting and even vicious attacks on the man and his cause.

128. Since I contend that Whitefield's growing Calvinism was a factor in Franklin's change of mind about him, it might be well to

	(1)	(2)	(3)	(4)	(5)	(6)	(7)	(8)	(9)	(10)	(11)	(12)
Before June 1741												
Pro GW and GA	127	104	52	11	—	52	14	87	18	10	85	13
Anti GW and GA	14	20	35	4	—	11	3	2	2	3	41	6
Total	141	124	87	15	—	63	17	89	20	13	126	19
After June 1741												
Pro GW and GA	27	18	51	10	11	49	18	3	—	5	12	—
Anti GW and GA	55	9	48	3	2	36	19	0	—	3	17	—
Total	82	27	99	13	13	85	37	3	—	8	29	—
Total Pro	154	122	103	19	11	101	32	90	18	15	97	13
Total Anti	69	29	83	9	2	47	22	2	2	6	58	6
Total	223	151	186	28	13	148	54	92	20	21	155	19
Pro GW or GA before first negative item appeared	46	19	3	1	—	2	2	21	0	10	6	3

1. *Pennsylvania Gazette*, 15 September 1739-23 June 1743
2. *American Weekly Mercury*, 17 May 1739-11 August 1743
3. *Boston Evening-Post*, 17 September 1739-8 August 1743
4. *Boston Gazette*, 18 June 1739-13 October 1741
5. *Boston Gazette Weekly Journal*, 10 November 1741-30 November 1742
6. *Boston Weekly News-Letter*, 19 April 1739-23 June 1743
7. *Boston Weekly Post-Boy*, 16 July 1739-30 May 1743
8. *New England Weekly Journal*, 12 June 1739-8 September 1741
9. *New York Gazette*, August 1739-19 May 1740. (Begins with a negative item; very fragmentary.)
10. *New York Weekly Journal*, 10 December 1739-15 February 1742
11. *South Carolina Gazette*, 14 July 1739-1 August 1743
12. *Virginia Gazette*, 1 June 1739-1 February 1740

mention Paul Dudley's view of the orator. Dudley was a latter-day Puritan who hated passionately those who disagreed with his notions of orthodoxy. Yet he accepted and even admired Whitefield as "a very Extraordinary man full of zeal to promote the Kingdom & Interest of our Lord Jesus & in the conversion of Souls." To Dudley, Whitefield's preaching seemed "like that of the old English puritans." Dudley, who was born in 1675, knew what he was talking about. He had not only heard, among others, Increase and Cotton Mather, but was allied with them against the liberalism of Leverett at Harvard. His comparison of the young Anglican with the old Puritans went beyond affecting delivery. Dudley was happy to note that Whitefield's sermons were on "the nature & necessity of Regeneration or Conversion, and Justification by the Righteiousness of xt as recd by faith alone." See Dudley's Commonplace Book. Harvard Archives.

129. *Works*, I, 22.
130. *Papers*, II, 202-4.
131. *Papers*, III, 88.
132. *Papers*, III, 26-27.
133. *Papers*, XI, 231-32.

134. In the winter of 1750 Whitefield expressed his grief that religion was "at so low an Ebb" in Philadelphia. G[eorge] W[hitefield] to William Bradford, February 24, 1750. Miscellaneous Manuscript Collection. APS.

135. *Papers*, III, 383. There had been so much backsliding that the Philadelphia Grand Jury, of which Franklin was a member, called on the mayor and the recorder to rid the city of "Tipling Houses . . . many of which . . . are little better than Nurseries of Vice and Debauchery" and helped give rise to the growing problem of swearing on the streets. See *Papers*, III, 9-12. Whitefield, in the same letter of 1750 to Bradford noted above, hoped fervently that he would, upon arriving in Philadelphia, be able to create another revival.

136. *Papers*, III, 467.

137. *Papers*, IV, 343.

138. *Autobiography*, pp. 201-2.

139. James H. Hutson has suggested that the Presbyterians united only in the middle of 1766, in opposition to English policies and the threat of having an American bishopric established in the colonies. See *Pennsylvania Politics*, p. 210.

140. *Writings*, VIII, 647.

141. *Writings*, IX, 256.

142. *Writings*, IX, 318-19.

143. *Writings*, IX, 640-42.

144. *Writings*, IX, 26.

Notes   Chapter V

1. *Papers*, III, 318.

2. *Papers*, III, 118-19.

3. *Papers*, III, 272-73.

4. *Autobiography*, pp. 161-62. Also see p. 163, where he comments, in 1788, that "I am still of the opinion that it was a practicable Scheme . . ."

5. *Papers*, III, 385.

6. *Papers*, III, 404.

7. *Papers*, III, 413.

8. For a more complete discussion of Franklin's search for the proper man to head the school, see Melvin H. Buxbaum, "Franklin Looks for a Rector," *Journal of Presbyterian History*, 48 (1970), 176-88.

9. *Papers*, IV, 222n.

10. *Samuel Johnson, President of King's College: His Career and Writings*, ed. Herbert W. and Carol Schneider, 4 vols. (New York, 1929), II, 18.

11. Johnson's chief opponent among Presbyterians had for years been Jonathan Dickinson. See Dickinson's letters to Thomas Foxcroft, January 21, 1746, and April 9, 1746, Thomas Foxcroft Correspondence, 1740-1759. Princeton University.

12. [Samuel Johnson], "Advertisement" to *Ethices Elementa* (Boston, 1746), [p. 6].

13. Ibid., pp. 33-34, 35, 36.

14. [Samuel Johnson], *An Introduction to the Study of Philosophy*, 2nd ed. (New London, 1743), pp. ii-iv.

15. *Samuel Johnson*, I, 33.

16. Joseph Shippen, Jr., to Edward Shippen, Sr., November 5, 1750, Shippen MSS. Princeton University. Shippen was a Presbyterian supporter of the College of New Jersey, but the Anglican William Smith, whom Johnson recommended to Franklin for the Philadelphia position, also disparaged Johnson's abilities as a teacher, moralist, and thinker. Smith was capable of ingratitude and intrigue, but since he was writing to another Anglican, Richard Peters, who had reservations about the young Provost, it would seem that Smith either had to have sufficient proof for what he said, or that he was relying on Peters to agree with what may have been a fairly general belief. See William Smith to Richard Peters, July 18, 1754, Peters Papers. HSP.

17. Buxbaum, "Franklin Looks for a Rector," pp. 185-87. The quote is from Alison's undated manuscript, "Of the Rights

of ye Supreame Power, & ye Methods of Acquiring It," which is in PHS.

18. *Papers*, VI, 174.

19. The sensitivity of Anglicans on the matter of anti-Presbyterianism in the Philadelphia school is expressed as late as 1774 in the Reverend Jacob Duché's anonymous work, *Observations on a Variety of Subjects, Literary, Moral, and Religious; In a Series of Original Letters* . . . (Philadelphia, 1774), pp. 24-25.

20. *Samuel Johnson*, I, 399.

21. Ibid., I, 33, 35, 106-7.

22. Ibid., III, 353.

23. Ibid., I, 105.

24. Ibid., III, 20, *passim*.

25. Ibid., III, 41.

26. *Papers*, IV, 37-40.

27. *Papers*, IV, 41.

28. *Papers*, IV, 260-62.

29. Even before he officially took Anglican orders Smith was singled out by the Archbishop of Canterbury as an excellent candidate for the position in Philadelphia. The Archbishop, however, very likely knew that Smith was intending to be ordained. See the Reverend Thomas Herring, Archbishop of Canterbury, to Thomas Penn, September 19, 1753, Penn MSS, Private Correspondence, IV. HSP; Thomas Penn to Richard Peters, March 9, 1754, Letters of Thomas Penn to Richard Peters, 1752-1772. HSP.

30. William Smith, "A General Idea of the College of Mirania," *Discourses on Public Occasions in America* (London, 1762), pp. 41-42. There has recently been published a Johnson reprint edition of this work. The edition is handy and quite clear, but the introduction to it is virtually useless.

31. Smith, *Discourses*, p. 43.

32. Ibid.

33. Ibid., pp. 44-45.

34. In his unpublished manuscript, "On the Liberty of the Press," Smith argued that a free press, "the noblest Privilege purchas'd by our brave & worthy Fathers, with the Toil & Blood of Ages," could never injure Christianity. According to Smith, those who attacked Franklin's friend and partner, James Parker, who printed a deistic piece in his *New York Gazette*, actually "wreak their Private Resentment" and express their lack of charity to "an innocent Man" while wearing a "mask of Zeal" for Christianity. Such people "do more real Dishonour to the Name of Christ" than any deistic writings. The manuscript is dated July 28, 1752, William Smith Papers. HSP. It seems likely that Franklin found out about Smith's defense of Parker, though Parker did not publish it. If so, Smith's piece was bound to make Franklin think well of the young man. See *Papers*, IV, 310-12; also Alfred Owen Aldridge, "Franklin's Deistical Indians," *Proceedings*, APS, 94 (1950), 398-410.

35. *Papers*, IV, 475-76.

36. *Papers*, IV, 512.

37. *Papers*, IV, 512.

38. *Papers*, V, 59. Also see Albert Frank Gegenheimer, *William Smith, Educator and Churchman, 1727-1803* (Philadelphia, 1943), pp. 36, 37.

39. *Papers*, V, 331.

40. *Papers*, V, 331.

41. *Papers*, V, 263.

42. Penn expressed his political-religious plan for the College in letters to James Hamilton, October 18, 1760, and to Richard Peters, December 10, 1762, Letterbooks. HSP.

43. Francis Alison was so thorough and effective a Penn supporter and opponent to Franklin that in 1772 Governor John Penn rewarded him with a "splendid tract of one thousand acres at the confluence of the Bald Eagle with the West Branch of the Susquehanna," Dr. Francis Alison, 1705-1779. Records from Notebook. PHS.

44. There were many reports that Smith was seeking the institution and position of American bishop, and according to one writer he was opposed even by Thomas Penn. *Journals of Charles Beatty*, ed. Guy S. Klett (University Park, Pa., 1962), p. 118.

45. Smith and Franklin both originally thought that the English school and the charity schools were eminently useful. The latter were to be used to "Anglify" the Germans

and to insure their loyalty to England. See Whitefield J. Bell, Jr., "Benjamin Franklin and the German Charity Schools," *Proceedings*, APS, 99 (1955), 381-87; Glen Weaver, "Benjamin Franklin and the Pennsylvania Germans," *William and Mary Quarterly*, Third Series, 14 (1957), 536-39; *Papers*, V, 203-18.

46. *Writings*, X, 9-31, esp. 15-21.

47. *Papers*, VII, 12, 50.

48. Hanna, pp. 5-6, 22, 36.

49. [Smith], *Brief State*, pp. 13-14. This piece appears in *Sabin's Reprints*, No. IV (New York, 1865). Smith had already created a commotion with the pamphlet by May 1, 1755; see *Papers*, IV, 52 n.

50. Ibid., pp. 16, 26.

51. *Papers*, VI, 169, 216. On November 27, 1755, Smith reported that he and Franklin were still friendly. He renewed his promise, though, to work for Penn "against a levelling & licentious Race of Republicans," William Smith to Thomas Penn, November 27, 1755, POC. HSP.

52. *Papers*, VI, 213.

53. [Smith], *Brief View*, p. 23. The piece was sold by Bradford in Philadelphia.

54. Ibid., p. 19.

55. Ibid., p. 53.

56. Ibid., pp. 6, 12-13. Smith failed to mention, however, that the Assembly had on occasion appropriated money for defense; nor did he discuss the penuriousness of Thomas Penn that held up such funds.

57. John Pemberton to John Gurney, December 13, 1754, Pemberton Papers. HSP.

58. *An Epistle from our General Spring Meeting of Ministers and Elders for Pennsylvania and New Jersey, held at Philadelphia, from the 29th of the Third Month, to the 1st of the Fourth Month, inclusive, 1755.* The letter was addressed "To Friends *on the Continent* of America," Pemberton Papers. HSP.

59. Henton Brown to James Pemberton, June 11, 1755, Pemberton Papers. HSP.

60. William Logan to Israel Pemberton, November 12, 1755, Pemberton Papers. HSP.

61. Thomas Willing to Walter Sterling, May 19, 1756. HSP.

62. Isaac Norris to John Fothergill, June 16, 1756, Logan Collection, Isaac Norris Letterbook, 1719-1756. HSP.

63. Robert Foster to John Pemberton, July 29, 1756, Pemberton Papers. HSP.

64. Richard Peters to the Reverend Samuel Chandler, June 28, 1756, Peters Papers. HSP.

65. *Papers*, VI, 169, 216. Earlier in his career Franklin, as J. A. Leo Lemay observes, was no enemy to the Proprietary Party. See "Franklin's Suppressed 'Busy-Body,'" *American Literature*, 37 (1965), 309.

66. *Papers*, VIII, 188-90.

67. *Papers*, X, 78n.

68. According to Thomas Penn, Norris was opposed to imprisoning Smith. If Penn is correct, then the members of the Assembly who insisted on jailing the Provost were even greater enemies to him, and possibly the College, than Norris. One of the few men capable of pushing through legislation over even nominal objection by the speaker was the powerful and influential Joseph Galloway, Franklin's chief political ally and William Franklin's close friend. Thomas Penn to Richard Peters, July 20, 1759, Letterbooks. HSP.

69. *Papers*, VII, 385. Charles Moor to William Smith, January 12, 1758, William Smith Papers, I. HSP; Jacob Duché, Jr., to Richard Peters, May 10, 1758, Peters Papers. HSP. Thomas Penn also wrote on this matter charging that Franklin's animosity toward the Provost was so great that he even sought to undermine the efforts to Anglicize the Germans through the charity schools because Smith and other proprietary figures were involved in the scheme. Earlier, of course, Franklin had given his complete support to the plan. Thomas Penn to Richard Peters, May 13, 1758, Letterbooks. HSP.

70. *Papers*, VII, 385. Edward Shippen, Jr., reported to his father that the affair "put every thing into a Flame," Edward Shippen, Jr., to Edward Shippen, Sr., January 28, 1758, Balch Papers, Shippen Papers, I. HSP; Thomas Crosby to James Pemberton, May 13, 1758, Pemberton Papers. HSP; John Hunt to James Pemberton, May 27, 1758, July 14 and December 12, 1759, Pemberton Papers, Box 3, folder entitled "John Hunt Corre-

spondence." HSP; Last Will and Testament of Rev. Dr. Wm. Smith, November 27, 1758. HSP.

71. *Papers*, VII, 385-86.

72. The Reverend Thomas Barton, missionary at Carlisle, often complained bitterly of the unrelenting hostility of the Presbyterians, especially the New Side, toward the Church of England. See, for example, his letters to the Secretary of the Venerable Society for the Propagation of the Gospel in Foreign Parts for December 6, 1760, November 8, 1762, June 28, 1763, November 16, 1764, and November 15, 1768, *Historical Collections*, II, 293-95, 343, 347-49, 366-72, 436, 437.

73. Penn, however, had to move cautiously for political reasons in supporting Anglicanism in the school. See Thomas Penn to Richard Peters, April 13 and December 12, 1761, Letterbooks. HSP. Penn's lack of respect for Presbyterianism can be gleaned, for example, from his criticism of Samuel Finley, New Side minister who, in 1761, would become President of the College of New Jersey. Thomas Penn to Richard Peters, May 26, 1758, Letters of Thomas Penn to Richard Peters, 1752-1772. HSP.

74. William Allen to Thomas Penn, October 21, 1764, POC. HSP.

75. *The Pennsylvania Journal and Weekly Advertiser*, 20 May 1756.

76. The Reverend Samuel Chandler, according to the proprietor, did, however, want Smith "to avoid controversy" and insisted that he end his political-religious machinations for the good of the school. Thomas Penn to William Smith, October 6, 1756, Letterbooks. HSP.

77. Thomas Penn to Richard Peters, October 9, 1756, and Richard Peters to Thomas Penn, February 14, 1757, Letterbooks. HSP; Thomas Penn to Richard Peters, May 14, 1757, Peters Papers, V. HSP.

78. *Papers*, VIII, 415-16.

79. [Duché], *Observations*, pp. 23-24.

80. Thomas Penn to Richard Peters, March 9, 1754, Letters of Thomas Penn to Richard Peters, 1752-1772. HSP. Further, when Smith was recommended for the degree of Doctor of Divinity, the Archbishop of Canterbury wrote that Smith accepted the position of Provost "on Condition of being allowed to enter into holy Orders." If the recommendation by the Archbishop is accurate, and he should have known the situation because of his private conference with Smith before he undertook to head the school, then it is almost certain that Franklin was not entirely surprised by Smith's ordination. See "The Recommendation of Wm. Smith to the University of Oxford, by the Archbishop of Canterbury & others, March 12, 1759." HSP.

81. Gegenheimer, *Smith, passim*.

82. *Historical Collections*, II, 391.

83. Richard Peters to William Smith, May 28, 1763, Dreer Collection. HSP. This letter has been published in *The Pennsylvania Magazine of History and Biography*, 10 (1886), 350-53. Also see [Duché], *Observations*, pp. 25-26.

84. Just how effective the trustees were in maintaining Anglican control of the school is expressed in a letter of Richard Peters to William Smith, June 10, 1762, William Smith Papers. HSP.

85. Horace W. Smith, *Life and Correspondence of the Reverend William Smith, D.D.*, 2 vols. (Philadelphia, 1880), I, 143.

86. Penn had to appear at least reasonably fair to other groups in Pennsylvania. His problems were compounded when some of his staunchest Presbyterian allies came to see that he was prejudiced in favor of his own church. Thomas Penn to William Smith, October 12, 1764, and Thomas Penn to William Allen, April 16, 1768, Letterbooks. HSP.

87. *Records*, p. 206.

88. *Stiles*, ed. Dexter, p. 428. Five years earlier, however, Alison had hopefully included the College of Philadelphia, along with those in New Jersey and New Haven, as "our Colleges," meaning those controlled by Dissenters. Francis Alison to Ezra Stiles, July 10, 1761, Alison MSS. PHS.

89. *Benjamin Franklin and the University of Pennsylvania*, ed. Frances N. Thorpe (Washington, D.C., 1893), pp. 79-80. Also see Thomas H. Montgomery, *A History of the University of Pennsylvania from Its Foundation to A.D. 1770* (Philadelphia, 1900), p. 424.

90. Penn had long hoped that the more serious Quakers could be attracted to the

College and under its influence be "drawn insensibly from little peculiarities" and brought into the Proprietary Party. Thomas Penn to James Hilton, October 18, 1760, and Thomas Penn to Richard Peters, December 10, 1762, Letterbooks. HSP.

91. Richard Peters to Thomas Penn, June 20, 1752, POC. HSP.

92. Richard Peters to Thomas Penn, November 5, 1753, POC. HSP.

93. William Smith to Richard Peters, [1765], Peters Papers. HSP.

94. *Pennsylvania Archives*, ed. Samuel Hazard, 12 vols. (Philadelphia, 1852-56), III, 450-51.

95. *Historical Collections*, II, 394.

96. Richard Peters to William Smith, May 28, 1763, Dreer Collection. HSP. Smith later worked against the fund-raising efforts in behalf of the Baptist College of Rhode Island (Brown), even after having received help from Philadelphia area Baptists in collecting for the College of Philadelphia. Smith was upset that the Church of England did not play a major role in the administration of the school and therefore advised the proprietor against doing anything substantial by way of helping the institution. William Smith to Thomas Penn, February 16, 1767, POC. HSP.

97. William Gordon to Charles Beatty, December 24, 1763. HSP. William Smith to Richard Peters, November 23, 1762, and February 12, 1763, William Smith Papers. HSP. Smith worked through Penn and the Reverend Samuel Chandler to overcome the hostility of Presbyterians toward him resulting from Beatty's charge. Thomas Penn to Richard Peters, December 10, 1762, Letterbooks. HSP.

98. *Records*, p. 206. Jonathan Dickinson, President of the College of New Jersey, made it quite clear that the "great and chief Design of erecting the College is for the Education of pious and well qualified Candidates for the Ministry." Jonathan Dickinson to ____, March 3, 1747, General Manuscript Collection. Princeton University.

99. On the continuing tensions between Presbyterian factions, see Hugh Williamson to the Reverend Andrew Elliot [sic], May 29, 1762, Andrews-Eliot Papers. MHS. The implications for the colleges of the continuing animosities are clear. The conflict, while it could be fought out verbally every year in the Synod, would eventually be resolved in the colleges, which were turning out ministers.

100. Richard Peters to Thomas Penn, December 23, 1754, POC. HSP. Aaron Burr, President of the College of New Jersey, pointed out that his school had many enemies among the Old Side and "among our Episcopal Brethren" who were "envious at the growing State of the Dissents." Aaron Burr to Dr. P. Doddridge, May 31, 1750, Aaron Burr Collection. Princeton University. Although most Anglicans in the Middle Colonies were sympathetic to the Colleges of Philadelphia or New York, Daniel Roberdeau, a prominent Philadelphia Anglican, sent his son to the Jersey school. Moreover, he disobeyed the wishes of a friend that Roberdeau send the man's son to the College of Philadelphia by sending the boy to the College of New Jersey. Roberdeau was an ally of Franklin and had deposed against Provost Smith in the libel case. Daniel Roberdeau to William Turnbull, May 16, 1769, and Daniel Roberdeau to Francis Frett, Jr., May 16, 1769, Letterbook of Daniel Roberdeau, 1764-1771. HSP.

101. Richard Peters to Thomas Penn, December 23, 1754, POC. HSP.

102. Richard Peters to Thomas Penn, December 23, 1754, POC. HSP.

103. William Smith to Thomas Penn, April 10, 1755, POC. HSP.

104. Quoted in Edward P. Cheyney, *History of the University of Pennsylvania, 1740-1940* (Philadelphia, 1940), p. 40.

105. Smith, *Smith*, I, 103, 104. President Samuel Finley of the College of New Jersey struck back. Writing to an English correspondent he denied Smith's promotional claims for the College of Philadelphia and said that the school was insignificant in America. Samuel Finley to William Hogg, June 27,

1764 (typescript), General Manuscript Collection. Princeton University.

106. Ibid., pp. 103-6.

107. Ibid., pp. 104-5.

108. The influence of the Church of England in the College of Philadelphia was so great that the Archbishop of Canterbury thought it within his province to influence the choice of persons who were to receive honorary degrees and to make certain that not too many were granted to Presbyterians. William Smith to Richard Peters, August 25, 1763, William Smith Papers. HSP.

109. *Stiles*, ed. Dexter, p. 429.

110. Ibid., p. 558.

111. Ibid., pp. 554-58.

112. Ibid., p. 559.

113. Ibid., p. 435. Two years earlier, however, Alison had complained that his New Side brethren "reviled" him "as an enemy to Christ." The change in his sentiments expresses, I believe, his frustrations over Anglican control of the College of Philadelphia rather than any change in his feelings about the New Side or its school. Further, although Alison was an ardent supporter of the proprietor, he believed Thomas Penn to be very reluctant to grant Presbyterians the same privileges and advantages he gave readily to Anglicans. *Stiles*, ed. Dexter, pp. 431-32.

114. Alison sent two of his former students, John Ewing and Hugh Williamson, to raise funds for the Academy which, after it moved to Newark, became the University of Delaware. Thomas C. Pears, Jr., "Francis Alison, Colonial Educator," *Journal of the Presbyterian Historical Society*, 29 (1951), 213-25.

115. Yet its anti-intellectual origins that went back to Gilbert Tennent and other of his evangelical followers from Log College later caused discomfiture to cultivated and educated Presbyterians. William Shippen argued against the fashionable genteel preachers, who were polished rather than pious, but he still hoped that the Jersey school would "produce a few Collegians who [would] make a Figure and speak as gracefully as their Neighbours, notwithstanding they have had the chief part of their

education at Nottingham." William Shippen to Edward Shippen, Jr., April 10, 1761, Shippen Papers. HSP.

116. Even such a good, if not altogether trusting, friend as Ezra Stiles recognized that Franklin was hostile to Presbyterians. Stiles, not knowing the full story, though, conjectured that Franklin's antipathy resulted from politics alone. See *Papers*, XVI, 123-25.

117. Ewing tried to further this goal by advocating that the Presbyterian Church purchase as much land as possible so that it could have "Power" in general. But the key, at least initially, to fulfillment of his dream was the control of the schools. John Ewing to Andrew Eliot, August 6, 1766, Andrews-Eliot Papers. MHS.

118. Cheyney, p. 61.

119. Thomas Penn recognized that a collection in England for the College was necessary as early as 1760. Thomas Penn to William Smith, May 10, 1760, Letterbooks. HSP. He did not want Smith to go to England for the purpose, however, fearing that the Provost would use the occasion to get himself a deanery in England and leave the College. The proprietor was both relieved and surprised to discover that he had mistaken Smith, in whose integrity he had little faith. Thomas Penn to James Hamilton, March 6, 1762, and Thomas Penn to William Smith, February 15, 1765, Letterbooks. HSP.

120. Joseph Yates Brinton, "Introduction" to *The Collection Books of Provost Smith* (Philadelphia, 1964), p. 7.

121. Cheyney, p. 171.

122. *Papers*, VII, 201.

123. *Papers*, VII, 201n. Franklin had ordered £150 worth of scientific apparatus for the Academy in 1755, but he donated nothing. See *Papers*, VII, 50, 286.

124. *The Pennsylvania Journal and Weekly Advertiser*, 30 November 1758.

125. Ibid.

126. Ibid., 1, 8, 22 February and 1 March 1759; Thomas Penn to William Allen, July 11, 1759, and Thomas Penn to William Smith, October 18, 1760, Letterbooks. HSP. It should be pointed out that Quaker

abhorrence of lotteries was, at least later, not too great to prohibit some of the Society of Friends from buying tickets and from trying very hard to collect their winnings. John Kilden to John Pemberton, September 5, 1767, Pemberton Papers. HSP.

127. Letter of William Franklin, December 28, 1759. The original is at Yale University, but there were two copies made of it. I have used the one belonging to APS.

128. Letter of William Franklin, December 28, 1759. APS. Duché, a prominent Anglican, had come under Calvinist influence to such a degree as to cause Presbyterians to think he might leave the Church of England and join them. See Samuel Finley to Joseph Bellamy, November 10, 1763, Gratz Collection. College and University Presidents. HSP.

129. Richard Peters to Thomas Penn, June 1, 1756, POC. HSP.

130. Smith, *Smith*, I, 284. The Provost, however, had planned carefully on his own for this trip and, in fact, had been thinking about raising funds in England for the school as early as 1759. William Smith to Richard Peters, June 9, 1759, Peters Papers. HSP.

131. Smith, *Smith*, I, 335. According to James H. Hutson, once the Provost discovered for certain that Franklin had tried to sabotage the collection he retaliated by working with Thomas Penn to have William Franklin's recent appointment as Royal Governor of New Jersey annulled. To accomplish this end, Smith and Penn broke the story that William was illegitimate and would therefore prove unacceptable to the people of New Jersey. James H. Hutson, "Benjamin Franklin and William Smith, More Light on an Old Philadelphia Quarrel," *Pennsylvania Magazine of History and Biography*, 93 (January 1969), 109-13. In a letter that Mr. Hutson cites, Smith wrote to Peters that he had "taken Care to say Nothing in the Affair [of William's birth] except letting Gilbert Eliot Know." Smith also notes that Eliot said it was "too late" to do anything about the appointment. The letter to Peters was written about two weeks after the time that, ac-

cording to Dr. Hutson, Smith began to spread the report about William's birth, on April 5, 1762. Mr. Hutson may be assuming that the Provost was lying to cover up his activities, and Smith was, indeed, capable of doing so.

132. *Collection Books*, pp. 19-20, 25-26.

133. William Smith to Richard Peters, April 5, 1762, William Smith Papers. HSP; Gegenheimer, *Smith*, p. 150.

134. William Smith to Richard Peters, August 14, 1762, William Smith Papers. HSP; Gegenheimer, *Smith*, p. 151.

135. William Smith to Richard Peters [undated], William Smith Papers. HSP. Someone noted on the manuscript that Smith most likely wrote the letter in March 1762. This date is surely incorrect if as late as August 14, 1762, the Provost believed that Franklin might once again take a "lead" in the school. It is perhaps a commentary on the hostility between Anglicans and Presbyterians, as well as on the bitter rivalry between the Philadelphia and Jersey schools, that William Allen had to warn Smith about secretly working against the Presbyterian college. Thomas Penn to William Smith, February 15, 1765 (in reply to Smith's letter to Penn, December 19, 1764), Letterbooks. HSP. Smith's sensitivity on this matter is understandable, as is his natural desire to warn Peters about Franklin's charges. Yet there is some confusion about this whole matter. Smith's letter to Peters, which he received on October 2, 1762, is undated. I have contended that the letter must have been written after August 14, 1762, since Smith at that time thought Franklin might once more become a force in the school. Yet Smith had evidently met George Hanna, who claimed to have been told that the College was "an Instrument of Dissension," early in the spring, for the Provost's *Collection Books*, No. 2, p. 1, indicate that "George Hanna Esqr." contributed £25 to the institution, and the entry of this gift is dated April 22, 1762, or five and one-half months before Peters received the above-mentioned letter from Smith. The most plausible explanation seems

to be that Smith did learn by April 22 what Hanna had been told about the College, but that he refrained from accusing the Franklins or anyone else of having injured the institution until he had investigated the whole matter carefully, as his detailed letters show he had. He still did not realize on August 14 where Hanna received his information and so merely advised Peters to be cautious in dealing with the elder Franklin about the school. Smith's second collection book breaks off after August 17, 1762, and the next entry is dated October 10, 1762. On September 29 of that year he left London for Edinburgh and northern Scotland to collect money for the College. He must have discovered the truth about Hanna's source of information after August 17 but long enough before he left London for Peters to receive the news on October 2. It does not seem likely that Smith would have waited any longer than necessary to tell Peters of his discovery. Not only did he want to protect the College against Franklin, but he had to clear its reputation in Great Britain.

136. *Collection Books*, p. 14.

137. *Papers*, X, 108n.

138. *Papers*, X, 3n.

139. John Ewing to Andrew Eliot, August 6, 1766, Andrews-Eliot Papers. MHS.

140. *Papers*, VII, 134-35.

141. *Papers*, X, 143.

142. *Papers*, X, 169.

143. Fearing that the College might suffer from Presbyterians trying to control it or from Franklin and his supporters striving to undermine or seize it, Thomas Penn pleaded with Peters, who was resigning as his secretary, to remain active in the school and protect it from its enemies. Thomas Penn to Richard Peters, December 12, 1760, Letterbooks. HSP. When Peters had been offered a position in Antigua, Penn again reminded him of his obligation to protect the College in Smith's absence. In fact, Penn worked through English connections in the Church of England to insure that Peters would remain in Philadelphia to defend the institution and to educate "our young Men . . . for the Church." Thomas Penn to Richard

Peters, April 13, 1761, Letterbooks. HSP. Smith echoed the proprietor's fear and desire and insisted that it was Peters' obligation as an Anglican minister and trustee of the College to see that "our National Church" kept control of the school. William Smith to Richard Peters, April 24 and June 17, 1763, William Smith Papers. HSP. Peters and Smith both feared that the Presbyterians were taking advantage of Smith's absence to take over the College through their strength on the faculty. William Smith to [Richard Peters], February 15, 1763, William Smith Papers. HSP.

144. William Smith to Richard Peters, [September] 14 and November 23, 1762, William Smith Papers. HSP; Gegenheimer, *Smith*, pp. 151-52; Smith, *Smith*, I, 335, 336. It is interesting that the Provost's *Collection Books* do not indicate that the Dissenter ever actually fulfilled his promise.

145. Smith later complained that Dissenters had given very little to the school, in spite of Alison's connection with it and his letter supporting the collection. William Smith to Richard Peters, February 14, 1764, William Smith Papers. HSP. Though Franklin's efforts against the collection hurt the school, so too did Smith's activities against Beatty and his reputation of being anti-Presbyterian.

146. Once he returned to Philadelphia and saw the political situation for himself, Franklin, according to Smith, persisted in working against the fund-raising drive in letters to England. William Smith to Richard Peters, April 23, 1763, William Smith Papers. HSP.

147. *Papers*, VII, 12.

148. *Papers*, VIII, 415-16.

149. Richard Peters to William Smith, October 12, 1762, William Smith Papers. HSP.

150. William fell in love with England soon after he arrived there, as he reported in a letter to Elizabeth Graeme, an American girl he was about to jilt. He later married an English woman. See *Papers*, VII, 289.

151. "Letters from William Franklin to William Strahan," ed. Charles H. Hart, *Pennsylvania Magazine of History and Biography*, 35 (1911), 44.

152. *Papers*, VIII, 408.

153. Francis Alison to Ezra Stiles, August 7, 1766, Alison MSS. PHS. To what degree Alison actually believed in these sentiments is debatable, for they are evangelical positions of an earlier day, and ones to which he had been considered an unflinching enemy. Francis Alison, "Reasons for Dissenting from the Church of England," [n.d.], Alison MSS. PHS. It should be pointed out, however, that New Side adherents as early as 1757 had expressed their skepticism about revivals and their determination not to permit again the wild excesses of the Great Awakening. Reports spread that there was a mild, student-inspired revival in the College of New Jersey and that it was spreading throughout the colony, "especially among the young people." So great was the fear of another wave of hysteria that some parents of students threatened to remove their sons from the school. Further, Samuel Davies felt compelled to defend the college and the revival to his Virginia congregation. See Samuel Davies, "Little Children invited to Jesus Christ: A Sermon Preached in Hannover County, Virginia, May 8, 1757," *Sermons* (London, 1758), pp. 30-31.

154. *New Jersey Archives*, First Series, ed. William Nelson (Patterson, 1880-86), XXV, 317.

155. *New Jersey Archives*, First Series, ed. William A. Whitehead, VII, 579-80; Aaron Burr to Joseph Stennett, November 9, 1751, Gratz Collection, College and University Presidents. HSP.

156. William was also hostile toward the College of Philadelphia, a fact which is made clear in his denial of the use of his father's name to a revived or new version of the American Philosophical Society. He thought, in 1768, that the Society was merely a more prestigious arm of the proprietary-controlled College. [Cadwallader Evans to William Franklin], January 25, 1768. APS.

157. *Stiles*, ed. Dexter, p. 25.

158. Ibid., p. 555.

159. *Papers*, XI, 168-69.

160. *Stiles*, ed. Dexter, p. 555. See also *Letters of Benjamin Rush*, I, 40, 42.

161. Thomas Jefferson Wertenbaker, *Princeton, 1746-1898* (Princeton, 1946), p. 87. Franklin's plan was echoed by the attempt of an Anglican Tory to work through Joseph Galloway, a nominal Quaker who also proved to be a Tory, to encourage the Pennsylvania Assembly to take the College of Philadelphia under its protection. The Anglican, the Reverend Duché, feared that Presbyterian patriots were gaining control of the school. See [Duché], *Observations*, pp. 26-27. As governor and an interested party in the affairs of the Jersey school, William certainly knew that there had been going on for at least a year an awakening among the students at the school. The revival, according to President Samuel Finley, was providing a good number of additional Presbyterian ministers. Given his hostility toward Presbyterianism, the revival may have furnished William an additional motive for trying to get the school away from the Presbyterian trustees. The governor, of course, knew that the financial problems of the College persisted and were, in fact, aggravated by the refusal of the Old Side to help the institution without controlling it. See Samuel Finley to Joseph Bellamy, November 10, 1763, Gratz Collection. College and University Presidents. HSP; Francis Alison to Ezra Stiles, June 4, 1768, Alison MSS. PHS.

162. *New Jersey Archives*, First Series, VII, 579-80; Wertenbaker, *Princeton*, pp. 30-31.

163. *Letters of Benjamin Rush*, I, 40; John Ewing to Andrew Eliot, August 6, 1766, Andrews-Eliot Papers. MHS.

164. Ibid., p. 42. It should also be noted that William Bradford rather than Franklin and Hall received the printing business of the College of New Jersey. Samuel Finley to William Bradford, Collection of Papers Relating to Colonel William Bradford of Philadelphia, I, 109. HSP.

165. *Letters of Benjamin Rush*, I, 40, 42, 43, 45n.

166. *Stiles*, ed. Dexter, p. 555.

167. *Papers*, XIII, 319-20.

168. William Allen to Thomas Penn, November 12, 1766, POC. HSP.

169. *Historical Collections*, II, 327, 367.

170. *Ecclesiastical Records ... New York*, VI, 4,040, 4,048, 4,084.

171. John Penn to Thomas Penn, October 19, 1764, POC. HSP.

172. Richard P. McCormick, *Rutgers: A Bicentennial History* (New Brunswick, 1966), p. 8.

173. The elder Edward Shippen, a staunch friend to the College of New Jersey, favored building it at Princeton rather than at New Brunswick to avoid having to compete with King's College. Edward Shippen, Sr., to Joseph Shippen, May 7, 1752, Shippen MSS. Princeton University.

174. John Witherspoon to Dr. Rush, February 8, 1768 [sic] 1769, Witherspoon Collection. Princeton University.

175. *The Independent Reflector*, ed. Milton M. Klein (Cambridge, 1963), pp. 38, 46.

176. Aaron Burr to Thomas Foxcroft [n.d.], Thomas Foxcroft Correspondence, 1740-1759. Princeton University.

177. *John Witherspoon Comes to America*, ed. L.H. Butterfield (Princeton, 1953), pp. 16, 17.

178. *Stiles*, ed. Dexter, pp. 554-55.

179. Ibid., pp. 558-59.

180. *New Jersey Archives*, First Series, ed. Frederick W. Ricord and William Nelson, X, 339-42.

181. Varnum Lansing Collins, *President Witherspoon, A Biography*, 2 vols. (Princeton, 1925), I, 209-12.

Notes   Chapter VI

1. Richard Peters to Thomas Penn, January 30, 1751, POC. HSP.

2. Thomas Penn to James Hamilton, June 13, 1764, Letterbooks. HSP; Thomas Penn to John Penn, April 13 and July 13, 1764, Letterbooks. HSP; Hanna, pp. 46-47.

3. Scrupulous Friends had, however, been pressing their brethren to at least reduce their participation in government since it was compromising their peaceful testimony. See Jack D. Marietta, "Conscience, the Quaker Community, and the French and Indian War," *Pennsylvania Magazine of History and Biography*, 95 (January 1971), 11-13.

4. Israel Pemberton to John Pemberton, December 8, 1753, Pemberton Papers. HSP.

5. Isaac Norris to Charles Norris, October 5, 1755, Logan Collection, Isaac Norris Letterbook, 1719-1756. HSP.

6. Yearly Meeting of Ministers & Elders held in Philadelphia, 20th 9th Mo. 1755, pp. 372, 378, and 380. Yet James Pemberton felt nothing but contempt at this time for the opposition of Presbyterians. [James Pemberton] to Richard Partridge, October 7, 1755,

Pemberton Papers. HSP; [James Pemberton] to Henton Brown, October 7, 1755, Pemberton Papers. HSP.

7. "A Brief Memorandum for those who have been Educated among the People called Quakers, but have swerved from the Divine Principle of Grace & Truth in the Soul which has been an Inlet to great Deviations ..." (1752). Pemberton Papers. HSP.

8. John Pemberton to John Gurney, December 13, 1754, Pemberton Papers. HSP.

9. Samuel Fothergill to Israel Pemberton, April 6, 1755, Pemberton Papers. HSP.

10. James Pemberton to Dr. John Fothergill, November 27, 1755, Pemberton Papers. HSP. Fothergill and other English Friends, who were often less concerned about strict pacifism than the general political, economic, and social health of the Society in England and the colonies, had been working in England on a compromise that would enable Pennsylvania Quakers to resign temporarily from the Assembly, pay taxes in support of defense, and then return to the legislature when peace was established. John Fothergill to Israel Pemberton, March 6 and April 3, 1756, Pemberton Papers. HSP; Marietta, pp. 7-8, 19-23.

11. James Pemberton to John Fothergill, November 27, 1755, Pemberton Papers. HSP.

12. Robert Pleasants to James Pemberton, September 10, 1755, and William Logan to Israel Pemberton, January 11, 1755, Pemberton Papers. HSP.

13. [James Pemberton] to Richard Partridge, October 7, 1755, Pemberton Papers. HSP; also see part of an unsent letter, perhaps by James Pemberton to John Fothergill, November 27, 1755, Pemberton Papers. HSP.

14. *Papers*, VI, 266-73. The bill was ineffective and was disallowed by the Board of Trade and the Privy Council Committee that considered it. The Assembly did not present a new bill until March 1757 and when Governor Denny amended it on important matters that body vetoed his changes. *Papers*, VII, 52-53n.

15. James Pemberton to John Fothergill, November 27, 1755, Pemberton Papers. HSP.

16. Thomas Willing (Philadelphia) to Thomas Willing (London), November 22, 1755, Letterbook of Thomas Willing, November 30, 1754-May 1, 1757. HSP.

17. Thomas Willing (Philadelphia) to John Perks, June 10, 1756; Thomas Willing (Philadelphia) to Thomas Willing (London), June 15, 1756; Thomas Willing (Philadelphia) to Robert Morris, November, 1756. All the letters are in the Letterbook of Thomas Willing, November 30, 1754-May 1, 1757. HSP. Willing had additional reason for hating Quakers, since as a trader he suffered from their unwillingness to employ privateers to retaliate for French privateering. Thomas Willing to Christopher Scandrett, September 29, 1757, Letterbook of Willing and Morris, May 1, 1757-1761. HSP.

18. Samuel Fothergill to James Pemberton, June 23, 1755, Pemberton Papers. HSP; Henton Brown to James Pemberton, March 11, 1756, Pemberton Papers. HSP; [John Fothergill] to Israel Pemberton, February 21, 1757, Pemberton Papers. HSP.

19. MS Sermon of Francis Alison, February 29, 1756. PHS. The sermon is based on Nehemiah 2.3,4,5: "Why should not my Countenance be sad when the City the Place of my fathers Sepulcres lieth waste & the gates thereof are consumed with fire. . . ."

20. *The Burd Papers. Extracts from Chief Justice William Allen's Letter Book*, I, ed. Lewis B. Walker (Pottsville, Pa., 1897), 25.

21. *The Pennsylvania Journal and Weekly Advertiser*, 10 June 1756.

22. John Fothergill to Israel Pemberton, July 8, 1755, Pemberton Papers. HSP.

23. William Allen to Samuel Chandler, February 4, 1758, and William Allen to Ferdinand John Paris, February 4, 1758, POC. HSP.

24. *Burd Papers*, I, 49.

25. *Papers*, VIII, 81. Contrary to Hutson's claim (*Pennsylvania Politics*, pp. 4, 240) that the Presbyterian Party was a distinct group from any other in the province and that it emerged only in 1770, it had become commonplace to refer to the Proprietary Party as the "Presbyterian Party" and to the opposition party as the "Quaker Party." Penn, in fact, worried about the political and religious consequences of the practice and pleaded privately that it cease. Thomas Penn to John Penn, December 14, 1765, February 26, 1766, Letterbooks. HSP. When his pleas were ignored, the proprietor wrote again to his nephew, the Governor of Pennsylvania, reiterating his request on May 10, 1766, Letterbooks. HSP. Years earlier Penn expressed displeasure with the fact that the backbone of his party was Presbyterian, for he had little regard for or trust in the denomination. He bewailed the support Franklin had from about half the Anglicans in Pennsylvania and complained that this fact made him very dependent upon Presbyterians. Thomas Penn to Richard Peters, May 13, 1758, Letterbooks. HSP. When Quakers, therefore, referred to Penn's supporters in 1774 as the "Presbyterian Party," they were expressing a fact that was already almost twenty years old. Abel James and Henry Drinker to Benjamin Booth, August 30 and October 4, 1774, Henry Drinker Letterbook, pp. 107, 115. HSP.

26. See the minutes of the various Meet-

ings for Sufferings for Pennsylvania and New Jersey, held in Philadelphia, in 1756 and 1757, pp. 2, 3, 4-7, 8, 9, 10, 11-12, 13, 14-15, 18, 24, 25, 35, 47-48, 51, 65-66, 71-72, 78-79, 116, 383. FHLS. As part of the pacifist effort, Daniel Stanton and John Pemberton visited 560 families and individuals between 1757 and 1760, encouraging them to preserve orthodoxy and the Society. "An Account of Friends and Families belonging to the Monthly meeting of philadelphia, & some few Families not altogether in Unity, Visited by Daniel Stanton & John Pemberton." HSP.

27. Jonah Thompson to John Smith, June 26, 1756, Correspondence of John Smith, 1740-1770. HSP. John Fothergill to [Israel Pemberton], August 2, 1756, Pemberton Papers. HSP; Samuel Foulke, "A Collection of some Scripture Texts & a few remarks thereon recommended in Brotherly Love to ye Consideration of Friends in Pennsylvania, especially those who appear dissatisfied with the late act of Assembly made for granting a Sum of Money to ye King's Use . . . , 2 mo 10th 1756." FHLS; Minutes of the Philadelphia Monthly Meetings for 1756, pp. 213, 221, 227; Jonah Thompson to Anthony Benezet, January 31, 1758. FHLS.

28. Richard Peters to Thomas Penn, February 14, 1757, Peters Letter Book. HSP; Marietta, p. 18.

29. *Pennsylvania Archives*, Eighth Series, V, ed. Gertrude MacKinney (Harrisburg, 1931), pp. 4,245, 4,250; Minutes of the Yearly Meeting for Sufferings, 1756, pp. 1, 2, 42-43. FHLS; William Logan to John Smith, October 1, 1756, Correspondence of John Smith, 1740-1770. HSP; Charles Norris to James Wright, June 3, 1756, Norris of Fairhill MSS., Miscellaneous Volume. HSP; James Pemberton to Samuel Fothergill, November, 1756, Pemberton Papers. HSP; Robert Foster to John Pemberton, September 9, 1756, Pemberton Papers. HSP; Henton Brown to James Pemberton, August 17, 1756, Pemberton Papers. HSP; Israel Pemberton to Samuel Fothergill, January 11, 1757 (draft), Pemberton Papers. HSP.

30. William Smith to Mr. Vernon, October 15, 1756 (copy). HSP.

31. James Pemberton to Samuel Fothergill, November, 1756, Pemberton Papers. HSP.

32. [Israel Pemberton] to John Fothergill, July 1, 1757, Pemberton Papers. HSP.

33. Thomas Penn to Richard Peters, May 14, 1757, Peters Papers. HSP.

34. Thomas Penn to Richard Peters, May 14, 1757, Peters Papers. HSP; James Hamilton to Thomas Penn, November 21, 1762, POC. HSP.

35. John Hunt to Israel Pemberton, August 30, 1759, Pemberton Papers, Box 3, folder entitled, "John Hunt Correspondence." (Hereafter JHC.) HSP. Hunt's efforts were opposed also by Quakers, as he himself noted. John Hunt to John Pemberton, July 7, 1758, JHC. HSP; [Israel Pemberton to John Hunt], May 31, 1758, JHC. HSP.

36. John Hunt to Israel Pemberton, December 12, 1759, JHC. HSP.

37. [Israel Pemberton] to John Fothergill, December 17, 1755, Pemberton Papers. HSP.

38. Minutes of the Yearly Meeting for Sufferings, 3rd of 5th Mo., 1756, p. 10. FHLS.

39. Minutes of the Yearly Meeting for Sufferings, 3rd of 2nd Mo., 1757, and 10th of 2nd Mo., 1757, pp. 50, 60. FHLS.

40. Isaac Norris to John Fothergill, June 16, 1756, Logan Collection, Isaac Norris Letterbook, 1719-1756. HSP.

41. Minutes of the Yearly Meeting of Ministers & Elders . . . Philadelphia, 30th of 5th Mo., 1756, pp. 380-81. FHLS; *Papers*, VI, 246-48. For a different opinion on this point, see Marietta, p. 26.

42. James Tasker to John Pemberton, March 18, 1759, Pemberton Papers. HSP; Minutes . . . Yearly Meeting for Sufferings, 2nd of 7th Mo., 1756, pp. 34, 36, 37, 39. FHLS.

43. William Logan to James Pemberton, October 1, 1761, Pemberton Papers. HSP.

44. John Hunt to Israel Pemberton, August 30, 1759, JHC. HSP.

45. Richard Peters to Thomas Penn, June 5 and October 30, 1756, POC. HSP; Robert H. Morris to Thomas Penn, October 23, 1755, POC. HSP; and also see *Papers*, XI, 375-76, 382, for early expressions of

Franklin's disgust with Quaker politics; Thomas Penn to Richard Peters, April 8, 1758, Letterbooks. HSP; Thomas Penn to William Smith, October 6, 1756, William Smith Papers. HSP.

46. William Franklin to [Joseph Galloway], December 28, 1759, William Franklin Papers. APS. (Copy from original in Yale University Library.)

47. George Thomas to John Penn, November 4, 1740, Thomas Penn to Ferdinand John Paris, April 24, 1741, and Richard Peters to John Penn, November 20, 1741, POC. HSP.

48. Thomas Penn to Richard Peters, August 13, 1755, Letters of Thomas Penn to Richard Peters, 1752-1772. HSP.

49. James H. Hutson is surely correct in pointing out the importance of the tax dispute in the attempt to make the province a Crown colony; however, to argue, as he does, that it was a catalyst, indeed the chief reason for that effort, is to distort the situation, I believe. Moreover, such an interpretation of events essentially ignores the great significance of the religious and social issues involved in the campaign, and these were the critical ones for most Pennsylvania groups. See *Pennsylvania Politics*, pp. 18-24, 90-92, 113-21.

50. In the pamphlet war that followed the murders and march on the city, it was the Presbyterians who were accused of the bloodshed and riot, though Germans were involved in the march and apparently supported the action. The Reverend Thomas Barton of the Church of England was happy to report that no Anglicans were involved or attacked. Thomas Barton to Thomas Burton, November 16, 1764, in *Historical Collections*, II, 367.

51. Excellent essays on the Paxton affair have been written by Brooke Hindle, "The March of the Paxton Boys," *William and Mary Quarterly*, Third Series, 3 (October 1946), 461-86, and by John R. Dunbar in the "Introduction" to his edition of *The Paxton Papers* (The Hague, 1957), pp. 3-51. The editors of the Franklin *Papers*, XI, 22-29, 42-47,

69-75, provide a useful summary of the murders.

52. James Pemberton to John Fothergill, March 7, 1764, Pemberton Papers. HSP. Pemberton puts the number of Quakers bearing arms at about 200, and noted that most of them were young people.

53. Until recently it has been assumed that the bulk of the marchers' support in Philadelphia came from the workers at the lower end of the social scale. Though the Paxton Boys did have such support, they also had enemies among the pro-Franklin ships carpenters known as the White Oaks. See James H. Hutson, "An Investigation of the Inarticulate: Philadelphia's White Oaks," *William and Mary Quarterly*, Third Series, 28 (January 1971), 10-11.

54. Hindle, pp, 483-84.

55. *Paxton Papers*, p. 36.

56. Ibid., p. 46.

57. See, for example, the following: Edward Shippen to William Allen, July 4, 1755, Shippen Papers. HSP; John Harris to Richard Peters, July 26, 1755, Peters Papers. HSP; letter of Edward Shippen to his "Cousin," August 10, 1755, Shippen Papers. APS; William Allen to Ferdinand John Paris, October 20, 1755, Letterbook of William Allen. HSP; Edw[ar]d Shippen to John Alford, July 28, 1756, Shippen Papers. APS; John Elder to Richard Peters, July 30, 1757, Peters Papers. HSP; James Hamilton to James Burd, February 22, 1760, and Edward Shippen to William Allen, March 18, 1760, Shippen Papers. HSP; Edw[ar]d Shippen to Joseph Shippen, January 11, June 13, July 21, August 31, October 17, December 19, 20, 1763; January 1, 4, 1764, Shippen Papers. APS; Thomas McKee to James Burd, July 9, 1763, Shippen Papers. HSP; Edw[ar]d Shippen to James Hamilton, October 29, 1763, Shippen Papers. APS; John Penn to Thomas Penn, November 15, 1763, December 18, 1763, POC. HSP; John Harris to James Burd, December 2, 1763, Shippen Papers. HSP; Joseph Shippen, Jr., to James Burd, January 3, 1764, Shippen Papers. HSP; James Burd to William Allen, January 10,

1764 (Copy), Shippen Papers. HSP; Sam-[u]el Hunter to Edward Shippen, February 22, 1764, Shippen Papers. APS; *Paxton Papers*, pp. 16-18, 19n., 20, 21, 22, 23-24, 27, 35; Benjamin Lightfoot to Israel Pemberton, October 12, 1761, and John Pemberton to Rachel Pemberton, August 27, 1762, Pemberton Papers. HSP; James Hamilton to James Burd, June 13, 1763, Shippen Papers. HSP; John Penn to William Johnson, February 2, 1767, Penn Papers. HSP.

58. *Paxton Papers*, p. 85.

59. Ibid., pp. 104, 205, 210, 339, 375-76.

60. [Israel Pemberton] to John Fothergill, April 26, 1756, Pemberton Papers. HSP.

61. Israel Pemberton to John Hunt, October 8, 1763, JHC. HSP; Israel Pemberton to John Pemberton, February 7, 1764, Pemberton Papers. HSP.

62. John Hunt to Israel Pemberton, December 10, 1763, JHC. HSP; William Logan to John Smith, December 30, 1763, Correspondence, 1740-1770. HSP; John Hunt to John Pemberton, March 1, 1764, JHC. HSP; "On the Massacre at Lancaster, 12 mo. 1763," Miscellaneous Papers, 1724-1772, Lancaster County. HSP; Deborah Logan, "Extracts from the 'Selections' of James Logan," James Logan Papers, pp. 347-49. HSP; "Journal of Roda Barber" (1830), [pp. 15-20]. HSP.

63. Edward Bond to Israel Pemberton and Jonathan Leams, January 9, 1764, Pemberton Papers. HSP.

64. J[ames] P[emberton] to Robert Valentine and Richard Downing, December 29, 1763, Cox-Parrish-Wharton Papers. HSP.

65. James Pemberton to John Fothergill, March 7, 1764, Pemberton Papers. HSP; [James Pemberton to John Hunt?], April 11, 1764, JHC. HSP.

66. James Pemberton to John Fothergill, March 7 and June 13, 1764, Pemberton Papers. HSP.

67. George Churchman to Israel Pemberton, January 18, 1764, Pemberton Papers. HSP.

68. Elizabeth Wilkinson to John Pemberton, April 14, 1764, Pemberton Papers. HSP.

69. Susanna Wright to Isaac Whitelock, January 16, [1764], Pemberton Papers. HSP.

70. Samuel Wyly to Israel Pemberton, April 20, 1759, Pemberton Papers. HSP.

71. Conference of Friends with the Red Indians, 4 mo 19-5 mo 31, 1756. FHLS.

72. [Smith], *Brief State*, pp. 16, 26; [Smith], *Brief View*, p. 53; anonymous article attributed to Smith in *The Pennsylvania Journal and Weekly Advertiser*, 10 June 1756.

73. *Paxton Papers*, pp. 85, 104, 205, 210, 339, 375-76.

74. Ibid., pp. 88-90, 133-38, 155-64, 168, 180, 226, 277, 282, 285-86, 330-31, 339, 369-70, 375-76, 380-82.

75. "Fragments of a Journal Kept by Samuel Foulke, of Bucks County, While a Member of the Colonial Assembly of Pennsylvania, 1762-3-4," *Pennsylvania Magazine of History and Biography*, 5 (1881), 70.

76. *Paxton Papers*, pp. 155-64.

77. Ibid., p. 168.

78. Ibid., p. 89.

79. Ibid., pp. 89-90.

80. Ibid., pp. 282, 285-86, 369-70, 380-82.

81. Ibid., pp. 226, 330-31.

82. Ibid., p. 227.

83. *Papers*, XI, 47.

84. *Papers*, XI, 48.

85. *Papers*, XI, 48.

86. *Pennsylvania Colonial Records*, ed. Samuel Hazard, 16 vols. (Harrisburg, 1852), IX, 103-4.

87. *Papers*, XI, 48-49.

88. *Papers*, XI, 49.

89. *Papers*, XI, 49.

90. *Papers*, XI, 49.

91. *Papers*, XI, 49.

92. *Papers*, XI, 50.

93. *Papers*, XI, 50.

94. *Papers*, XI, 50.

95. *Papers*, XI, 50.

96. *Papers*, XI, 52.

97. *Papers*, XI, 52-55.

98. *Papers*, XI, 53.

99. *Papers*, XI, 55.

100. *Papers*, XI, 55-56.

101. *Papers*, XI, 56-64.

102. Smyth and others have "Christian." I have not seen the original used by the editors of the *Papers*.

103. *Papers*, XI, 66.

104. *Paxton Papers*, p. 246.

105. Ibid., pp. 246-47.

106. Ibid., p. 249.

107. Ibid., pp. 369-70. For the comments on the letter to Allen and Chandler, see Thomas Penn to John Penn, June 8, 1764, Letterbooks. HSP; Gilbert Tennent, Francis Alison, and John Ewing, "A Circular Letter," March 30, 1764 (copy); Samuel Purviance to James Burd, September or December 20, 1765, Shippen Papers. HSP; Correspondence, 1763-1768, reprinted in Dietmar Rothermund's *The Layman's Progress* (Philadelphia, 1961), pp. 185-88. On Franklin's political alliance with Galloway, see Benjamin H. Newcomb, *Franklin and Galloway: A Political Partnership* (New Haven, 1972), esp. pp. 136-60.

108. *Paxton Papers*, p. 255.

109. Ibid., p. 309.

110. Ibid., p. 301.

111. "Powell-Roberts Correspondence, 1761-1765," ed. Charles M. Smith, *Pennsylvania Magazine of History and Biography*, 18 (1894-95), 41.

112. James H. Hutson contends that the Quakers, particularly those in the Philadelphia area, supported the effort to gain royal government. While many Friends did back Franklin on this matter, numerous members of the Society gave only extremely cautious and half-hearted support, making a brave show to frighten Thomas Penn into compliance with the Assembly, and others, especially the pacifists, refused to help or were openly hostile to the campaign. The lack of enthusiasm among Quakers doubtless helps to explain the relatively few signatures Franklin and his allies were able to procure despite their intense effort to impress the Crown and Ministry with the widespread desire to bring the province under the Crown. Hutson is led to misstate the issue, it seems, because he fails to account for the ambiguous relationship between Quaker politicians who followed Franklin and those, like the Pembertons, who

opted for pacifism rather than power. Lumping together all Quakers under the rubric of the "Quaker Party" at this time, as Hutson does (p. 130), distorts the facts and ignores the tightrope Friends had to walk to avoid both alienating their political allies and wrecking themselves as a religious entity. While Franklin controlled the Assembly more than any other person, it was a combination of Quaker instinct for survival and Proprietary Party politicians that prevented Franklin's lieutenant, Galloway, a strong advocate of the change of government, from succeeding Norris as Speaker of the House, when the older man retired out of anger with Franklin and because of illness. Instead, Joseph Fox, who was completely opposed to royal government, was appointed Speaker. The Assembly helped save the relationship between Quaker groups by forcing its leader, Franklin, as he was about to depart for England, to realize that it would not let him throw away Quakers' or any other groups' liberties and privileges for the sake of Crown government. While Franklin was clearly the head of the Assembly and generally gave it direction, it was not merely a rubber-stamp matter. See Hutson, *Pennsylvania Politics*, pp. 123-33, esp. pp. 129-31.

113. James Pemberton to Samuel Fothergill, June 13, 1764, Pemberton Papers. HSP.

114. Mary Weston to John Pemberton, September 25, 1755, Pemberton Papers. HSP. The following letters are from the Pemberton Papers: Israel Pemberton to [Mary Pemberton], May 5 and May 28, 1757; James Pemberton to John Pemberton, July 28, 1757; James Pemberton to Hannah Pemberton, August 3 and August 4, 1757; John Griffith to John Pemberton, February 9, 1758; Thomas Crosby to Israel Pemberton, February 10, 1758. HSP; John Hunt to [Israel Pemberton], October 8, 1763, JHC. HSP.

115. The fullest account of the petitions appears in Hutson, *Pennsylvania Politics*, pp. 125-27, 167-68.

116. James Pemberton to John Fothergill, November 27, 1755, Pemberton Papers. HSP.

117. Robert H. Morris to [Thomas Penn, 1756-57]. HSP.

118. Ferdinand John Paris to William Allen, February 14, 1756, POC. HSP.

119. John Hunt to [Israel Pemberton], February 23, 1758, JHC. HSP.

120. William Logan to "Dear Coz," February, 1761. HSP; William Logan to James Pemberton, April 17, 1761, Pemberton Papers. HSP. Also see John Fothergill to Israel Pemberton, April 19, 1759, Pemberton Papers. HSP; The Meeting for Sufferings in London to the Meeting for Sufferings in Philadelphia, September 7, 1759 (copy), Pemberton Papers. HSP.

121. William Logan to John Smith, February 20, 1761, Correspondence of John Smith, 1740-1770. HSP. For other information on Quaker efforts to oppose such of Franklin's schemes as were thought detrimental to the Society, see Thomas Crosby to James Pemberton, February 26, 1762, Pemberton Papers. HSP; Israel Pemberton to John Hunt, October 8, 1763, and John Hunt to Israel Pemberton, December 10, 1763, JHC. HSP.

122. John Hunt to James Pemberton, January 21, 1764, and [James Pemberton] to John Hunt, April 11, 1764, JHC. HSP; James Pemberton to Samuel Fothergill, June 13, 1764; James Pemberton to Henton Brown and John Fothergill, December 17, 1765; and [James Pemberton to John Fothergill?, 1766?], all in Pemberton Papers. HSP; [Hanna Griffith], "Sylvania's Complaint, Address'd To Those who Signe'd the Petition for a Change of Government," [1764] (copy). HSP. Thomas Crosby to James Pemberton, May 22, 1764, Pemberton Papers. HSP; John Griffith to John Pemberton, June 23, 1764, Pemberton Papers. HSP; [Israel Pemberton] to David Barclay & Son, November 6, 1764 (copy), Pemberton Papers. HSP; Elizabeth Wilkinson to John Pemberton, January 18, 1765, Pemberton Papers. HSP; William Peters to Thomas Penn, June 4, 1764, William Allen to Thomas Penn, September 25, 1764, and John Penn to Thomas Penn, November 22, 1764, POC. HSP; William

Allen to Thomas Penn, May 25, 1767, POC. HSP; Thomas Penn to John Penn, November 8, 1766, Letterbooks. HSP; John Penn to Thomas Penn, September 12, 1766, Penn Papers, Additional Miscellaneous Letters, II. HSP; William Logan to John Smith, 10 month, 22, 1764, Correspondence of John Smith, 1740-1770. HSP; Benjamin Lightfoot to "Dear Friend," November 11, 1763. HSP.

123. [James Pemberton] to David Barclay, Sr., November 6, 1764, Pemberton Papers. HSP.

124. William Logan to John Smith, April 12, 1765, Correspondence of John Smith, 1740-1770. HSP.

125. William Allen to David Barclay & Sons, September 25, 1764, and May 19, 1765, and William Allen to David and John Barclay, November 7, 1769, William Allen Letterbook. HSP.

126. David Barclay [Sr.] to Israel Pemberton, July 5, 1764, Pemberton Papers. HSP.

127. David Barclay, Sr., to Israel Pemberton, July 8, 1765, Pemberton Papers. HSP.

128. John Fothergill to James Pemberton, May 10, 1766, Pemberton Papers. HSP.

129. John Fothergill to James Pemberton, February 13, 1765, Pemberton Papers. HSP. Also see Israel Pemberton to John or Robert Pleasants, April 22, 1765, Pemberton Papers. HSP.

130. John Fothergill to James Pemberton, April 8, 1766, Pemberton Papers. HSP.

131. [James Pemberton] to John Hunt, April 11, 1764, JHC. HSP.

132. *Papers*, XI, 422-26.

133. [James Pemberton] to John Fothergill, December 18, 1765, Pemberton Papers. HSP.

134. Edw[ar]d Shippen to [Joseph Shippen], May 29, 1764, Shippen Papers. APS.

135. Edward Burd to "Dear Sister," March 7, 1765, Yeates Papers. HSP.

136. Samuel Purviance to James Burd, September 10, 1764, Shippen Papers. HSP; Thomas Penn to William Smith, October 12 and December 7, 1764, February 9, 1765,

and April 1, 1766, William Smith Papers. HSP; William Allen to Thomas Penn, March 11, 1765, POC. HSP; Thomas Penn to John Penn, November 8, 1766, Letterbooks. HSP.

137. Thomas Penn to William Smith, October 12, 1764, William Smith Papers, II. HSP; William Strahan to David Hall, February 14 and April 11, 1767, "Account Book of David Hall, 1767-1771" (copy). APS; David Hall to Benjamin Franklin, January 27, 1767, *Papers*, XIV, 16-18. Hall continued to hold Franklin in high regard, but he was hurt and resented the tactics. See Robert Hurd Kany, "David Hall: Printing Partner of Benjamin Franklin," Diss., The Pennsylvania State University, 1963, p. 3 (copy). APS; William Strahan to David Hall, undated letter reprinted in *Pennsylvania Magazine of History and Biography*, 13 (1889), 484-85. Though undated in the journal, the manuscript has, perhaps since 1889, been dated twice. The first attribution is obviously incorrect, placing the letter in 1751, but the second one, suggesting a date of February 14, 1767, is plausible. In fact, in a letter of April 11, 1767, Strahan refers to "my letter of Febry. 14th," and goes on to add to the earlier letter's discussion of Hall's difficulties with the Assembly.

138. *Papers*, XV, 71-73; Henry Drinker to Pigou, Jr., and Robinson, April 30, 1764, Henry Drinker Letterbook. HSP; Abel James and Henry Drinker to Neate, Pigou, and Booth, November 6, 1764, James and Drinker Letterbook. HSP; Henry Drinker to Samuel Emlen, Jr., September 20, 1766, Henry Drinker Letterbook. HSP; Petitions for Royal Government, 1764 (typed copies), Franklin MSS. HSP.

139. John Reynell to Mildred & Roberts, November 23, 1764, John Reynell Letterbook, 1762-1767. HSP.

140. Henry Drinker and Stephen Collins to Israel Pemberton, September 25, 1766, Pemberton Papers. HSP.

141. James Pemberton to John Fothergill, 13 6 mo. 1764, and September 3, 1764, Pemberton Papers. HSP.

142. James Burd to Samuel Purviance, September 17, 1764, Shippen Papers. HSP.

143. Thomas Penn to Richard Penn, October 11, 1764, Letterbooks. HSP; Also see Thomas Penn to William Allen, November 10, 1764. HSP; James Pemberton to John Fothergill, December 18, 1765, Pemberton Papers. HSP; William Allen to Thomas Penn, October 8, 1768, POC. HSP.

144. *Papers*, XI, 77.

145. *Papers*, XI, 107.

146. *Papers*, XI, 101-5.

147. *Papers*, XI, 180-81.

148. *Papers*, XI, 161.

149. *Papers*, XI, 162-69.

150. *Papers*, XI, 158.

151. *Papers*, XI, 160.

152. *Papers*, XI, 185, 189, 239, 256, 264, 313, 328, 332-33, 355-56.

153. *Papers*, XI, 287, 304-5.

154. *Papers*, XI, 169-70. Galloway, too, was very hostile toward Presbyterians and blamed them for his political troubles throughout his career. See Newcomb, pp. 132, 164, 222, 271, 272, 296.

155. *Papers*, XI, 239.

156. *Papers*, XI, 125, 290, 327, 369, 389, 485.

157. *Papers*, XI, 332.

158. William B. Reed, *Life and Correspondence of Joseph Reed*, 2 vols. (Philadelphia, 1847), I, 34-35.

159. Samuel Purviance to James Burd, September 20, 1765, Shippen Papers. HSP.

160. Joseph Shippen to Thomas Penn, September 25, 1765, POC. HSP.

161. [James Pemberton] to John Fothergill, October 11, 1764, Pemberton Papers. HSP.

162. James Pemberton to Henton Brown and John Fothergill, 12 mo. 17, 1765, Pemberton Papers. HSP. Though Friends defended Franklin's character from unfair attack, they continued to resist his attempts to bring the province under the Crown. See John Fothergill to James Pemberton, 27th 2 mo. 1766, POC. Henton Brown and John Fothergill to James Pemberton, April 8, 1766; James Pemberton to John Fothergill, July 8, 1766, and 11 mo. 14, 1766, Pem-

berton Papers. HSP. Henry Drinker to Samuel Emlen, Jr., September 20, 1766, Henry Drinker Letterbook. HSP.

163. *Votes and Proceedings of the House of Representatives of the Province of Pennsylvania, Met at Philadelphia* (Philadelphia, 1764), pp. 14-15. The "Remonstrance" is reprinted and discussed in *Papers*, XI, 402-6.

164. *Papers*, XI, 408-12.

165. *Burd Papers*, I, 81-85.

166. *Papers*, XI, 434.

167. *Burd Papers*, I, 118-19.

168. *Papers*, XI, 457, 467, 524, 526.

169. *Papers*, XI, 457.

170. *Papers*, XI, 467, 472, 522-23.

171. *Papers*, XI, 484-85.

172. *Papers*, XII, 67-68, 172-73.

173. Samuel Purviance to James Burd, September 20, 1765, Shippen Papers. HSP.

174. See, for example, Edward Shippen to Thomas Penn, September 25, 1765, and John Penn to Thomas Penn, September 12, 1766, POC. HSP. For William Franklin's reply to these and other charges, see his broadside, *The Answer of His Excellency ...* (Philadelphia, 1765). As might be expected, the bulk of his enemies were Pennsylvania and New Jersey Presbyterians. On the Act itself and Franklin's role in its repeal, see Edmund S. and Helen M. Morgan, *The Stamp Act Crisis: Prologue to Revolution* (Chapel Hill, N.C., 1953).

175. For background on the controversies over the bishopric, see Arthur L. Cross, *The Anglican Episcopate and the American Colonies* (New York, 1902), particularly Chapters IV, VIII, and IX; and Carl Bridenbaugh's *Mitre and Sceptre: Transatlantic Faiths, Ideas, Personalities, and Politics, 1689-1775* (New York, 1962), especially Part Two. Stiles' calculation of the Anglican population in America is in Bridenbaugh, p. 179.

176. William Atlee to James Burd, September 20, 1765, and September 26, 1768, Shippen Papers. HSP.

177. *Letters of Benjamin Rush*, I, 40, 42, 48.

178. *Stiles*, ed. Dexter, pp. 434-35; Richard Peters to William Smith, April 28, 1763, William Smith Papers. HSP.

179. Francis Alison to Ezra Stiles, June 19, 1767, Alison MSS. PHS.

180. [James Pemberton? to John Fothergill?, 1766?] and October 20, 1768, Pemberton Papers. HSP; John Ewing to Andrew Eliot, August 6, 1766. MHS.

181. James Pemberton to John Fothergill, 14 11 mo. 1766, Pemberton Papers. HSP.

182. Thomas Penn to William Allen, May 19, 1767, Letterbooks. HSP.

183. [Duché], *Observations*, pp. 62-63.

184. *Papers*, XIV, 117; XV, 131.

185. *Papers*, XIV, 145-47, 193-200; XV, 99; Thomas Penn to Richard Peters, May 18, 1767, Thomas Penn to Benjamin Chew, July 31, 1767, Thomas Penn to William Allen, July 31, 1767, Thomas Penn to John Penn, May 7, 1768, and Thomas Penn to James Hamilton, February 4, 1769, Letterbooks. HSP.

186. *Papers*, XV, 128-30. BF to Joseph Galloway, August 20, 1768, *Papers*, XV, 189-90. It is the letter to Galloway that leads Hutson to believe it signaled the end of Franklin's quest for Crown government. The letter itself indicates, however, that Franklin did not relinquish all hope on August 20, 1768. Instead he told Galloway they would have to await a favorable change in the Ministry before pursuing their plans. Moreover, Thomas Penn's letter to Hamilton of February 4, 1769, cited above, shows that at least as far as the proprietor himself was concerned, Franklin continued his efforts. Hillsborough resigned only in August 1772, when Franklin no longer desired the change and, indeed, when such a suggestion would have been incredible. See *Pennsylvania Politics*, pp. 227-29; Thomas Penn to James Hamilton, February 4, 1769, Letterbook. HSP.

187. *Writings*, VII, 186.

Notes Epilogue

1. William Allen to Thomas Penn, October 12, 1768, POC. HSP. Also see Allen's letter to David Barclay, Sr., and John Barclay, November 7, 1769, Letterbook of William Allen, HSP, in which he writes that private squabbles among Pennsylvanians "are quite Subsided," since the "wrong-headed Schemes on your Side of the Water have fully taken up our Attention."

2. *Papers*, XVI, 125; XVII, 227 n., 228-29.

3. *Papers*, XVI, 10-18. Even earlier, in the letter to John Ross of May 14, 1768, Franklin had expressed his shock and utter dismay over the London riots and the inability of the government to maintain peace.

4. *Writings*, VII, 348.

Index